Acting
Skills
for
Life

This book is dedicated to Lloyd,
to the memory of my parents, Philip and Barbara,
and to my circle of friends and students
in deep appreciation of their gifts to me

Ron Cameron

Acting Skills
for
Life

THE DUNDURN GROUP
TORONTO · OXFORD

Editor: Cheryl Cohen
Design: Scott Reid
Printer: Transcontinental Printing Inc.

Canadian Cataloguing in Publication Data
Cameron, Ron, 1944-
Acting skills for life
3rd ed.
Includes bibliographical references and index
ISBN 0-88924-289-5
1. Acting — Study and teaching. 2. Drama in education. I. Title.

PN3171.C35 1999   792'.028'07   C99-932883-2

1   2   3   4   5   03   02   01   00   99

THE CANADA COUNCIL | LE CONSEIL DES ARTS
FOR THE ARTS | DU CANADA
SINCE 1957 | DEPUIS 1957

We acknowledge the support of the **Canada Council for the Arts** for our publishing
program. We also acknowledge the support of the **Ontario Arts Council** and we
acknowledge the financial support of the Government of Canada through the **Book
Publishing Industry Development Program** (BPIDP) for our publishing activities.

Printed and bound in Canada.

Printed on recycled paper.
www.dundurn.com

Dundurn Press	Dundurn Press	Dundurn Press
8 Market Street	73 Lime Walk	2250 Military Road
Suite 200	Headington, Oxford,	Tonawanda NY
Toronto, Ontario, Canada	England	U.S.A 14150
M5E 1M6	OX3 7AD	

Table of Contents

Acknowledgments

In my adjudication work, I have often said only half-jokingly "all theatre is theft." If that is the case, this book is a good example. The exercises that I have used in this book have come from a variety of sources, the origins of many lost in the nether regions of my mind. Some, I specifically remember, were exercises in which I participated at the Banff Centre; others date from my days at the Guildhall School of Music and Drama in London, England. Still other ideas come from professional colleagues, in discussion or participation in workshops. The balance is material which I have either read somewhere and incorporated into my own classes at Sheridan College, or devised myself to fulfil specific needs within my courses. Several exercises are contributions from workshop participants, anxious to share their particular favourites. Several improvisation suggestions are drawn from particularly memorable classroom work created by former students.

To all these professional sources, to all my former students who have taught me the truth of Joseph Joubert's comment that "To teach is to learn twice," I extend my thanks and appreciation. Where possible, I have endeavoured to give credit to specific people important ideas that have made an impact on my own teaching and these are acknowledged in the Bibliography at the end of this book.

If I have omitted extending appropriate credit, such an oversight is unintentional. I apologize and plead my overriding belief that all theatre involves sharing. As Christopher Newton, long-time Artistic Director of the Shaw Festival at Niagara-on-the-Lake, Ontario, once said: "Give me a group of people who share a generosity of spirit and we will create new worlds for you."

Thank you to Marian M. Wilson for initiating a project that simmered in the back of my mind for several years. I am grateful for the impetus, guidance, and sound advice she provided in developing this book. I would also like to thank Frank English and, in particular, Harriet Law who helped to organize and shape the original edition of this book. I would like to add a special thank you to Kirk Howard of The Dundurn Group for the total support he has shown in developing this third edition; Barry Jowett, Editorial Co-ordinator, for his assistance; Cheryl Cohen, for her superb clarity, insight, and detailed work in copyediting; my brother Harold for his work with the index.

I deeply appreciate the work of the readers who worked on this project. Drawn from various backgrounds — teaching, professional acting, and former students, friends, and colleagues — they share my love of theatre and recognize its role in our personal development. My special thanks to each for their advice, encouragement, ideas, criticism, suggestions, and time: David Eden, Liz Flynn, Christina James, Paul Lampert, Lloyd Lewis, Antony Parr, Frances Rustom, Art Southcott, Ian Waldron, Ken Watts, Chris Worsnop, and the late Jean Burgess and Christopher Covert. Four people deserve special mention for their help:

- Christopher Covert for his invaluable suggestions on content and concept. His insight and professional criticism provided a firm and steady perspective on this project.
- Ian Waldron, whose knowledge of theatre was surpassed only by his eagle eye watching my grammar and spelling.
- David Eden for his careful attention to so many aspects of the manuscripts and scenes.
- Lloyd, for his forthright honesty and superb computer skills.

Finally, I would like to thank the thousands of students I have worked with over the years. My personal credo is that the purpose of life is to learn, and you have each taught me so much.

Foreword

W hen I first began to work on this book in the mid-1980s, it was a very different world.

The students I encounter today in the Music Theatre Department at Sheridan College in Oakville, Ontario, have been raised surrounded by a whole new set of influences. Pop culture has expanded exponentially and modern students don't remember life before video games, satellite dishes, cell phones, compact discs, and music videos. The widespread integration of computer technology has shaped their education and experience. The Internet has expanded rapidly into an extraordinary information-gathering research tool. Major changes in the multicultural face of Canada continue to alter the nature of our society and our classrooms. As well, political decisions affecting education are escalating change at all levels of public education.

The students I now teach at Sheridan College have grown up with Much Music; as a result, they bring a heightened sense of imaginative visual presentation to their performance work. Teaching is a two-way street and such influences have, in turn, affected the content and style of my teaching. In fact, increasingly I have found myself teaching acting classes in the television studio at Sheridan, where I have adapted some of my exercises and methodologies.

During the years since the first edition of this book was written, Sheridan College has phased in a joint program in Theatre and Drama

Studies with University of Toronto at Mississauga. Students in the TDS program study academic subjects at UTM three days a week, and get practical acting training at Sheridan two days a week. These students are increasingly involved in the formation of new experimental theatre companies that have been achieving solid results in theatre competitions, fringe festivals, and summer festivals. Again, the imagination and commitment these students bring to their work with me has affected my work and inspired my thinking.

An interesting life — just like good acting — cannot be trapped by the enticing security of the status quo. That is why it's time to undertake a serious revision of my book. I hope those of you who knew the original version find some interesting new ideas in this, the third edition. To those of you who are new to *Acting Skills for Life*, welcome aboard.

Ron Cameron
August 1999

Introduction

Preface: to the teacher/director

An overview

This book provides a transition from creative drama to formal play production for novice performers in secondary schools, colleges, and the community. It is a book for classroom teachers who have creative drama training and wish to guide the preparation of student plays and school assemblies, or supervise theatre festival entries. It is also a book filled with practical suggestions for the director of community theatre plays.

You will find exercises for group work and creative problem solving are blended with script interpretations, exercises, acting theory, and historical plays. The intention is to integrate personal growth and the process of creative drama with the more formal skills required for successful stage production.

In this book, teacher/directors as well as students are encouraged to wear many hats/masks: author, actor, director, technician, designer, producer, and informed member of the audience. Trust develops when all parties share a wide array of practical tasks in the process of creating a production. You will become more inventive and creative in your work and thus, as a teacher/director, a more valuable resource to your students and community.

The acting exercises in this book are construed as opportunities for discovery rather than imitation of the emotional centre of an event, feeling, or concept. Choice of the exercises is contingent upon the unique interests and capabilities of individual students, rather than hierarchical levels of difficulty. The emphasis, then, is on craft as an extension of both intuitive and learned abilities. You will find exercises for characterization, personal and dramatic conflict, comic principles, acting styles, script interpretation, and the Canadian contribution to a literary and theatrical heritage.

Acting teachers must carry around in their heads about 20 times the amount of material required for each class. An experienced acting teacher must be able to build on what comes out of any classroom situation. Making decisions about the choice of material is really a matter of personal instincts, the needs of student actors, the general theme of recent classes, current events in the outside world, and the pressures of time.

How to use this book

Although you may be working on material early in the book, feel free to pick and choose exercises or theory from elsewhere in the book and, indeed, connect them with material from other writers. Borrow, steal, and adapt ideas that will help your students better understand the material with which they are dealing, much as I have done over the past 30 years. The theory and exercises in this book are drawn from those that have proven most effective in my own classroom experience. Wherever appropriate, they are tied into excerpts from Canadian plays contained in the two accompanying scene study books called *Behind the Scenes, Volume One* and *Volume Two*. Those books contain material from a wide range of Canadian plays, for one to five characters, dealing with communication problems and conflict in life. Both volumes include a variety of background information and practical advice.

The Table of Contents outlines three major areas of study:

1. **The Actor's Instrument:** developing the student's freedom and flexibility, physically and vocally
2. **The Actor Beginning Work:** initial steps in creating a character
3. **The Outside Eye:** looking at acting from the viewpoint of the teacher/director/guide/audience

I have not included a glossary because each of the terms and definitions is explained within the context of the work. However, for easy reference, there is an **Index** at the end of the book to enable you to find the pages that deal with any subject contained here. Important subjects are printed in boldface, and a **Bibliography** has been included at the end of the book to provide you with further sources of reading or research.

Guidelines for teaching acting

In conclusion, I have three pieces of advice that collectively provide a "guide" to teaching acting — at least, they articulate the guidelines that have worked best for me over the years. However, every teacher/director must find what works best for him or her.

1. Encourage your actors to make their own discoveries. No matter what time constraints exist, avoid giving them line readings or instructing them to mimic your physical action. They must find their own interpretation, not an imitation of your interpretation. Allow actors in rehearsal to discover the text, character, and physical action as much as the realities of time will permit. It is harder work for the teacher/director in the beginning, but the results will be exciting and the actors will have total commitment to the production.

2. Encourage the idea that the process is actually more important than the product. When a student gets up to present a speech in class, he or she will often view the experience as a performance when, in fact, it should be seen as simply another development of the rehearsal process. This is especially true when the material is being presented for the first time. Such pressure will often create unreal expectations founded on a belief that the presentation is all that counts and, unless the student is particularly intuitive or skilled in technique, he or she may be unhappy with the results.

    For this reason, I encourage my students to repeat lines — several times over if necessary — when they are first working on their speeches or scenes. They need to take that time in early performance work to find the truth of the lines. I don't give out gold stars for finishing a scene quickly, for parroting lines perfectly, or for allowing internal pressures to overwhelm performance. I do, however, give praise for exploring the text and subtext of the scene; for discovering its energy; for sustaining character throughout (regardless of what happens); and for finding the natural beginning, middle, and end of the piece. The exploration may take place individually, in small groups, a classroom group, or a larger group dealing with one particular scene.

3. Encourage a classroom/rehearsal atmosphere that is open and safe. This involves deconstructing the barriers of power structures created by social convention. Discard the role of teacher as authoritarian figure, the student as passive receiver of wisdom, and others as detached observers. Perhaps more than any other subject in the curriculum, theatre breaks down artificial barriers between "teacher" and "student." Trust is based on mutual respect, which is fostered through the creative process and shared discoveries.

Good manners are the foundation of civilized society, and healthy theatre can flourish only in a civilized society. Thus, it is essential that theatre classes be founded on honesty, respect, and commitment to the shared tasks and goals.

Preface: to the student actor

Some reasons for studying acting

Acting provides you with an understanding of self, position in society, and the universality of human experience (both in time present and time past). Whether you are doing creative drama, improvisations, scene study work, or fully mounted productions, theatre opens up new worlds for you. It forces assessment of past experiences in the light of new — and often opposing — ideas and values. Time and thought must also be spent in discovering the mental and emotional barriers that the actor personally has acquired throughout life. Such barriers provide the biggest stumbling blocks to emotional honesty, both in acting and in life.

We have all learned to "act" in our daily lives and, whether or not we realize the extent to which we use these acquired skills every day, acting for the stage is mostly an organized extension of both natural and learned abilities. One cannot really "learn" acting. One can, however, learn craft: knowledge of staging, dramatic conflict, characterization, comic and dramatic principles, style, dramaturgy, script analysis, and an understanding of our literary and theatrical heritage.

Acting skills, then, prepare us for life because acting develops personal and social skills. Every theatre teacher or acting instructor can give numerous examples where acting experience has improved students' sense of poise and confidence. If you can get up in front of a group of your peers and present a monologue or scene, you will be less inhibited later in life by a situation where you must address a group in public, or face an intimidating stranger during a job interview.

Acting can teach you to control nervous energy and to channel that energy into your performance. Acting teaches an awareness of physical and vocal selves — how we move, what messages we project, how we command attention. Such knowledge will give you both an added vocal authority and a physical presence that is comfortable and relaxed even in the most stressful situations.

You will be asked in improvisations, acting exercises and scripts to put yourself into a wide range of characters and situations, often with little preparatory time. Such enriching experiences teach you to "think on your feet." They also make it a little easier to handle such real-life improvisations as negotiating a bank loan, looking for an apartment, buying a car, and dealing with intimidating people in a variety of situations.

If a young actor is cast as an applicant for a job, whether in a situational improvisation or in a scene study, that "dry run" experience will be carried over into real life one day. Insight and knowledge gained from the acting class will make the real-life situation a little less overwhelming than it might otherwise be. It might even provide the edge that will allow you to land the job, rather than lose out to another applicant.

On the other hand, if cast as the prospective employer, you will be interviewing the applicant from a different perspective. You may have been given advice in the past that you have rejected — "get your hair cut, wear neat clothes, speak clearly and positively, get an education!" But now, facing these ideas from another person's perspective and experiencing the opposite viewpoint, you may be more likely to understand and accept the reasoning behind such advice. The confidence acquired from such acting training will equip you for many life experiences.

Acting deepens your understanding of all individuals in the present and in the past. Learning what makes other people tick can provide insight, not only into our own natures but also into the motivations of people whose actions have touched our lives. The field of understanding is deepened when scripted plays become part of the theatre experience.

The playwright brings a perspective on life that is normally outside the range of experience of the general student body. This exposure forces you to address new ideas, new relationships, new values, new motivations, new needs, and new goals. The playwright and the script offer you the chance to experience something beyond the situations and dialogue that emerge from classroom improvisation.

We can often analyze two characters in conflict within a play more easily than we can analyze our own problems in life. Such parallels are important. Understanding the "hows and whys" of real relationships may come more easily as a result of theatrical experience.

Individual prejudices, fears, values, morality, and assumptions can all be put to the test.

Through analyzing, rehearsing and presenting scripts dealing with a wide range of subjects, we can learn to talk about subjects that — in the ordinary creative drama situation — we may not have had to address. They may frighten, amuse, or anger us, but we will learn from them. We can clarify our understanding of ourselves and of others.

For after all, if we — as individual human beings — are the sum total of our life's events, we have much to gain by increasing our range of experience. Understanding ourselves may be painful at times, but learning about acting helps explain us to ourselves.

The process of studying acting

Developing acting skills does not happen in logical sequence, nor does it progress neatly from point A to point B to point C, as do some other academic subjects. The study of acting is scattered by its very nature. What you get out of any exercise depends upon who you are and what you have experienced thus far in life, the values you embrace, and the understanding you already possess. These factors will colour what you bring to each stage of acting training.

Learning to act is not a steady, slow, uphill climb. It is more like a merry-go-round ride perched on top of a roller-coaster ride, because:

- Sometimes you don't know which direction you're going in.
- Sometimes it's fun.
- Sometimes you feel disoriented.
- You simply have to trust that it is worth the ride.

Of great importance in acting training is distillation time. This is the period of reflection where you process — consciously or subconsciously — what has been learned. Allow for that time. Trust that your subconscious mind will eventually make sense out of apparent chaos.

Remember that it is very easy to see improvements in other people, but not necessarily those that are occurring deep inside you. You can be impressed with the skill of one classmate in picking up mime. You can hear the improvement in another's singing voice over the course of a school semester. You can be moved by the advanced acting work of another individual during a particularly powerful scene. But rarely can you see the improvement within yourself.

This depressing fact of life leads many students to feel from time to time that they are not progressing in their acting work, to doubt that they are actually learning any new skills in acting. If they grow to accept and believe these doubts, the insecurity will in turn create barriers to further development.

If you can see improvement in acting skills happening in others, you simply have to trust that it is happening inside you as well.

Part One

The Actor's Instrument

Chapter One
An Introduction to Acting

Learning through doing

M any students have studied creative drama in a school subject and the experience has stimulated them to want to discover more about acting. The "act" is defined by the *Gage Canadian Dictionary* as "the process of doing." Acting allows us to explore life interpretations and "become" another person for a while. In doing so, we experience another person's point of view, which in turn creates dramatic fictions, provides an opportunity to learn and grow, and gives us poise to meet everyday life situations.

Consequently, this book is based on the following premise: acting skills are required every day of your life. Learning to act for theatre is not really a question of acquiring an entirely new body of knowledge. It is certainly not a matter of sheer memory work. Rather, it is a process of:

- creatively revealing much of what you already intuitively or instinctively know
- sharing your understanding of yourself and others
- expressing personal insight with physical and vocal clarity

The study of acting is as erratic as the process of living through a day: you can never predict what will be in 10 minutes, an hour, or an afternoon.

If you were to imagine the two major elements of acting, the actor and the character, as if they were part of a pinball machine, you might come close to visualizing my approach to acting exercises. Picture a pinball that represents the current exercise or assignment on which you are working. It spins up the side of the machine, bouncing off obstacles labelled "fear," "bad mood," or "peer-group pressure" and so forth. It may also locate moments of "courage," "understanding," or "independence."

The pinball will sometimes hit one part of the "actor circle," making it light up. Another time it will hit the "character circle" and make that light up. You never know just where the pinball is going, what it will strike, or what will light up.

Like the pinball, acting exercises and tasks are meant to be experienced rather than to achieve "expected" results. The pinball machine is an image that, for me, sums up the complex subject of acting and character exercises.

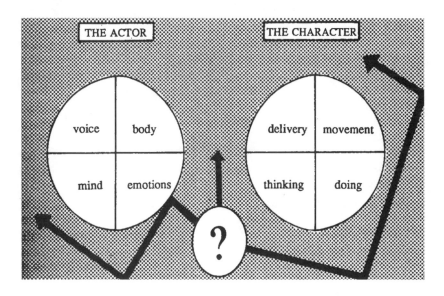

Acting and life

Whether or not you realize it, you have already acquired a number of acting skills from the time you were a child. You play several roles in different relationships and situations. Think about it. Are you the same person with a parent or employer as you are with a close friend?

From our earliest childhood, during our teenage years, and throughout our adult lives, each of us learns to act. We recognize early that there are numerous situations in life where certain conduct is expected and, for the most part, we go along with the expectations. We learn from our families, school experiences, cultural background, and our gradual socialization which roles suit specific situations. We learn to dress to suit an occasion such as a wedding, or to express a feeling such as compassion, and we may even rehearse lines before an important event, such as preparing to deal with an irate parent who wants to ground us.

Children, of course, are constantly using acting in their play: pretending to be Mummy or Daddy, role-playing in "good guy/bad guy" games, bestowing life on stuffed toys, and using their imaginations to fantasize real problems. Child psychologists view such play as children's work. It is part of the child's process in gaining control of his or her world. As children, acting out events helps to prepare us for life in our society.

We are all nervous of — or frightened by — things that we don't know or have not yet experienced. A wise parent will prepare his or her child for life through role-playing games — for example, when street-proofing the child. Upcoming visits to the hospital or the first day of kindergarten can be made less intimidating by acting out the events with the children's dolls. This allows the children to verbalize and visualize the approaching events and to assimilate the information into their egocentric view of the world.

As we get older, the processes are similar but increasingly complex. For example, we have one way of acting when we are applying for a job that we need urgently. Yet we have another very different way of acting later that same day when we are out for an evening of fun with old friends. We demonstrate still a different mode of behaviour when stopping by a funeral home to extend sympathy to a family for whom we care. In this situation, our mere presence and body language can transcend our awkwardness of speech. Again, there is still another way of behaving when we meet someone who sets our hormones aquiver. Unanticipated chemistry in a relationship can cause considerable disruption in our lives, profoundly affecting patterns of behaviour that others have come to expect of us. Nevertheless, through trial and error, most of us become quite skilled at understanding the various kinds of role-playing that life demands of us.

In each of these real-life situations, there is a different setting, audience, script, costume, physical energy level, vocal rhythm, and projection of character that is acceptable within our community: in short, all the components of theatre are present.

Memory work: one kind of work

Yet, when you are in a theatre arts class, or just beginning to participate in a community theatre group, and you are handed a script and told to prepare a character in a scene, all this life training generally goes out the window. What is the novice actor's reaction?

"Oh no! Look at all the lines I have to memorize!"

We focus only on memorizing the lines, forgetting about the richness of our life experiences that could enhance our interpretation of the role. A newcomer may have some vague awareness of staging the scene, such as the use of blocking, costume, and props. Often, however, he or she is totally caught up in an overwhelming dependency on getting the lines memorized and reproduced as accurately as possible. Panic takes over, we lose confidence, and we forget to draw on our own insight and intuition.

Remember, good memory work doth not an actor make. There is much more work required to bring acting off the written page and into life as a fully textured, believable performance. Indeed, half the actor's work should be done long before there is any conscious attempt to memorize the text. In this book, you will be shown the steps that an actor follows. The process begins with discussion of each scene and its goal within the framework of the play. Then you will learn to analyze what your character is really trying to say, stating intentions in your own words, not those of the character. When the time comes to begin to learn the lines, the job will be much easier because of the insight you have gained into the character's objectives and motivation.

Acting helps you move from the **particular** (just you) to the **universal** (the rest of humanity) and back again. When you understand yourself, you can more easily understand others. Through learning about others, you gain further insight into your own nature. Thus, learning to act demands that you come to know yourself thoroughly. That is the difficult part of acting. Honest self-evaluation can be a painful experience for each of us, but it is necessary to our development and maturity on and off stage.

Often your problems in acting will reflect the problems you are dealing with in life. More will be said about this later, but acting can help you identify and deal with your problems.

The nature and elements of theatre

The components of theatre vary widely. But there are common elements to the elaborate, spectacular productions of such works as the modern high-tech musical or the complex symbolic staging of Kabuki theatre; alternative theatres performing experimental works; and simple classroom productions presented in most schools throughout the country. For each production:

- There is a story to tell.
- There is at least one performer involved in the telling of the tale.
- There is an audience watching the story unfold.

As the story begins, the audience takes a magical first step as its contribution to the occasion. Samuel Taylor Coleridge described this step of poetic faith as "the willing suspension of disbelief." This simply means that we in the audience accept the conventions of the show — whether on the street, in the classroom, or in a theatre — and join in with the performers as they communicate their message to us. This sharing of an unspoken commitment fuels both the audience and the actors. It creates the dramatic energy of the occasion.

First, then, an understood contract exists between the actor and the audience, one that is based on centuries of ritual. For hundreds of years, theatre has helped explain us to ourselves, whether we are on stage or in the audience. Second, theatre takes us to places, situations and relationships far beyond our own experience, allowing us safely to escape our own circumstances and be entertained, often illuminating our lives and giving us a new understanding of ourselves. Third, it can stimulate the imagination and the emotions, thereby enriching us in the process.

As performers, acting lets us become all types of people in the world, in time past, time present or time future. We experience their ideas, emotions, and inner conflicts. We see at work the principle of cause and effect in personal and political relationships, along with the consequences arising from decisions we make and actions we take.

External and internal conflict

The essence of good theatre, whether comic or dramatic in form, is conflict. Conflict leads to the discovery of the action of the play. There are two types of conflict: external and internal.

External conflict is generally provided by the playwright and is created by the mere presence of a character (or characters) representing a differing point of view. Conflict between characters is expressed verbally and/or physically. Good, well-written drama will involve two or more characters with opposing intentions in every scene.

External conflict provides the humour that we see in farce or slapstick (as with the Three Stooges) and much of the drama of Shakespeare. Modern films have realized the importance of action to explore external conflict. Look back to the swashbuckling films of the mid-20th century and you will see how conflict is expressed through physical action. More recent action films, often dressed up with animation and special effects, still rely on the dramatic excitement provided by contrasted characters physically expressing opposing points of view.

Internal conflict involves the mental and emotional turmoil within a character. It comes partly from script analysis and partly from the insight provided by the actor. Through studying your character, you will be discovering both the internal and external conflict of an individual: understanding how it came about and then developing it within the dramatic action of the scene.

Probably one of the most famous examples of internal conflict is the great psychological study of *Hamlet* by William Shakespeare. Hamlet is so full of conflicting ideas regarding which course of action he should pursue in avenging his father's murder that he is virtually paralyzed by the inner turmoil. His soliloquies reveal his dilemma. Other writers such as Henrik Ibsen and Anton Chekhov explore the use of inner psychological conflict in their plays. Since the late 19th century, when "modern" playwriting began to grapple with difficult themes and situations, writers everywhere have tried to incorporate internal conflicts to enrich the characters in their plays.

One of the first steps an actor takes in approaching a play or scene, then, is to search out the internal and external conflicts confronting the character. These can be made more easily identifiable through analyzing each character's objectives and obstacles, scene by scene.

Objectives and obstacles

Every character in every scene in every play has an **objective**, a specific goal that provides the character with motivation to achieve that end. Romeo's objective on the way to the Capulet ball is to enter forbidden territory and have fun. Once there, his objective is to meet Juliet, whose mere appearance has so thoroughly captivated him.

Often a character will have several objectives, one of which is generally more important than the rest. Sometimes these objectives provide a conflict themselves as one need "battles" with another. Often they change within a scene. Rarely in a play are all the character's objectives achieved. (Think how many objectives we may have in real life, how often they war with each other, and how few of them are ever realized.)

In addition, each character generally encounters an **obstacle** that interferes with the easy achievement of an objective. Sometimes obstacles are external, created by other people or groups. Other times they may come from within a character. Obstacles may be created by fate, religion, or social convention.

Conflict is created when the obstacle gets in the way of the objective:

TEENAGER: "Hi, Dad. I'm going out for a while. Can I borrow the car?"

FATHER: "No. You should have thought of that earlier when you said you were too tired to cut the lawn."

We've all experienced similar examples of conflict in our lives. Such conflict can be physically expressed in numerous ways, and physical action will be different for each pair of speakers delivering these same lines. The truth and believability of the movement comes from the actor's understanding of the conflict. This applies equally to real-life situations, improvisations, and scripted work.

Often the obstacle isn't an external one but rather an internal one: it is part of the character's inner psychological make-up. Neither do objectives and obstacles remain constant. How often in life have you craved something that, once acquired or achieved, didn't seem to be important to you after all?

Characterization will require a great deal of script analysis in your search to achieve understanding. This is one of those initial steps that novice actors often skip over, particularly if they are gifted with fine, intuitive ability.

Yet deliberate, serious script analysis is the foundation of rich acting. The role-playing we do in everyday life flips constantly from relationship to relationship, situation to situation. So it does in acting, and script analysis will provide clues to help you understand the finer nuances of the character you are preparing to play. Each time you read or rehearse a play, you will find new insight into your character's objectives. You will discover new obstacles as your fellow actors bring fresh ideas to each rehearsal. The search for objectives and obstacles never stops, and choices you may have made early in rehearsal will change (often dramatically) as you approach performance deadlines.

The late Dr. Hans Selye, noted Canadian authority on stress and its effects on the individual, was once asked to sum up in one sentence his life's work — his years of scientific studies, his many medical textbooks, numerous learned papers delivered to international medical conventions, and his practical clinical experience. His answer was very simple: "It's not so much what happens to you throughout your life that counts, but how you cope with it."

It is how we cope with life that reveals our character to others around us in the everyday world. Through script analysis, we can discover how our character in a play copes within the action of the script, and this provides us with the keys to explore a believable, dynamic character on stage.

Now that we have discussed some of the basics involved in acting (both in life and on stage) and why acting fulfils an important need for many people, let's take a look at the first steps in developing some performance skills.

Chapter Two
Overcoming Personal Obstacles in Acting

Fears and acting

Many situations that student actors deal with in exercises, improvisations, and scene study are based on real-life situations. For this reason, training in acting is an excellent process to prepare you for the more stressful moments that are inevitable in daily life: school examinations, first dates, pressure before an important game, sibling rivalry, or emotional conflicts with authority figures.

Think of the shy child hiding behind a parent, withdrawing from an opportunity to participate in a game with new friends. That's fear at work. Even the most outwardly successful business executive may be inwardly terrified of entering a room full of strangers at a business conference.

Exercises:

- Ask the most successful people in your life about their inward fears.
- Have every student in an acting class write down his or her single greatest fear on a piece of paper — using disguised handwriting and leaving the statement unsigned. The teacher can read the responses aloud, making sure that total anonymity is guaranteed and destroying the papers after the class is over.

Some of the most stressful situations are those created by your perception of the expectations of others — parents, teachers, friends. Actors discover only too well how other people's expectations create barriers that serve only to generate fear of:

- judgments being made on your acting
- failure in public
- true physical and vocal release
- exploring your own emotions
- thinking about the "one deepest secret" that lies buried inside each of us

Every young actor faces problems of insecurity, nervous tension or even blind panic when first approaching acting. Yet, at the same time, there is a special thrill that performing provides for actors, singers, dancers, and entertainers. The continuing search for this thrill drives us onward. It enables us to transcend our insecurities and seek out further performing opportunities and experiences.

Difficult as it may sometimes be, we must shake off constraints created by these mental barriers. Acting exercises can help us achieve freedom from our fears, as we learn to overcome our insecurities one step at a time in the supportive environment of the acting class. This freedom can give us greater courage for dealing with stressful situations in our personal lives.

As an individual and as an actor, you can be working hard to overcome one anxiety when suddenly another one pops up to take its place. The process is reminiscent of the story in Greek mythology of Hydra, the many-headed serpent of the marshes of Lerna. This monstrous creature had nine heads; where one of them was cut off, two more sprang up. Addressing our personal and acting fears can seem just as overwhelming.

It is generally easier to avoid a stressful situation than to deal with it. Many of us devote inordinate amounts of time trying to find graceful, believable justifications that allow us to avoid certain situations in life because of our own internalized fears. Improvisations in this and other acting books can help individuals cope with everyday life.

Ghosts that constrain us

Do you recall comments like these from your past?

1. "Nice girls don't shout like that."
2. "I never want to hear you use language like that again!"
3. "Honestly, you're so clumsy."

We've all had variations of these served up to us in childhood or teenage years by different authority figures in our lives. If such comments have a lingering effect, they can limit our freedom in acting.

Example 1: Every acting teacher has encountered the student who, after years of daily conditioning, is reluctant to increase vocal projection to the degree necessary to fill a theatre. To that student, speaking even at a "normal" level of projection sounds like shouting. Such people feel uncomfortable projecting to a full classroom, and they feel even more inhibited when they are required to fill a theatre space. The student must work hard to undo years of habit and conditioning until other volume levels "feel right."

Example 2: This leads to students who "absolutely never swear." They will generally pull back from using foul language in a script. This can originate from an acquired distaste for what the words represent (we all have three or four swearwords which particularly offend us). Or perhaps our aversion stems from an excessive apprehension of what others might think if we use "those words." In either case, the student never completely distinguishes between his or her own character and that of the character in the play. The student must understand that they are — and must be — two separate, distinctive beings.

Example 3: A person who is repeatedly called "clumsy" can become very inhibited physically on stage. Natural inhibitions are magnified when you think that everyone is staring at you. This is an especially difficult problem for anyone who has suddenly grown several inches in height in less than a year of adolescence, and hasn't yet become accustomed to the new proportions of this alien body. Natural grace can be acquired at any age, however, and the type of physical exercises that actors undergo can help individuals become more comfortable with their body size and shape.

Ridding yourself of fears

First, you need to identify how and in what form such outside opinions get in your way and inhibit your freedom in acting. Then dump those external authoritarian influences. Get rid of them. Let them assume an importance in your personal life if you insist, but don't allow them to mess up your performance work.

Identify and rid yourself of the inwardly imposed expectations that you demand of yourself. Such expectations, whether stated or implied, can profoundly affect your behaviour and potential.

1. "I know I'll never get that line right. I can never remember how it goes."
2. "I'm going to show them how funny I can be when I want to be. Then they'll see."
3. "Oh, I could never play a sleaze like that!"

The "I can never remember" person is almost guaranteed to blank out at the same point in the speech each time in rehearsal, as if deliberately fulfilling his or her own prophecy. This actor must work extra hard to find the transition in the script between one thought and the next. (More is said about transitions later in the book.) Remember, too, that memorization is a skill and therefore improves with the type of practice that comes with acting training.

The "I'm going to show them" actor will generally bring a forced feeling, even a quality of desperation, to the comedy of the scene, which can throw other actors off guard. However, quite the opposite delivery is required. Timing and deftness are what make comedy work successfully, and good theatre depends on teamwork, rather than solo work.

The person who says, "Oh, I could never do that" will speak the lines and walk through the movement, but we in the audience won't believe a word. Emotional honesty and truth of character are glaringly absent, as the actor safely avoids playing "the sleaze" despite the apparent attempt. You will eventually learn to fully embrace all aspects of a character, finding the rewards to be much greater when a total commitment is made to the material at hand.

To be successful in acting, you must free up your own natural intelligence and creativity. This can be accomplished through improvisation, exercises, experience and time. Improvisation and exercise ideas, such as those found throughout this book, will help. Acting training and distillation time will further develop skills necessary for successful acting. Good training provides opportunities to grow, to think, to assimilate experiences, to understand your own character, and to reflect on and integrate everything you've learned to date.

Improvisation and theatre exercises don't follow the traditional educational sequence in the acquiring of skills. They differ in approach, for example, from beginning to use a computer or learning to swim, which share a "step one, step two, step three" method of skill development. Theatre work is much more erratic — and a little harder on your emotions as a result. It demands things of you in a personal way that few other activities do, and it will not allow you to hide from yourself.

Six important acting principles

1. There are no rights and wrongs in acting, just choices

Like all generalizations, this one isn't entirely accurate, but it remains a very good motto for the novice actor to adopt. You could say, "Well, I'm going to do this scene with a bag over my head." It's a choice all right, but it won't necessarily lead to effective theatre. You might say, "I think Hamlet is really suffering from an Oedipus complex and is passionately in love with his mother, Gertrude." This may be fine in theory, but it may or may not hold together in practice. I have adjudicated quite a few plays that expounded a theory that did not completely hold up within the full context of the show. Many variables must come together for a successful final result.

Some choices are better dramatically than others, but when you are just beginning to learn about acting, try to avoid the absolute terms of "right" and "wrong." Omit them entirely from your rehearsal vocabulary and don't let others apply the terms to your work either. "Right" and "wrong" carry judgments that will cloud your creativity.

2. Be able to justify your choices

Justification is the root of clarity in theatre. If you cannot answer questions about your performance, don't expect your audience to be clear about your intentions. Find answers to these basic questions:

- Who are you?
- Where are you?
- When is this taking place?
- What is your character feeling?
- Why is your character saying these words? (What is my motivation?)
- What is happening in this scene? (What is my obstacle and what creates the conflict?)
- How does this scene fit into the overall action of the play?

Many times in my classes, student actors have missed some of these basics and, when questioned, have been vague and insecure in their responses. Know your answers to these questions. Make sure you have carefully considered every aspect of your interpretation of character and the staging of your scene, if you hope to understand and grow as a performer.

Be specific, not general. Be able to explain or verify the choices you make. To do anything less is to cheat yourself and your audience. Whatever choices you make must be well considered if you expect your work to be believable. But don't be afraid to find a new interpretation to a character. This world would be a dreary place indeed if there were only one way to present any given character or play.

3. Understand the fundamentals of theatrical presentation

These fundamentals will give you the groundwork on which to build your craft. Your understanding of theatrical presentation should encompass:

- an honest awareness of yourself (vocally, physically, emotionally and intellectually)
- your understanding of the creation of a character
- some knowledge of the function of setting, costume, props and other technical components
- the actor's use of space in that setting and theatre
- inherent components of the style of the play
- the interdependent roles of everyone involved in mounting the production
- theatre etiquette

The same principles are found in every type and style of performance, whether high comedy, serious drama, or night-club cabaret. Just don't do your serious drama as high comedy, however, and expect it to meet with universal approval. You may occasionally see plays that use visual physical slapstick where the play is written with a more gentle and subtle comedy. This type of production has ignored both principles 2 and 3.

However, for virtually every theatrical principle you learn, there is an equally correct occasion — in a certain scene, at a specific moment — when you are wise to break that "rule" of theatre.

4. Keep yourself open, flexible, and vulnerable

The best actors are those with accessible, inquiring minds. They don't react defensively to hearing value judgments of their work either in rehearsal or later during performance. You won't get very far if you reject criticism of your work, if you remain closed to suggestions, or if you continue doing only the kind of acting in which you feel "safe." This leads to acting by personality rather than acting by character.

An example of a "personality actor" in films is the late John Wayne: you will find limited variety from one character or film to another. (Personality actors can often be very successful in their careers and make a great deal of money, nevertheless.) On the other hand, actors like Robert DeNiro, Dustin Hoffman, and Meryl Streep go to great lengths in preparing for each new role. They thrive on total immersion in the character and material, and sometimes we can barely recognize them in a new film because they are so successful at illuminating yet another character.

Sometimes our fears lead us to put ourselves down or apologize, often in subtle ways:

- "Oh, I only do serious drama. I don't have any time for the silly froth of comedy."
- "Me? Sing? Never! I couldn't carry a tune if it had a handle. You should hear me ... I sound like a screech owl."

These are both forms of protection against the fear of failure that every performer experiences at one time or another. Every honest actor struggles with identifying personal anxieties and overcoming these blocks every time he or she prepares to go onstage. Generally, insecurity eases with experience, and others will help you during the training and rehearsal process. But don't rely upon your acting coach or your fellow students to carry you along. You must take responsibility by remaining open, flexible and vulnerable.

Remember, too, that whether in a classroom or a theatre, an audience gets to see and hear something only once. How many times have you missed a key line because of fading vocal energy or been unable to see a piece of staging because of muddy blocking? It requires a lot of work on the actors' part to achieve physical and vocal clarity. The best actors develop their mental, physical, and vocal flexibility to meet all kinds of challenges.

5. Don't play last night's performance

This is an interesting way to express a problem that many new actors encounter. During a performance, if an actor gets a certain audience reaction one night — such as the drawing in of breath at a particularly dramatic moment — there is often a temptation to anticipate the same reaction the next night. If instead a giggle breaks out in the audience, the actor can become upset with the audience. This can be the kiss of death for the actor's performance that night.

Worse still, the actor sometimes forces the buildup to that moment, thereby destroying the expected reaction. It's somewhat reminiscent of the joke-teller who says, "You're going to love this," but then is laughing so hard that he or she can't get the punchline out. Unfortunately, no one else enjoys the joke at that point. In fact, we — as the supposed audience to the joke — can feel miffed that we missed out on the fun.

When an expected reaction doesn't materialize, the performer feels a variety of emotions ranging from irritation with the audience to self-pity. There is always a momentary loss of concentration or confidence.

Principle 5 can also be applied to classroom work. Often while rehearsing at home in the evening, you will achieve a certain standard of performance that eludes you the next day during presentation to the class. A line that every acting teacher knows only too well (generally accompanied by huge sighs and a bit of a whine) is, "You should have seen me do my monologue last night at home in front of the mirror."

Try not to become preoccupied with what you achieved once, for you will end up merely attempting to create an exact reproduction of a single occasion. Instead, view each rehearsal and presentation as a fresh exploration of the emotional elements of the scene. Even during the run of a show, actors will continue to refine moments of their work as they discover fresh nuances, performance by performance.

It is doubly important in classroom work and rehearsal to keep yourself flexible so that you can adapt your work to a variety of circumstances.

6. If anything can go wrong, it will

Always remember this old rule of the theatre. It barely needs explaining. Anyone who has worked in theatre can tell endless horror stories of things that went wrong during a show. Actors forget lines, sometimes jumping over pages of dialogue and throwing other actors and stage crew into panic. They occasionally miss entrances entirely, leaving other actors desperately ad-libbing while stalling for the overdue entrance. Technical cues sometimes fail, props get lost, costumes rip or get caught on furniture, and parts of the set have been known to collapse. The list of theatrical crises is infinite.

One of the most important things you can do during the rehearsal process is discover the points in the play where you are most likely to encounter problems, whether this involves lines, physical action or other actors. Then devise ways to deal with each problem (plan A, plan B, and plan C) and use your subsequent rehearsals to try out those solutions. This will give you added confidence to help you face the special pressures of opening night.

The more resilient and imaginative the performer, the more likely it is that accidents can be covered up successfully. Contrary to popular belief, you can fool most of the people most of the time if you know what you're doing — and it can be a wonderfully exhilarating experience to know you've kept the show going, supported your fellow actors, and sustained the illusion.

The building-block approach to acting

Every acting teacher has his or her own series of favourite exercises — and sequence of experiences — which are designed to challenge and stretch the individual.

Learning to act depends heavily upon the dynamics of the theatre class, the backgrounds, interests and levels of experience of other members of the group, and the variety of material brought into the classroom. No two acting classes will achieve the same result from any given improvisation. No two individuals will progress at the same rate, even though they are in the same class and appear to be receiving identical training, because acting draws upon life skills and life experiences, which vary greatly from one individual to the next.

41

Learning to act is not a steady, slow uphill climb. It often appears to follow a haphazard path, in the same way that events in life affect us at random intervals.

For these reasons, acting exercises are often self-contained. Each class period should be viewed as a brick or a building block. It has a purpose and a function in its own right, but it also will ultimately become part of a larger whole — whose shape and objective may not be evident at the time of construction.

You just have to trust that eventually your building blocks will create a well-rounded actor.

Chapter Three
Relaxing the Actor's Body

Tension centres

The less experienced you are in performing, the more likely it is that physical agitation will take over in performance and manifest itself as nervous physical mannerisms. This often occurs at the most unlikely moments and in the most extraordinary manner.

Have you ever seen people who worry the side of their jeans with nervous fingers while standing up to speak, or who continually clear their throat? Or the person whose leg constantly jiggles, or whose face freezes in panic, or whose eyes dart all over the place?

Onstage, such physical mannerisms generally work against our intended presentation. Since actions are stronger than words, the audience's focus is drawn to our physical mannerism and away from what we are saying. This is the principle behind what is referred to as upstaging: drawing the eye of the audience away from an intended focal point, whether this is a prop, another actor, or a technical effect.

If our body is tight, our voice may also be tight and lead to vocal tension problems, especially as the shoulders and neck are our most common areas of retained tension. Problems can include mumbled delivery, speech that is trapped in the upper register, or talking with an excessive hissing sound on the letter "s" (which is called oversibilance.) This is why actors need to do a warm-up before going on stage. They need to relax their bodies and focus attention on vocal delivery.

Sometimes tension is visible right from the beginning of our work, but at other times it simply appears halfway through our performance without our being aware of it. Students are often amazed at how easily an experienced teacher/director can determine when and where they blanked out on their lines. The answer is simple: it can be found in the sudden reappearance of inappropriate physical or vocal tension habits.

To the experienced eye, it is obvious that an actor has not done a warm-up when the individual "slips into" a role, taking the first two, three, five or more minutes of work to begin to become the character. Up until that point, there is too much of the student visible in the performance and not enough of the character. This is a common problem among novice actors.

Unfortunately, no actor can afford the luxury of "slipping into character," especially when auditioning for entrance into programs of higher training, for important roles, and/or for professional work. Therefore, as an actor, you owe it to yourself to learn techniques that will help you be relaxed from the first moment. Warm-ups must be an ongoing, disciplined activity for the actor because until we achieve a truly neutral state, we cannot begin to create a new character.

As is often the case, self-knowledge is the first step to improvement. We need to discover our own physical and vocal tension centres because each of us has our own way of channelling discomfort. Then we must acquire a series of exercises to help overcome our individual problems.

How to avoid tension in performance

When there is tension in the shoulder and neck, muscles used in breathing and voice production become tight. This adversely affects the quality of the spoken word. We have all seen this problem demonstrated when an obviously nervous person stands up to speak before an audience and suddenly his or her voice comes out as a squeak over which there is little control.

Before a rehearsal, an audition or a performance, it is very important for any actor to do a complete personalized physical and vocal warm-up. Start with physical exercises involving the arms and legs, then progress toward the trunk of the body. When the torso is free and comfortable, move on to exercises involving the head and face. Then begin to warm up the voice with exercises in breathing and resonance. Spend some time flexing the facial muscles used for clearly produced speech.

Everyone has favourite relaxation exercises gathered from a variety of sources, and exercises for theatre often overlap with techniques used in dance, gymnastics, or singing. Use warm-up time to listen to your body. Whether you are working individually or with a partner, concentrate actively on the exercise and what you are getting out of it physically. Let go of the events of the day. Leave your mind outside the room and simply focus on the muscles and ligaments inside your body.

Individual exercises:

Many relaxation exercises can be done solo. One of the most common of these is to actively increase tension in a specific part of the body. When you are finally allowed to let go of that tension, the sense of release is very noticeable. This is a bit like the old joke of bashing your head against a brick wall: it's so wonderful when you stop.

The principle remains, however, that many relaxation exercises alternate between increasing physical tension (and locking the breath) then suddenly letting everything go. It's a fast way to discover a state of relaxation. This group of exercises is called tension/relaxation or TR exercises. They don't require much space, can be done individually and can even be done backstage while in costume. They are useful not only before a rehearsal or performance, but also in real life — for example, when you are having trouble getting to sleep before a major examination. In a modified form, they can also help you before you go into a job interview, or perhaps prior to an appearance on local cable television, or for any other stressful situation where you are concerned about appearing visually comfortable.

Group exercises:

Other exercises require one partner or more. They take a bit longer because everyone has to have a turn. A word of caution, however: any group exercise will be only as valid as the least-committed member of the group will allow it to be. One joker can ruin an exercise for several people and any student who cannot enter into the spirit of an exercise should be unceremoniously dismissed from the room.

Advice:

If you feel any physical or mental discomfort, such as dizziness during breathing exercises, sit down where you are and wait for the next exercise.

If emotional distress or concentration problems begin to appear, stop doing the exercise, withdraw to the edge of the room without interfering with anyone else and wait quietly until you have recovered. Above all, do not berate yourself as if you have "failed." Problems with involvement happen to everyone at some point. If you can figure out what got in your way, you will have discovered something important about yourself.

General limbering exercises

1. *Rag dolls/toy soldiers:*

This simple kindergarten game is actually a classic example of a tension/relaxation exercise requiring a deceptive amount of concentration.
For the rag-doll exercise, the body collapses as follows:

- feet locked at the ankles
- knees bent and spread
- arms hang down almost to the floor
- the head falls forward between the knees
- use only the minimum number of muscles to keep yourself from falling over

The toy-soldier position is the exact opposite:

- stand totally erect
- knees locked
- fists clenched rigidly at the side
- chest out and chin in
- every muscle as tense as possible

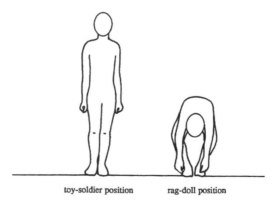

toy-soldier position   rag-doll position

The leader of the group simply calls out "rag doll" or "toy soldier" in a sharp, brisk manner, but in random order. The fun happens when participants try to anticipate which instruction is coming next, get caught copying someone else's mistake, or get fooled by repetition and erratic alternation of commands.

2. Hand shakes:

This exercise is particularly good for people who worry their fingers when they appear in front of an audience or fiddle with costumes during a scene. It can be done as a last-minute reminder by an actor standing in the wings before an entrance, or immediately before entering an office for a job interview.

Before you begin this exercise, take off any loose jewellery. Begin to shake your hands in front of you. Once you have achieved a rapid action, double the speed. Without losing speed, begin to raise your hands above your head and hold them there for several seconds. Then let your arms totally collapse beside your body without stopping the hand shakes.

Alternate between the raised-arm position and the collapsed-arm action several times, all the while keeping the hands moving as fast as possible. Then gradually slow down the intensity of the action, much as a swing slows when someone stops pushing it. Eventually, stop shaking and just allow the arms to swing a bit. As you wind down, you will begin to feel heaviness in the fingertips, and a very relaxed feeling in the hands.

3. Tension/relaxation with body isolation:

Ideally, this exercise should be done lying on the floor in a relaxed state with shoes off and overhead lights dimmed. Because it involves very little movement, it can be adapted to daily life situations. It is a good exercise to practise at different times of the day until you can almost call upon it at will. In such cases, it can be done while seated: in a waiting room when applying for a job, for example.

Begin by making a fist with one hand only, sustaining the tension for five to 10 seconds, then relaxing briefly. Almost immediately squeeze the fist again, harder than before if possible. Try not to let any of the tension creep into another part of the body such as the forearm.

Once you have worked on one fist, try it with the other while ensuring that the original hand remains relaxed. Repeat the exercise, tensing both hands simultaneously. Then proceed to tense one forearm

47

without allowing tension to creep back into the hand or the upper arm. Repeat the exercise with the other forearm, then with both. Move to the upper arm and follow the same pattern.

Then move to the feet, the calves, the thighs, and the buttocks. Next, isolate each part of the torso without allowing tension to creep back into the limbs or up into the neck. Keep the head gently rolling while the upper torso and shoulders are being dealt with, to ensure the neck remains loose. With the rest of the body remaining relaxed, work on isolating the neck, the jaw and the face.

Finally, sum up the whole exercise by tensing every muscle in the body and sustaining it for 15 seconds. During this count, do a mental checklist of each part of your anatomy to ensure you are integrating "total body" tension. Relax briefly before repeating the sequence with double the intensity for another 15 seconds. Then allow yourself the luxury of simply lying (or sitting) there and enjoying the sensation of total relaxation.

4. *Head rolls:*

Now we come to an exercise to relieve tension in the neck. If you find you have some stiffness in one particular part of the neck, consciously try to relax the area with some preliminary massage. This exercise works best if you are standing with your feet at least shoulder-width apart and the rest of your body in a neutral position, though head rolls can be done seated. Do a slow, 30-second rotation of your head while allowing your jaw to relax and fall in whatever direction it wants. Try to focus on the muscles of your face sagging toward the ground. Feel them being pulled by gravity — stretching is important in this exercise — and do not rush the head roll. Reverse direction after each rotation to avoid dizziness.

5. *Six separate stages of tension and relaxation:*

This tension/relaxation exercise introduces the subject of movement involving all parts of the body. Each sequence should involve every part of the body in random order at one point or another. It involves a lot of free movement, so make sure there is sufficient space between all participants to prevent one person accidentally hitting another. You may close your eyes on the first step and the last one; the rest of the time you'll need them open to make sure you don't collide with a neighbour. (Make sure the floor is clean so that no one is reluctant to use it when necessary.)

(a) *The stretch:* Before you begin, take a moment to check the points of your body where you feel stiff or tight and see whether or not by the end of the stretch you have released some of the tension you're holding. Close your eyes if it helps your concentration. This allows you to focus more clearly on the messages from your body. Start from a standing or seated position.

Begin with one hand: stretch each finger of the hand very slowly, one at a time. Add the palm of the hand into the action, then the wrist. Rotate the wrist, then add in some forearm action. Explore your space in every direction, gradually adding in the entire arm and shoulder until you are extending into the very furthest areas you can reach. Repeat the action with the other hand and arm.

Apply the same technique to the feet and legs, beginning with the toes and extending through the entire leg. First, work on one side of the body, then the other. Explore a good stretch of the torso and head (including the face). Imagine making your entire body yawn and verbalize that yawn, if you like. Yawning brings oxygen into the body, helping circulation and relaxation of the voice.

Once you have warmed up your body, begin to change your breathing pattern with the movement of the stretch. Focus on each breath in and out as you stretch. Add a sound to each exhalation. This should be thought of not as a "note" but simply as a natural yawning sound. Don't feel you must isolate each part of the body. Rather, move whatever part of the body wants to move. Continue for a couple of minutes.

(b) *The swing:* Begin this step of the exercise with just one part of the body, then add in other parts as you build the movement. Start with the arm again. Think of large circles and try to imagine your arm is going to swing in several of the biggest possible circles. Sometimes it will make the complete circle, while other times it won't quite manage to do so and will come falling back in the reverse direction.

Enjoy the sensation of swooping, swinging, and swirling. Do you notice that a momentary sense of floating accompanies the highest point of the swing? You may also notice a heaviness in your fingertips as this exercise progresses. As you add in different parts of your body, you may want to move around the room. You could make complete spinning motions as you move. Just keep thinking of circles, in every possible direction.

When you move, begin to think of your breath patterns. Vocalize the circular movements, realizing that different movements will create different qualities of sound. Again, do not think of the "note" of the voice but rather of matching raw sound to the energy of the swing.

(c) *The bounce:* Bouncing should be a loose, up-and-down action that you will perform successfully only if you retain the looseness you have acquired in the first two stages of this exercise. Keep your knees bent to absorb the shock of the movement and land on the balls of your feet every time. Remember, not all bounces require your feet to leave the floor. Don't overdo the action of the bounce. Keep it small and specific to one part or another of your body.

Experiment with different rhythms and degrees of bounce, but make sure your bouncing retains an easy energy. Try it standing, crouching, and then bent over. Try it with one part of the body, then another. First bounce tight and low, then high and free with arms extended above your head. Be imaginative. Think of part of your body bouncing like a basketball, then another part like a ping-pong ball, while yet another bounces like a medicine ball.

After a minute, begin to vocalize the actions that your body is creating. Add increasing amounts of sound carried on the breath. Once again, the release of sound is more important than the quality.

(d) *The shake:* This stage of the exercise begins to add further tension to parts of the body. The shake is similar to the bounce but it is a tinier action, much faster and with more tension. Begin as usual with one specific part of the body and develop a shake — first in one direction, then in another. Move from side to side, up and down, and back and forth. Don't let action or tension creep into another part of the body. Let speed and tension appear in the breath and voice that you add to this stage of the exercise, but try not to fall into a stereotyped "shiver" voice.

(e) *The blow:* Attack is the name of this stage of the exercise. All movement is sudden, sharp and short. Imagine you're an expert in martial arts and each part of your body is a lethal weapon. Isolate each part of your body so that movement is happening just in one place at a time for the first while. Don't think about where you are going to move next. Just let it happen. Use all your space, but remember to keep your movement restricted to short distances. Add in awareness of your breath patterns after a minute or so, then vocalize the various energies of the blow.

(f) *The collapse:* Allow yourself one minute to go from your last position in the blow sequence to a total collapse on the floor. The moment the signal is given for this final stage of the exercise, freeze. Analyze the position of all parts of your body. Allow yourself to be drawn down by the force of gravity, but control the speed with which this happens.

The collapse begins with the part of your body that is highest in the air: a finger, an elbow, or the head. Feel the energy drain out of those muscles bit by bit. Enjoy the sensation of relaxing and let this relaxation be reflected on the breath. When your arms have dropped, let your head get heavy and begin to pull you forward toward the ground. This basic rag-doll flop should be familiar to you now, so just continue to be pulled down by gravity. Think of the movement of the vertebral column as you bend over deeper and deeper, and begin to vocalize the breath at this point.

Finally, fade into the floor from the rag-doll flop position as if it were a slow-motion slide (and try not to land on your kneecaps). Don't worry about landing in a certain position. Just end up wherever you melt. Once you are on the ground, let each muscle relax one at a time until you feel your are dissolving into the floor.

6. *Rag-doll slow flop:*

This exercise involves the whole body and introduces the subject of combining breath work with relaxation. The beginning position is similar to that in the first exercise, but your feet should be about shoulder-width apart. Knees should be bent and the body flopped loosely forward so that the hands are just brushing the floor. In this position, get an image in your mind of the shape of your spine, and continue to visualize the movement of your vertebrae for the duration of the exercise.

Slowly begin to raise yourself, one vertebra at a time, allowing the spine to gradually straighten from the lowest vertebra first. Take at least 30 seconds to rise up, making sure that your arms and head hang loosely until the last possible moment. The second-to-last action is the rolling back of the shoulders to a comfortable, dropped position. The final moment involves slowly raising your head while keeping your face as relaxed as possible.

Once you have completed this movement, reverse it. Let your head get heavy and fall forward without the rest of the body becoming involved yet. Remain there for a few seconds before allowing the weight of the head to draw the shoulders and torso slowly downward again. Allow your breath to leave your body with a freely released sound as you collapse. Ultimately, you will return to the beginning flopped position. Repeat the exercise three or four times.

Variation — rag-doll fast flop: Repeat the exercise, but speed up the second half. Collapse abruptly and allow air to escape with a rushing sound, but retain the slow upward rising action.

Variation — rag-doll breath flops: Repeat the rag-doll fast flop but this time focus on the rhythm of inhalation and exhalation. To start, get rid of as much breath as possible and begin from the flopped-over position. As you rise, try inhaling in one long, slow breath through the nose. When you collapse, allow the air to leave suddenly and noisily through the mouth. Inhalation may take upward of 20 seconds, while exhalation takes only two or three seconds.

Now try the same thing with the rag-doll slow flop. Instead of releasing air in a rapid collapse, allow the body to fall back slowly and deliberately into the starting position. First, feel the head get heavy, then let the shoulders fall. Gradually the entire body collapses forward with one long, sustained exhalation. Visualize breath leaving the mouth. Keep the mouth relaxed and let the sound come out as a sustained "fffff." On the next slow collapse, allow the breath to come out of the body like a moan on a sustained "mmmmm" sound of no fixed pitch.

Remain in the flopped-forward position for a few complete in-and-out breath cycles. Although this is an awkward physical stance that seriously restricts upper-chest breathing, you will discover some expansion takes place in the most unexpected part of your anatomy: the lower back. While you hang there breathing in and out, place your hands on the small of your back to feel just how much physical action can be detected as you inhale and exhale. This exercise helps to free up deep-body breathing to provide good breath support for an actor or singer.

Variation — balloon breath: When you have completed the rising action from the initial rag-doll flop position, continue the upward movement. Raise the arms and reach for the ceiling. Imagine yourself as a balloon. Once your arms are completely extended and tension is building in the entire body, rise onto your toes and hold this position for as long as possible. Collapse quickly, letting sound escape as you flop forward. (This is another example of a tension/relaxation exercise.) Try to complete the exercise in one inhalation/exhalation cycle to build up your breath-holding stamina.

7. The next two exercises are particularly good for dealing with shoulder tension:

Shoulder rolls: Stand with your feet approximately shoulder-width apart and put your hands on your hips. Slowly rotate one shoulder backward in a circle several times, allowing yourself to feel each stage of the action: up, back, down, forward. Then reverse the direction of the shoulder roll: forward, down, back, up. Repeat these steps with the other shoulder. Now alternate between the two shoulders: first one back, then the other one back, first one forward, then the other one forward. If you speed up a bit or do it to music, you will feel a bit like a "hoochy-koochy" dancer.

Shoulder drop: This basic TR exercise simply involves raising your shoulders as high as possible and keeping them raised as long as you can. Do not allow tension to creep down into your arms. You can avoid this by allowing your arms to swing gently by your body. Your shoulders will almost touch your ears and, when they are finally allowed to drop, you may experience a sensation that your neck is twice as long as it might normally feel.

Alternate between the shoulder roll and the shoulder drop (which is also called the "No-Neck Monsters," for obvious reasons and thanks to Tennessee Williams's *Cat on a Hot Tin Roof*).

Advanced torso warm-up exercises

The following exercises, while not initially appearing to be more difficult, tend to require a greater degree of concentration. As you become increasingly skilled at listening to your body and learning to heed its messages, your powers of concentration and focus will be sharpened. Not only do these exercises have an application in acting work, but also they are very efficient at helping the body relax before bedtime — especially the night before a major audition or examination.

Rehearsal warm-up exercises are designed to help you forget about the activities of the day:

- the bus that infuriated you by pulling away as you ran to catch it
- the frustration of forgetting your wallet
- insecurity you experienced in dealing with someone who intimidated you
- embarrassment of being caught in a white lie
- guilt over cheating on your diet
- the exhaustion of a long, hard day
- the misery brought on by not dressing sensibly enough, so that you arrived cold and wet at rehearsal

All these issues can get in the way as you begin acting work. There is a direct ratio between anxiety and concentration: as anxiety goes up, concentration goes down. You don't lose skills, but you do lose psychological control. Warm-up exercises will help you forget the myriad of daily frustrations. They will begin to release tension from physical and vocal centres that are deep inside you, and allow you to focus on your physiological make-up.

The first two exercises represent a most efficient method for ridding the torso of tension. The torso is the centre of breath work, and breath is the source of all energy in characterization.

1. *Spinal roll:*

This exercise will help you discover how much tension is carried throughout the entire torso. As stress accumulates through the average day, we often become increasingly aware that our neck muscles tighten and contract to the point where we get tension headaches. Although we are rarely aware of it, a great deal of tension is also held in the spine. The spine changes its alignment as physical tension creeps into the muscles of the torso. This subtle change of alignment affects the way we stand, sit, move, or perform any physical activity.

A curved spine generally means muscles are locked, which can have a negative impact on your breath work. To illustrate this point, try taking a deep breath while standing in a deliberately exaggerated sway-backed position. You will find it is very difficult to inhale a substantial amount of air.

The principle behind the Alexander technique of movement (a set of exercises with which every actor, in time, should become familiar) deals with lengthening the spine by using the head as the initiator of all movement. The head moves upward and away from the body as the body lengthens. More importantly, the muscles used in breathing are attached to the spine. Therefore, the actor must learn to relax muscles along the spine in order to free the breath.

The spinal roll involves lengthening and flattening the spine while lying on the floor.

Choose a clean, carpeted surface or a gym mat, if possible. Otherwise, a coat on the floor will provide some protection for the spine. Make sure no bright overhead lights are shining in your eyes. Stretch out flat on the floor with your legs extended. Do you notice that there is a curve in the small of your back? Most people can slide a hand between the arch of their spine and the floor. If you raise your knees and bring your feet in close to your torso, this space decreases. The leg action has helped to straighten the spine. Consider this position of lying with your knees bent as the starting point for this exercise.

(For safety's sake in real life, remember to bend one knee when lifting heavy objects. Let your legs do the lifting where possible. For example, place one foot on the bumper of a car when removing luggage from the trunk. If you lift from that position, you will substantially ease the muscular strain on your lower back.)

To begin the spinal roll exercise, hoist your body up onto your shoulders and over so that your feet come over your head and practically touch the floor. Keep your knees close to your face and set each vertebra down on the floor one at a time, taking as much time as possible. Visualize in your mind's eye the action of each vertebra.

Your hands will do a great deal of the work to keep you in control and moving slowly. Keep your knees and legs close to your body and allow your knees to part as they pass by your face. Don't let your legs rise away up in the air or you will end up working the tummy muscles more than the spine. Complete the action of setting each vertebra on the floor and return to the original starting position — with knees bent — so you can keep the spine flat. Repeat this exercise several times.

Feel the spine pressed against the floor. Breathe in and out deeply and as low in the body as you can manage. See whether or not you can make the small of the back expand with each inhalation. Feel it flatten against the floor with each breath taken in.

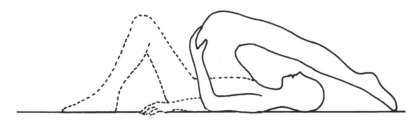

flattening the spine: spinal roll

Variation #1: If you are wearing a skirt and cannot do the exercise without compromising your modesty, or if you have trouble getting up and over onto the shoulders, try this method. The beginning position is the same: flat on the back, knees bent. Keep your feet in place and hoist your weight up onto your shoulders. In this position, your only points of contact with the floor will be your shoulders and your feet. Everything else will be raised off the floor and supported by your thighs.

Allow your thighs to do all the work as you lower your body to the floor, one vertebra at a time. You will find that in this variation you cannot get as high up onto the top of the spine as with the previous exercise. On the other hand, you will have more control over the speed with which you set each vertebra in place.

spinal roll variation #1

Variation #2: The same exercise can be done in full costume, as you stand in the wings of a theatre waiting to go onstage. Stand about 30 centimetres away from a smooth wall and spread your feet shoulder-width apart. Lean back so that only your head touches the wall. Begin the same action of setting one vertebra at a time against the wall, taking at least a minute to reach the final position where your spine is pressed flat against the wall. Your legs will automatically bend and take the weight of the body as you flatten the spine.

Variation #3: You can also reverse the direction of the exercise in *Variation #2.* With your feet in the position discussed above, place the small of the back against the wall while allowing your head and shoulders to hang down. Place one vertebra at a time against the wall until you reach the top of the spine. Lengthen the neck as much as possible before allowing the head to touch the wall.

2. *Shoulder drop:*

This exercise will enable you to release a surprising amount of tension across the back and neck. It should generally be preceded by the previous exercise, the spinal roll. That exercise was designed to flatten and lengthen the spine, while the shoulder drop is meant to rotate the spine gently in order to release back tension.

Start by lying on your back with raised knees. Gently roll over onto the right hip. In this position, draw your left leg over so that the left knee is touching the floor, or as close to the floor as you can comfortably reach. Let the left shoulder fall behind you toward the floor. You will find that

allow shoulder to relax toward the ground

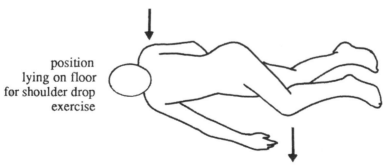

position
lying on floor
for shoulder drop
exercise

allow knee to relax toward the ground

you cannot make both the knee and the shoulder touch the ground at the same time — unless you are double-jointed — but your task in this exercise is to try to do so. Don't force your knee and shoulder to drop, though. Let it happen through relaxation and release of tension.

As you are lying there, close your eyes and breathe in and out deeply and slowly for at least two minutes. You will find it is impossible to use your upper chest to breathe, for it is held in a rigid state. You will be forced to breathe from your lower abdominal area.

Visualize any part of your body where you feel tension. With each exhalation, try to release just a little more tension from that specific part of your body. Enjoy the feeling of relief that comes with each exhalation. Feel tension flowing outward and visualize it leaving your body.

As you get rid of tension in one area, you may become aware that another part of your body feels tense. Although you are focusing on the torso, tension may be discovered in an arm or a leg as well. No matter where it appears, focus on it and breathe it out of your body. Listen to what your body is telling you.

A few things to watch for:

- Don't let your top foot rest on your lower leg.
- Keep both feet touching the floor.
- If you begin to feel pins and needles in your lower leg, adjust your position on your hip by rolling a bit more in one direction or another.
- Allow your arms and hands to collapse in a comfortable position, so long as they don't rest on your body.
- If an arm begins to go to sleep, adjust its position.
- With each breath, keep monitoring feedback from your body.

Once you have completed that stage, roll back slowly into the starting position, taking at least 20 seconds to get there. Use the minimum amount of energy to complete this action. Then roll onto the other side and repeat the exercise for another couple of minutes.

When you have finished breathing out tension from the other side of your body, slowly roll over onto your front and lie there for a moment or two. Keep one knee bent to the side of your body to retain the flattened-spine feeling. When you are ready to get up (as before, using the minimum amount of energy), slowly draw yourself back onto your haunches much like a cat stretching after lying luxuriously in the sun. Sit there for a while and enjoy the physical sensation of relaxation until you feel like returning to the real world.

It is important to move as slowly as possible in order to keep your body as relaxed as possible. Your aim should be to sustain the feeling of total relaxation for as long as you can.

Exercises for evening rehearsals

The following are very efficient group relaxation exercises that can be a particularly refreshing treat at the beginning of an evening rehearsal, especially after a difficult day. They rapidly rid the body of the day's tension, foster group cohesiveness, and offer a popular incentive for the first few people who show up on time for rehearsal.

1. *Group back-pats:*

The exercise is designed to release tension from the back, arms, and legs. One person is selected to be in the middle of a circle formed by four or five others. The subject in the middle should remove any loose jewellery, eyeglasses, or anything bulky in pockets such as wallets or combs. The subject has but one job: to remain in the basic rag-doll position described earlier with feet shoulder-width apart, knees bent to absorb physical action, head loosely hanging forward, and arms practically touching the floor.

The rest of the group, having removed all rings and bracelets, gather around and assume comfortable positions either standing or kneeling by the subject. With the flat of the hand, lightly and rapidly begin to pat the broad area of the subject's back. Make sure you keep all hands moving, rather than lingering in one specific spot, to avoid pummelling someone's kidneys or tailbone.

It is really important that no conversation take place. Communicate within the group by facial expression, because chattering is very distracting for the person on the receiving end of this exercise.

Work down the legs and arms as well, ensuring that you keep patting rapidly. Once you have been at it for 30 seconds or so, you might be able to increase the intensity somewhat (that will vary depending on the body structure and body weight of the subject). It is common for the subject to sag a few centimetres lower toward the floor as he or she begins to relax and unwind.

Don't touch the subject's head or neck. There is only one exception to this rule: if the subject begins to raise his or her head, thus putting tension back into neck and shoulder muscles, lightly touch the top of the subject's head as a gentle reminder to let the head flop forward. Once the subject's head is loose, the body can relax again.

Sustain the hand pats for a couple of minutes or so. Then, by mutual unspoken agreement, stop and step back a couple of paces to wait. After a moment or two, the subject begins to rise slowly; others should be prepared to catch him or her if dizziness occurs.

In rising, try to imagine there is a string between your shoulder blades that is pulling you upward like a puppet. Come up slowly. Thirty seconds is not too long but a minute is even better. Use minimum energy to rise because you don't want to put tension back into your body:

- Slowly unfurl the spine vertebra by vertebra.
- Allow the shoulders to drop.
- Gently raise the head using the minimum number of muscles.
- Stand tall and relaxed.

If the person in the centre is rising too quickly, one member of the group can slow down the action by "walking" his or her fingers up the subject's spinal column, thereby controlling the speed of the vertebral action. The others remain still and silent while this is happening.

Repeat this exercise so that everyone in the circle gets a chance to be in the middle — returning the favour to each other, as it were. This exercise is particularly effective because the subject cannot anticipate where the pummelling action of the hands will go next. The body has no option but to release tension from the torso muscles.

2. *Group neck massage:*

This exercise is based on relaxing one part of the body (the neck) while keeping tension in another part (the hands). It involves concentration to sustain these two separate messages to your body.

Everyone in the group stands in a circle facing inward with their shoulders almost touching. Then everyone turns in the same direction with their feet approximately shoulder-width apart to brace themselves. The idea is that each person massages the individual in front of him or her — along the neck, down the shoulders to mid-back and the upper arms — while the person behind is doing the same thing for you.

In an exercise like this, you must really concentrate on relaxing every part of your body, except for the forearms and hands, which will be working energetically in the massaging action. Silence is important so that participants can focus upon their individual body tension and breath patterns.

If you are too far away from the partner you are meant to be massaging, the temptation is to move a step forward into a better position. That would create the same problem for the people behind, however, and the problem would spread round the circle. Instead, move that part of the circle a step in toward the centre and everyone will be satisfied.

When this exercise has continued for a couple of minutes or so, everyone should stop working, turn 180 degrees, and return the favour to the person behind.

3. *Head pivot manipulation in pairs:*

This exercise builds on the previous two and is especially good for releasing neck tension. Match people according to height and designate a manipulator and subject within each pair. The manipulator sits on a chair or the floor, while the subject sits on the floor in front, leaning securely back into the manipulator's body for support. All the subject must do is to relax completely and allow the manipulator to do all the work.

In each of us, there is a central point where the head balances on the top vertebra of the spine inside the skull. Ultimately, the manipulator's goal is to find this balance point. However, it can only be found if the subject is capable of totally releasing all tension in the neck and head.

The manipulator can begin with a gentle neck and shoulder massage if desired. But the manipulator's principal function is to take the subject's head and move it slowly and gently in a variety of directions. The subject must not do any of the work. There is a real temptation, especially in certain types of people, to not relinquish control of the head. It is up to the manipulator to sense this and to coax the subject into letting go of such tendencies. Gently murmured comments may be helpful.

To help the subject give up control, the manipulator can try confusing the direction of the head movement. If you lift the subject's head and you feel he or she is taking over the action, just let go of the head. It should fall forward. The next time, roll it back and forth instead of raising it up. Keep the subject confused about which direction, when, how, and how often you manipulate the head.

Sometimes a short pause to massage a stiff tendon will assist the subject in letting go. After a couple of minutes of allowing the subject's head to relax — and this is a condition that can be felt but not easily described — you should begin to feel for the central balance point. You will know you have found it when the subject's head is completely relaxed yet remains upright as you remove your hands.

When the head and neck are truly relaxed, the manipulator will notice how heavy the head feels. It can be moved gently from one side to the other with no resistance. If a full feeling of security and trust has been achieved, the subject will discover the sense of relaxation is wonderful, quite unlike that achieved in any other warm-up exercise.

Reverse the roles.

This is one exercise where you can learn as much by giving as you can by receiving. Usually, repeating this exercise a second time around permits the subject to apply what he or she has learned through functioning both as manipulator and as subject. Much deeper results can then be achieved.

When followed by vocal resonance work, this is a particularly good exercise to help you get in touch with the relaxed yet flexible state that radio and television work demands.

Facial relaxation

We carry a lot of tension in our faces; these exercises will help you discover where you retain tension and how to release it.

1. *The jaw:*

The muscles of the jaw often hold a surprising amount of facial tension. Remember that in all jaw relaxation work you must keep the action of the jaw up and down, not side to side. Cattle were made to chew cud in a sideways action, but the human jaw is not designed for that range of motion and you do not want to cause harm by inappropriate movement. If you are wearing orthodontics, you may want to adapt the following exercises to your own situation.

The first stage of jaw relaxation is done by self-massage. Feel where the upper and lower jaws are joined at the hinge by a large muscle. Using three fingers of each hand, begin to massage this muscle in either a pulsing action or a circular motion. Allow the jaw to open as you work vigorously at releasing the tension. Because the jaw is a major area of retained tension, even more exercise may often be necessary to rid the face of unwanted discomfort.

Next, lean your head forward so that it is parallel to the ground.

Grab a good pinch of each cheek in the middle of the face. With a vigorous action, in either a side-to-side or up-and-down direction, shake the face as strongly as possible. Ensure that your jaw is relaxed and ignore any funny sounds that emanate from the mouth. Repeat this action grasping different places along the jaw and lower-lip area.

Now, grip your jaw between your thumb and forefinger and move the jaw open and shut. The catch here is to make sure your hand does the work, not your jaw. If your jaw is truly relaxed, you can hear the "clink-clink-clink" sound of the upper and lower teeth contacting. The more you increase the speed of this action, the easier you will discover whether or not your jaw is taking over the movement.

2. *Facial massage:*

This exercise will help to release tension in a variety of places. It involves the same physical action as the jaw massage: three-fingered pulsing actions or circular motions. Begin this movement at the jaw muscle for several seconds before allowing your fingers to move up toward the temples. Linger there for a moment or two. Then proceed along the upper-brow ridge until your fingers meet in the middle of the forehead just above the nose. Let the action move toward the hairline, along the edge of the scalp and back to the temples. Continue down toward the cheekbones, being delicate of touch as you work around the eye. Proceed along to the nose, down to the lower lip, and around the mouth. (Remember to let the mouth move freely as you massage.) Finally, complete the action back to the starting point at the hinge of the jaw.

Once you have made this circuit, repeat the exercise using as rapid a pit-a-pat action as possible. Let the fingers of each hand delicately and rapidly beat out a raindrop pattern over the face. Repeat the same circuit as the massage, but let the fingers completely fill in over the forehead, nose, lips, and cheeks.

Having completed this second stage, lightly draw the fingers of both hands down your face, beginning at the scalp line and continuing right over your face to the throat. Enjoy the feeling of the last bit of tension being drawn out of your face. Repeat this two or three times.

3. *Peanut-butter face:*

This full-face exercise is simple and self-explanatory. Imagine your mouth is overstuffed with sticky peanut butter and you are having a difficult time trying to eat it. Exercise every part of the face while doing this, including the eyes, eyebrows and forehead. This will give the entire face a workout.

A variation on this is the "Ugly Face Contest," which also leads to some strenuous stretching. This gives you a chance to make all those hideous faces that you were forbidden to make as a child in case the wind changed direction and your face remained forever fixed in a grimace.

4. *The lips:*

Lip exercises are designed to release tension around the mouth. Every actor must strive for the greatest clarity in articulation and it is for this reason that lip exercises are included in physical warm-ups. Try doing them one after another, three times through.

These "fish face" exercises tend to make one look bizarre and feel even sillier. If you have trouble concentrating, close your eyes. What you can't see won't bother you:

- *Angelfish:* Draw your cheeks in as far as you can, using the teeth to keep the face in shape. Make what is left of the upper and lower lips touch as quickly as possible 25 times.
- *Blowfish:* Blow the air out of your mouth, using fat cheeks and vibrating lips.
- *Kissing fish:* Pucker up the lips and stretch them as far forward as possible. Make them extend far beyond your nose.

Now vibrate the lips, deliberately trying to create spray and to make engine-type noises. Try to imitate a horse whinnying. Then make various sounds like a motorcycle. In each of these exercises, you should endeavour to relax the lips. The more relaxed they become, the more sustained the noise will be.

5. *Tongue tension:*

Curious as it may seem, the tongue holds a great deal of residual tension even when the rest of the body is fully relaxed. The next time you are having trouble getting to sleep at night, notice how much tension remains held at the root of your tongue. If you consciously focus on relaxing your tongue, you'll fall asleep before you know it.

Inappropriate contractions in the muscles of the tongue can lead to distortion of the shape of the mouth cavity. This in turn can affect our speech; think how we stumble over words with a thickened tongue when we are nervous. Tongue tension can also affect the quality of sound passing through the larynx, so we lose control of our pitch. When some people become nervous, tension may go to the tongue tip and create an overly sibilant sound. An actor should try to eliminate these problems through exercises as illustrated here.

A word of warning: tongue tension exercises tend to make us look silly as we are doing them, but there are a couple of ways to minimize the problem:

1. Close your eyes. If you can't see what other people look like, you won't waste time thinking how foolish you yourself may look.
2. Put all your attention into the physical sensations you experience in each of the following exercises.

Before you begin, make an exaggerated hissing sound and sustain it for 30 seconds. Impose as much tongue tension as you can muster. Do it till it hurts. Feel what happens to the tongue, especially how it bunches up in the back of the mouth. Become aware of the position of the tongue tip in making this overly sibilant "s" sound. Do you see how much tension also goes into the face and the neck? File this information away so that you have a point of comparison when you discover the difference a relaxed tongue can bring to your entire jaw and neck.

(a) *Tongue stretch:* This exercise involves extending the tongue as far as it will reach. Fight to keep it stretched there until the position becomes painful — for at least 15 seconds. Then let your tongue slowly relax and slide back into the mouth to its natural resting place. Don't let it retreat into your mouth any farther than that. You will discover that the tongue rests much farther forward in the mouth in a relaxed state than in a tense one. The blade of the tongue rests on the lower teeth, while the tongue tip actually falls slightly over the lower front teeth.

Repeat this tension/relaxation exercise several times. If you are ever required to do radio, microphone, or television work, this is an excellent exercise to do a few minutes before you begin to speak, even as you sit waiting in the studio.

(b) *Tongue extension with counting:* Repeat the tongue extension

65

described above. With the tongue fully extended, begin to count as follows:

1
1 - 2
1 - 2 - 3
1 - 2 - 3 - 4
1 - 2 - 3 - 4 - 5 ...

and so on. Work your way up to 15, ensuring that the tongue remains fully extended the entire time. It's very hard to talk with the tongue in this position and you will find that the tongue will ache after a period of time. Fight against the pain. Don't let the tongue withdraw into the mouth under any circumstances. You may also discover that you begin to drool as you are counting, because the regular swallowing action that rids us of excessive saliva is impossible under these circumstances. Keep a tissue available.

Although this exercise is very simple to do, it requires maturity and discipline to execute. Remember the above advice about keeping your eyes closed, if necessary, to improve concentration. But plug your ears as well. This will block out all external stimuli and allow you to focus on your own physical sensations.

Once you have finally reached the number 15, begin to let the tongue relax and slide back into its natural resting place in the mouth. This exercise is a perfect example of putting excessive tension in a specific part of the body in order to achieve a high degree of relaxation when the tension is relieved. If you suffer from a great deal of tongue tension, you should add this TR exercise to your vocal warm-up procedures.

(c) *Th - into - S:* The following exercise builds on the previous two and is designed to help the speaker discover a fully relaxed "s" sound with no trace of excessive sibilance.

Repeat the tongue-extension exercise once and discover the fully relaxed sensation when the tongue draws back to its resting-place. Feel the blade and tongue tip resting on the lower teeth. Keep the mouth as relaxed as possible and begin to make a "th" sound.

Slowly withdraw the tongue into the mouth, keeping it as

fully relaxed as possible. As soon as the "th" begins to turn into an "s" sound, stop the tongue but sustain the sound. Don't let the tongue withdraw any further into the mouth. Feel how the tongue and face are relaxed, and hear how the "s" is easy and soft. Remember this sensation and realize you can control the formation of this very difficult consonant.

Now take a tongue twister with a lot of "s" sounds in it. For example: "Sister Suzy sews some shirts for some soldiers." Isolate every "s" sound in it, and it reads like this:

S - is - ter S - uz - y s - ew - s s - ome sh - irt - s for s - ome s - oldier - s

Say the sentence using a "th - into - s" sound before each and every "s" in the sentence. It reads in a silly manner, but this represents an approximation of the sounds:

Th - s ith - s ter	Sister
th - s uth - s y	Suzy
th - s ew th - s	sews
th -s ome	some
th - sh irt - **th - s**	shirts
for	for
th -s ome	some
th - s oldier **th - s**	soldiers

Keep the tongue relaxed at all times during this exercise. Stop the movement of the tongue at the very moment the "s" sound begins to be heard. Once you have worked your way through the line, say the entire sentence using the minimum amount of "s" sound for each word. Don't let tension creep back into the tongue or face.

As you say the sentence in its entirety, without any tension in the tongue, you will likely hear that the line sounds dead and flat. This is because vocal inflection is missing. Try to say the sentence now, getting the happy balance between life and colour on the one hand, and a relaxed non-sibilant "s" on the other.

If you discover that oversibilance is your own particular problem — through this exercise, from your teacher or friends, or by listening to yourself on a tape recorder — begin to assemble your own list of similar tongue twisters. Make up your own tongue twisters using as many "s" sounds as possible in one extended sentence. When you work at the problem on a daily basis, eventually you will be aware of the correct physical sensation and tongue placement in making "s" sounds. It takes a long time and diligent practice to overcome excessive sibilance — because it's usually a deeply ingrained habit — but it is necessary for anyone aspiring to performance work.

(d) *Tongue stretches:* Extend the tongue far forward and alternate several times between rounding (or pointing) it and flattening it. Don't cheat by using your fingers or teeth to help you. This is an exercise purely for the muscles of the tongue. Close your eyes if you have concentration problems with these steps. Next, with the tongue extended, see if you can make it reach your right ear, your nose, your left ear, and your chin. Repeat this sequence a few times, keeping your attention fixed on stretching the tongue as far as possible. Next, extend the tongue, flatten it, and flip it first to one side and then the other. Don't use the teeth to do any of the work.

Now try vibrating the tongue tip on the roof of the mouth. When unvoiced, it sounds like Eartha Kitt's famous purr. When voiced, it resembles the noise of a motorcycle. Voice the sound and imagine you are shifting gears up and down a hilly landscape.

Not everyone can perform various tongue exercises, due to genetically inherited factors. Approximately one person in four, for example, is missing the muscle structures that allow the tongue tip to vibrate. Very few people can make the flattened tongue flip equally well in both directions. If you have trouble with one particular tongue exercise, substitute another tongue-strengthening exercise that you can, in fact, manage.

6. *Larynx tension:*

Finally we come to the last of the physical warm-up exercises that are designed to prepare the actor for a vocal warm-up. This exercise deals with the larynx (commonly known as the "voice box"), which can hold residual tension. This exercise of laryngeal manipulation should be the last stage of physical warm-up. It is a serious exercise and should be approached with a mature attitude.

Tension in the larynx tightens the vocal folds which, in turn, inhibits their easy and free use. The voice sounds tight. Lower resonators of the throat and torso become blocked by tension in the larynx, which means that the lower notes of the voice will be missing or weak.

Having first thoroughly relaxed the neck, shoulders, and face, tilt your head slightly forward. Allow your fingers to rest on either side of the larynx. You will discover that you can actually move the larynx, surrounded by its cartilage, from side to side. Begin with the gentlest possible push — just a fraction of a millimetre. Push it to one side, then the other. Keep the action delicate, slow, and gentle.

You may feel a sensation and, indeed, even hear a popping sound as the larynx moves from one side to the other. Don't be alarmed; as you achieve complete relaxation, the sound diminishes and the movement of the larynx becomes freer and easier. This exercise is a real test of relaxation in the throat area.

These introductory exercises are helpful in loosening up the body before other acting exercises. There are numerous other such exercises, so begin to accumulate a sequence of those that are most effective for you personally. Try to set aside a certain period of time each day to apply them, to understand how your body functions, and to learn how best to deal with your own personal tension centres.

If you find an exercise is helpful under ordinary circumstances, think how wonderful it will be when you have had a particularly stressful day and really need to shake off the day's tensions before beginning rehearsals.

Chapter Four
Voice and the Actor

Vocal analysis

Do you remember how startled you were when you first heard yourself on a tape recorder or video? The voice we hear inside our head bears little resemblance to the voice that is actually projected through space to other people. Take some time to listen to the vocal delivery of your friends, your family members, and actors from the world of film and television. Notice the many assumptions we make about other people based on how they speak.

Speech is a learned skill, and we pick up other people's vocal patterns in childhood without being aware of it. Often, these deeply ingrained habits can get in the way of what we really mean to communicate. Vocal delivery can also reveal some of our insecurities, and we can project incorrect information to others. For example, sloppy speech can make us appear dull, lazy, or ill-educated. Bombastic or aggressive delivery can alienate listeners. Voices that trail off suggest we don't believe what we're saying. A flat voice can sound unemotional and boring, so the listener's attention will easily waver. Rising inflection at the end of every thought suggests you are asking for confirmation or approval.

Because vocal problems are interconnected with physiological and psychological sources, training the actor's voice should be viewed as part of training the whole person: a synthesis of voice, movement, thought, and emotion. That does not mean, however, that vocal training should neglect the value of repetition and practice drills.

Self-awareness is the key to improving our level of vocal skill. A first step is to tape record your voice and analyze the results. As an actor, you must begin to view your voice as an instrument, and practise daily vocal exercises with the same discipline that a violinist or pianist practises scales and musical pieces in preparation for performance. Your voice is the instrument with which you will carry the language of the play and the subtext of your character to the back row of the theatre. (Remember this old theatre saying: there is a slightly deaf person seated in the back row at every performance of every show. Learn to project to the full extent of the theatre space.)

Speech delivery, for stage and for daily life, will vary depending on:

1. the size of the space in which you are working
2. the number of people you are addressing
3. the nature of what you are saying

We also have different styles of speech for different occasions in life, and speech for the theatre should not try to impose something unnatural on the actor's personal life. Keep your vocal delivery flexible and appropriate to the occasion.

The purposes of voice study for the stage are quite simple:

- to improve flexibility of your vocal range
- to aid projection without relying on microphones
- to improve clarity of speech

If you do not develop your full vocal potential, you run the risk of short-changing your audience, whether on stage or in everyday situations.

Influences on vocal sound

Our speech patterns are learned habits that directly reflect a number of life factors, such as:

- the speech patterns in our families
- influences of our peer groups
- educational and/or religious background
- individual susceptibility to slang and "sub-cultural" language

- an "ideal" sound based on voices we may consciously or subconsciously admire

Some people are easily influenced by these factors, while others remain rigidly fixed in early speech patterns. Many of us have a sympathy for or aversion to specific vocal sounds because of early childhood influences, most of which are buried in our subconscious mind. For example, if your favourite babysitter spoke with a pronounced Italian accent, you might retain a love of the rhythm that is the essence of that accent. Perhaps you could even make a respectable stab at the accent yourself, years after that person has left your life.

Speech patterns also may reflect a number of personal factors that can vary from one day to the next, or one moment to the next. These can include:

- general state of health
- energy level
- emotional condition
- reaction to other people or events around us at the moment
- what we want

In addition, each of us has certain limitations that are dictated by our physiological structure. No amount of exercise can alter inherited features such as the specific sizes of body cavities where resonance occurs, the vocal folds themselves (contained in the larynx), the muscle structures of the tongue tip, and so forth.

An actor must be aware of his or her own vocal patterns and personal habits before beginning to create those of another character. If you impose your own vocal patterns onto a character, you will bring a similarity to every character you develop in scene study or performance. When we first become aware of the manner in which we use (or under-use) our voices, many of us are alarmed to find that we do not project the quality of sound that we believed we were producing. Let's look next at the process of producing and developing sound.

The sequence of voice production

There are five general areas of vocal development for the stage. They follow a logical sequence, namely the order of voice production itself: **relaxation**, **breathing**, **resonance**, **articulation**, and **vocal variety**.

1. Relaxation

Remember what happened when you had to get up in front of a class or at the school assembly? Without any warning, your voice was pitched much higher than usual. Fear made your throat dry out and your knees began to tremble. Not only do the muscles in our limbs go tight, but also the muscles affecting the neck are tensed. This stress in turn leads to tension in the vocal folds within the larynx, which results in lack of control of the voice. Sometimes the voice breaks, projection fails, or we lose control of the pitch. We trip over simple combinations of words, compounding our pressure and feeling even more foolish afterwards.

So before you can begin to discuss good voice work, it is important that you are loose and limber. No tension should be found in the neck or face, especially the parts of the mouth used in articulation. The vocal folds in the larynx must be relaxed in order to release a full and natural sound.

2. Breathing

Without good breath support, a speaker can often run out of breath before the end of a line. Sometimes this makes it difficult for listeners to hear every word, especially toward the ends of sentences. Poor breath control also leads to a very "breathy" voice, almost whispery, which doesn't project well in a large space. The need for good breath support becomes evident when you work in large theatres or "gymnacafetoria."

But breathing for vocal projection is a bit different from breathing for jogging, dancing, or strenuous physical activity. Aerobic activity is not necessarily connected with vocal projection. It is designed to keep one moving throughout strenuous physical activity.

Speech for theatre, however, demands a fluid communication of emotions. The actor's emotional release and interpretation of character must be tied into well-supported breath work. Good breath control is essential to sustain appropriate energy in the voice, whatever the emotional content of the spoken word and whatever the size of the audience. Breath and sound are the keys to the actor sharing his or her emotions with an audience.

3. Resonance

Defined as the amplification of the voice, resonance allows the actor to project his or her voice to fill a large theatre without placing undue strain on the larynx. Resonance can best be understood by comparing the voice to a musical instrument. If you strum a string on a guitar, you can hear the sound increase within the wooden body of the guitar. If you beat a drum, the sound reverberates within the drum to amplify or increase the power of the sound.

By the same token, the human voice resonates or reverberates within the cavities and bones of the body — particularly in the mouth, nasal cavities, throat, and chest. Remember the last time that you had a bad cold? The quality of your speaking voice changed dramatically from the sound you were used to hearing in your head, because the sinuses and nasal cavity filled with fluid, thereby preventing normal resonance from taking place. The degree of resonance is governed by several factors that will be discussed later.

Resonance is carried on the vowel sounds in the human voice, so all resonance exercises involve the vowels — *a, e, i, o, u* — and combinations of vowel sounds. Vowels can be divided into three types:

- *Monophthongs* are one-syllable vowel sounds, such as is found in "oh."
- *Diphthongs* are comprised of two interdependent vowel sounds together in one sound. An example can be found in the combination of "ah" + "ee" in the pronoun "I." In the study of accents and dialects, you'll see that vowels are often distorted — elongated or shortened — from one region to the next.
- *Triphthongs* are much less common. They are made up of three interdependent vowel sounds together within one overall sound, such as the "i" sound in "fire." This sound is made up of "ah" + "ee" + "uh," the final sound being a throwback from the consonant *r*.

4. Articulation

This simply means clarity in the formation of the consonant sounds using the organs of speech — specifically, the lips, tongue, teeth, hard palate, and soft palate (the palate is the roof of the mouth). Clarity and crispness of speech depend on precision of articulation. Skills can be developed by exercises that strengthen the contact points used in forming consonants.

Variations of articulation can be found between one person and the next for a variety of reasons, including where we were raised, family speech patterns, and individual physiological structures. Listen to the speech patterns of those around you. Do some of your family and friends have particular ways of speaking specific consonants?

Each language has its own combinations of consonant sounds, so a person who begins life speaking one language often has difficulty with a few specific sounds in a second language. Sometimes one language will simply not have a particular consonant sound (or combination of consonants) that is common in another language. Often an alphabetical letter in one language is not found in other languages or, if it exists, it is pronounced quite differently. It can be very difficult for us to shake our recognizable "first language" accent when we learn a second language after we reach adulthood. Children are generally more adaptable than adults when learning new languages, and assimilate more easily.

Another reason for differences in articulation comes from peer-group vocal patterns.

Some of these factors change as we progress through different phases of our lives, and we are continually being exposed to new influences and experiences. For example, many teenage boys begin to speak less clearly when their voices start to change during adolescence. If they can't trust their voice to sustain the sound, it's safer (and less embarrassing) to mumble a bit. But once the voice has settled, confidence and clarity generally return.

5. Vocal variety

Vocal variety allows us to express a wide array of emotions, interpretations, and colour with our voices to reflect the true meaning of what we are saying. It involves:

1. rate of speech
2. pace of dialogue
3. use of pause to point words or moments
4. inflection or musicality
5. volume
6. pitch

It is important to understand each of these terms clearly. For example, rate and pace are often confused. In theatre terms, **pace** really deals with the overall shape of a speech, a scene, an act, or the entire play. It depends upon a number of factors, such as the various rates of speech, the use of pause, the speed with which cues are picked up, and the tightness or looseness of vocal and physical action. **Rate**, on the other hand, means the speed of delivery. It is dictated by two factors: the nature of the piece itself and the capabilities of the speaker. Never try to speak faster than you can clearly articulate and make sure your rate reflects the emotional content of the piece.

You may know that the musicals of Gilbert and Sullivan demand a fast rate of delivery even when you speak, rather than sing, the lines of their songs. If you cannot move your mouth clearly and quickly, you will soon scramble the words.

Pause, meaning to dwell or linger for a moment, is one of the most effective ways of marking a word in order to give it a particular importance.

Inflection is the rise and fall of the voice within a range of pitch, and provides colour and energy to the voice. Inflection can be anything from a simple upward lilt of the voice to a compound — and very musical — embellishment of sound.

As a rule, Canadians use very little inflection. We suffer from The Great Canadian Monotone: the voice continues along on one eternal droned note, rising only at the end of the line with the infamous spoken or implied *"eh?"* When such a speaker begins to use more inflection, it often sounds unreal or forced to him or her (although not to an audience). This is hardly surprising if the speaker is changing speech patterns after many years.

Pointing is simply a combination of inflection and pause. (The issue is discussed more thoroughly in chapters 6, 19, and 20, where it is applied to delivery of classical text.) Generally speaking, there is one key word in every spoken line. The meaning of a line can be severely altered simply by choosing to point a different word by inflection and pause. For example, take the line "I spoke to him yesterday." Depending on which word you choose to point, you can completely change the intention of the sentence:

- **I** (as opposed to **you**) spoke to him yesterday.
- I **spoke** to (as opposed to **saw**) him yesterday.
- I spoke to **him** (as opposed to **her**) yesterday.
- I spoke to him **yesterday** (as opposed to the **day before**).

Volume depends on the degree of support behind the voice (that is, the energy of the breath) and the degree of resonance achieved. It encompasses everything from a bellow to a stage whisper.

The **pitch** is the note of the voice. There are many pitches in a musical sense, but in speech we talk about three general notes. The mid-note is the most common, while the lower pitch is used for a change of emotion, and a higher pitch permits further variety. Sometimes the nature of the piece itself demands a specific pitch be used. Just listen to the pitch used on television by a reporter covering a major tragedy, and then note the pitch change as the announcer switches to the exciting sports finals.

For the actor, a "pitch switch" generally occurs with a new thought, a shift of emotions, or when using an "internal" character voice. Do you remember your favourite babysitter telling the story of *The Three Little Pigs and the Big Bad Wolf?* The more vocal variety the reader achieved in pitch and emotional intensity, the more captivated you were by the story.

You will find a wide variety of speech habits among your family and friends, films actors, and television personalities. Note how diverse speech patterns can be, and how voices that are alive with colour, energy, and variety are the most interesting to listen to.

Listening is a skill that is critical to an actor, both for exercise purposes and in real life. We are often selective in what we hear in daily life. Instead of concentrating on what someone is saying, our mind races ahead to another thought or how we plan to respond to the speaker. As an actor, try to develop your listening skills, because good acting depends on the ability to focus your attention to the full meaning of what is being said and how it is being delivered.

Common vocal patterns

There are several common problems that can be identified in the untrained speaking voice. When these are repeated over and over, they form a vocal pattern that becomes evident to a skilled listener after a period of time. Often, it is difficult for people who are listening to vocal patterns to hear clearly what is being said, and their attention starts to wander. For an actor, it is dangerous to let an audience member's attention drift away from the action of the play.

1. Fading tone ... or unfinished business

The problem: This begins when the voice runs out of volume before the end of the line. It is caused by difficulties in sustaining breath support throughout the spoken line. You actually have a lot more breath inside you than you really need in order to speak. However, you must learn to trust that it is there, then discover how to employ it. (See also point 3.)

The solution: Daily exercises will help. Practise counting from one to 10 while gradually increasing the volume as you speak. Repeat this several times until you learn to keep sufficient breath in reserve for the final numbers that, of course, require the greatest energy. Then substitute words for numbers, practising with nursery rhymes or simply structured poems. Practise with different volumes, pitches, rates of delivery, and types of material.

2. Rising inflection ... or "Am I pleasing you?"

The problem: A habit that is common to the tentative, diffident or approval-seeking personality is the continued rising inflection at the end of every word. It suggests or implies a number of subtext messages: "Is this right? Am I understood? Am I pleasing you with what I'm saying?" The speaker appears to lack confidence. Some actors put a question after their own names, or pepper their speech with irritatingly repetitive phrases such as "you know?", "um," and "er."

The solution: Learn to state everything, not ask it. Consciously bring the voice downward at the end of every line in an authoritative, confident manner. Practise with a variety of scenes and speeches. Work with a tape recorder. Practise with improvised dialogue where you are recounting stories from real life. You can overcome this problem in time.

3. Falling inflection ... or negative music

The problem: This habit occurs when the cadence of the voice falls at the end of a few words. This is usually accompanied by a decline in energy and breath support (see point 1 above, "Fading tone"). Imagine speaking the sentence "I'm having fun" with a downward inflection. In a longer sentence, falling inflection signals that the speaker is concluding a statement. Repeated "false endings" interfere with open conversation, for the listener is never sure when to jump into the dialogue.

This vocal fault is particularly dangerous in comedy, for the key to successful comic delivery is to keep the voice alive and energetic to the last word in the line. Very often it is the final word of a comic line that triggers the laugh. Try this exercise: tell your favourite joke but deliberately drop the energy on the last word of each line. Then tell the joke again, emphasizing the last word in each line. Do you hear the difference this makes to a simple joke? Imagine the difference it can make to the successful delivery of dialogue in a comedy.

The solution: Look for opportunities to use upward inflection in the voice through a line of speech. Develop breath support in conjunction with smooth phrasing and sustain the breath phrasing to the end of the line. Particularly watch that you stay open and responsive in improvisation, and that you do not block others with an implied negativity at phrase endings.

4. Gusting ... or "I'm so excited"

The problem: Speech in which most of the energy bursts forth at the beginning of the line, before the speaker slows down to complete the balance of the thought, leads to "You-rushing-all-your-words-together-in-a-bunch-a-little-bit-like-this." Finally you begin to slow down to a normal rate of delivery for the last part of the line. With every new breath you take, you rush and elide initial words together, thus interfering with clear speech.

The solution: Discover the natural rhythm of the line. Counting exercises are good, and the use of a metronome will help keep your rhythm consistent. Explore your text for the important words that appear at the beginnings of lines. Practise throwing attention onto those words for a while, until you become accustomed to giving due credit to every important word in the line.

5. Equal pauses ... or "Sssh, I'm concentrating"

The problem: This occurs when you have begun to memorize your piece and are pausing at the end of every line in the speech. It goes against all natural speech patterns and gives a mechanical or practised sound to what you are saying. What is actually happening is that you are subconsciously taking a moment to think of the first words of your next line. However, some actors often retain this vocal pattern well into the run of a show.

The solution: Rewrite. Punctuate. Take your speech and change it so that the punctuation matches your character's intention and energy. Inevitably, this will result in several sentences being delivered as if they were one long sentence, while pauses may often appear in the middle of lines in front of important pointing words. Keep your interpretation of lines and words open and experimental in rehearsal. Avoid "locking in" to repetitive line readings, and don't settle for dull patterns of speech. The time will come when you have conquered this problem; then you can revert to the punctuation suggestions of the writer.

6. Grocery lists ... or "Sing me a song"

The problem: A sing-song type of delivery occurs when the actor is not thinking of the emotional subtext behind certain types of lines. Words come out in a parroted fashion. Each word is spoken with an identical sound, as if the actor were reciting a grocery list of: "apples, oranges, bananas, sugar, bread, milk, and tea." Sometimes the grocery-list delivery happens when there is a series of words on a related theme, as is common in Shakespeare's plays.

This habit becomes especially noticeable in a speech that deals with repetitive words. If there is a repeated word or phrase, the actor will latch onto it as the key to the vocal delivery, when, in fact, the emphasis should be placed on other words in the line.

A common example is found in three lines spoken by Sophie in Neil Simon's play *The Star-Spangled Girl*. Each line begins with "I have tried to be...." When emphasis is placed on those initial words, the listener hears only those words. But the real meaning of the line emerges when you place the emphasis on the other contrasted words: "neighbourly," "friendly," and "cordial."

The same principle is found with repeated pronouns such as "I," "she," or "you." Repeated words may also include "always," "never," or "horrible." Playwrights often repeat words for a specific effect, but an untrained actor will over-use those words in delivering the speech. In fact, the emphasis should be placed elsewhere.

The solution: Early in the rehearsal period, long before actors become fixed in speech patterns, they should look for any repeated words and pronouns. Find other words to point, and lightly score a line through as many pronouns as possible.

These are a few of the more common vocal faults. There are others, such as weak articulation of final consonants, or overly resonant sound. You can discover these patterns in your own voice.

- Use a tape recorder to hear yourself as others hear you. In preparation for rehearsal, tape yourself delivering your lines in practice at home.
- Keep a tape recorder running through your next improvisations or discussions with friends, then play the tape back to hear your speech patterns that emerge from unstructured dialogue.

- Make a tape of yourself sight-reading three or four different items from a newspaper or magazine. Leave the tape alone for a while so that you can't clearly remember what you read — sometimes the subconscious mind will fill in missing consonant sounds if you can easily recall what you have read. Some days later, play the tape back and make note of which sounds seem unclear.
- Check each of the five stages of voice production. Do you sound relaxed? Do you have a natural, sustained breath support throughout? Is your voice resonant? How clear are the consonants? Is your voice varied and pleasant to listen to?

Everyone has the potential to develop his or her voice beyond the demands placed on it in everyday speech. If you really want to develop your voice, you must allow for a certain amount of daily practice time.

The physiology of voice production

Here is a diagram illustrating the parts of the head used in speech work, and some definitions and explanations to help you get even more out of this and other vocal exercises.

The "contact points" in speech involve the tongue, teeth, lips, and hard and soft palate. (The palate is the roof of the mouth. The hard palate is the forward two-thirds of the mouth and is divided from the nasal cavity by bone. The soft palate is the soft tissue at the rear third and ends in the uvula — the dingle-dangle that cartoonists love to focus on in close-ups of screams!)

Each consonant is classified according to its sound and the parts of the head used in forming the consonant:

- *Labial* sounds are made with the lips.
- *Lingua-dental* consonants are formed by contact of tongue and teeth.
- *Lingua-palatal* sounds involve contact of the tongue with the hard or soft palate.
- *Guttural* sounds are created by the contact between the back of the tongue and the soft palate.
- Some consonants (such as *t*) are *voiced.*
- Others (like *h*) are *unvoiced.*
- Some (such as *b*) are "stopped" sounds and are called *plosives.*

The physiology of voice production

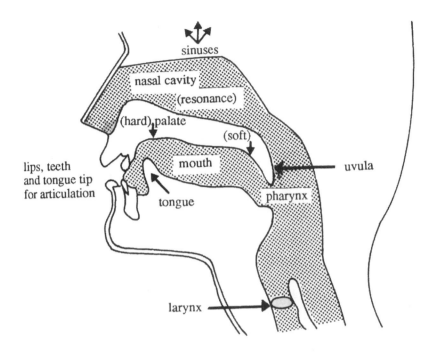

- Others (like *s*) are *continuants*.
- *Fricatives* are sounds created by forcing the breath through a narrow space, as when forming an *f.*
- *Sibilants* (such as *s*) have a hissing quality.
- *Blends* are sounds that start with an explosive quality but immediately soften. An example of a blend is found in *j.*
- *Glides* and *nasal sounds* are easy enough to understand.

In North America, we tend to be very sloppy with our final consonant sounds. (Exercises for this problem will appear later in the book.) Experiment to discover which consonant sounds you find most difficult to form. If you were to make a list of that consonant sound as it appears at the beginning, in the middle, and at ends of words, you would more easily be able to strengthen your own articulation. For example (using *b*):

- *b*oy, a*b*out, and so*b*

Finding the natural note of the voice

<u>What you need to know</u>:
The first step in producing the voice is to get in touch with your natural speaking note, which is called the **optimum pitch**. This is generally not the note you use during most of the day but is, in fact, a couple of notes lower.

If you think back to the early moments of your day and recall the deeper-pitched sounds you made as you were fumbling about in the kitchen trying to find the coffee pot, you will be remembering your optimum pitch. The problem is that as we progress through the day, we use energy to project our voice. This energy automatically makes us work our way up the scale a couple of notes, and sometimes by late in the day we become aware that our voice is pitched higher than we'd like it to be.

<u>What you can do to apply this</u>:
To reacquaint yourself with your optimum pitch, put fingers in both ears to block out other sounds. This also helps you hear a more accurate sound of your own voice. Keep your mouth open and your jaw slack, and don't let any tension creep into the neck area. Next, pick a note that is about halfway up the scale you normally use for speech. Using open "ah" sounds, let the voice simply fall or "slide" down to the lower end of your range. Repeat a few times.

The sound should be continuous rather than a note-by-note "singing scale." You'll notice a bit of "dive-bomb" quality to the sound — all the more reason to keep your fingers in your ears if several of you in a class are doing this at once.

As you listen to your own voice with your fingers firmly planted, try to visualize the shape of the sound you are making, much like the following illustration depicts. It's hard to describe, but you should be able to hear that very near the bottom end of your dive-bomb, the "ah" sound seems to spread, becoming fuller and more pleasant. This note is the optimum pitch and it occurs at almost the last stage of the glide, immediately before vocal quality dissipates into hoarseness or raggedness.

As you repeat this step several times, recall the final note that your voice rests upon. Repeat the exercise, but sustain that lower sound when you reach it. Do this several times. Then make another dive-bomb to see if the final note is perhaps a bit lower than the one you last reached. In many cases, as the voice relaxes within this exercise and tension diminishes, the optimum pitch note is actually discovered to be somewhat lower than originally thought.

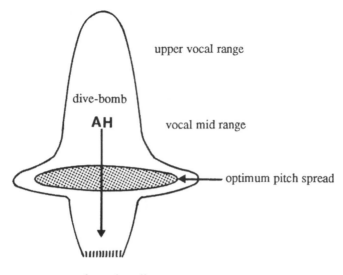

There are several other ways to discover optimum pitch. One is to speak the word "her" repeatedly in a rather potted version of Tarzan pointing at Jane. Another is to repeat the word "he" with a lot of attack, almost like a cough. Another way is to imagine you are passing a bakery just as fresh bread is taken from the oven. You take a big sniff and say "mmmm." The lower end of that sound is the optimum pitch. Alternatively, say an exaggerated "uh-uh" as if you mean "no way." Again, the lower end of that sound is your optimum pitch. Finally, if all else fails, the lower note of a yawn may get you in touch with the pitch.

Once you are relaxed and have renewed your acquaintance with your optimum pitch note, it is time to begin working on building that note through resonance. Resonance will allow you to create a stronger, fuller sound in your body without putting extra strain on the larynx.

Developing resonance

<u>What you need to know</u>:
Resonance occurs in several places within your body: the mouth, nasal cavity, pharynx, sinuses, throat, and chest. If you want to develop greater ability in vocal projection, experiment with resonance to discover how it sounds and where you can feel it reverberate within you. These next exercises are designed to help you achieve better resonant sound and you should add them to your daily vocal workout. The greatest resonance will

take place in your head because the largest resonators are found there.

<u>What you can do to apply this</u>:
1. Mouth resonance:

To discover mouth resonance, direct the sound to the front of your mouth. Before beginning, make sure your mouth is open about the width of two fingers, and the lips remain drawn gently over the teeth. Don't let tension come into your lips or jaw, but rather let your face feel slack as the lower jaw drops naturally down and back. In fact, don't try to "open the mouth," for that puts the emphasis on the lower jaw and builds tension. Instead, concentrate on lifting the upper jaw from far back inside the mouth in order to ease the strain on the jaw. Alternatively, you can allow the jaw to go totally slack. If you feel tension building, yawn a couple of times to stimulate the circulation and to stretch and condition the jaw muscles.

If the teeth remain close, the sound will simply bounce off the back of them, preventing total mouth resonance. (This is the situation we find at work in someone who talks through a clenched jaw. The sound is never fully released.)

Begin with a few dive-bombs. Let the sound of the optimum pitch build within the mouth on a continuous "mmmm" hum. After a short time, you will discover that there is a tingling feeling around your lips and nostrils, which means that the exercise is on track and effective. This sensation is created by the vibration of resonant sound in what is called the "mask" of the face.

Build the volume level without putting undue strain on the larynx and see how the quality of the sound varies. Experiment with an "ah" sound instead of the hum. Try different pitches and perhaps a couple more dive-bombs. Use simple words that combine the "m" sound, such as "Mom," "memory," and "Mammy."

2. Nasal resonance:

Another type of head tone comes from nasal resonance. Start by keeping your mouth almost closed while making the sustained "ng" sound that is found in words such as "sing" or "song." You will feel that at the back of your mouth the soft palate is connecting with the tongue, thus preventing the sound from entering the mouth. The sound has no option but to go up into the nasal cavity, where it reverberates in turn within the sinuses above the nasal cavity. Do you feel the difference in sound quality, placement, and vibration?

If you have heard yourself on a tape recorder and believe that your voice sounds too nasal, what is happening is that the soft palate is being lazy and remaining dropped. The problem can be helped by learning to open the mouth wider as you speak. This action raises the soft palate, thus permitting the sound to exit through the mouth. You cannot sustain a nasal sound in your speech when the soft palate is raised (as it should be in normal speech).

If you are having trouble feeling the action of the soft palate — as many people do — imagine you are singing the highest possible note you can reach. Don't actually sing; just pretend you are doing it while you keep your lips closed. You shouldn't have too much trouble feeling the soft palate lift. Try this again with your mouth open while looking at your reflection in a mirror, so that you can actually see the soft palate lift.

Try practising the words below. Make sure that you open up fully after each "ing" or "ong" sound by making a deliberate open "ah" sound. Thus:

- *sing-song* becomes *sing-ah-song-ah*
- *King Kong* becomes *King-ah-Kong-ah*
- *Hong Kong* becomes *Hong-ah-Kong-ah*
- *ding dong* becomes *ding-ah-dong-ah*

Practise these over and over until you feel the action of the soft palate. Then go on to incorporate these words into sentences. Listen to how the quality of sound changes with this different placement of mouth and nasal resonance. Now try to combine both mouth and nasal resonance into one full head sound without putting any extra strain on the larynx. Continue to vary the pitches and sounds you produce. Close your lips and let the sound amplify within your head on an internal hum.

3. Throat resonance:

A third area of resonance can be found in the throat. Resonance here can be discovered not on the closed "mmmm" sound, but rather on open vowel sounds. Begin by resting a hand lightly on your throat so that you can feel vibrations there as you form the vowels. Start with some mouth resonance on a hum and experiment with dive-bombs on different notes. Now sustain the hum for five seconds on your optimum pitch note before opening the mouth and releasing the sound freely on the "ah" sound. As you gradually open out this sound, you should feel an increase in the vibration within the throat.

4. Chest resonance:

Some people can also discover chest resonance. This is the natural vibration of sound that occurs lower in the body. Once more, place your hands on your body to feel the vibrations: one hand on the chest, and (believe it or not) the other on the small of your back. Chest resonance is most easily felt when you open the mouth to release the sound on a vowel such as "ah" or "oh."

If you have done a thorough relaxation warm-up program with lots of torso limbering and flops, you will have loosened the muscles in your back sufficiently to enable you to feel some residual vibration low in your body. Don't worry if you cannot feel it there the first few times you try. Few people manage to do so right off the bat. In fact, a great deal of vocal work takes months and years to understand fully. Just keep coming back to this exercise later in your acting work. Perhaps by using other exercises in this series (such as the initial rag-doll exercise where you place your hands on the small of your back while hanging over doubled up), you will discover chest and low-back resonance and be able to employ it in your vocal projection work.

Exercising the resonators

<u>What you need to know</u>:
Now that you have experienced the increased fullness that resonance can bring, experiment with different vowel sounds. You will find that some vowels are formed naturally in certain parts of the mouth. Sometimes a diphthong begins to form in one part of the mouth, then moves to another part of the mouth for the completion of the sound (as in "ah" + "ee" of "ice"). You may discover that one vowel resonates more easily in one specific part of the body than another.

For example, the following words contain vowel sounds that are formed in the front of the mouth: please, pill, bake, passed, them, glad. Vowels formed in the middle area of the mouth include: cup, father, fur. Back vowels include: are, want, ball, sold, cook, do. Some diphthongs that move from one place in the mouth to another are: play, I, coin, ewe, cow, blow.

<u>What you can do to apply this:</u>
Bearing in mind that resonance is carried by the vowel sounds, try this exercise. Take some poetry with lots of open vowel sounds, such as these lines from William Wordsworth:

> "On either side the river lie
> Long fields of barley and of rye ..."

Follow these steps in sequence:

1. Read the sentence normally.
2. Exaggerate all the vowel sounds and mouth action as you read the line, continuing to form the consonants but greatly underplaying them.
3. Drop the consonant sounds completely so that the line sounds like this:
   O ei-er aye uh i-er aye aw ee uh ah-ee a uh aye.
4. Allow the sounds to flow in one continuous but ever-changing sound. Combine this with breath support work, trying to increase the length of time that you can keep the sound flowing without running out of air.
5. Separate each sound and precede it with a resonant hum on an "mmm" or "nnn" sound:
   Mmmo mmmei-mmmer mmmaye mmmuh mmmi-mmmer mmmaye mmmaw mmmee mmmuh mmmah-mmmee mmma mmmuh mmmaye.
   Alternatively, you can follow each vowel sound with a resonant "mmm" or "nnn."
6. Combine these vowels with optimum-pitch work in a series of dive-bombs.

Try placing a cork between your teeth to keep sound from being trapped in the mouth (a cork will allow some slight tightening of the teeth without causing any damage). In the absence of a cork, place two fingers between the teeth to prevent the teeth from tightening up. In either case, try not to tighten the jaw. Keep it relaxed despite the awkwardness of the physical position of the mouth. If you feel tension creeping into your jaw, stop and get rid of it before continuing with resonance exercises.

Now that you have discovered the function of optimum pitch and its relationship to resonance, practise the exercises several times more in the privacy of your own home, but with a variation. (You may want to choose a time when everyone else is away from home, or they will wonder what you are up to with all the strange noises you will create.) Try doing your resonance exercises in the bath. Everyone knows that the sound they produce in the shower is fuller than normal. This is due to several factors:

- Hard tiles bounce the sound.
- Warmth relaxes the larynx and resonators very efficiently.
- Sound is carried better through humidified air. (Remember how loud the party sounded across the lake last summer? That was the humidity factor at work.)

Continue to practise each of these exercises in turn on a daily basis. You will soon discover how to use your resonators, thereby saving strain on the vocal folds. In time, you will learn what each feels and sounds like. These are the first steps in improving the quality of the sound you make.

Lastly, just for fun, there are some tongue twisters that are particularly good for resonance work because of their particular combinations of sounds. Try some of these, gradually increasing your rate as you repeat each one 10 times over. Linger on each of the "n" and "m" sounds:

- Niminy-piminy (remember to move the lips as you do this one).
- Niminy-moominy-piminy-piminy-moominy-niminy (this involves mind over matter — begin very slowly and concentrate on each word in turn).
- Many mighty men making mounds of marvellous money in the moonlight.

Group vocal exercises:

1. *Resonance circle:* It is best to perform this group exercise on a wooden floor because wood is a natural resonator that dramatically enriches the quality of shared vocal sounds. The exercise works best with only six or seven people. Before you begin as a group, make sure that:

    (a) your spine is lengthened and flattened to free up the muscles of the torso, and
    (b) you have explored a full optimum pitch.

Sit in a circle, facing outward. Appoint one person to arrange the position of everyone in the group. Ultimately, you will be lying on your back with your spine pressed against the floor, your knees bent, and your head aimed toward the centre of the circle. Each person's head should just touch the heads of both neighbours, lightly contacting above the temple area. This tangible connection promotes resonance. Avoid awkward overlapping or bumping. (If one were to look down from ceiling height, the array of bodies would resemble the outwardly radiating petals of a daisy.)

Reacquaint yourselves with your optimum-pitch notes. Focus on relaxing your jaw and allowing your mouth to open at least the width of two fingers.

The object is to begin a simultaneous group resonance exercise with individual, rapid breaths being taken whenever necessary. The group sound should be continuous and of a steadily improving quality — gradually lowering in pitch and increasing in volume — and sustained for at least three minutes.

During that time, be aware of various individual sounds and the collective group sound. Ensure that your mouth remains comfortably open, so that the maximum sound can be fully released. Otherwise the sound will be locked behind your teeth, reverberating only within your head and not joining in the collective sound. Complete three minutes of pure resonant sound, then compare notes with the group.

The most noticeable effect will likely be the communication of each resonating note around the circle so that another person's sound often seems to be coming from inside your own head. In addition, a natural harmonious sound or a common group sound generally emerges after a while.

If the members of the circle have kept their mouths relaxed and well open, the sound often seems to have a circle of energy that appears to hover about a couple of feet above the heads of the participants. (Remember not to strive for expected results, however. Just do the exercise and discover whatever you can from it.)

2. *Paired resonance:* In this exercise, two people are matched up according to their height from hip to shoulder. The exercise demonstrates both the sharing of resonance and the principle of sympathetic resonance.

Sympathetic resonance is the sound that occurs on a second — and immediately adjacent — piano when a chord is played on the first piano. If you listen very closely beside the second piano, you will hear tiny echoing vibrations along the strings inside, note for note the same as the original chord. This exercise applies the same principle to the human voice.

Again, try to do this exercise on a wooden floor to improve the acoustic quality of the sound. Before beginning, take a moment to rediscover your optimum pitch, preferably starting from the lying position on the floor.

Sit back to back with your partner. Position yourselves for maximum physical contact, placing tailbone to tailbone and spine to spine, aligning the shoulders, and expanding the torsos. Link arms in this back-to-back position if you like, for that will minimize the risk of slipping out of position.

Now begin optimum pitch work. Try to resonate as fully as possible, opening up the sound within your own body to its maximum. Experiment with different notes. Remember to keep your mouth open and relaxed. Sometimes you can work the same note as your partner, while at other times you will be working in different pitches.

What often happens in this exercise is that the actor discovers how deeply he or she can resonate within the body. While we are often unaware of employing deep body resonance on our own, when you are sitting back to back with another individual, sympathetic vibration can be felt down at the lower back. Of course, sympathetic resonance occurs elsewhere within the two bodies. It is possible to pick up head tones as well as chest tones.

The quality of sound you achieve in this exercise and the areas of the body that resonate will vary from partner to partner. Repeat the exercise two or three times with different partners. This will expose your resonant sound to other notes and contrasting body structures, and help you discover the variety of changes that occur from one individual to the next.

Improving articulation

<u>What you need to know</u>:
There are many excellent exercises to improve articulation, a lot them involving tongue twisters. The principle behind articulation work is to

strengthen the muscles and contact points in the mouth that are used to form consonants. To achieve this, we go to a degree of exaggeration far beyond the demands of normal speech work. Drills and repetition are the keys to developing clarity of speech.

Each of us has particular strong and weak consonant sounds in our everyday speech, largely dictated by social, educational, and cultural influences; regional or ethnic dialect differences; and the specifics of our own facial structure. Learn to identify which sounds or combinations of sounds create problems for you. Devise your own personal warm-up drills based upon those observations.

T and *d* create problems of clarity for most people. "What a cute little kid" is colloquially spoken as "Wha' duh cu' liddle ki.'" Similar problems happen when people don't clearly distinguish between the allied sounds of *f* and *v*.

Elision, which is the dropping of certain consonant sounds, makes the problem worse. An example of elision can be found in this series of contractions: "I do not know" becomes "I don't know," which in turn becomes "I dunno," which ultimately ends up as the half-shrugged and mumbled "I'n'uh." Weak articulation is probably the single greatest problem for novice actors, but like any other problem, awareness and practice can correct the situation.

<u>What you can do to apply this</u>:
Here is an exercise to help strengthen the contact points in articulation and to assist you in identifying your own personal weak-consonant sounds.

Take the following five vowel sounds:

- *oo* as in "soon"
- *ah* as in "saw"
- *eh* as in "say"
- *i* as in "is"
- *ee* as in "see"

Run through the sounds and think about the shape of your mouth in forming the sounds. Discover the position of the tongue for each sound, and ensure that your jaw does not tighten, particularly on the last two sounds. Make your tongue and lips do the work. (If you tend to close your mouth on "i" and "ee," use a cork between the upper and lower front teeth in order to become familiar with a more open jaw position.)

Now practise the same five sounds preceding each one with the consonant *b*. This makes the line read:

- Boo, bah, beh, bih, bee

Repeat the exercise with the *b* following the vowel:

- Oob, ahb, ehb, ib, eeb

Now combine a separate *b* both at the beginning and at the end of each vowel sound. If you want to make sure that each sound is totally separate, add an aspirate "uh" between the five sounds, like this:

- Boob-uh-bahb-uh-behb-uh-bib-uh-beeb-uh

Continue in this fashion with every hard consonant sound in the alphabet — *c, d, f, g, j, k,* and so forth. When you apply this to soft consonants like *h* and *y* you may choose either to skip over them or to give them a hard, guttural attack. Experiment with combinations of hard consonant sounds such as "tch" in "church." Ignore the fact that occasionally you will create a slightly rude word. With each consonant run through the exercise three times:

1. beginning with the consonant
2. ending the vowel sound with that consonant
3. placing the consonant both at the beginning and the end of each vowel sound

Ultimately, this will help you discover your own strong and weak consonants. Sometimes you'll be fine with a particular consonant at the beginning of the vowel, but you'll have a harder time achieving clarity when the same consonant concludes the vowel sound. It is this type of self-observation that will help improve your articulation.

Tongue twisters are a lot of fun to speak — and they help improve the clarity of speech. Once you have identified your own weak consonant sounds, look for tongue twisters that focus specifically on certain tricky sounds and combinations of consonants. Here are a few pointers on how to avoid tripping up:

1. Tongue twisters can sometimes be difficult to speak because the eye

works faster than the mouth. We skim along to the next word before we have finished the one we are trying to pronounce. This inevitably leads to confusion in the brain. So, if you want to fool the eye, try reversing the syllables.

Here is an example: "The sea ceaseth and sufficeth us." That line can be quite intimidating to the novice actor, but see what happens when you reverse it. Take your time with each syllable, exaggerate the movement of the mouth and in particular the tongue tip, and build the sequence like this:

- Us
- Eth - us
- Ice - eth - us
- Suff - ice - eth - us
- And - suff- ice - eth - us
- Eth - and - suff - ice - eth - us
- Cease - eth - and - suff - ice - eth - us
- Sea - cease - eth - and - suff - ice - eth - us
- The - sea - cease - eth - and - suff - ice - eth - us

If you have trouble, try putting an aspirate "uh" between each syllable. Remember this tip in rehearsals when you find you consistently stumble over a phrase. The solution is to practise speaking the line backward, one syllable at a time.

2. Tongue twisters depend upon the rapid alternation of (generally) two confusing sounds. Begin slowly when you read the tongue twister, concentrating on accuracy of sound rather than speed, and build up the rate as you become increasingly confident. Discovering the natural rhythm to a line will help.

In English, we often encounter adjoining words with duplicated or allied consonants. **Duplicated consonants** can be found in the phrase "hot tea," where the *t* must be repeated twice in articulation exercises. An example of **allied consonants** is found in "hot dog." This common term is generally spoken with the tongue starting to form the *t* sound but not really completing it. Instead, the strength of the sound comes from the *d* of "dog." In articulation exercises, however, make sure you keep the *t* and *d* sounds separate and clearly formed. It sound like as "hot-uh-dog" with an aspirate "uh" between the two words for clarity's sake.

3. Exaggerate the formation of the consonants to help get you through the line. For example, if you were to say the following tongue twister (which is in the *Guinness Book of Records* as the most difficult tongue twister in the English language), you would discover that there is an obvious difficulty: "The sixth sick sheikh's sixth sheep's sick."

This particular tongue twister depends upon the alternation of the "th" and *s* sounds. When forming the "th" sound, stick the tongue tip through the teeth so that it extends quite pronouncedly. This isn't so difficult when a word begins with that sound (as with "**the**"), but when the sound comes at the end of the word (as in "six**th**") there is a real temptation to let the tongue remain behind the teeth. You can test yourself by placing a finger half an inch in front of the mouth so that the tongue tip must touch it on every "th" sound.

(Note: there are two slightly different "**th**" sounds in this line. "The" contains a voiced fricative and words like "sixth" have unvoiced fricatives. In both instances, you should exaggerate the extension of the tongue tip.)

4. For each new tongue twister, try this sequence:

(a) Read it naturally the first time.
(b) Exaggerate all consonants so that the sentence sounds over-articulated.
(c) Really exaggerate all mouth movements, all the contact points and the tongue action. At the same time, virtually remove the vowels from each word.
(d) Do a voiceless articulation exercise, in the following manner. Move the mouth (still using exaggerated mouth action) and try to spit out each consonant or combination in turn with maximum strength. Do not vocalize any vowels. All that you will hear are the popping and spitting sounds of *p, t,* and *d* for the hard consonants; the soft consonants like *h* and *l* involve little or no contact but should be shaped by the mouth anyway.
(e) Speak the sentence normally, but repeat it over and over. Begin to build up the rate of delivery to the maximum combination of clarity and speed.

Here are some tongue twisters to practise. Repeat shorter lines several times through:

1. a hot cup of coffee from a proper copper coffee pot
2. six slim saplings
3. a critical cricket critic
4. six slippery seals slipping silently ashore
5. six selfish shellfish
6. black bug's blood
7. six thin thistle sticks
8. truly rural
9. shining soldiers
10. toy boat
11. unique New York
12. poor food for four poor mules
13. coop up the cook.
14. lemon linament
15. red leather, yellow leather
16. Peggy Babcock
17. Cuthbert's custard
18. The Leith police dismisseth us.
19. Some shun sunshine. Do you shun sunshine?
20. She says Susie shall sew a sheet.
21. The rat ran by the river with a lump of raw liver.
22. She stood upon the balcony, mimicking him hiccuping, and amicably welcoming him in.
23. The bootblack brought the black boot back.
24. Can you imagine an imaginary menagerie manager imagining managing an imaginary menagerie?
25. She shall share the shrimp.
26. Theophilus, the thistle sifter, while sifting a sifter full of thistles, thrust 3,000 thistles through the thick of his thumb.
27. This is a zither.

In conclusion:

You can use the exercises in this chapter not only to prepare yourself for performance, but also to develop your voice for real-life situations. There are many instances in life where we are called upon to speak — sometimes without warning — and if we draw upon the full power of the voice, our presentation will be stronger.

Anyone who is about to enter a job interview, or any situation in which the presentation of one's self is very important, should spend a bit of time beforehand practising clarity of speech. Keep your speech clear, positive, and dynamic. If it gives you the edge over the next job applicant, surely it is worth trying.

Chapter Five
Developing the Actor's Voice

Group vocal exercises

The following exercises for group voice work are excellent as company vocal warm-ups for cast members prior to rehearsal or as self-contained exercises in vocal range. They encourage an imaginative use of the human voice, help us get away from The Great Canadian Monotone, and encourage an awareness of the demands of ensemble voice work.

1. Vocal variety

Experiment with a number of different readings (see below) to explore variety in inflection. Listen to different types of inflection you can use with various words. Some inflections are simple, involving just a mere hint of an upward or downward movement of the voice, while others are more complex.

Match people in pairs and have them work out their own interpretation of this dialogue:

    A: Is it black or white?
    B: It's blue. Yes.
    A: Blue? Really ...

B: I think so ...
A: Well!

2. Inflection circle

Form a circle with everyone seated on the floor. Each person in turn says the same word or phrase (see the list below for examples or ideas), but everyone tries to repeat it in a fresh way. Keep the sound moving around the circle. If you dry, or if your idea has already been used by another person and you have yet to think of a new one, just say "Pass" so as not to lower the energy of the exercise.

This game will exercise your ability to stretch your voice through the endless colour of inflection, pause, breath, pitch, rate, pace, sounds, noises, volume, and repetition. Sometimes, people are reluctant at first to exaggerate their vocal range and an inflection circle will barely make it twice around before running out of ideas. But the more you practise it, the more skilled you become. It is possible to keep an extended inflection circle going for several minutes. Suggestions for inflection circles:

- Each person, one at a time, says "yes."
- Then try going round the circle using the word "no."
- Say "yes "or "no," or any combination up to three times. Colloquialisms and sounds can be substituted for the sake of increased variety. If the energy of the circle is strong, it will often be possible to create little "stories" from the exchanges of words around the circle.
- This exercise is a variation on an early Mike Nichols and Elaine May comedy skit. Form a circle alternating males and females. The females may say only "Oh John"; the males, "Oh Marsha." Considerable vocal variety is possible within this limitation. Stories and relationships will emerge, especially when the speed of delivery is kept moving rapidly round the circle.
- Try this sentence to see how many possible meanings you can find: "I don't know what you mean when you say that."
- Create a circle using **noises**. These are the endless range of sounds that individuals make, from "tsk-tsk," through sighs, to soft whistling.
- Develop a circle using laughter. Individuality expressed in laughter is just as varied as that revealed by the spoken word.

3. Dialogue

Here is a slice of dialogue without a context of time, place, or character. It can therefore be given a wide variety of interpretations. Divide the group into pairs and devise your own vocal delivery for these lines. Explore the use of generous pause and/or overlapping voices. When you are ready, present the dialogue as a radio play to the rest of the class. There are two ways of doing this. In either case, the end result throws emphasis onto the spoken word:

(a) Have the audience close their eyes so they have no sense of visuals to assist them in creating the scene.
(b) Alternatively, the speakers sit at the back of the room out of sight of the audience.

Dialogue for two characters:

A: Well ...
B: It's not quite what I expected ...
A: No ...
B: No ...
A: Still ...
B: Yes.
A: Yes.
B: It's nice.
A: Well ...
B: Yeah.
A: It makes you think.
B: Hmmm ...
A: Well.
B: I can't believe it.
A: It's great. I love it.
B: I can't believe it.
A: Well ...
B: Well ...
B: Yeah.
A: Yeah.

4. Individual vocal masques

A **masque** is an art form that was popular in the 16th and 17th centuries at European royal courts. It involved the integration of poetry, music, and dance, along with elaborate spectacle in sets, costume, and special effects. Masques were theatre by the aristocracy and for the aristocracy. Often ,extraordinary sums of money were spent to stage them. They were only ever performed once, generally at a celebration such as a royal wedding.

The idea behind the vocal masque is similar in its commitment to embellishment. The aim is to experiment and stretch the voice, creating an individual "script" from a variety of sources, and to present it with as much vocal colouring and nuance as possible.

First, pick a topic. It can be a general subject such as babies, wintertime, witchcraft, or money; emotions such as love or envy; or even specific persons such as the Marx Brothers or the Prime Minister.

The individual components of a vocal masque include:

1. a definition
2. a song
3. a ditty or saying
4. various sound effects
5. a poem
6. rhythm
7. a Biblical quotation
9. a tongue twister
10. a list or patter
11. a selection of prose
12. a Shakespearean selection
13. a limerick
14. repetition of a word or phrase

You will require some time to research and prepare a vocal masque. However difficult it may be to search out appropriate material for your topic, it is essential that vocal masques contain every element listed above to ensure sufficient variety and colour. Books like *The Concise Oxford Dictionary of Quotations* will help speed up the process. The different elements can be ordered in any number of ways, linked by sound effects and music, or perhaps with random thematic words connecting the sections.

When vocal masques are presented, sound is the key to judging their success. Vocal masques must be read as radio plays following the suggestions in the previous Dialogue exercise.

Here is a short example of a vocal masque based on the topic of "baby." Begin by assembling the information on the list of contents, then organize the material into a running order of your own choosing.

Definition
Baby: (noun) a very young child, the youngest of a family or group, a person who acts like a baby, childish person; *(adjective)* small for its kind; *(verb)* treat as a baby, pamper.

Song
"Rock-a-bye baby on the treetop
When the wind blows the cradle will rock
When the bough breaks, the cradle will fall
And down will come baby, cradle and all."

Saying
"Any man who hates dogs and babies can't be all bad."
(W.C. Fields, 1939 speech)

Sound effects
Create various baby sounds: gurgling, guttural, little exclamations.

Poem
"I like it best when the baby sleeps
But this one cries, he screams and weeps.
My mom says I must mind the brat.
Now why must I put up with that?"

Rhythm
Develop a rhythm to a baby's cry.

Biblical quotation
"And this shall be a sign unto you; Ye shall find the baby wrapped in swaddling clothes, lying in a manger." *(St. Luke, 2:12)*

Tongue twister
Rubber baby buggy bumpers

List

Baby, kid, infant, newborn, suckling, little one, toddler, babe, tot, nursling, bambino, bratling, babe in arms, sweetheart, pamper, the first year of life

Selection of prose

"I thought having a baby sister was supposed to be fun. I had organized all my favourite toys to show her. Mr. Bartholomew Bear was the most important, of course. But when they brought her home from the hospital, I wasn't very impressed. All she did was squint and make faces. Little red, wrinkly, ugly baby faces. So I held out Mr. Bartholomew Bear and tickled her face with his paw. Then she grabbed his paw and stuck it in her mouth. She made a funny twitchy move with her whole body and barfed up some guck on him. Oh ugh!"

Shakespearean selection

"Peace! Peace!
Dost thou not see my baby at my breast,
That sucks the nurse asleep?" (*Antony and Cleopatra, II, ii*)

Limerick

There was a young girl who said "Maybe
I'd like to have one little baby."
The result of her sins
Was quadruplets not twins
And a very surprised midwife lady.

Repetition of a word or phrase

"It's like taking candy from a baby."

Use repetitive words, phrases, and sounds to link the excerpts. When choosing the running order of the pieces, try to alternate styles of writing and attitudes toward the subject matter. Change vocal delivery with each new section and use all ranges of your voice, including singing, humming, and whistling. The possibilities are endless.

Here is a suggested "script" for the baby vocal masque. Remember, though, that no two people will come up with the same script even using identical material, because the way each person chooses to arrange and deliver the material will be unique to him or her. Such is the creativity of theatre.

Open with sounds of baby crying ... develop into a rhythm.

There was a young girl who said "Maybe
I'd like to have one little baby."
The result of her sins
Was quadruplets not twins
And a very surprised midwife lady.

"Any man who hates dogs and babies can't be all bad."

"Rock-a-bye baby on the treetop
When the wind blows the cradle will rock
When the bough breaks, the cradle will fall
And down will come baby, cradle and all."

"Peace! Peace!
Dost thou not see my baby at my breast,
That sucks the nurse asleep?"

Baby: a very young child, the youngest of a family or group, a person
who acts like a baby, childish person; small for its kind; treat as a
baby, pamper.

Repeat sounds of baby crying.

"Any man who hates dogs and babies can't be all bad."

"I like it best when the baby sleeps
But this one cries, he screams and weeps.
My mom says I must mind the brat.
Now why must I put up with that?"

Baby sounds: gurgling, guttural, little exclamations.

"And this shall be a sign unto you; Ye shall find the baby wrapped in
swaddling clothes, lying in a manger."

"... babies can't be all bad."

Rubber baby buggy bumpers *(repeat three times, fading gradually)*

Baby, kid, infant, newborn, suckling, little one, toddler, babe, tot, nursling, bambino, bratling, babe in arms, sweetheart, pamper, the first year of life.

"I thought having a baby sister was supposed to be fun. I had organized all my favourite toys to show her. Mr. Bartholomew Bear was the most important, of course. But when they brought her home from the hospital, I wasn't very impressed. All she did was squint and make faces. Little red, wrinkly, ugly baby faces. So I held out Mr. Bartholomew Bear and tickled her face with his paw. Then she grabbed his paw and stuck it in her mouth. She made a funny twitchy move with her whole body and barfed up some guck on him. Oh ugh!"

"It's like taking candy from a baby."
" ... can't be all bad."
(repeat) Rhythm of baby crying

5. Group vocal masques

Vocal masques can be presented individually, in pairs, or in small groups of four to six people. With group vocal masques, the ingredient components listed above remain the same, but the scope of the exercise can be expanded according to individual talents, time, and the number of participants. Because several voices are available, you may want to expand the amount of material. For example, use segments of three or four songs instead of just one. One or two people might choose to sing solo, while others would be more comfortable in choral selections.

At the time of presentation, people should exploit the theatrical opportunity provided by the larger group. Look for moments of dramatic vocal contrast, musical harmony, and overlapping dialogue. The expanded vocal masque form lends itself to being staged, as opposed to being presented as a radio exercise.

6. Vulnerability exercise

One of the most difficult states for an actor to achieve is the sense of complete openness: communicating with others while feeling totally relaxed, free of tension, and secure within the work at hand. Openness in acting allows you to be sensitive to others. Without it, an actor's work can be mechanical, forced, predictable, and out of tune with others in the scene or play.

This next group exercise deals with the technique of achieving openness. Although the exercise is relatively simple to describe, it is difficult to perform. It is called "Row, row, row." One person is chosen to begin and the others encircle him or her. Make yourselves comfortable, because you'll be there for some time. The actor in the centre is simply to say the words to this childhood song:

> "Row, row, row your boat
> Gently down the stream
> Merrily, merrily, merrily, merrily
> Life is but a dream."

This seems simple enough, but there are several important elements to add — each of which makes the exercise increasingly demanding:

(a) The actor must be warmed up and comfortable. Good preparatory work on optimum pitch should be explored as part of the group warm-ups so that the performer is easily in touch with the fullness of that note.

(b) The actor must sustain each syllable using the optimum-pitch note for the full duration of the sound. One sustained breath is used for each syllable, with the sound continuing as long as the breath lasts. This means an exhalation period of 30 seconds or more, not a mere 10-second stab.

(c) A word with more than one syllable must be broken down into individual sustained breaths for every syllable of the word. Sustain the vowels as long as possible and only add the consonants very near the end of the syllable, taking a fresh breath before beginning the next syllable. The poem then reads like this:

Rooooooooooooooooooooooooooooooooooooooooooooooooooooow
Breath
Rooooooooooooooooooooooooooooooooooooooooooooooooooow
Breath
Rooooooooooooooooooooooooooooooooooooooooooooooooow
Breath
Yooooooooooooooooooooooouuuuuuuuuuuuuuuuuuuuuuuuuur
Breath

Boooooooooooooooooooooooooooooooooooooooaaaaaaaaaaaaaaaaaat
Breath
Geeeeeeeeeeeeeeeeeeeeeeeeeeeeeeeeeeeeeeeeeeeeeeeeeeeeeeeeeeeen
Breath
Tleeeeeeeeeeeeeeeeeeeeeeeeeeeeeeeeeeeeeeeeeeeeeeeeeeeeeeeeeeeeee
Breath
Dooooooooooooooooooooooooooowwwwwwwwwwwwwwwwwwnnnn
Breath
Theeeeeeeeeeeeeeeeeeeeeeeeeeeeeeeeeeeeeeeeeeeeeeeeeeeeeeeeeeeeee
Breath
Streeeeeeeeeeeeeeeeeeeeeeeeeeeeeeeeeeeeeeeeeeeeeeeeeeeeaaammm
Breath
Meeeeeeeeeeeeeeeeeeeeeeeeeeeeeeeeeeeeeeeeeeeeeeeeeeeeeeeeerrrrr
Breath
Iiiiiiiiiiiiiiiiiiiiiiiiiiiiiiiiiiiiiiiiiiiiiiiiiiiiiiiiiiiiiiiiiiiiiiiiiiiiiiiiiiiiiiiiiiiiii
Breath
Leeeeeeeeeeeeeeeeeeeeeeeeeeeeeeeeeeeeeeeeeeeeeeeeeeeeeeeeeeeeee
And so forth ...

(d) The actor must establish eye contact with each individual in the circle, locking eyes with one person at a time throughout one sustained note. Under no circumstances should concentration be broken. Eye contact is the key to believability in acting, and this aspect of the exercise challenges the actor's eye focus.

(e) During this contact time, an exchange of emotion might occur. (If it doesn't, don't worry about it.) The emotional connection should not be based on a preconceived idea or existing relationship between the two individuals. Rather, it should happen spontaneously.

(f) Occasionally, the emotional exchange will shift slightly from one emotion to another par way through sustained eye contact. Sometimes the emotions that are triggered may surprise the people involved. Don't worry if this happens to you. This is not an exercise in rights and wrongs, but rather one of self-discovery.

(g) The final aspect of this exercise concerns tension. Above all, this is an exercise in keeping the body free and relaxed regardless of what happens. If you feel tension beginning to build while performing this exercise, get rid of it quickly. Don't let it build or get in the way of your work.

Always try to monitor your own performance. Keep close watch on what you are doing, how you are doing it, and what you are discovering about yourself in the process. Through non-stop analysis, you can identify your own tension-centre problems. You must begin to alleviate or eliminate them or they will continue to creep into all your acting work and hinder your freedom, flexibility, and development.

Variations: If everyone gets really bored with "Row, row, row your boat" (and some groups likely will), you can always substitute a similar ditty, such as "Happy birthday to you."

Occasionally, time poses a problem. There may be too many individuals in the class to allow each person to have a stab at "Row, row, row your boat." If so, you can substitute this sentence: " My name is ... *(insert own full name)."* Members of the group with polysyllabic names will be most unhappy with this variation, quietly regretting as they wait their turn that their families gave them elaborate names.

Dialects and accents

The study of dialects and accents is fascinating and a natural area of interest for the young actor. In North America, there are many regional variations in the speech patterns of the English language. Britain — composed as it is of England, Wales, Scotland, and Northern Ireland — contains even more diverse regional speech patterns. The many English-speaking countries around the world add still further colour to our common language.

Strictly speaking, there is a distinction between dialect and accent. A **dialect** is the regional variation within a language's speech patterns, which are formed by such factors as geography, social background, educational influences, and peer-group pressure. Therefore we have a cockney dialect, a Texan dialect, or a Newfoundland dialect: each one with its distinctive sound and vocabulary. We all speak one dialect or another.

Accent, on the other hand, refers to the variations in speech patterns that can come about by learning English as a second language. Thus we say someone has a French accent, a German accent, an Italian accent, and so forth. Each accent brings its own special sound to the English language, influenced by the vowel and consonant formations of the mother tongue.

In everyday usage, the terms "accent" and "dialect" are freely interchanged. It is possible, of course, to speak with both a recognizable accent and a distinctive dialect, e.g. if one has learned English as a second language (providing the accent) in an identifiable region of the country (providing the dialect).

Slang words particularly alter the colour of our daily speech, coming in and going out of fashion regularly and rapidly. Few things will date a play or a character as rapidly as slang words. Science and technology consistently add new words to our language. Think of the range of new words and terminology that developments in computers and space exploration have brought about in this generation alone.

Pronunciation of words changes over time, too. Regional dialects spoken all around the world today are a little bit different from those spoken even 100 years ago, let alone several centuries back. Authors from past centuries offer tantalizing clues to such changes in speech.

Some factors are common to all dialects and accents. Every actor must understand these elements in changing his or her own speech habits. In addition, learning to analyze different dialects and accents — in real life, on television, in movies — will help train your ear to listen.

1. Rhythm and musicality

Every dialect has an inherent musical rhythm. For instance, the rhythm of an Irish dialect is different from a Texan drawl. The **rhythm** comes from stress patterns and pauses, while **musicality** comes from the use of pitch and inflection. Sometimes inflection is very elaborate and embellished, as in the Edinburgh or Southern Welsh dialects, and other times it is as flat as a pancake. Think of The Great Canadian Monotone discussed in Chapter 4, with its flat sound and upward inflection on the word "eh?" Accents, too, contribute their own musicality. For example, the Swedish and Welsh accents are very pronounced and lilting.

Exercise:

Find a sentence that captures the rhythm, musicality, and voice placement of the accent or dialect you're preparing. It may come from a movie, television show, dialect tape, or a friend. Ask for suggestions from your class, cast, or circle of friends and assemble a list of "buzz phrases." When you are rehearsing your script and you don't feel you've spoken a line with its true dialect sound, repeat the strongest buzz phrase in your head to reconnect with the natural rhythm. Then repeat your lines using those cadences.

2. Diction

Diction correctly means choice of words. For example, your English teacher might have asked you to say what was special about a poet's diction (or choice of words). When we apply the word to a study of dialect, diction includes the expressions, slang words, buzz phrases, and local expressions that give a particular dialect its own colour and individuality. For example, look at the number of ways the idea behind a phrase like "Please stop that" can be treated simply through the choice of words:

Stop it, eh?
Cool it.
Knock it off, now.
Pleeeeease ...
Chill out.
Thanks all the same, but ...
Give over.
Enough.
No ...
Excuse me, but do you mind?
Hold on.
Get off my case.
That's quite sufficient, thank you.
... and the list can go on and on.

In a well-written script, a playwright will use believable regional diction and a sense of rhythm within the dialect, which will make the actor's job only half as difficult. However, if you are involved with group improvisations, then you — the actor — are left with the responsibility of choosing the words that your character speaks. This problem is compounded if you are creating your own class play from improvisational sources, or if you are developing a docudrama in which you play numerous cameo roles. You may want to make your characters "sound" different, so you use an accent or a dialect (don't let yourself rely too heavily on such a potentially superficial device).

Diction can be very helpful to an actor in creating a sense of specific setting. Time, place, mood, and atmosphere can all be carried on the words that an improvisational actor or playwright uses. For example, look at the plays of Tennessee Williams and you'll find it's hard to read them without a Southern drawl. David French and Michael Cook have finely tuned ears for the Newfoundland dialect with its Irish roots. George Bernard Shaw's play *Pygmalion* deals comically with the subject of dialect, and contains the rhythms and diction appropriate to each dialect used by the characters.

When you are applying diction to the study of accents, be aware that the choice of words in one language is often very different in another language and culture. For instance, the Inuit language has nearly 50 words to describe snow, but only one for automobile. Those of us farther south have many more than 50 words to describe specific models and types of cars, yet very few words for snow. Consequently, it is no surprise that people often have trouble searching out the correctly applicable word in another language.

A good playwright will know how to apply this principle when scripting an accent or a dialect. An improvisational actor will have to research his or her language.

Exercise:

Take a simple sentence such as, "Pardon me, ma'am, but can you tell me how much this dress costs?" Translate this into three contrasted dialects or accents. "Pardon me" can become everything from "Hey lady" to "Excuse me, madam," while "this dress" can become "this here outfit" or "this little frock."

3. Placement of the voice

In some dialects and accents, the voice is placed forward in the mouth. Usually, this is accompanied by careful articulation and the sound comes from the mask of the face. Other accents are very guttural and emerge with a throaty sound. In such cases, articulation is generally sloppy and sound is often cut off with what is called a **glottal stop**. (The glottal stop occurs when you don't use the lips and teeth to form the words, but instead cut the sound short in the throat.)

For an example of this, consider the cockney dialect. Owing to the placement of sound nearer the throat than the mask of the face, the cockney dialect appears very lazy in its attention to articulation: some letters and entire syllables are dropped from words. One word generally melds into the next in a continuum of sound — this is known as the cockney glide. The sound tends to come from the back of the throat and travel out through the nose. Therefore in a cockney glide, "bottle" becomes "bah-ohl."

On the other hand, the standard British dialect is placed forward in the mouth and is well articulated. The expression "a stiff upper lip" for the British doesn't apply only to their sense of fortitude. If you'll notice, sometimes there is a certain amount of tension in the upper lip in Standard British speech which makes it necessary for the tongue tip and bottom lip to take care of most of the movement in articulation.

Some dialects and accents are more nasal than others, which gives them a distinctive quality. Rural dialects, for example, often take on a flatness of sound and there can be relatively little flexibility when so much sound is placed in the nose. Therefore, specific words are generally emphasized using stress rather than inflection.

Exercise:

Take two lines of poetry and speak them aloud in your natural speaking voice. Repeat these lines with a greater awareness of your resonators, allowing the sound to reverberate in the mouth, nasal cavity, and torso. Now repeat the same lines several times through, placing the voice in a different part of your body each time:

- the mask of the face
- the nasal cavities
- the back of the mouth
- the throat

Feel and hear what happens to the quality of sound in each of these areas. What springs into your mind with each of these sounds? Does your image of yourself change from one placement to the next?

4. Consonant alterations

Sometimes it helps to understand the sounds of a particular accent by going back to the original language. For example, the original Hawaiian language is made up of just over half the letters we know in the English alphabet, so English words translated into Hawaiian have to be broken down into the nearest equivalent. Therefore, "Merry Christmas" becomes "Mele Kalikimaka." Various Chinese dialects again lack one or two consonant sounds that are common in English.

Consequently, people raised in one language often have trouble forming foreign consonant sounds in another language. When you add voice placement to this factor, it is easy to understand, for example, why so many people have trouble rolling their *r*'s with the blade of the tongue, as in the Parisian manner in the French language. Therefore, consonant formation will have a strong influence in the study of certain accents.

Exercise:

Go through the consonants in the alphabet slowly and experiment with each one in turn. Within your class circle of experience, how many consonants in our language create problems for people learning English as a second language?

5. Vowel alterations

One dialect will often differ from another because of the changes made in the vowel sounds. An "oh" sound in Standard British will be altered from a **monophthong** (that is, a one-sound vowel) to a **diphthong** (a two-sound vowel) or **triphthong** (a three-sound vowel) within the cockney dialect, and emerge as "aow." In other dialects, diphthongs will be shortened to monophthongs.

The vowel sounds produced — and the alterations necessary from one dialect to another — will be integrally bound up with the placement of the voice.

Exercise:

Try saying a monophthong "no" placed in the front of the mouth. Now say it as a triphthong "naow" beginning at the back of the throat and proceeding up through the nose. Hear the difference. Feel the difference. Play around with this idea, varying the accents and dialects you imitate and varying the placement of the voice.

Repeat this with other vowel sounds: the "a" sound in "eh?", the "e" sound in "he," the "i" sound in "hi" and the "u" sound in "up."

Tips on developing an accent or dialect:

We have seen how the five components of dialect affect the study of any accent or dialect. But where does an actor begin to learn a new set of speech patterns? There are many excellent sources for learning a dialect or accent, but the best one is to search for the original sound.

Try to find someone with the distinctive accent or dialect sound you wish to emulate and persuade him or her to read the script into a tape recorder. Play the tape over, analyzing the placement, rhythm, and variations in the voice. Repeat what you hear word for word and phrase for phrase.

If that isn't possible, there are many films, records, and tapes that can help the student actor. Perhaps a late-night movie will feature a character with the specific dialect you want to learn. Sometimes a recording of a play or a taped series of poetry readings will involve the dialect in question. Then there are many books, records and tapes of dialects and accents that are marketed specifically for theatrical purposes. They are easy to learn to use and very helpful, although generally quite expensive.

One of the problems in studying accents and dialects is that the actor often becomes more involved with how the sound comes out than with the reasons why the character is saying those specific lines (losing track of the character's objectives). In many instances, a dialect or accent can be an unnecessary red herring. For example, many students will try to do a character from the plays of Michel Tremblay with a Québécois accent. However, the character types that Tremblay depicts are found in English-speaking Canada as well as Quebec.

Translated plays should never be done with an accent, because characters are meant to be speaking their own language; we hear what they are saying with all the truth of our language. There should be no barrier between the actor and the audience. The solution to doing a scene from Michel Tremblay is to transpose the character into English-speaking terms and avoid the entire problem of learning a Québécois accent. After all, there are many more important challenges facing the actor in a Tremblay play.

The problem of dialect becomes even worse when you look at Shakespeare. Many students will attempt a generalized British pronunciation in presenting a Shakespearean scene, usually listening repeatedly to BBC recordings of the play and then slavishly reproducing what they hear.

Why try to emulate plummy vowels? Why choose to worry about the effect of the language rather than the cause or intention behind the words? After all, Shakespeare's characters are universal: their vitality, humour, energy, and emotions are common to all humanity four hundred years after they were written. Almost every character Shakespeare created can be performed with a regional or localized dialect within any language. Before an actor begins work on a dialect or an accent, he or she should take a little time to think whether the character can be translated into a regional dialect.

The care and treatment of the actor's voice

Actors are notorious for developing vocal problems during the rehearsal period of a play. It is surprising how the incidence of colds and flu within a performing company multiplies in direct proportion to the advance of opening night. There are many explanations for this phenomenon. However, there are several steps that you can take to either minimize the chance of becoming ill or enable you to continue through the run of the show, despite vocal problems.

In rehearsals:

1.   This point is so obvious it shouldn't even have to be mentioned: ban smoking from the rehearsal area. Apart from the disservice smoking does to one's own larynx — both on the way into the lungs and again on the way back out — the odds are that one or more other members of the company are allergic to the second-hand smoke.
2.   Make sure you are dressed appropriately so that you can dress up or down according to the (often-fluctuating) temperature of the rehearsal or performance space.
3.   Do not share food, coffee, or soft drinks with other company members. Don't use mugs that have not been thoroughly washed, and preferably use disposable cups.
4.   If you are not well, stay at home and keep your germs to yourself. The show can't go on if your illness strikes down the rest of the cast. Consult your doctor regarding the demands on your time and energy. Perhaps with medical approval, taking an anti-stress multivitamin every day will help. Pamper yourself with adequate rest and eat well.
5.   Do a sensible and complete vocal warm-up before rehearsals so that you don't strain your voice.

During the run of the show:

1.   In addition to the above advice, avoid drinking dairy products before a performance. Milk coats the throat and increases the amount of phlegm generated in the throat. Coffee is not much better for you. Stick to water, natural fruit juice, or fresh oranges.
2.   Do not share make-up supplies. Not only will this prevent cold

germs being transmitted from one actor to another, but also it will stop the spread of skin infections.

If you come down with a sore throat and the show must go on:

1. Gargle with salt and water as frequently as possible.
2. Try gargling with a mixture of apple-cider vinegar and honey diluted with warm water.
3. Drink a mixture of fresh lemon, honey, and hot water shortly before you go onstage.
4. If laryngitis strikes, try the following technique to arrest the minute muscle spasms that laryngitis creates deep in the muscles of the larynx. Apply an ice-cold compress to the larynx area while drinking a beverage that is as hot as you can manage to swallow. Then reverse the procedure and apply a hot compress to the larynx while drinking a glass of ice-cold water. Repeat these steps several times.
5. Bring a small humidifier into the dressing room and keep it as close to you as possible when you are not required onstage. If you are really unwell, pull a towel over your head and lean over the humidifier to get full advantage of the warm, humid air.
6. If you suffer from nasal congestion as well, here's a method of reducing the problem prior to going onstage. Place the middle finger from each hand on the fold between the tip of the nose and the nostril. Next, place the fourth finger of each hand higher on the nose near the bridge of the nose. The index finger then sits just below the mid-point of the eye, just touching the cheekbone. With the fingers positioned this way, begin to massage your face with rapid, tiny circular motions. Continue for a couple of minutes. Now bend over from the waist, allowing your head to hang freely upside-down, and repeat the massaging action for another two minutes. This action will loosen the buildup of sinus congestion and allow freer breathing and resonance to occur.

There is no guarantee that following this advice will prevent you from catching a virus but, should you become unwell, it will help you to uphold the old adage that "the show must go on."

Chapter Six
Voice and Text

In this section, the student will begin to explore written material with a view to applying some of the knowledge and techniques discussed in earlier chapters. Contemporary plays are written in **prose**, which is the type of everyday form of written language used in this sentence. However, some plays are written in **verse** (or poetry) where the lines have a regularly repeated stress and often a rhyme pattern. Well-written verse expresses thought that is charged with heightened emotion and enlightened with imagination. This chapter will address exercises for both prose and verse.

Much of Shakespeare's writing was in verse form (chapters 19 and 20 provide further study on the variety of verse Shakespeare used in his plays). During the course of their training, actors will be exposed to all types of writing and, it is hoped, will become increasingly comfortable with many literary styles.

It all begins with reading.

We are a generation devoted to the visual rather than words. Television, music videos, and the film industry have replaced radio plays, stories, sermons, and the written/oral traditions of yesterday. Nevertheless, reading is a critical skill for anyone who is genuinely interested in proceeding in theatre. It must be developed as fully as the performer's spoken and singing voice, body flexibility, dance movement, and creative imagination.

Sight-reading

Sometimes in life we are called upon to read material that we have not had time to prepare. It may be something as simple as being asked to read a poem aloud in class, or it may be in an audition where you are asked to read a scene from a play that you've never read.

In preparation, you can work on improving sight-reading skills. Read some scripts aloud and continue this practice for a given period of time each day to increase your confidence. Explore as wide a stylistic variety of plays as possible. There is a wealth of material to explore in the two accompanying *Behind the Scenes* volumes. However, there are other types of writing you should look at as well. A book such as *Caught in the Act* by Corey Reay, published by Simon & Pierre of Toronto, is an ideal practice text for it offers a wide range of characters written in a flexible and amusing free-verse style.

If you are asked to sight-read at an audition, you will likely be allowed a little time to glance over the material you are to read — sometimes 30 seconds, sometimes five minutes. If this opportunity isn't offered, ask if you can take some time. Most auditioners are reasonable and, time permitting, will agree to give you a few moments to glance through the material.

Your request will at least demonstrate your respect for the script and your desire to do the best possible reading. Here is some advice for sight-reading:

Preparing to read

1. Use the preparatory time to skim the piece for the general style of writing, especially focusing on the emotional state of your character, the mood, atmosphere, and the dramatic shape of the piece:

    • What is the scene about?
    • Who is your character?
    • What is he or she feeling?
    • Where is the climax of the piece?
    • Where do you begin to build to that?

2. Look for the **universals**, the emotions that are common to all humanity — pain, anger, sadness, etc. — to make the piece real for you and for your audience. Search out the **particulars**, the

words that serve as valves to release the emotions you have identified. An example of a valve can be found in this excerpt from the opening Chorus speech of Shakespeare's *King Henry V:*

"O for a Muse of fire, that would ascend
The brightest heaven of invention!"

The opening "O" is not a mild "oh!" In fact, it is a sound that can be expanded and sustained, arresting the audience's attention and allowing a powerful build into the balance of the line. Explore such words to the fullest.

3. Consider the address of the piece. You will have a different manner when addressing a single five-year-old child than when addressing 5,000 union members who are considering strike action. If you are reading an introductory monologue in a children's play, your address will differ from that found in a social comedy of manners. Identify this element of your script and apply the appropriate vocal energy.

4. Consider, too, how you want the audience to react; this will help you find your point of view. Do you want to frighten them, to amuse them, to instruct them? Don't let an "expected" response assume too much importance, but be aware of its function in theatre.

5. Look for the "**hitching posts**," the words that indicate what is coming next. These words are the keys to the story of the piece. For example, if you were reading from a murder mystery, you would naturally emphasize words and phrases that help to move the story along: "then suddenly that night ..." or "in the cold light of early morning." These words provide guideposts for the audience, as surely as if you were describing to friends in a car what lay around the corner of a country road that they had never travelled before. A reader is taking the audience down a road that he or she alone knows.

6. In an audition, people will be watching how effectively you establish a rapport with the other people with whom you are reading. Be aware of character relationships, which are the heart of acting. Ask yourself questions such as:

   • What is my relationship with others in this scene?
   • What do I want from each of them?

- What am I about to do to achieve my goals?

If the answers are not clear, make an immediate choice and go all the way with it in your reading. It is better to be courageous and miss the mark than to play it safe. Ignore the unfamiliar, the difficult. Go with what you recognize.

7. Try to scan the piece in **thought units**. Most playwrights tend to use punctuation as an accurate reflection of natural speech rhythms. Generally, they don't base their punctuation choices on strictly grammatical grounds because they are writing for the spoken — not written — word. Use this concrete help the writer offers you, for it is likely that more time was spent selecting the most effective punctuation than you have had to prepare to read.

The reading begins

1. When you are asked to begin, assume a comfortable stance with no tension in the body. Take a few deep breaths to help you relax, to enable you to build your breath, and to allow you to sustain emotion at the appropriate level for the first lines. Don't let anybody — or your own built-in sense of urgency — rush you in achieving this breath control. Otherwise, you will feel unprepared and will likely begin badly. Part of what people look for in sight-reading is your ability to take control.

2. If you want to incorporate movement within your reading, do so, but remember that the auditioners are more concerned with the insight and interpretation you can bring to the piece. If you use any movement, it should be appropriate to what you are reading. If you are unsure how and when to move, stand still because inappropriate physical action will pull focus from your reading. If you are prone to overly fussy habits, do a shakeout or some relaxation exercises before you begin.

3. Try to establish as much eye contact as possible with the other character(s) in the scene. This helps you to develop a relationship with others or to underscore and share an important moment in the scene. As an added benefit, lifting your face to make eye contact helps vocal projection, too.

4. Read at a slightly slower rate than usual. This advice is difficult to put into practice because of increased adrenaline in your

system. Being nervous often makes people talk faster than they actually want to. But reading more slowly than usual has several advantages:

- It will give you more time to scan ahead to look for the key word that will unlock the emotional content of the line for you.
- It allows you to discover the units of thought or phrases so that you read smoothly, not erratically.
- It will let you identify and explore images that help to make the piece more vivid and real for you.
- It will give you more time to establish eye contact with other people involved in the reading.
- It minimizes the possibility of stumbling over the text or mispronouncing unfamiliar words.
- You will be less likely to drop words, be sloppy with final consonants, or elide words; instead, you will achieve a greater degree of vocal clarity.

5. Try to use all ranges of your voice. Release your imagination and fill the space you are working in. Use pause and inflection to point key words and remember to vary the pitch when required. Let the volume level be appropriate both to the environment you're in and the emotion of the moment. Don't be afraid of overdoing something vocally. For every individual who overdoes a moment, a hundred miss it. After all, how else can you show emotional release while reading except by using all the range and power of your voice?

6. If you come to a difficult word that you don't understand or recognize, plough right through it with confidence. As a general rule of thumb, when in doubt regarding pronunciation, put the stress on the first syllable and let the rest of the word remain unstressed. This works in three cases out of four, proving that you can fool most of the people most of the time. If you trip partway through a word or realize that you have mispronounced something, repeat the word only once. Anything more creates a bumbling effect. The more you repeat it or try to correct your pronunciation, the more the problem is compounded. Your audience begins to worry about that particular word itself and ultimately loses the train of thought in the balance of your reading.

7. If you have built up to a strong conclusion, or have worked carefully to establish a certain mood, hold that moment and savour it. Don't break instantly. Raise your eyes from the page for a moment and sustain the effect you have created. Think of this as your silent round of applause from your listeners. Linger in the moment before allowing yourself to break and return to the relative safety of your seat.

Reading is a skill that will enhance innumerable personal and career experiences throughout your life.

Advice for oral presentations

Many of us are called on in everyday life to give presentations as part of our employment. Students are often required to give oral reports — increasingly so, as they work their way through senior levels of education. Although our written work may be in good shape, sometimes our presentations or seminars are less dynamic than we would wish.

Some of the following advice for oral speakers is similar to points mentioned above for sight-readers. The biggest difference is that the oral speaker is responsible for creating what will be read aloud, which gives him or her much more control over the situation. Another difference for the oral speaker is that presentations require committed eye contact with every member of the audience. This can spook some people. Special techniques can be helpful when preparing notes for verbal presentation. It can be worthwhile to look at these.

Preparing your material

1. Remember that when someone is reading your written work, they can reread it if they become lost or confused. When listening to you, however, they cannot revisit what you have said. While you are preparing your written notes, keep your "ears" alive. Imagine how effectively your comments would carry in a darkened room where people could only hear you. Let this thought guide you in assembling your ideas on paper.
2. Keep your sentences short, direct, and to the point. Long sentences are difficult for listeners to follow. Stick to points or bullets.
3. Sometimes it is helpful to write key points on small file cards so

that you are not upstaged by larger pages of notes. A nervous speaker will often end up shuffling papers needlessly. In extreme cases, quivering hands will set papers rattling. This will pull the audience's focus away from the speaker.

4. Identify moments in your presentation where you can remind your audience of the key points of your content. Repetition keeps the listeners on track. Here is a useful formula that teachers know well:

   1) This is what I'm going to tell you.
   2) This is what I am telling you.
   3) This is what I've just told you.

5. If you have complicated issues to discuss, discard all unnecessary points. Stick to the major issue of the through-line and don't try to include too much material. Many presentations fail because the speaker tries to share interesting but irrelevant information.

6. Be very careful with numbers and statistics. It is particularly difficult for listeners to absorb many numbers in a short time frame, so take the time to think of other ways of expressing the point you wish to make. Perhaps you can reinforce the impact of statistics by using repetition, or by tying numbers into concrete facts, percentages, or points of comparison.

7. Think about how to make your presentation special and memorable for your audience. This may involve the use of visual aids — ranging from slide shows generated by computer software to something as simple and charming as hand-drawn cartoon figures or flash cards.

8. Understand the audience. Are they third-year sociology majors in a university seminar setting, or are they a group of young teens being trained for part-time work? Adjust your material to their point of view and level of understanding, even as you assemble your points on paper.

Presenting your material

1. Before you get up to speak, organize your notes in sequence and make sure you can read them easily.

2. The room may not be set up in the best way for your presentation. If the placement of people in the room can be adjusted to make

your delivery more effective, take charge and rearrange people and/or furniture before you start to speak. Use a little banter to help you work off your nervous tension and allow the audience to see a lighter side of your character.

3. Engage your audience. Make eye contact with each person as often as possible. Play to your full audience, not just half of the room (you'll be surprised how frequently speakers fall into this trap).

4. Assume a position of secure physical comfort. You must appear to be comfortable even if you don't feel it. Your anxiety enables an audience to become detached from what you're saying. We begin to feel uncomfortable on your behalf and worry that you won't make it through your presentation. Here is a checklist:

   • Keep your feet on the floor, distribute your weight evenly, and don't let yourself sway or twitch.
   • Avoid shifting your weight too frequently; it projects discomfort.
   • Don't creep in toward your audience — people will be intimidated if you invade their space.
   • Watch out for repetitive physical mannerisms, because they can distract your audience.

5. Express yourself in your own personal way. Use your own strengths and develop your own style. Don't try to be someone you're not or imitate the work of others. Your own natural charm will draw the audience in. Just be yourself.

6. Try to overcome your nerves. Breathe your way through your anxiety before you begin, and/or use breath technique to calm you during your presentation.

7. Keep vocal energy alive and colourful. Watch that you don't let your voice fade out at the end of sentences (all the more reason to keep your written text brief and to the point). Avoid upward inflection, and learn to "state," not "ask." After all, you are considered the authority of the moment, so let your voice reflect that confidence.

8. Find moments of natural fun, enthusiasm, and excitement for your topic. Remember how frequently we use humour in our everyday discussion. Why should you settle for a lesser amount in your presentation?

9. Don't be afraid to adjust your presentation partway through.

Sometimes speakers run short of time. If you sense an audience is getting restless — for any number of reasons — it may make sense to trim the comments from what was planned to something more appropriate to the changed circumstances. Give yourself permission, deep inside, to make such executive decisions partway through your presentation. Keep in mind that no one else has the script in front of them, so you can encapsulate your comments as you go and no one will be the wiser.

10. Never apologize for yourself. You don't have to explain to the audience that you have a cough, or that you feel nervous, or that you don't believe yourself to be as expert as the previous speaker. If you plant a negative idea in people's minds, it will become a self-fulfilling prophecy and may undermine the effectiveness of your presentation.

11. If you can't think of anything to say, don't say anything. This means avoiding "ums" and "ers" and such related filler sounds. These are acquired nervous habits that generally become more pronounced or frequent under stressful conditions. Remove these from your delivery and you will immediately sound more authoritative and in control. It's an interesting point that when a speaker pauses for a moment, the audience assumes that he or she is searching for the most precise word to use. We are content to wait for you to discover the best phrase to express yourself; at the same time, such effective use of pausing gives an erudite quality to your presentation.

But ... um ... if... ah... you put ... um ... fillers ... er... ah ... back into ... ah ... er ... your presentation ... uh ... you ... uh ... will ... uh ... immediately... uh ... sound... ah.... er... less authoritative.... and ... uh ... not in ... ah ... control.

Choral speech

One excellent warm-up exercise for improving individual vocal technique is to rehearse material using group choral speech. It is particularly useful when beginning work on children's theatre or the docudrama form of theatre — both of which provide lots of opportunity for group speaking. There are several advantages to this exercise, apart from the most obvious one of expanding your knowledge of poetic themes, forms, and styles of writing.

Advantages of choral speaking

- It develops an awareness of the full range of your individual voice and the power of the collective voice.
- It trains your ear to listen to other voices.
- It helps you to connect with the emotions and energy that have been fed to you with your cue.
- It develops an ensemble sound, which is important in plays requiring unified speaking or chorus work — such as those by T.S. Eliot, Christopher Fry, or James Reaney, as well as original ensemble productions. A lot of children's theatre lends itself to choral speech.
- It exercises concentration skills.
- Shyness is more easily overcome in group voice work and the accompaniment of other voices gives you the "protection" to help cover your initial "mistakes" or insecurities .
- It develops your ability to read a dramatic or comic piece of writing, to know what to look for in the text.

How to do choral readings

Begin by looking at a wide variety of styles of material, such as the sonnets that follow later in this chapter. When each cast or class member in turn provides a poem — interpreting and teaching it to the others at the beginning of each rehearsal — the shared responsibility and free choice will provide that a broad range of material is explored over time. This will also ensure the greatest voice demands are made on each person.

1. Divide yourselves into three or four groups, according to the nature of individual voices. This will vary with the numbers of people in the group, the male-female ratio, the lightness or darkness of individual voices, and the nature of the poem you will be addressing.
2. Place each vocal group in a different area of the room so that like-sounding voices can rely on others in their group without being distracted by different sounds immediately beside or behind them. Identify each group by an initial:

   - A = lighter female voices
   - B = deeper female voices

- C = lighter male voices
- D = deeper male voices

3. Break the poem down into sections that are allocated to various groups. Perhaps groups A and C will read the first three lines, everyone will join in on the next two lines, D voices will read the next line and a half, and B will conclude the stanza.

4. Assign specific words or phrases to individual voices. This will break up the pattern of speech and allow solo character voices to be used at effective moments.

   A leader is chosen to begin inhalation. Others join in on cue to create a smooth opening breath. With practice, the ensemble will sense when to begin to speak. The first time through, speak the poem together so that those of you with stronger voices will help the less trained readers to discover the structure of the written lines and the rhythm of the piece. Practise each stanza in turn so that everyone clearly understands when and how he or she must speak in order to achieve the desired impact of the words. Build the poem, verse by verse, until a complete reading of the entire work is fluid and well rehearsed.

Now it is time to stage the reading. This should not be elaborate; blocking moves should be kept to a minimum (if, indeed, any are needed). However, in addition to the individual and collective vocal improvements that choral speaking can provide, staging of the choral speech will heighten everyone's awareness of:

- the power and effectiveness of simple groupings
- the use of levels
- economical choices of gesture
- facial expressions
- group and individual focal points

Poetic forms

Writers use many literary devices to increase the effectiveness and emotional impact of their work, particularly in verse. Actors should look for these devices in their scripts, because strong writing serves the action of the play and (as with the above exercise) provides clues to strengthen the power of the actor's delivery.

For ease of reference, these terms are listed alphabetically. (You will see in the following section on sonnets how literary devices help the actor analyze and understand verse. Later, chapters 19 and 20 explore Shakespeare's plays from the actor's point of view. There you will find even more occasion to work with these terms. At that point, you may want to refer back to the following definitions.)

alexandrine: A line with 12 syllables, or six iambic feet, usually containing a slight pause (or caesura) after the third foot,
e.g. "He **con**/jures **might**/y **spells**, / to **troub**/le ev/il **minds**/."

allegory: A sustained metaphor with an underlying moral meaning different from the surface meaning.

alliteration: Repetition of the initial letter or sound in words that are in close juxtaposition, e.g. "the snake slowly slithered."

antithesis: The contrast of opposite ideas, which is expressed vocally by a combination of inflection and pause:
single antithesis: I asked for tea, not coffee.
double antithesis: I asked for hot tea, not cold coffee.
triple antithesis: I asked for hot, sweet tea, not cold, unsweetened coffee.
implied antithesis: I asked for hot tea …

assonance: Internal rhyme of vowel sounds, e.g. "lone" and "show."

bathos: Dullness of speech that immediately follows elevated speech, e.g. "the exile returned home, wounded, exhausted and hatless."

blank verse: Lines that follow a regular iambic pentameter rhythm but which are without rhyme (see the definitions below for "iamb" and "pentameter").

cacophony: Dissonant or harsh, discordant sound, e.g. "he snapped at a flat-fish."

caesura: A natural pause, which may occur anywhere in a line.

couplet: Two identically formed lines of poetry that rhyme.

dimeter: A line of verse with just two feet of iambic rhythm,
e.g. "To **go** / or **stay**/."

end-stopped: A line that ends with a definite pause, indicated by a punctuation mark.

euphony: Sounds that are agreeable and pleasing to the ear when spoken in sequence.

feminine ending: An extra unstressed beat that occurs at the end of a line of verse.

foot: The unit of measurement in a line of poetry (the end of each foot is denoted by an oblique line, as you will note throughout):

iamb: one short (unstressed) beat followed by a long (stressed) beat, e.g. "but **wait**"

trochee: one long (stressed) beat followed by a short (unstressed) beat, e.g. "**ne**-ver"

anapest: two short (unstressed) beats followed by a long (stressed) beat, e.g. "in-ter-**sperse**"

dactyl: one long (stressed) beat followed by two short (unstressed) beats, e.g. "**ten**-der-ly"

spondee: two strong (stressed) beats, e.g. "**King Kong**"

pyrrhic: two weak (unstressed) beats, e.g. "uh huh"

free verse: Poetry written in lines of unequal length and in which the metre or cadence continually changes, instead of following a fixed pattern.

gerund: A verb used as a noun, ending with "ing." When a gerund appears in the first foot of verse, do not place emphasis on the "ing" part of the word. Today, as in Shakespeare's day, we say we're going "**hunt**-ing, **fish**-ing and **shoot**-ing," not "hunt-**ing**, fish-**ing** and shoot-**ing**."

imagery: Pictures created in the mind through descriptive figures of speech, such as comparisons made with similes and metaphors, reinforced by carefully selected choice of words.

liquid consonants: Softer consonant sounds — like *l, m,* and *n* — that bring a fluid quality to several words spoken in sequence.

metaphor: An implied comparison between two different things, e.g. "a copper sky" or "a heart of stone."

metonymy: The use of one thing to naturally suggest something else, e.g. "The pen is mightier than the sword."

metre: The measure of rhythm indicating the number and kind of feet in a line, e.g. dimeter, trimeter, tetrameter, pentameter, iambic, trochaic.

oblique mark: The stroke (/) that indicates the end of each foot of verse, e.g. " But **soft**, / what **light** / through **yon**/der **win**/dow **breaks**?/"
It may cut through a word without interfering with the delivery of the word.

onomatopoeia: The naming of a thing or action by imitating the sound associated with it, e.g. "shriek," "murmur," "buzz," "hum."

oxymoron: A figure of speech in which two contradictory words are placed together, e.g. "O loving hate."

pathos: A quality of the text that creates feelings of pity or sadness.

pentameter: From the Greek word *penta* meaning "five," this means a line of verse written with five repeated feet. Thus, iambic pentameter is a line with five iamb, such as in Romeo's line,

e.g. "But **soft**, / what **light** / through **yon**/der **win**/dow **breaks**?/"
(Oblique marks indicate the end of each foot.)

personification: Representation of an idea or thing with human characteristics, e.g. "duty calls."

prosody: The study of poetic metres and versification.

repetition: Repeated use of consonants, words, or phrases providing a stronger, driven impact in spoken verse.

rhyme: Identical sounds in words placed at ends of lines:

feminine rhyme: a rhyme of two syllables where the second syllable is unstressed and the actual rhyme occurs on the first stressed beat, e.g. "**hur**ry" and "**wor**ry"

masculine rhyme: a rhyme that occurs only on accented syllables, e.g. "re**frain**" and "dis**dain**"

internal rhyme: rhyming of the last word of a line with another word near the middle of the line

rhythm: The alternation or repetition of stronger and weaker stresses, beats, or accents that creates a musical flow of prose or verse.

scansion: The study of the form of verse, i.e. the division of a line into feet, the marking of accented syllables, unaccented syllables, and caesura; and the identification of the metre (see the section on scansion in Chapter 19 for further details).

simile: A figure of speech that expresses comparison between two unlike things, using "like" or "as," e.g. "a face like marble."

suspensive pause: (also called **enjambment** or **run-on** line) This occurs where there is no punctuation at the end of a line of poetry, yet the thought and meaning of that line continue into the next. When speaking verse, the actor marks the suspensive pause by a slight "leaning" on the last word of the line and no breath should be taken.

tetrameter: A line of verse with four feet,
e.g. "And **thrice** / a-**gain**, / to **make** / up **nine** /"

trimeter: A line of verse with three feet, e.g. "I **would** / I **knew** / thy **heart** /"

Sonnets

A **sonnet** is a personal form of verse written in 14 lines. When you first start to explore classical verse — every actor will, in time — it can be useful to begin with a study of Shakespeare's sonnets. It's easier to become comfortable with the idea of speaking verse when you are restricted to 14 lines, rather than facing an entire five-act play.

In Shakespeare's day, the mark of an educated man was that he could sit down and write a perfect sonnet to his love. The worthiness of a suitor was assessed by how frequently and how well he wrote. Shakespeare himself wrote 154 sonnets during the course of his life, and he created a particular structure and rhyme scheme that bears his name today. The Shakespearean sonnet form consists of three **quatrains** (four lines of poetry with a cohesive thought) and a **rhyming couplet** (two lines of verse that sum up the previous 12 lines). Shakespeare's sonnets were generally written in iambic pentameter verse.

Almost all of Shakespeare's sonnets follow this pattern (there are a couple of exceptions, so don't be alarmed if you encounter a discrepancy in the structure of a sonnet you're studying):

- **The first quatrain (Q1)** outlines the opening thought of the sonnet in four lines. It has a rhyme scheme of A-B-A-B.
- **The second quatrain (Q2)** takes that idea and slightly shifts the focus of the issue. The verse speaker should take a brief beat between quatrains to allow a connection with the shift in emotional development. The rhyme scheme here is C-D-C-D.
- **The third quatrain (Q3)** moves the discussion in yet a different direction. Again, the speaker will take a moment between Q2 and Q3. The rhyme scheme in Q3 is E-F-E-F.
- **The rhyming couplet (RC)** has a rhyme scheme of G-G. It sums up the previous 12 lines and either reaches a conclusion or introduces a new, final argument. On the written page, the rhyming couplet is always indented to the right of the rest of the verse so that it stands apart from the quatrains in style as well as in content. The speaker should definitely take a moment to change emotional notes before speaking the rhyming couplet.

Here is a Shakespearean sonnet to illustrates the structure of the quatrains and rhyme scheme:

Sonnet 30

When to the sessions of sweet silent thought	(Q1)	A
I summon up remembrance of things past,		B
I sigh the lack of many a thing I sought,		A
And with old woes new wail my dear time's waste:		B
Then can I drown an eye, unused to flow,	(Q2)	C
For precious friends hid in death's dateless night,		D

And weep afresh love's long since cancell'd woe,		C
And moan the expense of many a vanish'd sight;		D
Then can I grieve at grievances foregone,	(Q3)	E
And heavily from woe to woe tell o'er		F
The sad account of fore-bemoaned moan,		E
Which I new pay as if not paid before		F
But if the while I think of thee, dear friend,	(RC)	G
All losses are restored and sorrows end.		G

The first step in working on a sonnet is to **paraphrase** the work by "translating" Shakespeare's lines into your own words. Use contemporary language and wherever possible avoid using words that Shakespeare himself chose. When paraphrasing sonnets, honour the structure of the verse by addressing each quatrain and couplet in turn, i.e. don't let the paraphrasing of Q1 run into that of Q2. Try to include every phrase that Shakespeare used, and avoid oversimplification.

Here is another example, Sonnet 91. It follows the traditional Shakespearean form illustrated above. Following the sonnet is an example of paraphrasing:

Sonnet 91
Some glory in their birth, some in their skill,
Some in their wealth, some in their body's force,
Some in their garments, though new-fangled ill,
Some in their hawks and hounds, some in their horse;
And every humour hath his adjunct pleasure,
Wherein it finds a joy above the rest;
But these particulars are not my measure;
All these I better in one general best.
Thy love is better than high birth to me
Richer than wealth, prouder than garments' cost,
Of more delight than hawks or horses be;
And having thee, of all men's pride I boast:
Wretched in this alone, that thou mayst take
All this away and me most wretched make.

Paraphrasing

Q1: Some people are proud of their family background, others are vain about their abilities. Some are arrogant about the money they have, or how physically strong they are. Some are vain about their clothing, no matter how unflattering the style may be. Some relish their status-symbol hawks, dogs and horses.

Q2: Every type of personality has an accompanying enjoyment of one thing in life more than other things. But this isn't the way I rate things myself, because I have one thing that tops them all.

Q3: Your love is more precious to me than a privileged background, more than money or expensive clothes, and brings me more pleasure than expensive birds and animals. And because I have you, I am prouder than anyone else could be.

RC: The only thing that terrifies me is the realization that you could take all this away from me, and thereby devastate me.

Now you can see more clearly how the first quatrain outlines the basic idea of the sonnet. The thought and direction shift between one quatrain and the next, while the rhyming couplet arrives as a bucket of cold water on Shakespeare's reverie. The next step is to create a **summary** where you reduce each quatrain and couplet to one sentence. Here is a summary for Sonnet 91:

Summary

Q1: Many people are vain about material things, their own circumstances or abilities.

Q2: Everyone loves something special, though I have a higher standard.

Q3: Your love is better than social position, money or possessions, and makes me prouder than everyone else.

RC: My only fear is that you can take this away from me and destroy my happiness.

Now that you have a clearer understanding of what Shakespeare's language means, it is time to begin looking at scansion; that is, the structure of the rhythm. Scansion provides major clues for the actor on how to speak the lines.

If you were learning a song, you would naturally learn the lyrics, melody and rhythm. However, if you were to learn just the lyrics and melody and ignore the rhythm as written, your listeners might not even recognize the song. It is the same thing for actors when approaching Shakespeare. Because his sonnets are written in verse (as are the overwhelming majority of his plays) the speaker needs to understand rhythm and give it due credit in preparing to learn the material. If you learn your lines with an incorrect interpretation of the rhythm, you will find it very difficult to "unlearn" the pattern. So the next step after paraphrasing and summary work is scansion.

As mentioned at the beginning of this section, Shakespeare's sonnets were generally written in iambic pentameter verse. This selection, Sonnet 29, employs a number of exceptions and appears here twice: once as written, and the second time, marked with scansion and notations. Sonnet 29 was chosen because it is *not* written in pure iambic rhythm and, since you will definitely encounter the odd discrepancy of rhythm in Shakespeare's sonnets, you might as well see how and why certain rhythmic changes were employed. Irregularities are numbered at the side of appropriate lines, and explanations follow the sonnet:

Sonnet 29
When, in disgrace with fortune and men's eyes,
I all alone beweep my outcast state
And trouble deaf heaven with my bootless cries
And look upon myself and curse my fate,
Wishing me like to one more rich in hope,
Featured like him, like him with friends possess'd,
Desiring this man's art and that man's scope,
With what I most enjoy contented least;
Yet in these thoughts myself almost despising,
Haply I think on thee, and then my state,
Like to the lark at break of day arising
From sullen earth, sings hymns at heaven's gate;
      For thy sweet love remember'd such wealth brings
      That then I scorn to change my state with kings.

The same sonnet is marked below so that you can see the pattern of stressed and unstressed beats, with each foot marked by oblique lines. In this example, stressed beats are written in boldface. But when a student is marking a script with stressed and unstressed beats (in pencil, so mistakes can be erased), unstressed beats are more easily marked with a squiggle (like the "~" found in some Internet Web site addresses). Stressed beats are marked by a strong left-to-right mark. These are a little awkward to do on a computer — boldface is much easier than squiggles — but here is an example using the first line of the sonnet.

˘ - / ˘ - / - ˘ - / - - / ˘ - - /
When, in / disgrace / with for/tune and / men's eyes /

Each foot in each line of verse is always separated from the next foot by an oblique mark, and this pattern should follow the last word of the final foot (as above). An oblique mark can cut through the middle of a word without problem, as with the word "for/tune" in the first line of the sonnet. Throughout this book, every time an oblique mark cuts through the middle of a word, no spaces exist on either side of the line. The placement of oblique marks has nothing to do with how an actor speaks the line or how the word is spelled. It simply allows you to note the end of a foot of verse.

Scansion (noting points of interest)

Sonnet 29
When, in / disgrace / with **for**/tune **and** / men's **eyes**,/
I **all** /alone / beweep / my **out**/cast state/
And **trou**/ble **deaf** / heaven **with** / my **boot**/less **cries**/ (Line 3)
And **look** / upon / myself / and **curse** / my **fate**,/
Wishing / me **like** / to **one** / more **rich** / in **hope**,/ (Line 5)
Featured / like **him**, / like **him** / with **friends** / possess'd,/ (Line 6)
Desir/ing **this** / man's **art** / and **that** / man's **scope**,/
With **what** / I **most** / enjoy / conten/ted **least**;/
Yet **in** / these **thoughts** / myself / almost / despi(sing),/ (Line 9)
Haply / I **think** / on **thee**, / and **then** / my **state**,/ (Line 10)
Like **to** / the **lark** / at **break** / of **day** / ari(sing)/ (Line 11)
From **sul**/len **earth**, / sings **hymns** / at **heav**/en's **gate**;/
 For **thy** / sweet **love** / remem/ber'd **such** / wealth **brings**/
 That **then** / I **scorn** / to **change** / my **state** / with **kings**./

Rhythmic clues for the actor discovered through scansion

Line 3: In the third foot of this line, the word "heaven" is elided into one unstressed sound. This pronunciation occurs very often when scanning Shakespeare's plays and poems, and provides a clue to how the word was likely spoken in his day. Singers with experience in traditional choral work know the word "heaven" is often sung as a one-syllable word, too, in classical music.

Line 5: "Wishing" is a gerund. As discussed in the definitions above, when a gerund appears at the beginning of a line of verse, the stress falls on the first part of the word and the "ing" remains unstressed. This foot is a **trochee** (see definition above), not an **iamb**. When you combine the first two feet of the line — the trochee and the iamb — the rhythm creates a "galloping" feeling. Repeat it several times over to hear how this sounds: "**Wish**ing me **like**, **wish**ing me **like**, **wish**ing me **like**." Shakespeare used variations in rhythms to throw emphasis onto key words and ideas. Here, the galloping rhythm marks the beginning of Q2 and helps propel a new energy into the delivery of the text.

Line 6:   This line, too, begins with a trochee and, in combination with the iamb of the second foot, creates another example of the galloping rhythm. This expresses the deeper emotional turmoil of the second quatrain.

Line 9:   The final word of the line, "despising," is an example of a **feminine ending** (see definition above). Marking it with brackets helps remind you the unstressed final syllable is "thrown away" when speaking the verse.

Line 10: Here again, the first foot begins with a trochee and the second foot is an iamb, creating a third example in this sonnet of the galloping rhythm. It is interesting to note that the stressed beat in "**hap**ly" follows the unstressed beat provided by the feminine ending in the previous line. That is not uncommon in Shakespeare's writing.

Line 11: There is another example of a feminine ending in this line. That is hardly surprising, because when you look at the rhyme pattern of the sonnet, "despising" and "arising" form the "EE" of the rhyme scheme. In analyzing Shakespeare's sonnets, it is to be expected that if one line has a feminine ending, its counterpoint rhyming word will also have a feminine ending.

Several reasons why actors begin their work with scansion are discussed in Chapter 19, where iambic pentameter verse is applied to Shakespeare's plays. But one major reason needs consideration here: scansion helps the speaker discover **pointing words** (see Chapter 4 for definition and Chapter 19 for examples applied to Shakespeare's plays).

Pointing words

Pointing words in verse always fall on a stressed beat, never on an unstressed beat, and there are generally one or two pointing words in every line of verse. Here is Q1 from Sonnet 29:

When, **in** / dis**grace** / with **for**/tune **and** / men's **eyes**,/
I **all** /**alone** / be**weep** / my **out**/cast **state**/
And **trou**/ble **deaf** /heaven **with** / my **boot**/less **cries**/
And **look** / u**pon** / my**self** / and **curse** / my **fate**,/

Only the words written above in boldface can be emphasized in delivery. If a word contains both a stressed and an unstressed beat, such as "disgrace" and "fortune" in the first line, then the word may or may not be a pointing word: it depends entirely on the choice of the speaker. Experiment with different choices of stressed beats to see which work best in delivery for you.

A stressed word that falls at the end of an unpunctuated line of verse must, by definition, be used as a pointing word because there is a suspensive pause at the end of the line. In the above example, "state" (at the end of Line 2) and "cries" (at the end of Line 3) are followed by suspensive pauses. Because the speaker must "lean" on the word to indicate the suspensive pause, the resulting delivery automatically transforms the word into a pointing word. One or two other words in the line may also be pointing words, as long as the words contain a stressed beat.

An unstressed word — such as "when," "with," and "men's" in Line 1 — should not be used as a pointing word; neither would "I" at the beginning of Line 2. To do so would imbalance the natural rhythm of the line. If a speaker completely ignores the rhythm of verse and uses pointing words at random, the verse ends up sounding like prose. A trained actor knows the difference between prose and verse, and uses vocal technique to serve the integrity of the writing.

The next step is to examine the sonnet for its poetic form, to discover key words and analyze images and literary devices. These clues will help the speaker make the presentation dramatic and effective.

Sonnet 55
Not marble, nor the gilded monuments
Of princes, shall outlive this powerful rhyme;
But you shall shine more bright in these contents
Than unswept stone besmear'd with sluttish time.
When wasteful war shall statues overturn,

And broils root out the work of masonry,
Nor Mars his sword, nor war's quick fire shall burn
The living record of your memory.
'Gainst death and all-oblivious enmity
Shall you pace forth; your praise shall still find room
Even in the eyes of all posterity
That wear this world out to the ending doom.
    So, till the judgment that yourself arise,
    You live in this, and dwell in lovers' eyes.

Literary analysis

Here is a line-by-line analysis of notable literary devices contained in the 14 lines of Sonnet 55, and some comments on how these might affect the speaking of the verse:

Quatrain 1:

Line 1: Assonance is found in "not," "nor," and "mon-uments."
Liquid consonants run through the line.
Personification of marble and gilded monuments.
Line 2: Assonance continues from Line 1 with "of," "out," and "pow-erful."
Line 3: Alliteration is found in "shall shine."
"Con-**tents**" has a double meaning that is illuminated by iambic rhythm.
Line 4: Repetition of the *s* sound is found in four words in this line.
Cacophony runs through this line, in contrast to euphony of opening lines.
General: The speaker can linger easily over many words and phrases in this quatrain. There is an overall use of *o, s* and "*s*-combination" sounds that provides continuity through this quatrain. A sense of texture and colour is provided by words such as "marble," "gilded," "shine," and "unswept stone." Suspensive pauses occur at the ends of lines 1 and 3, thus placing breath support demands on the verse speaker.

Quatrain 2:

Line 5: Alliteration of *w* is found in the first three words.
Assonance is found in "shall" and "statues."
War is personified.

Line 6: The play on *o* sounds brings euphony to the line.

Line 7: Assonance is found in "sword nor."

Note the impact of the series of monosyllables in this line.

General: There is a sense of attack and determined energy in the words used in this quatrain. The classical allusion to Mars brings a strong image to the verse, and many strong, aggressive words fill this quatrain. Articulation requires a lot of lip movement in delivery of this quatrain, particularly with *r* and *w* sounds. The speaker should "taste" the words and savour powerful images. Note the suspensive pause at the end of Line 7.

Quatrain 3:

Line 9: Death and enmity are personified.

Line 10: Assonance is found in "pace" and "praise."

Repetition of the word "shall."

Note the use of single-syllable words though this line.

Line 11: Assonance of *e* sound in the first three words and last syllable.

Posterity is personified.

Line 12: Repetition in first four words of "th" and *w* sounds.

Assonance in "to" and "doom."

General: The feeling behind many of the words in this quatrain is more relaxed than in the previous quatrain. Words can be elongated to reflect mood shift, now that the theme of eternity is introduced. Note that elision of "Even" occurs in Line 11, so the word is pronounced as "e'en." There are suspensive pauses at the end of lines 9, 10, and 11, so the verse speaker is allowed only one breath (at the punctuation mark in the middle of Line 10).

Rhyming couplet:

Line 13: "So" falls on an unstressed beat, but the comma lets the speaker linger for a moment.

Line 14: Assonance of sound in "live in this."

General: The couplet is filled with vowels and consonants that permit the speaker to extend key words and linger over emotional moments.

Conclusion

Several sonnets have been used here to illustrate the beginning steps an actor follows when working on delivery of verse: sonnet structure, paraphrasing, summary, scansion, and analysis of literary devices. These steps will help you understand the meaning of the verse, find clues for pronunciation and delivery, and gain a comfort level in speaking classical text.

You are now well on the road to applying the actor's preparatory steps when working with Shakespeare's language. More will be said of this in chapters 19 and 20, when we address classical plays.

Part Two

The Actor Beginning Work

Chapter Seven
Working with the Five Senses

Having looked at the physical and vocal preparation that every actor must undergo in order to be flexible and ready for work, it is time now to begin looking at steps that actors follow in creating a character. Developing an awareness of the five senses, for example, helps the actor believe in the "pretend world" of the stage. Sensory work is the foundation of many of the exercises and methods that follow in this book.

Using sensory work in acting

We live in the physical world and have an understanding of that world through innumerable messages sent to and received by the brain. Just as our minds lets us perceive the world intellectually, our bodies know the world through the senses. The messages that our senses receive are sent to the brain, where they are interpreted in the context of what we have already learned or experienced in life. However, there are so many sensory stimuli around us all day that the mind tends to block out the vast majority of them, simply to function efficiently.

For example, our earlier life experience lets us look at a pan of boiling water and know that it is hot. The sight and sound of bubbles and steam give us the necessary visual and auditory information. We don't have to plunge our hand into the water to know the water is boiling.

In rehearsal and performance, an actor can apply his or her own experience of the physical world and make acting more "real" through heightened sensory awareness. The actor draws upon present and past experiences involving sight, sound, touch, taste, and smell. These sense memories are then incorporated into the actor's work and become the foundation for the creation of images.

Images

Images — the pictures visualized by the actor — are the key to the actor's success in creating and sustaining the make-believe world of theatre. The stronger and clearer the images become for you, the easier it is to believe the text and relate to the character you are portraying.

When you are training seriously for a particular sport, you repeat the same exercise hundreds of times. As your body performs a sequence of functions over and over, it "remembers" the action in a physical sense until it can follow very complex sequences of movement without you once having to think consciously of each step. The term "muscle memory" is used to describe how such physical action affects the brain. The body simply remembers.

Similarly, the mind remembers. We recall collective sensory experiences of the world through sense memory recall. Every actor should attempt to reawaken familiarity with the physical world, to recall past sensory experiences — pleasant or otherwise — and to incorporate these elements into acting work. A number of such sensory exercises follow.

Being attuned to our five senses is only part of the actor's job, however. The next responsibility is to search out sensory images in the words of the script. Discover and analyze each of them. Then proceed to find the images within the "unscripted" part — that is, the creative ideas that the actor adds to the script to enrich his or her personal interpretation of the text. Use of the five senses will also help you create a strong, believable awareness of the setting before you say the first word of your scene. Sometimes strong sensory work will help you find the most effective unspoken transition between two lines of dialogue. It can heighten a dramatic or comic moment in the physical action of the play.

Sensory exercises

You may wish to begin with a general sensory exercise. On a nice warm day, find a relatively isolated place outdoors where you are prepared to spend 15 or 20 minutes. Map out a space that is no more than two metres square. As you sit in that space, watch the world in miniature unfold around you. Take care to consider each of the five senses in turn, and discover how they are integrated within that space. Examine everything within that area for colour, texture, insect life, and soil composition: in short, everything visual.

Then pick up several items and examine them closely, thinking not just of sight but also of the sense of touch. Don't be afraid, for example, to taste a blade of grass or whatever you find. Is there a fragrance coming from the earth itself? Perhaps some smells enter the area from nearby. Are there any sounds emanating from your space? What kinds of sounds passing through your space can you identify?

These are some of the questions you can ask yourself, but it is essential that you spend a certain amount of time specifically examining each of the five senses. After you have passed your allotted time, go indoors and find a private place. Sit down again and recreate everything you can remember from your space. Try to visualize the entire scene. Recreate from your sense memory whatever life you observed: pick up the imagined items, examine them, relive each sensory element in turn. Make the setting as real as possible by drawing upon all five senses.

Here are some specific exercises designed to heighten awareness of each of the five senses. They are also very good concentration workouts because of the demands they make on specific mental and sensory functions.

Sight exercises:

1. On a table, place 15 random objects donated from peoples' pockets and purses. Allow everyone two minutes to closely examine the items without touching them. Then have everyone look away while the objects are rearranged on the table and one item is removed. Allow participants 20 seconds to discover which item has been removed, then give them another minute to jot down every detail about that item. Repeat the exercise several times, constantly rearranging the items and removing a different object each time. Sometimes, for a twist, it's fun to not remove an object.

2. Sit in a comfortable circle so that each of you has a clear view of the others. Depending on the number of people in the circle, allow yourselves about two or three minutes to study one specific person in a detailed way and the others in a general manner. Then close your eyes. One person is selected to describe as accurately as possible the individual upon whom their attention

was focused. The rest of the group keep their eyes shut in order to help them visualize each detail and to prevent their vision from filling in the missing pieces. Once a member of the circle realizes who is being described, he or she is to point in the direction of that individual.

There are two ways of deciding on the effectiveness of this exercise: one is based on how quickly people zero in on the correct person, the other on how accurately the individual was described.

3. Give one person from the group a book containing a large colour photograph. (Art books or photography books work well for this exercise.) That person must then describe the picture in as much detail as possible to the rest of the group: subject matter, size, composition, colours, relative proportions, emotional atmosphere and other relevant points. When that person has exhausted the descriptive elements in the picture, the others are shown the picture to see how closely their visual mental picture matches the original item being described.

    This sounds like a simple exercise, but it is surprisingly difficult. One omitted element can totally confuse everyone and a skimpy description will result in an even skimpier image. The key is to give the broadest possible description first, before systematically filling in the details.

    Allow several people to try this exercise, for it not only tests the group's ability to visualize images, but we all discover how the limitations of our vocabularies can frustrate an entire group. Precision in choice of words is critical. Not surprisingly, people are often more receptive to vocabulary games after this exercise.

4. We have all been through experiences that remain etched in a visual memory on our brains, usually as a result of a heightened emotional moment. We can see ourselves years later in that situation, in the middle of a traumatic or exciting experience. In the same way, this individual exercise deals with a specific memory-recall image. (It may also become a barrier-breakdown exercise for some people.)

    Allow the members of the group a minute to think back to a particularly vivid moment in their lives. They must imagine themselves in that setting and try to recall every detail that surrounded them at that time: the physical setting, others who were present, what each person (including themselves) looked like, and so forth. Make the visual pictures as real and complete as possible.

The exercise is approached as a tableau or a frozen moment in a film clip. Although other senses can come into it, the memory recall should focus on the sense of sight. No dialogue is allowed.

You may wish to relive the situation physically in a tableau with limited movement. Movement should arise from the emotions that are triggered by the images rather than trying to "copy" a remembered movement. This may give the exercise a stilted appearance but, by limiting movement to the minimum, you can focus on the sensory images and the emotions they trigger.

You may choose to add one sound or an audible breath at the most emotional moment of the improvisation. The point of the exercise, however, is to use sense memory recall in order to create a dramatic or comic moment that is real and believable to the subject. (If you find it hard to deal with this heightened emotional experience, relax. Choose a less emotional image; explore, for example, the physical setting of your bedroom exactly as you left it this morning.)

5. Select a ten-square-centimeter area of the room: floor, wall, or objects such as an exercise book, desk, or chair. You must be able to focus closely on that space. Look as closely as possible at that area to discover how many different hues and tones go into the making of one general colour. See the effects of wear and tear on that space. Note the quality of light and texture and their changes as you move about. Then turn away and try to recreate the picture in front of you. Place it in different locations around the room. If you have trouble projecting this image, turn back to the original object and refresh your senses.

This type of exercise can be used at random moments of the day. Carefully study the salt shaker on the cafeteria table and see how well you can recreate it a few minutes later. You will improve this ability with daily practice. Continue to challenge your powers of concentration and search for increasingly complex objects to study.

Sound exercises:

1. This is an individual exercise in observation of sound. Sit as quietly as you can in the room for three minutes. Listen to the sounds outside the room as your first area of attention. From where do those sounds originate? What is the quality of each sound, and how

does that quality change through the duration of the sound? Is the sound pleasant or unpleasant? How does it affect you emotionally? Can you recognize what is making each sound? How many are continuous, repetitious sounds that you subconsciously blocked out before this exercise began?

Now think of your second space — the area within the room. Focus in turn on each sound that you hear and repeat the questions listed above.

The third focus of your attention is your own personal space, the sounds you are making yourself. Despite interference from other sounds beyond us, we can usually hear ourselves breathe. However, if the room is particularly quiet, try to hear your heartbeat. Try to recount the sounds in sequence after the exercise.

2. This kindergarten game is fun and it also underlines the importance of total clarity. The group sits in a circle and the leader whispers a sentence clearly into one person's ear. That person repeats the sentence, word for word, pause for pause, and inflection for inflection, into the next person's ear. In this manner, the sentence continues round the circle. No one may repeat the sentence a second time, so you must focus carefully on what you hear when it is your turn.

   When the sentence gets back to the original person, he or she repeats exactly what was just heard, then what he or she heard at the beginning of the exercise. Generally there is a substantial difference between the two sentences and it can be interesting to see where the distortions occurred. Often someone who mumbles, speaks too quickly, or perhaps is not prepared to receive the message can undermine this exercise.

3. Sort people into pairs and assign one individual in each pair to be the leader. The leader begins to speak but with certain provisos: speech must be slower than usual, it must be exaggerated in the movement of the mouth in order to facilitate lip reading, it should have lots of colour and energy, and it must be continuous. There should be no long pauses, or stalling for time to think of the next sentence in the story. Simultaneously, the other person is repeating exactly what is heard, word for word, stress for stress and inflection for inflection.

   When the exercise is over, the follower repeats the same story with word-for-word accuracy. Even if this instruction is not mentioned initially, most people can reproduce the story fairly accurately afterwards. Try this at home while listening to the radio or television to improve your imitative abilities. Speaking along simultaneously with a dialect is a good beginning for imitating the rhythm and musicality of a dialect.

4. This is a sound exercise to improve concentration abilities. Seat the group in a circle. Each person thinks of five totally unconnected, random words. This will ensure a good mix:

    - one noun
    - one verb
    - one adjective
    - one adverb
    - one gerund

The first person says a word. (Exercise your imagination in inflection, emotional subtext, volume, and pitch.) The next person repeats the first person's word exactly as spoken and adds a first word. The third person repeats the first two words identically and adds the next word. Continue round the circle, with each person accurately repeating all of the preceding words in sequence before adding his or her own contribution.

If the person immediately before you does not repeat a certain word with the same vocal qualities as the original person, you must still say the word as you heard it spoken originally by the initial speaker. The initial speaker also may correct the mispronunciation or inflection of his or her word by someone else.

You will discover as this exercise continues that you create your own pattern for remembering these random words, although there is no logical sequence to their meanings. If a person makes an error of omission — forgetting one of the words in sequence — he or she is eliminated from the circle. However, any words that this person has contributed remain in the spoken sequence. The object of the exercise is to be the last person left who can accurately repeat each of the random sequential words.

For added difficulty, try this exercise with a gesture or pose accompanying each word.

Touch exercises:

1. This is an individual exercise that shows the limitations of

depending on one sense, such as sight. Close your eyes and begin to explore your own clothing and external being from head to toe by means of the sense of touch. You should feel for such things as texture, temperature, and the wear-and-tear conditions of your clothing. Is there an emotional response to your discoveries? List the three most surprising aspects of what you find.

2. For the maximum benefit from this exercise, everyone should be barefoot. Close your eyes for greater concentration. Imagine you are walking over a variety of surfaces, each one lasting for about 30 seconds. As you encounter each, imagine yourself in a specific situation. Let your mind and body focus on the texture and temperatures involved. Feel each substance against your feet, and use the rest of your body as necessary within the setting you create.

   Walk barefoot over or through:

   - fresh-cut grass
   - soggy mud
   - a gravel laneway
   - a sandy beach
   - a cold stream
   - broken glass
   - hot tarmac
   - a giant spider's web
   - a waterbed
   - a pile of autumn leaves
   - clouds

3. You can perform this simple exercise at random times during the day. Take a small object from your purse or pocket and examine it carefully through the sense of touch. Close your eyes to prevent your sense of sight from interfering. Set your object down and then try to recreate its size, weight, dimension, and texture. Keep your eyes closed initially but when you feel you have achieved good concentration, open your eyes and try to visualize the object.

   This is an important exercise for the novice actor when rehearsing a domestic scene in a play. Such scenes thrive on accuracy of setting. Each object on a kitchen table, for example, should be thought of with care. The more truthfully you can create the sense of a physical object, the more believable your acting will be.

Generally, one of the least believable pieces of acting in rehearsal involves an actor making an entrance through a door. The mimed door often gets pulled off its imaginary hinges, or opens in different directions from one entrance to the next. This breaks the illusion of reality. The solution is to practise with a real door, carefully feeling each stage of opening and closing it. Turn away immediately and recreate the same movement accurately in mime. Alternate between the two actions until you achieve clarity and accuracy.

4.   For this exercise, divide yourselves into groups of three. One person is to be the blind sculptor, another the model, and the third the lump of clay. The blind sculptor's eyes are closed while the model strikes a pose that can be held for an extended period of time. The person who is the lump of clay should assume a seated position beside the model. Then the sculptor, keeping eyes shut throughout the exercise, assesses the physical position of the model simply through the sense of touch: the model's stance, body weight, angle of arms and legs, facial expression, head angle, and so on.

The sculptor turns to the lump of clay and forms the clay into the identical physical position held by the model. The person representing the clay must not, under any circumstances, assist or anticipate how the sculptor will manoeuvre various limbs or the sense of balance. The model, of course, must not alter a single aspect of the original pose. The exercise is a real challenge in physical self-control, for both the person playing the model and the person representing the clay.

The blind sculptor may turn to double-check a point on the model at any time and, indeed, will likely alternate regularly between the two people. But at no time may the sculptor open his or her eyes and look until an identical statue has been created. Reverse the roles twice so that each person gets to experience each of the three functions in this exercise.

Taste exercises:

1.   Close your eyes and use your imagination to take you to another time and place. Draw on your own experience or visualize a situation to help make the sense of taste as real as possible for you. Imagine tasting each of the following items. Take 30 seconds for each one and linger over the sense of taste and texture:

- ice-cream sundae
- blowing dust
- pickle
- raw oyster
- salt
- toffee apple
- burnt toast
- slice of lemon
- maple leaf
- curry dinner
- piece of gum
- malted milkshake
- peppermint toothpick
- bran muffin
- peanut butter
- hardrock candy
- toasted marshmallow
- rancid milk
- hamburger (from each of the major burger chains)

Parts of the mouth react differently to sweet flavours than to tart ones. How does the sense of taste or texture change within your mouth?

2. The sense of taste is often under-used in acting exercises. Daily observation at mealtimes can help to heighten your awareness of taste and the discovery of where sweetness, tartness, saltiness, and so forth actually are sensed within the mouth.

Decide on two items of food: one is your favourite food of all time and the other is the worst thing you've ever had. Take a moment to visualize the foods in your mind. Establish that one of them will be to the right and the other to the left. Now imagine that the two foods will grow in size, much as things and people changed size in Lewis Carroll's *Alice in Wonderland*.

Once you can visualize the foods clearly, open your eyes. When your concentration is strong, begin to smell the two items in deep, long breaths, and alternate your attention between them. If you don't see the food first and then smell it, we who are observing you will not believe you actually taste it. Do this in slow motion with a fair degree of exaggeration. Allow free release of any sounds that reveal your emotional response to each food.

Begin with one complete bite of your favourite food. Savour each change in flavour, texture, and temperature. Really let your face and body reflect your enjoyment. By making the action larger than life, you will make it more real for yourself. Now take one equally large, exaggerated bite of the other food. Identify each of the unpleasant elements of the food —such as flavour, texture, and temperature — and overplay your emotional reaction. Alternate between the two foods.

If you have trouble concentrating, go back to the first steps in the sequence: imagine the food, see it, smell it, then eat it.

Afterwards, discuss what made you enjoy or dislike each food. Compare notes with others. You may be surprised to discover how many of our eating habits and our reactions to tastes are acquired from others: our families, peers, advertising campaigns, social environment. These influences change as we mature and all of us, over time, change our likes and dislikes of certain foods.

Smell exercises:

1. This exercise draws on memory recall. Close your eyes and take 30 seconds or so to recreate one specific smell. Place yourself in a setting with which you associate that smell. Once you have done this for 30 seconds, let go of it. Replace it with another specific smell. Alternate between pleasant and unpleasant smells. If you cannot go back into your own experience, create an imaginary situation from these suggestions. Let each smell suggest a specific situation that answers the major questions in acting: Where? When? Who? How?

   - fresh bread
   - ammonia
   - onions cooking
   - rotting fish
   - a new car
   - sea air
   - something burning on the stove
   - vinegar
   - freshly shampooed hair
   - a herd of cattle
   - the aftermath of a rainstorm

- cologne
- dirty laundry
- burning autumn leaves
- fresh garlic
- garlic on someone's breath the next day
- dusty attic
- scented rose
- freshly lit match
- a damp cave
- a skunk
- a freshly powdered baby

What emotional reaction do you have to each smell? Does this reaction alter? Does the quality of the smell change? Which is the strongest of the smells for you? Why?

2. The sense of smell is rarely called upon in our daily life, yet it can trigger strong emotional responses. Note moments during the day when you become aware of smell and determine which kinds of smells draw you out of your train of thought. Which emotional reactions occur within you as a result of each smell you encounter?

Imagine you are sitting down to dinner. Close your eyes and imagine a meal made up of your favourite foods. Once you have decided what you will be eating and where it will be in front of you, open your eyes. See each food on your plate in turn. Without touching it, lean close to it and smell it. Explore each item. Take enough time to make the food real for you. Now imagine you have the same food in front of you, but change one of the elements of the exercise. For example:

- Perhaps the meal has gone stale or even begun to spoil.
- Maybe you are recovering from an illness and have no appetite. Your taste buds are still out of kilter.
- Perhaps you are on a diet and have just eaten a surreptitious, illegal snack. You have no room left for dinner. However, imagine that the spread in front of you was put together by Your Most Favourite Person in the World and you do not want to hurt that person's feelings.

With some or all of these thoughts in mind, force yourself to explore the same foods concentrating on the sense of smell. What changes occurred in your image of the food, your emotional response to it and the quality of the smells you inhaled?

These exercises are designed to stimulate your awareness of the senses. Daily observation stimulates the five senses for an actor. The senses provide a believable foundation for images from which spring the emotional responses of your character in the play.

Different styles of plays contain varying degrees of opportunity for the use of sense memory. For example, abstract and absurdist theatre is relatively skimpy in this regard, but realistic and naturalistic plays abound with vivid, well-written images full of sensory opportunity. Whatever the genre, the actor can use creative imagination and careful research to bring a wealth of additional sensory work to a performance. This enriches the audience's understanding of setting, reinforces the emotional content of the scene, and makes the world of the stage believable.

The sensory notebook

An actor should try regularly to become sensitive to widely varying stimuli of sight, sound, touch, taste, and smell. Try choosing five different items per day for each of these five categories. That makes a total of 25 items to use in daily sensory observation.

Note down in a book a few words about your observations. Once you have used an object for one sensory observation, you should not choose the same item at a later date for another sensory category. After a couple of weeks, you may find you are running out of things to sample for this exercise. Use your imagination and continue to store away as many observations as possible. See if you can get six weeks' worth of images locked in your sense memory before you call it quits.

Exercise:

The next time you sit down for coffee, take time to examine it visually. See the mug, the colour of the coffee, the steam rising from it, the grains of sugar around the lip of the mug. Smell the fragrances, feel the weight and the temperature of the mug as you lift it. Hear the sound of the first sip, savour the coffee at each stage of the sip and swallow, notice the aftertaste and listen to the sound of the mug being set down.

Turn life's little moments into opportunities for observation, rediscovery and the reawakening of sensory stimulation. You can do this anywhere, anytime, and it will eventually become part of your daily activity.

Another good way to begin your acting preparation is by making a sense memory chart for a scene you are beginning to rehearse.

Sense memory chart

To create a sense memory chart, begin by highlighting or underlining every word or phrase in the scene that involves any of the five senses. Then list these words down the left side of a page, one word or phrase per line. If two or more words logically belong together in a phrase, don't separate them into individual words, for often an individual word will have a slightly different meaning than when it is used in a phrase. For example, "harvest moon" has one meaning, but if you were to isolate "harvest" and "moon." you would end up with an inexact — and incorrect — sensory description.

Across the top of the page, make five columns and label each one for a different sense: sight, sound, touch, taste, and smell. Now begin to look at each word or phrase running down the left column of the page. In a few descriptive words for each word or phrase, and considering each sense in turn, write down what you visualize. Watch that you don't spill over between one sense and the next. For example, it's a common mistake to describe texture under sight, and then forget to include it as well under touch.

Here is a section from *Canadian Gothic* by Joanna M. Glass, which can be found on page 62 in the accompanying scene book, *Behind the Scenes, Volume One*. Jean is remembering her childhood:

> Every day, before I started school, my mother took me past the city limits, to the fields around Cardigan. In the spring we collected wild prairie crocus. I wore dirndl skirts then. I'd lift the whole front of my skirt and fill it with stubby mauve crocus. When the skirt was full, and I couldn't bend down any more without the flowers spilling out, I stopped. She always hummed one song: "I Dream of Jeannie with the Light Brown Hair." When I couldn't hear it, I knew I'd strayed too far. We did the same thing with tiger lilies in the summer bringing them home and stuffing them into old honey cans and pickle jars. I never believed when they closed at night they'd open again in the morning.

The first step is to isolate or highlight the words or phrases which are connected to images. (There may be differing opinions on what constitutes a complete phrase with each of the images; that is a matter of individual choice.) This script is particularly rich with sensory words and images.

> Every day, before I started *school, my mother* took me *past the city limits,* to the *fields around Cardigan.* In the *spring* we *collected wild prairie crocus.* I *wore dirndl skirts* then. I'd *lift the whole front of my skirt* and *fill it with stubby mauve crocus.* When the *skirt was full,* and *I couldn't bend down* any more without the *flowers spilling out,* I stopped. She always *hummed* one song: "I Dream of Jeannie with the Light Brown Hair." When *I couldn't hear it,* I knew I'd *strayed too far.* We did the same thing with *tiger lilies* in the *summer* bringing them *home* and *stuffing them into old honey cans* and *pickle jars.* I never believed when they *closed at night* they'd *open again in the morning.*

Now begin to make a sensory chart from the list of words identified above.

Image words	sight	sound	touch	taste	smell
school	one-room wooden desks	kids playing bell ringing	painted wood blackboard		musty woodstove
my mother	pretty dark hair comfortably dressed	melodious gentle	warm safe		talcum powder
past the city limits	dusty road houses in distance	silence distant farm sounds	warm sun		spring flowers
fields around Cardigan	many shades of greens and yellows	wind rustling	brushing against grains of grass		sprigs new earth mixture of flowers
spring	birds buds on trees	birds singing	light breeze		fragrance on the wind
collected wild prairie crocus	mauves yellows green leaves shiny	snapping of stems	smooth slippery at stem when picked	bitter taste on fingers from the stems	floral scent like perfume

So it continues. Complete the description of each of the following words or phrases in a similar manner:

- wore dirndl skirts
- lift the whole front of my skirt
- fill it with stubby mauve crocus
- skirt was full
- I couldn't bend down
- flowers spilling out
- hummed "I Dream of Jeannie with the Light Brown Hair"
- I couldn't hear it
- strayed too far
- tiger lilies
- summer
- home
- stuffing them into old honey cans
- pickle jars
- closed at night
- open again in the morning

Some of these sensory images will be strong for you because of your past experiences in life. Others may be more difficult to understand immediately and may require some research. For example, you may not know what a dirndl skirt is, so you will have to look up the word "dirndl" in the dictionary. On the other hand, you may come from a background where every young girl in the family wore one. You may not be able to hum the tune of "I Dream of Jeannie with the Light Brown Hair." However, you might remember that it's a soft, romantic love song and therefore you can understand its purpose in this script. Research will help you find the lyrics and melody line, and thus you will discover the reason for the reference to the song in the scene.

The purpose of isolating each sense within an image is not to drive an actor mad with paperwork, but rather to rekindle and re-experience the world of the senses. The more vivid the sensory world becomes for the actor, the more easily he or she can identify with the character in the context of the play. These are devices to assist you when natural instinct and intuitive understanding seem to be letting you down during the rehearsal process.

Here is another excerpt, this one from the play *Gwendoline* by James Nichol. This selection can be found on page 82 of *Behind the Scenes, Volume Two*. Again you will notice that powerful images play a key role in this scene, which can help actors to apply sense memory.

GWENDOLINE: You dream about your mother?
DAVID: Yes.
GWENDOLINE: But you don't know what she looks like.
DAVID: She looks ...
GWENDOLINE: Yes? Go on, David!
DAVID: She looks a little like you ... and she's running. Her face is ... dark, and her hair is flying out. She's running away and I'm running too, but I'm not really running. I'm wrapped in a blanket against her and it's warm and ... everything smells warm. Sometimes we're running over the railroad bridge way above the river, right down the tracks, just like a train, and we're way up high! I told you it was stupid.
GWENDOLINE: What happens?
DAVID: Nothing. I wake up.
GWENDOLINE: I never dream about my mother. I dream about my father. He's always lying at the bottom of the stairs, dead. He's drunk. He's always drunk. Do you know what my father did?
DAVID: No.
GWENDOLINE: I found a rabbit's nest. It was right there, in the garden. It was in the very middle of the garden. I knelt down and I lifted off the fur and there were seven baby rabbits. They were all huddled up together and you could see their little hearts beating. I picked up one and I held him in my hand for a long while and then something made me look back toward the house. My father was watching me. He was standing right here at the window. I tried to gather them up. I tried to hold them in my dress, but I was too little and they kept falling and I couldn't get them! And then he was behind me. He said, Gweny, don't you know the rabbits eat the tops off the carrots? Don't you know they eat the lettuce? And he had the cat in his hands ... and he put the cat down ... and it began to eat them! It just held them down and ... my father put his arm around me ... and we watched! Don't cry, Gweny. Don't cry.
DAVID: I'm sorry.

Here is an extracted list of words and phrases that create the vivid images in the scene:

- dream
- your mother
- don't know what she looks like

- you
- She's running
- Her face is ... dark
- her hair is flying out
- She's running away
- I'm running too, but I'm not really running
- I'm wrapped in a blanket against her
- it's warm
- everything smells warm
- running over the railroad bridge
- way above the river
- the tracks
- train
- my mother
- my father
- lying at the bottom of the stairs, dead
- He's drunk
- found a rabbit's nest
- garden
- the very middle of the garden
- knelt down
- lifted off the fur
- seven baby rabbits
- huddled up together
- see their little hearts beating
- picked up one
- held him in my hand
- the house
- My father was watching me
- He was standing right here at the window
- tried to gather them up
- hold them in my dress
- I was too little
- they kept falling
- he was behind me
- rabbits eat the tops off the carrots
- they eat the lettuce
- the cat in his hands
- he put the cat down
- it began to eat them

- it just held them down
- my father put his arm around me
- we watched

The balance of the scene reads with equally strong images. You can see that the majority of the words in this scene are involved in some way or another with creating "time past" memories for both characters. The stronger the images (and hence the emotions) become for the actors, the more believable the world of *Gwendoline* becomes for them and us.

You will notice from these excerpts that we tend to rely heavily on two particular senses: sight and sound. We use those two most frequently in order to function in everyday life and they are the senses upon which playwrights generally rely in their writing. Consequently, these two columns will tend to fill up rather more quickly in most sense memory charts. The other three senses are used relatively less frequently in everyday life, but do not ignore their potential power.

Smell, for example, rarely appears in a sense memory chart. Yet the sense of smell can be a powerful tool for an actor. Everyone has a memory of at least one smell that reminds him or her of home, or of another person who is no longer around, which will help the actor unleash fresh and believable emotions. Smell can also be used to trigger a sense of revulsion, as anyone with a food allergy can confirm. The same principle can be used when we discuss the sense of taste. A sudden memory of a particular food, for example, can cause positive or negative feelings in us. Just because we don't use certain senses frequently in order to function in life doesn't mean that they are not important to us.

It is essential that actors regularly resensitize themselves to all five senses. It is especially important during the early stages of rehearsal, in preparing homework, and when taking "the moment before" as the actor prepares to present a monologue or scene.

Using the senses to create an environment

Research can make the actor's imaginary setting richer and stimulate strong feelings in "the moment before" the scene begins. For example, George Bernard Shaw's play *St. Joan* has a natural attraction for young women who are searching for material for scene study and monologues. The central character, Joan of Arc, is challenging and complex. She has some powerful speeches for audition purposes, and Joan's basic story has an appeal that transcends the centuries.

But in approaching a piece from this play, young actors rarely exploit sensory work in their preparation. An actor must be specific about Joan's world and the events that shaped her being. As an exercise, let's create Joan's prison cell because:

- The conditions of Joan's imprisonment are important in understanding decisions she takes during the action of the play.
- It is the Inquisitor's sentence of perpetual imprisonment that, in fact, leads her to recant her position, tear up her signed confession, and choose instead to be burned at the stake.

From an actor's point of view, those are strong motivating factors. Delving into Joan's prison life is one of the keys to understanding her character.

Begin by looking at some of the general questions to be asked when preparing a piece from this play, then research an accurate answer to each. What is the year? Which country is she in? Where is she being held prisoner? Who has her in custody and why? How long has she been there? What experiences has she gone through to this point?

Now look at some of the specific questions that will bring to life the reality of Joan's condition in this scene. This is where the actor's imagination kicks in. What is the courtroom like? Who is there? What do they look like? How is she treated during the trial? In this process, isolate each of the senses in order to focus specifically on each sense in turn. Now conjure up as vivid a prison cell setting as possible for Joan's "moment before" entering the courtroom.

Sight

- What are the dimensions of her prison cell?
- What is the source of light? (Is there a small window allowing in natural light, or do candles provide the only source of light? Describe the appearance of any window or candles.)
- Describe the walls, their surface, and anything found there: implements, insects, water seeping in, etc. Now describe the ceiling.
- What is the surface of the floor made of? Is it dry, damp, cold?
- Where specifically is the door?
- What is the door made of? Describe its surface. How many locks are there, and what do they look like? Are there hinges on the door?

- Is there any kind of peephole or window? If so, what specifically can you see beyond it?
- If there is a world outside the door, are there people there? Describe each of them. Discuss the hallway or antechamber.
- Is there an animal/insect world within the room, such as rats, lice, or spiders? Where are they found, and what traces do they leave behind?
- Is there any furniture in the room? Describe each piece in turn, such as a bench, table, or bed.
- Where does Joan sleep? Is there straw on the floor? Describe the texture of the blanket.
- Where does she eat? Describe a typical meal she might have, including the bowl, tankard, or plate on which it is served.
- What clothing is Joan wearing? Is she in breeches, or has she been forced to wear a skirt? Of what material is her clothing made?
- Have the authorities allowed her to wear a cross? If so, what is it made of? How elaborate or simple is it? Is she allowed a rosary?
- Are there any special personal items that she is allowed to have with her in the cell? Describe each item.
- Describe every aspect of her visual appearance, one part of the body at a time — hair, skin, hands, and so forth — as if looking at a reflection in a mirror.

Sound

- What are the sounds Joan would hear from outside the cell? Are the sounds sharp or muffled, regular or occasional?
- Are there soldiers moving around and talking? Are they at work or relaxing?
- Can you hear other prisoners beyond the cell?
- Do the kinds of sounds change with the time of day and, if so, which specific kinds of sounds occur under which circumstances?
- What sounds would Joan have heard within the room? Consider live noises such as those made by rodents, etc.
- Consider the sounds made by Joan herself: footsteps, furniture moving, a stone scraping a cross into the wooden door, breathing, the movement of clothing, or the rustling of rushes.

Touch

- What is the temperature of the room? This may change with the season in which you decide to set the scene, or the time of day.
- Is there a draft or is the room stuffy and airtight?
- Is there dampness seeping through the floor and into her clothing?
- Does a rat scamper over her foot? If so, describe the feeling.
- Does she feel infested with lice?
- What does it feel like not to have washed your hair or cleaned your teeth for months? Bearing in mind primitive dental care, how many teeth does she have left in her mouth?
- Was she perhaps allowed to wash regularly? If so, which parts of the body feel cleanest?
- What is the sensation of her clothing against her skin? How long has she been wearing that particular outfit? What is its texture?
- Does she have straw in her hair or prickling through her clothes?
- What does the surface of the wall feel like? The door, its peephole? The floor of the cell?
- Consider each of the articles (or props) in her cell.
- If you have decided there is a window or bars, how do they feel?
- What do the candle and candle holder feel like?
- Are there iron shackles in the room and what are their weight, texture, and temperature?
- What does her blanket or litter feel like at night when she goes to sleep?

Taste

- What is the taste inside her mouth?
- What did she last have to eat?
- Is there a salty taste from perspiration?
- Is there a taste from licking an insect bite or sore, perhaps?
- Is there any residual taste of soap or dirt in her mouth?

Smell

- Which smells come into the room from outside?
- Is there a smell from torches or candles from the outside world?
- There is always a smell of dampness when it rains. Sometimes one can smell a sense of the season, especially in spring or autumn. Do

any smells connected with the season or the weather enter the cell?

- Which smells exist within the room itself?
- Is there a different smell in the corners of the cell, such as mouldy dampness?
- Given primitive bathroom facilities in such a setting, are there smells connected with that area of the setting?
- Are there residual smells from the last meal?
- If there is a candle in the cell, does it have a smell?
- Which smells does Joan have surrounding her personally?
- Think of her clothing, whether she was allowed soap recently, and her state of cleanliness in general.

These are just some of the questions that could and should be asked before beginning to work on Joan's character. If you have done this background research work, you will have a clear understanding of Joan's passion in the trial scene. You will understand the motivation behind her words and actions, and thus be better equipped to portray her inner life. When Joan says to the Inquisitor, "Perpetual imprisonment! Am I not then to be set free?", the words will resonate in every part of your being.

Before you begin this scene in rehearsal, take a moment to look around and envisage everything you have selected in order to create Joan's world. See the setting in its entirety, take a breath, feel the temperature, hear the noises in the environment, and taste the dampness in the air.

If you have a problem making the setting seem real for you, go out and find the nearest modern equivalent to it. For example, while dungeons are in short supply in this part of the world and in this century, a basement cold-storage room might give you a feeling similar to the setting for Joan's cell. Find some appropriate contemporary equivalent and then renew your sensitivity to it. The more work you do of this nature, the easier it will become to recreate the reality of your setting, first in rehearsal and ultimately in performance. The fresher an actor's sensory resources remain, the more easily they can be employed in acting technique to:

- create and sustain images
- make the world of the stage become real for the actor
- trigger truthful, believable emotions in the actor

Chapter Eight
The Beginning Steps of Acting

Trusting others

Deep down under our protective layers, most of us are shy — although we are careful about when, where, and to whom we confess this. When actors gather to begin work on a new production, there is no place for shyness or inhibition. Rehearsal time is precious enough without taking weeks to get to know each other. Group improvisations and games help get inhibitions out of the way, especially in the first few days of working on a play. Experienced actors realize this and generally get right to work.

A series of workouts known as trust exercises are efficient and fun, especially for the novice actor. They provide an excellent way to break down barriers between people and give them a common basis from which to begin the creative work of acting.

Trusting yourself

When you begin to trust others in your acting class, you may have trouble trusting yourself. This is evident in scenes where actors are overwhelmed by their own nervous tension and rush through their work as quickly as possible.

For every action within an improvisation or a scene there is a natural beginning, middle, and end. This is one of the most important principles to learn in theatre, and at times it seems the most difficult. When we get nervous we feel vulnerable and self-conscious. We are anxious to get our performance or exercise over with as soon as possible so we can return to our seats, where relative safety and anonymity await us. This type of acting is known as "This is nice, wasn't it?" because your work is over and done with before it has been properly explored.

You can sometimes see actors "click off" within the last line or two of dialogue, even if they are not that obvious about it. Yet every scene has a few lingering moments that last beyond the final words in the text, so that the audience can absorb the impact of the scene in its entirety. Rushing the ending could sabotage your own efforts to make an impact.

Here are some exercises to help develop trust externally with others and internally with yourself. They will also reinforce two concepts: nothing should be rushed in theatre, and the actor should constantly search out the natural life expectancy for every action.

Trust exercises

1. *Trust circle:*

This exercise allows you to fall in any direction, secure in the knowledge that you will be safely caught and supported by other members of the group.

The group forms a tight circle some two metres across, facing inward with shoulders touching. You stand in the centre of the circle fairly rigidly, with hands folded across the chest like an Egyptian mummy. You then gently fall backward and are caught by the people behind you, who slowly push you back upright.

You then begin to fall in another direction — to the side, the front, or any way you please. (You can make it easier for the others if you don't buckle at the waist.) No matter in which direction you fall, hands reach out anticipating your movement; you will be caught and returned to an upright position by the people on that side of the circle. To gain the maximum benefit from this exercise, relax as much as possible while it is under way.

For safety's sake, everyone involved should be totally disciplined and no talking should take place during the exercise. Those who form the circle must co-operate in keeping the pace and momentum of this exercise as slow and gentle as possible. Sometimes the collective energy from one part of the circle makes the person in the centre move a little too strongly past the midpoint. The faster such momentum builds, the more difficult it becomes for the others on the opposite side of the circle to catch you safely. Try to avoid this problem. It undermines the feeling of security for the person in the centre and it inhibits group concentration.

Give everyone a turn in the centre of the circle. Many people will find they can relax and really enjoy this exercise, but a few will find it terrifies them. If you are particularly apprehensive when approaching the exercise, the participants can make the circle smaller by stepping in closer to the middle. Reducing the amount of distance to fall before you are caught can often alleviate fear.

2. Backward free-fall:

This exercise is performed in pairs. Match people according to approximate height and weight. Describing the exercise is easy, but relaxing while actually doing it can be a bit difficult.

One person (whom we'll call the subject) stands with feet together, arms outstretched, and back turned toward his or her partner (the catcher). The subject's job is to fall backward and be caught by the catcher several times. It will help if the subject doesn't buckle at the waist, because that lowers the centre of gravity and makes the subject's body seem twice as heavy. As long as the subject's spine stays rigid, the torso will be lighter to catch and the exercise will be physically much easier for the catcher. The catcher's job is to catch the subject and instill a sense of security and confidence that no accident will happen.

Both hands should always be positioned ready to catch the subject. Begin with limited space of five or six centimetres between the subject's back and the catcher's hands. The subject should initially try just a gentle tilt backwards. The catcher will catch the subject and safely stand him or her upright again. Once that part works to the satisfaction of both people, increase the amount of space between the subject's back and the catcher's hands. Continue to increase the open space according to how comfortable both parties feel. Only go as far as both people are willing to go.

Initially, the catcher can support the weight of the fall by using two hands to catch the subject's back. However, as the distance between the two increases, it will become necessary to catch the subject under his or her outstretched arms. The greater the distance of free-fall, the more the catcher should try to move with the momentum of the subject's fall.

It is quite possible to free-fall to very near floor level before being caught, but no one should go beyond his or her own physical and mental comfort levels. If someone is particularly nervous at the prospect of this exercise, set up two people to catch that individual — one on each arm.

Many people discover that as trust builds between partners, they will go beyond their initial fears and attempt even greater free-falls.

3. *Blind person/guide:*

This exercise requires the group to be divided into pairs. One person in each pair becomes the blind person; the other, the guide. (This exercise is included with trust exercises but, because it involves sight deprivation, it is also an effective sensory exercise. When we let go of the sense of sight, even for a short time, our senses of sound and touch are heightened.)

The guide offers an arm to his or her partner, and the blind person rests a hand lightly on the guide's arm. Then all the blind people close their eyes for the duration of the exercise. It is important that no one speak. The guides then lead the blind people around the room, ensuring that they do not bump into any furniture or other people. Move slowly at first, and progress only as quickly as the blind people permit. The exercise can be made more difficult by scattering furniture randomly around the room.

Although some people at first become tense when they can no longer see, because they feel they have lost control of their freedom, they still have control over their actions. Thus, if you feel insecure in the role of the blind person, lift your hand and stop moving. Sometimes shadows or sounds will briefly interrupt an otherwise smooth partnership. After a couple of minutes, reverse roles so that each person experiences being blind (and dependent upon a guide) as well as being responsible for another person's safety and security.

Variation #1: Change partners from the previous exercise so that you don't become dependent on one particular person. Following the same steps as above, repeat the exercise with only one finger resting on the guide's arm. Reverse roles later so that each person experiences both perspectives.

Variation #2: Change partners. No physical contact is permitted. Instead, the guide will talk to the blind person in a low, gentle voice, describing how many paces forward or sideways can be taken without hitting another person or some furniture. The blind person should move only when totally comfortable. If a direction is given in a confusing manner, the blind person should wait until it is repeated to his or her satisfaction. This provides the guide with immediate responses concerning the level of trust that is present.

For an added complication, have the blind people turn around three times with eyes closed in order to disorient them from their memories of the placement of people and furniture. While talking to the blind people, the guides should stay a couple of feet ahead of them and remember not to confuse instructions involving left and right: always speak to your blind partner in terms of his or her left and right.

Sometimes the blind people react very favourably to this variation because they feel they have total control over their own movement from the first moment in this exercise. If a sudden noise or unexpected shadow frightens them before they begin, they do not have to take a step. For the sake of the blind people, guides should keep their voices low enough to prevent a babble of sound from engulfing the room. Try to achieve the greatest amount of physical freedom as you guide or follow your partner around the room. Remember to reverse functions so that everyone experiences both roles.

4. Beginning, middle, and end:

This exercise begins with a large circle, with members of the group approximately one metre apart. Each person in the circle performs an action that has a beginning, a middle, and an end. The action will be passed in sequence from one person to the next, much the way a "wave" undulates around a sports stadium or a rock concert. One person is chosen to be the leader and that person turns to the right and strikes a pose. The leader's pose represents the end of his or her action. Freeze in this position.

Person #2 faces the leader and creates an exact mirror image of the leader's pose. This mirror image represents the beginning action for person #2. Once the second person has picked up the mirror image and begins to move away from the leader, the first person can come out of the freeze to relax and watch the progression of the exercise.

Person #2 gradually turns to face person #3 to strike a quite different pose (this is the second person's end action). Don't rush getting into this second pose. The transition between the two poses should take at least five seconds — longer would be good. This transition represents the middle action for person #2.

When person #2 strikes his or her end pose, person #3 in turn does a mirror image (which is in fact the third person's beginning action). And so the exercise continues: with a beginning, middle, and end to every action, passing from one person to the next in sequence, and at no time rushing any of the action. Here are some tips to help you with the exercise:

- Try not to have any preconceived idea of what pose you are going to assume when your turn comes. Simply move in a way that you feel is appropriate. Let the move itself be a smooth, fluid, unfolding, and natural type of action.
- Try to incorporate a sense of levels so that the visual picture constantly changes as the movement works its way round the circle. If your beginning action involves a gesture reaching upward, use your transition to let your body relax and conclude with an end pose that is low to the floor. (This exercise requires clean floors!)
- When you are passing your own physical pose to your neighbour, try not to repeat a similar kind of action to the one that you were originally handed.

Once you have fully understood the point of the exercise and your movements are clear and accurate, begin a second wave of motion round the circle. It is often possible for three or four separate actions to be worked into different points of the circle, depending on the number of participants and their level of achievement. Don't attempt to add a second sequence of action, however, until each person in the circle understands the need for a steady rhythm, accuracy of movement, and freedom of imagination.

Variation #1: Repeat the exercise, but add an emotion to the end action. Let a sound or breath accompany this emotion. You cannot anticipate what emotion you will receive or pass on to the next person. Don't think or plot. Simply react and trust your instincts. Keep a variety of levels, emotion, and physical action.

Variation #2: Add your name to this exercise, stating it within your chosen emotion. Each time it becomes your turn again, use a variation on your name: full name, nickname, or varying the first and middle names. Use your voice imaginatively. The person facing you must repeat your name identically, with the same emotion and body position, before proceeding through his (or her) own middle action. He then turns to his neighbour and says his name. (You will be surprised how many people mix up their own names in this exercise.)

Variation #3: Speak a sentence or phrase. When the person next to you repeats your words, his or her transition will become a period of absorbing the idea of the words and finding another phrase that builds upon the meaning in the original phrase. Stories can be built one sentence at a time as the exercise progresses round the circle. Emotions still play a large role. As each step becomes increasingly complex, the need to take your time during the transition — or middle phase — is obvious.

Concentration and focusing

A number of the exercises so far have required a lot of concentration, individually and collectively. For an actor, the ability to focus attention and energy at will onto any given subject is of great importance. Concentration is the foundation for building acting skills.

We all have times when daydreams and idle speculation are vastly more entertaining than our current real-life situation. However, the more involved we become in a subject or situation, the more focused our minds become. Obviously such control is a skill that is critical to any actor, not only for creating the imaginary world of a play in rehearsal, but also for the more mundane problem of memorizing lines.

Memorization is simply a matter of focusing attention. Just as with any skill, it improves with practice: the more consistently you practise concentration work, the better (and quicker) you will achieve results. It really does get easier with each show you do.

A problem for novice actors is that they worry more about what other people are thinking of them than about what their characters are experiencing. These anxieties begin in rehearsal and often continue through performance. Actors worry about the difficult upcoming scene. They become anxious that a scene partner will have line problems or jump a page of dialogue, or perhaps break character in the middle of a scene, or that a technical cue will not happen at the appropriate moment. During the run of the show, they are unsettled when audiences react in an "inappropriate" manner. There are endless reasons for line concentration problems at all stages of acting work.

There are numerous exercises that can help to sharpen concentration skills. Several are listed below. The most important thing, however, is to set aside time to practise these skills daily. A steady, disciplined approach will pay off in time. If you try to incorporate concentration exercises within the wasted moments of your day, it won't take long until your ability to memorize lines improves greatly.

We all have untold wasted moments during each day, perhaps when we are travelling on a bus, washing dishes after supper, shovelling snow, or jogging. We have periods of time every day where we can perform a boring or routine job while focusing our minds on a more challenging mental exercise. Identify your own wasted time — you may be surprised at how much time is available to you — and use it to your advantage.

Concentration exercises

1. *Head and tummy:*

This is an elementary kindergarten game, but it still requires real concentration. Your right hand pats your tummy while your left hand rubs a circle over your head. Proceed for a minute and then switch so the left hand pats the tummy while the right hand makes circles over the head. Change again so the right hand makes circles over the tummy while the left hand pats the head. Finally, the right hand pats the head while the left hand makes circles over the tummy.

2. *The manhole cover:*

This group exercise requires shared concentration. All stand in a circle and imagine you are surrounding an enormous manhole cover. On the signal to begin, everyone leans down, gets a grip under the lip of the manhole cover and begins to raise it to the maximum height you can collectively achieve. Once you have sustained this lift for a few moments, begin to lower the manhole cover until it rests on the floor again. This is a simple scenario, but there are a couple of added complications:

- No one is to speak. All stages of movement must be achieved by unspoken co-operative agreement within the group.
- Everyone must be very aware of his or her hands, specifically how their positions relate to people around them. Otherwise the manhole cover will end up with wavy edges, as if made of pliable rubber. All hands must be consistent in placement, tension, and height.

In a co-operative exercise like this, the manhole cover can be lifted only as high as the shortest person's reach. If the sense of group concentration is not strong during this exercise, repeat it once the problems have been identified. When successful group concentration has been achieved with the manhole-cover exercise, try a couple of other variations on group concentration work.

Variation #1: Imagine the group is watching a horse race. Establish the placement of the starting post and finishing post, and allow 20 seconds or so for the duration of the race. Not a word is spoken to initiate the race. The group must try to stay together as these horses approach, pass by, and then disappear toward the finishing post. Add words, sound and noises as appropriate.

Variation #2: Go back in time to the period of the French Revolution, centring action at a guillotine, and place each person as a character around the setting, individually or in clustered relationships. One person is chosen as the executioner whose job is to raise the guillotine to its maximum height, hold it for a few seconds, and then release the rope without providing a verbal cue. Complete the action with released breath and sound. Try to achieve a sense of reality within this shared collective improvisation.

3. *The tossing exercise:*

This exercise begins with everyone finding an object — preferably something soft, unbreakable and not valuable:

- Start by throwing the object in the air a few times and catching it. This warm-up will let you trust the dimensions and weight of your object, and you will develop a rhythm.
- Then throw your object in the air, and clap your hands once before catching it. Repeat this a few times.
- Choose a partner and face him or her with about two metres between you. The leader begins to count aloud, slowly and steadily: 1 - 2 - 3 - 4, 1 - 2 - 3 - 4, and so on.
- Both partners throw their objects to each other on every count of "4." It helps if you organize with your partner that one person throws high and the other low, to minimize the risk of objects colliding between you.
- Continuing the four-count, insert a hand clap between the time you throw your own object and the time you catch your partner's object.
- Then throw and catch on every second count (i.e. on "2" and "4"). Throw-clap-catch on 2 and 4 until you achieve a steady rhythm.
- Stop counting out loud and allow each pair to continue with its own unspoken rhythm.

(Anyone who drops an object must pick it up and resume the exercise as quickly as possible. Avoid the temptation, however, to hurl the object twice as hard as usual in order to make up time. Pay close attention to the actual count. Often, people anticipate the count and end up tossing their object before it is time.)

- Give the exercise a final complication by appointing a "speaker" and a "repeater" in each pair. The action resumes with an initial count to establish the rhythm. Then work in the throwing-clapping-catching action. Once this is operating smoothly, the speaker begins to tell a story — anything at all, from a fable to total nonsense to plans for the upcoming weekend. The repeater is to listen and repeat word for word what the speaker is saying, closely and accurately, and as near to simultaneously as possible. It is helpful if the speaker speaks much slower than usual and exaggerates the mouth action so that the follower can lip-read as well as listen to the spoken word. Reverse the functions of the two people after a few minutes so that the repeater gets a chance to be the speaker.
- When this is over, have the repeaters try to reproduce the dialogue they heard, as accurately as they can remember. It is surprising just how often total dialogue recall is possible.

Variation: Have the group form a circle, each person with his or her object. Repeat the same stages:

- Throw on a four-count, then add the clapping action, then reduce the time to a two-count.
- Each person should throw to the right, clap in the middle, catch from the left.

If one person drops an object, great skill is required to collect it again and pick up the rhythm without destroying the group concentration.

This exercise demonstrates an important principle of concentration. In real life, we often concentrate simultaneously on different mental levels. We can be performing a routine function, such as stirring soup on the kitchen stove-top, while talking on the telephone and watching TV in rapt deliberation out of the corner of our eye.

Such a skill, of course, is crucial in theatre. An actor must be able simultaneously to:

- concentrate on lines or lyrics of the moment
- listen to other actors or musicians
- stay in the correct lighting area on stage
- avoid tripping over the furniture
- pretend that the papier mâché prop is really solid gold encrusted with precious jewels
- learn to ignore the sweat dripping down the back of the neck or the butterflies in the stomach
- connect with the inner emotional life and intention of the character he or she is portraying
- be aware of the audience reaction to a moment
- experience each moment to its fullest

The more concentration work an actor experiences in the course of training, the more able he or she will be to execute a multitude of tasks with focus and commitment.

4. *The bag/rag exercise:*

This begins with the group standing in a circle. One person holds a jacket or sweater ("rag") and another person on the opposite side of the circle has a purse ("bag"). The object of the exercise is to pass these items from one person to the next without rushing or confusing the action and/or dialogue. (Remember the importance of a beginning, middle, and end to every movement.)

The person with the purse begins the dialogue, and others become involved:

A *(to B):* This is a bag.
B *(to A):* A what?
A: This is a bag.
B: Oh, this is a bag?
A: Yes. A bag!
B: Oh. *(then, to C)* This is a bag.
C *(to B):* A what?

So the dialogue repeats, continuing from one person to the next using "rag" and "bag" appropriately. The bag goes one way round the circle, while the rag goes the other. Eventually, one poor person gets caught with a bag coming from one side and a rag from the other and must take great care not to confuse or rush the two sequences of dialogue. If everyone can handle this much without trouble, try adding another two objects. These can be another "bag" and "rag" pair, or two other objects representing "hat" and "bat," for example.

5. *Emotion passing:*

This is another group exercise in concentration, but it also illustrates clearly how important breath control can be. When you are watching a film where the action is exceedingly tense or moving, you may have noticed how your breath patterns seem to match the person on whom your attention is riveted. When our breath patterns pick up those of a "larger-than-life" actor on a movie screen, we also pick up a deeper emotional response — a shared emotional bond within the movie audience. This device can be very effective in film work.

The following concentration exercise illustrates how this process can be created through breath work. One person is selected to be the leader and everyone else stands in a circle in the same "beginning" stance as that individual. The workshop leader whispers a word or phrase into the leader's ear — a simple emotion such as "loss" or "embarrassment," or a situational suggestion like "the beach."

The leader then visualizes a situation that the word or phrase suggests, projects it mentally, and begins to breathe as if he or she were in that situation and experiencing it. The rest of the people in the circle begin to copy the leader's breath patterns as accurately as possible. The leader can add sounds and, if so, these should be simultaneously copied by everyone else. However, no specific words should be spoken.

Develop the breath while the leader's imagined story progresses, ensuring that all breath levels are audible to the rest of the class. Naturally, movement has to be limited: if the leader turns around, so do all the rest of the people in the circle, thereby temporarily breaking the group concentration. Movement is best confined to a three-metre-square area. But feel free to explore all that space thoroughly.

When the exercise has reached its natural conclusion, share what each person felt emotionally by the end of the exercise. Often people will discover through this exercise that they are "on the same wavelength":

- In what situation did you envisage yourself?
- What emotions were triggered?
- How closely did you share the emotional experiences of the leader?

Occasionally, a leader will visualize a situation and emotions that personally are very strong but the rest of the group does not come close to experiencing the same emotions or images. This illustrates the difference between feeling something and accurately projecting it to others. In theatre as in daily life, we may occasionally feel we are expressing one emotion, yet in reality we are projecting something very different to others around us.

Confusion in this area can come from many sources, such as different cultural perspectives, individual values, or personal responses to particular emotions based on previous life experiences. For example, in real life one person may cry when lost, whereas another becomes fearful but brave.

If such a situation occurs within this exercise, try to identify the source of the confusion and repeat the exercise again.

6. *Wink:*

In this popular party game, everyone is seated in a circle and one person is selected to leave the room. That individual will be the detective. Everyone in the circle closes his or her eyes while the workshop leader walks around the outside of the circle. The leader simply touches one person lightly on the head to identify that individual as the murderer. Only the workshop leader (who is not involved in the game) and the murderer know the identity of the murderer. Once the workshop leader has completed the circuit, everyone opens their eyes, the detective is brought back into the room and the game begins.

The point of the exercise for the murderer is to "kill off" the other members of the circle without being caught. "Murder" is accomplished by establishing eye contact with others in the circle and winking at them. The murderer must try not to be caught in the middle of a wink, or the game is over. The detective's job is to find the murderer. If the detective guesses incorrectly, the game is over.

The rest of the group must try not to be killed — which is challenging, since they do not know the identity of the murderer either. They can't avoid looking at others but, if they must blink, they may avert their eyes momentarily toward the floor to prevent being accidentally identified as the murderer.

Because the group is made up of aspiring actors, it follows that when someone is "killed" by the murderer, he or she should die in a dramatic and theatrical manner. When you are shot, strangled, stabbed, or poisoned, a sequence of actions occurs. There is an initial point of focus, a slight sense of disbelief, sounds, breath exhalation, and a physical collapse — all of which happens in stages.

All these actions should occur in sequence and without rushing. Remember, find the beginning, middle, and end to every action.

By taking the "natural" time to die, the victim will also prevent an easy identification of the murderer. If the detective makes an incorrect guess, he or she dies. When the murderer is correctly identified, the game is over and another detective/murderer combination is selected.

7. *Babbling:*

This is a very noisy concentration exercise, so be careful about when and where you attempt it. Select one person to read an article aloud from a newspaper or book. Four or five of the group are to heckle and interrupt, causing as much verbal interference as possible. They are free to surround the individual, wave or tease — anything but physically touch or jostle the reader.

After a minute of this, stop all the noise — by a pre-arranged hand gesture or by flicking the lights in the room. Then see if the person who was reading can accurately repeat the text of the article. This is a difficult exercise in concentration, but useful in learning how to block out unnecessary information and focus attention on the task at hand.

The actor's journal

It is here in the actor's journal where results of sensory exercises, observation of real people in daily situations, insight concerning personal development or experiences, and pure reflective thought will become important tools for the creative actor.

An actor's journal is a cross between a diary and a notebook. It contains:

- acting class notes
- monologues and scenes you have worked on (are working on, want to work on)
- notes on plays you have read
- a list of plays you mean to read, so you know what to pick up on

your next trip to the library

- a selection of new monologues or scenes, so that you have lots of material from which to choose
- observations of real people from daily situations — the inner and outer impressions that you want to remember for future reference
- observations of other actors' work, whether in the classroom or in shows, especially ideas that you may want to borrow yourself one day
- script analysis questions and answers about each new character you are developing
- honest self-analysis
- discoveries you have made
- barriers you have encountered
- images and emotions that you want to retain for future work

The journal will be what you make of it, but it has the potential to be the actor's best friend. Bring your journal notes to every rehearsal. Don't trust that your memory alone will enable you to remember all your discoveries and all your problems in character work. If you keep it with you at all times you will never be without something to do when your bus is late. You will use those "wasted" moments during the day.

You will be ready with new material for every class or audition.

Chapter Nine
Acting and Physicality

The neutral state

An important first step for the performer is to develop the **neutral state**. Neutral is defined as being "neither one thing nor the other." You rid yourself of tensions, mannerisms, and personal quirks, while not yet beginning to assume any of those that belong to the character you are about to create. As you now realize, a series of physical exercises helps to achieve the neutral state. Trials and tribulations of the day are placed on the back burner, where they are less likely to interfere with the performer's creative processes.

One device to help the actor discover the neutral state involves the use of a neutral mask and full-length mirrors. A blank mask without expression can be bought at any costume supply house. (Mask exercises and building your own neutral mask are discussed in Chapter 15.) The blank expression on the neutral mask prevents our faces from expressing emotion, with the result that we can more easily see what degree of character is carried through our bodies. The term we use in acting for this corporal expression of emotion is **body language**.

Use of the neutral mask, a full-length mirror, and basic movement exercises are the foundation of all mime work. They help us discover and remove personal physical mannerisms that may be inappropriate for the character we are creating. Physical freedom is the foundation for unlocking the actor's creativity and imagination.

The actor's space and the use of levels

One difficulty in learning to act is to discover total personal freedom and comfort within the space around you. When people say "But I just don't know what to do with my hands," they are really expressing insecurity in the possession of their space. This next section discusses how to discover the actor's space.

The actor's space encompasses all the area around the actor that can be freely reached without moving the feet: up, down, to the sides, to the back — every possible physical extension. Children explore their space all the time regardless of the social setting in which they find themselves. As we grow up, however, we are inhibited from expressing ourselves physically within our space in everyday situations. Expectations are placed on us by others — parents, teachers, peer groups — and by ourselves. We become concerned about other people's opinions.

One of the components of the actor's space involves levels. There are three basic levels to consider:

- high (standing)
- medium (sitting)
- low (floor level)

In early rehearsals, performers often consider the use of only one of these areas. A common example is the actor who uses a comfortable sofa in rehearsal and is quite content to sit and deliver lines endlessly from this spot. If the actor explores only one level in this manner, he or she restricts the amount of action that can be expressed.

For the actor, physical action is the most important component of stage work because it allows you to express character in motion and space. However, actors must be careful not to distract the audience's focus improperly. If you are going to learn only one rule in theatre, it is this: **an action is stronger than a word.**

Remember, too, that we live in an age where we rely heavily on our sense of sight. Television has transformed our manner of assimilating information; once a society of active readers, we are now a society of passive watchers. To express their understanding of character and plot, actors must search out the balance between delivering lines and expressing body-language movement.

One of the director's jobs during the rehearsal of a show is to ensure that the audience's eye is drawn to the most important word or action of the moment. Upstaging is minimized when actors understand the principle of drawing focus, and when they achieve a heightened ability to listen to the action of the play, whether in rehearsal or performance. Good manners in acting allow no place for any deliberate pieces of upstaging.

Upstaging is different from searching out opportunities for action at all stages of rehearsal in order to keep the visual component of the show alive and moving. It is dangerous to stay fixed in one level, for you restrict the opportunity to express motivation, thought, and emotion if you remain rooted to one place. Don't rely on your director always to tell you when and where to move in rehearsal. Experiment.

However, everything must begin and end with your understanding of your character. For example, it would be entirely inappropriate to have Lady Bracknell in Oscar Wilde's *The Importance of Being Earnest* using the floor level at any point in the play. Her levels are strictly standing and sitting, for she is too imperious to do anything else. However, Joan of Arc would easily and freely use the floor level in George Bernard Shaw's *St. Joan*. Choices in levels, like all choices in acting, must come from the truth of the character at each moment in the dramatic structure of the play.

How does an actor discover opportunities to incorporate movement?

In any monologue or scene, search for moments where there is an emotional shift or change of subject matter. These **transitions** generally occur between the lines of the text as the character's mind moves from thought A to thought B to thought C, and so on. In real life, transitions are often made in split seconds: an idea is simply there in your head. However, when first working on a scene, actors should feel free to use rehearsal time to identify, explore, and expand transitions. Transitions provide the time and opportunity to experiment with blocking moves.

Because actions are stronger than words, you are wise to save blocking moves for moments where the dialogue is not critical to the plot. If you move on an important line, you will undermine its effectiveness. An experienced comic will tell you that the easiest way to kill a laugh is to move on the punchline, so save your move until the split second after the line has been delivered.

Pay particular attention to breath work at these points of transition, because breath carries the emotion of the moment. A change in breath patterns will express a lot of what your character feels during unspoken moments. There is always an energy shift of one type or another during transitions and, by changing breath patterns, the actor can reveal this change. More will be said later about breath work and acting technique.

Space awareness exercises:

For exercises in space awareness, dress comfortably in clothing that allows free movement and either wear ballet slippers or go barefoot. Shoes and tight clothing will restrict and/or inhibit you. It is very important that the classroom floor is clean. Otherwise you may pull back from using the floor level freely and comfortably.

These exercises are good warm-up concentration exercises as well. If you feel physically tight, daily practice will help free up gestures and make you feel more comfortable when expressing yourself in your space.

1. *Simple mirroring:*

Choose a partner and face each other about two metres apart, feet spread shoulder width apart. One person will be the leader and the other will be the follower. Try to sustain as much eye contact as possible to help develop communication. The leader's job is to move in a slow, fluid manner, initially using just the arms, but ultimately working in other body parts: legs, torso, and head. The follower's job is to copy each stage of the action identically, as if the two people were reflections of each other in a full-length mirror.

Once you have the idea of the exercise, reverse roles so that the leader becomes the follower, and vice versa. An extra person could circulate around the room trying to guess which person in each pair is the leader and which is the follower, or a third person can join one pair. In this instance, one person is the leader and the other two follow the movement simultaneously.

2. *Delayed mirroring:*

Change partners so you don't get locked in anticipated patterns of movement by working with one individual throughout. Instead of the action being simultaneous and continuous, it is divided into beats and freezes:

• The class leader counts out loud, slowly and steadily: one, two, three, four, (pause) one, two, three, four, (pause) etc.

- The leader of each pair then moves on the first four-count, freezes during the pause and stays in that position for the next four-count.
- The paired follower repeats the same action as the leader on the second four-count, finishing in the identical freeze position as the leader.
- The paired leader picks up again with the action during the third four-count, as the follower watches carefully.
- The follower repeats that movement on the fourth four-count.

Continue in this manner following the steady rhythm of four beats and a pause, with leader and follower continuously alternating roles. Eventually, having established a rhythm for the class, the class leader can stop counting aloud. You will discover in delayed mirroring that the leader may break eye contact, and even perform a complete turn if so desired. But all freezes must involve the re-establishment of eye contact that reinforces the unspoken communication between the two individuals. Make sure you reverse roles at some point so that each of you gets to try both functions.

Variation: Add a piece of music that has a strong rhythmic beat. Rock music will work because of its relentless four-count. Look at classical music, too, because it is easy to find slower excerpts that permit accuracy of movement. You may find the exercise less rigid with classical music and you can fill the whole musical phrase with movement.

3. *Opposites:*

Leave your partner for the moment and find your own space in the room. Imagine you are standing in front of a full-length mirror and you see your reflection as The Most Beautiful Person in the World. Take a moment to preen, to see what you are wearing, and to admire yourself from all possible angles.

Now step through the mirror and as you do you will become The Ugliest Creature in the Underworld. Examine how you have changed, what you are wearing, and allow yourself to explore every distortion in your appearance. Repeat the exercise once or twice, stepping back through the mirror again to become stunningly beautiful once more, then ugly again. Keep transitions smooth and steady.

4. Opposition mirroring:

Working in pairs, one person will move in one direction as the other instinctively moves simultaneously in the opposite manner. In this exercise, there are no rights or wrongs in the movement. For example, if the leader pulls back and up, the follower may choose to go down and in. But down and back is also acceptable.

The key to making the exercise work for the follower is not to think about what you are reacting to; just go with your instincts and keep your movement continuous and flowing. Intuition is a very useful tool for the actor, and these mirroring exercises will heighten your faith in your instincts. The more you learn to trust your intuition, the better your acting work will become.

Variation: Opposition mirroring can also be done in a delayed count as in Exercise 2 above, or performed to music as suggested in the variation to Exercise 2. Once again, reverse functions so that the leader has a chance to follow and vice versa.

5. The glass ball:

This exercise should be performed to music, preferably something classical, delicate and dreamy. The most effective piece I have found is the central theme music from the film version of *The Madwoman of Chaillot,* for it begins with lightly drawn strings, builds emotionally within the body of the music, and lasts about five minutes. Other pieces of music, such as Pachelbel's *Canon* or an instrumental version of Bizet's male duet from *The Pearl Fishers,* will do very well, too.

Begin with an individual exercise. Each person should find a starting place in the room and curl up into a little ball as tightly as possible. Sometimes it is helpful for concentration to keep your eyes closed in order to envisage each progression in the exercise. Imagine you are encased in an opaque glass ball. What does it look like? Is there a sense of colour or texture? You will discover as you begin to move that if you nudge it back, it will stay in that position. Perhaps it is more like a plastic substance than glass, for the texture appears different to each person. Begin to explore this phenomenon of the expanding glass ball, first with your hands, then incorporating all parts of your body.

Gradually expand more space inside this ball. First, focus on the space around you at floor level. Then discover you can crouch, rise, and stand up. From this point push back, out, forward, and up in all directions until you have expanded the space to the furthest part of your reach. Do you notice any changes in your space? Do you feel comfortable there?

Repeat the exercise to the same piece of music, this time pushing back stronger with your hands and getting up on your feet — but without rushing. Once you have claimed your full space, focus on your fingertips as you sweep your arms through this space. See whether you can draw an action simply using one fingertip, and then let the arm gently drop while following with your eyes the imaginary projected arc that the fingertip began.

In time, you can establish the confines of your space just by looking. See all the space behind you, above you, down around your ankles, everywhere that you can reach. Has it changed in quality since you were in the initial glass-ball stage? If you need reinforcement, reach out to touch it from time to time.

Now slowly begin to move, and you will find your space will move with you. If at any point you don't feel it is moving with you, stop, close your eyes, and go back to using your hands and arms to re-establish the full extension of your space. Proceed with each of these steps only as long as you believe in them. Eventually you will become confident that your space will stay with you. Keep looking at the space as you move so that you can see the full extension of your space.

As you move, you may find that other people pass through your space. Don't let that bother you, for you still have control over your space. You can allow other people or objects to pass briefly through your space without an encroachment on your sense of freedom.

Eventually, you can reach the stage where you no longer have to do the preliminary stages of this exercise. You may be backstage waiting to begin a rehearsal or performance and want to rediscover the authority this exercise can bring to your movement. Simply make a few fingertip sweeps to reconnect with your own sense of freedom and controlled space. See the full extension of your glass ball, and away you go.

6. *Glass ball mirroring:*

This exercise is performed to music and is a logical combination of all the above exercises. It begins from the individual glass ball position. What is different here is that you will begin to be aware of others in the room. There should be no verbal communication at any time and you should become involved only if you feel like it. Remember the following advice, not just for this exercise but for all acting exercises:

- Never let "anticipated" or "expected" results influence your work.
- Do what you feel or want, not what you think is expected of you.
- Do not force any stage of this (or any other) exercises.
- Do not worry if you don't get involved with anyone throughout this entire exercise.

During this exercise, however, you may establish contact with another person and choose to do a bit of mirroring with that individual. Here are some of the situations that may arise:

- You may become involved with simple mirroring, delayed mirroring and/or opposition mirroring.
- Your involvement may last just for one musical phrase or it may be extended.
- All action should have a natural beginning, middle, and end.
- Mirroring may involve one other person, two individuals, or a group.
- One person may communicate across a room to another regardless of intervening bodies.
- You may be oblivious to it, but someone behind you may be mirroring what you are doing.
- You may choose not to become involved with anyone at all, simply preferring to stay within your own space. That's all right too.
- Each individual will have a different idea of how to fill each musical phrase, the type and direction of movement; whatever feels right for them is right for them.
- Remember: there are no rights or wrongs, just choices.

Many people discover in this exercise that, from time to time, there may be a kind of unspoken sharing of emotions between individuals. This makes them want to become actively involved with others. This exercise helps to heighten non-verbal communication and concentration, as well as develop our sense of personal space. Sometimes people find themselves strongly affected by this exercise, being caught totally off guard by a sudden surge of strong emotions. One explanation is that the exercise triggers a strong sense of freedom.

Because most of us grow away from our childhood sense of physical freedom, re-experiencing it in this exercise can be quite exhilarating. Every performer, whether in serious drama or musical cabaret, should strive to sustain the sense of physical freedom that these exercises bring. Total physical freedom is a joyous experience, both in rehearsal and performance.

Mime

Mime is a type of international communication that uses gestures, movement and body language, but no sounds or spoken words. Most people have seen classical mime artists or even entire productions of mime plays, but have you ever noticed how frequently people use mime in place of speech and simpler body language in daily communication? How does:

- a student in class communicate surreptitiously with a friend several seats away?
- a teacher express unspoken displeasure when such an action is noticed?
- someone communicate with a person wearing headphones and a Walkman?
- someone behind a closed window call another person on the other side to the telephone?

People often use little snippets of mime to embellish a story, to substitute where words fail — either in a comic or dramatic manner — or to communicate with others despite obstacles such as distance or excessive noise. For mime to be effective, though, it should be simple. Too much movement, such as excessive waving of hands, can interfere with the real message being sent. This happens when the action is too fast. In such cases, the recipient sees only generalized actions. The physical movements lack tension, precision, and clarity.

For example, if one wanted to indicate through mime that a telephone call was being made on a rotary telephone, the average person would realistically dial seven or ten numbers. This increases the complexity of the action and diminishes the clarity of movement. In fact, the same message can be clearly established by picking up an imaginary telephone handle and using the index finger to make one simple dialling action.

When you first begin mime work, you should search for ways to simplify physical action. Remove unnecessary movement and find the fewest motions to clearly indicate what you are doing: simplify, control, and focus. Another key element in mime involves the sensory component: sight, sound, touch, taste and smell. The more you incorporate sensory work into your scene, the more fully you will believe in your mimed world and the more clearly the audience can experience its reality.

Mime exercises:

1. *Household chores:*

Each person in the group is to choose a household chore that can be executed simply. Devise a character who would be likely to perform this chore and let the group run through their individual actions simultaneously in mime. With each person performing his or her domestic action simultaneously with the rest of the group, try the same action three times:

> (a) in slow motion
> (b) at regular speed
> (c) at double speed

How does speed of action influence clarity of movement? Repeat the same action for two full minutes. During that time, your character is to age from three years to 95 years. With each repetition of the action, you should have a fixed age in mind so you can focus on the appropriate attitude to the task:

- What character changes occurred?
- Were there differences in rhythm?
- What were the effects on physical freedom?
- Did the attitude to the chore change over the years?
- Was there a change in the environment?
- Were there emotional changes?

2. *A circle of boxes:*

This exercise begins with everyone seated in a large circle. Imagine you have a box in front of you, which you will gift-wrap. See the box first and then decide what is inside because this will affect the size, weight, and shape of the box. Decide on the placement of wrapping paper, scissors, tape, ribbon, gift card, and pen before you begin. Start to wrap the present keeping all the above factors in mind. Reduce all movement to the minimum necessary to establish each step of the action.

Once you have wrapped the box, set it in front of you until everyone else has finished wrapping theirs. Each person then hands his or her present to the person on the right and accepts the gift being passed from the person on the left. Complete these actions in two steps so that you can clearly indicate to the person on your right all the specifics of your present. Similarly, you must receive the same information concerning the gift you are being given.

Now unwrap the gift you have just received. Regardless of your preconceptions of what was in the box, when you unwrap it you will find a pet animal of some description. Take the pet out of the box: see it, play with it, and get to know it. Take it for a walk and enjoy it. Once you begin to move with it, however, it starts to change size. As it grows larger and larger, it moves increasingly quickly. Both size and movement build to a very exaggerated state when suddenly, in a matter of seconds, the animal deflates to a fraction of its original size.

Examine this new version of your pet. The more you caress it, the larger it will grow until eventually it returns to its original size and weight. Take it back to your starting place and return the pet to the box.

There are three stages to this exercise:

- wrapping the present
- exchanging the boxes
- handling the *Alice in Wonderland* pet that insists on changing shape

In the first instance, you had total control over all the elements of the mimed action. In the second, you had to communicate in an unspoken manner with others. In the third, whatever you were creating was continuously changing on you.

Were all three stages of the exercise equally easy or difficult? If one was harder, why was it difficult for you? Repeat that part of the exercise which you found most difficult, focusing more carefully on keeping the physical action controlled and the sensory awareness as strong as possible, and being specific in all mimed movement.

3. *The hat box:*

This exercise illustrates the importance of consistency between two people in mime work. Choose one person in the circle to begin the exercise. That person visualizes holding a hat box while everyone else watches carefully.

Open the box and remove the hat. See the hat clearly before you put it on. Once you have done so, pass the empty box to your right, then remove the hat and pass it to the person on your left. Each recipient is to examine the object he or she has been given, either trying on the hat or looking carefully at all aspects of the hat box. Then in turn they pass their object along to the next person, and so the exercise continues round the circle.

Eventually, someone on the other side of the circle is going to receive two mimed objects at once. When this happens, don't get confused. Think "beginning, middle, and end," and don't rush or overlap the movements. Keep the objects in motion around the circle until everyone has examined both the hat and the hat box. Now begin to compare notes:

- Did the hat box change shape, size, or weight on its journey?
- What kind of hat was in the hat box?
- What colour was it?
- Were different people always putting on different hats, or was it possible to keep a consistency when passing an imaginary item between two individuals?

Having done this exercise once, repeat it with an added preliminary step. The person chosen to begin the exercise is to take a great deal of time verbally describing in detail both the hat and the hat box. Once everyone in the room is assured they are all seeing the same items and pertinent questions have been asked by the participants, begin the movement of the objects round the circle again. Keep total clarity of action uppermost in your minds. Discuss the difference between the two stages of this exercise.

4. *The memory box:*

This exercise incorporates both mime work and sensory elements, but extends them by bestowing emotions onto imagined objects. Visualize you have an old box in front of you that has been stored away for some time.

Where are you? Where did you find this box? Did you know it was there or did you discover it unexpectedly? Silently answer as many questions as possible before you begin.

The box contains five objects that belonged to someone you were very close to once. This person left your life some time ago, perhaps by moving away, or maybe it was a divorce or even death that separated you. Decide upon the person involved, your relationship with that person, and specifically what it was that separated you. How long ago did this happen?

Once you have made those choices, take a moment before you begin to imagine the five objects associated with that person. When you have made your decisions, pick up the box and set it in front of you. Bear in mind that the size, shape, and weight of the box depend upon the objects inside. Be meticulous and simple in every movement you make.

Now open the box and begin to examine each of those items. Keep sight, sound, touch, taste, and smell uppermost in your mind. In examining your five objects, incorporate as many senses as possible. Allow perhaps 30 seconds per item. When you have completed examining each object, return it carefully to the box, close the lid, and put the box away safely.

- What kinds of items were inside the box?
- How aware did you become of the sensory elements of each?
- Were you able to establish an emotional relationship with different objects?
- How vivid was the experience for you?

If you take one of your scene study rehearsals and devote it purely to exploring the potential role of mime, you may find the time spent will reward you in an unexpected manner. Because mime values simplicity, focus and clarity, it will help you discover the moments of repose that must be present in every acting piece. Some acting scenes fail because actors try too hard. They are too busy "doing" something rather than experiencing what it means. Through the silence of mime, you can discover:

- the inner symbols of reality
- the true impulse behind the words

Body language

The term "body language" is used a great deal by actors and directors in discussing how we express ourselves physically. We learn to "read" body language from early childhood, gradually acquiring over the years an ability to understand another person's mood, emotional balance, intention, or energy level.

Sometimes we are very aware of this information, but generally we do not stop to think about it. We simply determine without a word being spoken that a parent is annoyed with us, that a friend is excited, that another individual has a headache, or that a teacher is pleased with the answer we gave.

Therefore, the reading of body language — which is an acquired skill — is really a study in understanding an entire range of human emotions

197

and moods. These can be interpreted by watching facial expressions, tension, or freedom in each individual's body, closeness or distance between others and us, eye focus, various groupings of others, and the energy level of all physical action. Often the style and condition of the clothing that an individual is wearing is inescapably associated with these assumptions. In short, body language encompasses an entire visual picture.

Let's look at some exercises in body language awareness. Use your actor's journal to jot down notes about your observations, for these insights may become the basis for future character exercises in scene study, improvisations, and rehearsals.

1. Wander around a shopping mall, a hallway in a public building, or an airport terminal to see how many assumptions you can make about individuals you observe. Be aware that your impressions will reflect your own inherent personal bias or partiality, unless you make an effort to clear your mind of preconceptions. It is easy to assume from a style of dress that a certain individual is well-to-do, but that doesn't necessarily mean that the person is arrogant and cold; that's merely a stereotype. Look beyond the superficial aspects of clothing and veneer for the deeper emotional state of your candidate, the intention behind his or her actions.

2. Obtain a glossy black-and-white photography book from the library, featuring a variety of character studies. Work with a partner, and allow yourselves a fixed period of time (such as 30 seconds) to "read" each picture. Devise a brief history for the picture you are analyzing: who, what, where, why, how, when. Give your photographed character a name and past history. Then compare notes. See whether or not you are reading the same message from the identical picture. If you disagree, what led you to differing assessments of the character study?

Exercises in body language:

Alignment exercises are useful in taking an external approach to creating a character. Think how your body moves during each stage of the exercise. Be aware of the relationship between one body part and another.

First, get yourself into a neutral state through warm-ups. Any tension centre or alignment problem of your own that you bring to the exercise will interfere with your ability to achieve the best result. At the end of each stage of these exercises, return to a neutral physical position.

You will find that there are variations in each exercise depending upon the type of shoe you are wearing: its flexibility, type of heel, degree of newness, comfort and fit. If you are doing these exercises to help you create a specific character, make sure you are wearing the appropriate footwear and costume. Clothing can also have an effect, freeing or constricting various parts of the body. In general, it is a good idea to wear loose-fitting clothes and go barefoot for the following work.

For each of the exercises below, ask yourself the following questions as you complete each stage:

- What sort of things do I discover in changing the style of walking?
- Which characters do I envisage walking in these manners?
- In which situations would I use each manner of walking?

Remember how the movement makes you feel, so that you can use your discoveries in the future.

1. To understand the importance of foot placement in body language, walk a fair distance in the normal heel-first, toe-second manner. Return the same distance, reversing the placement of your foot, i.e. placing the toe on the ground first.
2. Now walk the same distance with your toes turned in; reverse the angle on your return so that the toes are turned out.
3. Walk with a natural alternation of leg and arm action, your right arm swinging forward when your left foot is brought forward, while at the same time the left arm is swinging back and the right leg, back. This should be done in a free, easy manner initially, then in a military manner on the return.
4. Now consider the hips and the shoulders. In the third point above, there was a natural alternation of the hip-and-shoulder action when you moved freely. Try to lock the right shoulder over the right hip, and the left one over the left hip. Your hands will naturally rest lightly on your thighs. (As you walk, you may begin to get the feeling you are at The Shoot-out at the OK Corral.)

Exercises in leading with parts of the body:

These exercises are based upon awareness that most of us consciously or subconsciously bestow a sense of importance on one aspect of our physical selves. For example, a "tough guy" projects a message through his body language by expanding his chest size. An importance is attached to one specific part of the anatomy. This varies from one person to the next and, in acting terms, is called the centre. The centre is the source of energy that fuels the physical and emotional action of the character.

An actor should be able to control the placement of the centre through concentration.

The exercises below are designed to give you a quick idea of how the placement of focus in the body can affect your body language and movement.

The next time you sit in a public place and watch people pass by, imagine there is a vertical line through which each of them must pass. You will notice in many cases that a specific body part passes through that line ahead of the rest of the body: this is the centre. It seems to have an importance or prominence that is observable by others, although often the person himself or herself is oblivious to it.

The following exercises are designed to make you aware of using different characters' centres and how these can help you sustain a character from one scene to the next. Discovering the correct centre for your character can be the key to feeling physically comfortable as your character. Remember that you may need to use a centre for only a few minutes, at various times throughout a show, or all the way through. It can be a useful device, but be selective about how and when you employ it.

If you have two or three cameo character roles to play within the same show, using different contrasted centres will allow you to achieve a distinctive physical presence for each one. You will not play the "same person three times over" if you have contrasted centres.

It is very important in the following exercises that you return to a neutral state at the end of each stage. Just take a big breath and shake out your body before assuming the next stage.

1.   Standing in a neutral position, imagine that you have the most wonderful nose. You have often been complimented on its aristocratic lines and you enjoy heightened abilities with your sense of smell. Focus all your energy on your nose. Then begin to walk while keeping all your attention placed there. See what it makes you feel, think about how your movement is affected, and ask yourself what kind of character you imagine yourself to be.

     The most notable "nose-centred" character in theatre history is surely Cyrano de Bergerac in the play of the same name by

Edmund Rostand. If you want to discover a wonderfully witty character, full of 18th-century swash and buckle, do read this script.

2. Now that you are back again in a neutral position, place all your energy on your stomach. Let your belly be as fat as possible and feel how your alignment changes. Your back will arch and the shoulders will be thrown back to counterbalance the weight of the belly. When you begin to walk you will find that the feet often turn out to steady a rolling gait. Who do you envisage yourself to be? What effects do these realignments have on your body?

   Shakespeare's Falstaff — found in *King Henry IV,* parts 1 and 2, and *The Merry Wives of Windsor* — is a good example of a stomach-centred character. His girth provides the basis for creating much of the visual humour of the plays.

3. Focus your attention now on your forehead and, once you have placed all your energy there, repeat the same stages of the exercise. Ask yourself the series of questions. How aware were you of the rest of your body as you moved across the room?

   This is the type of body language that is sent out by the typical absent-minded professor character, or the individual who is living more in the future than in the present. He or she is a common sight in the downtown areas of large cities: people rushing about, busily intent on where they are going rather than where they are.

4. Now try the same exercise while focusing on your chest. Let your torso swell up and discover what adjustments are made to the rest of your alignment. Go for a walk yet again and repeat the analytical questions. Did specific character types come to mind?

   A chest centre will have different results for males and females. With males, it tends to bring a swagger and a sense of authority; with females, it is associated with the breasts. In real life, we unfortunately tend to stereotype this centre very rapidly and often incorrectly: the tough guy or the sexually aware female. If you are not a chest-centred person yourself, you may find this exercise a bit uncomfortable at first. Just get a good image in your mind of a current Hollywood "stereotype" star and you will do well.

5. Place the energy now on your chin and, when you are ready, begin the exercise. Are certain emotions triggered by this particular placement? When the chin is tilted outward, it brings a sense of antagonism and aggression into the personality.

   Think of some gangster movies you have seen. Do specific characters come to mind?

6. Split focus between the teeth and the eyes. It is possible to do one without the other, of course, but the two are a natural combination. (One of the secrets in getting performers to smile believably during musical numbers is to engage their eyes with their smile. If their eyes are dead, no amount of bared teeth will convince the audience that the chorus line is happy.)

   Eyes truly come to life only when there are clear images behind them. To make this exercise work well for you, imagine specific pleasurable things and let your eyes and smile reveal your emotional connection to those images. Begin by imagining you have been complimented many times over the years on how lovely your smile is and how beautiful your eyes are. As you begin to move, keep all your attention focused on those areas. What does this do to your self-image and emotional state? Does your energy level change?

   Almost every dancer in *A Chorus Line* presents a centre of "teeth and eyes" to Zach when first appearing at the audition for the show. Their centres may change during the course of events, but their eyes and smiles are what the dancers hope will make an impression during the interview.

7. There are many other variations on this exercise. A crotch centre will totally alter the physical and psychological sense of character and in fact can be the key to help an actor express the sexuality of his or her character — often the most difficult aspect of characterization for a novice actor.

   Centres in the knees, Adam's apple or toes will again change your character. If you centre yourself in the balls of your feet, you will automatically acquire a bounce in your step. Focus on one finger of one hand and see what happens. The more you practise, the more sophisticated your choices can become. Try centring yourself on just one ear lobe and see how strongly this will alter your self-image. Try to catch the film *The Prime of Miss Jean Brodie* on late-night television just to watch where Maggie Smith centres herself: it's all in one wrist, and there is one particular shot of her walking down a corridor that is very funny simply because of this choice.

To be able to apply the technique of centres, you must understand your own personal centre. Have you ever watched an actor's work with growing unease over time and not been able to figure out what the problem is? The actor's work always seems the same no matter what character he or she is presenting. It may be a problem with centring. Sometimes actors make the mistake of applying their personal centre to every character they approach. Often it works for the character under study but at other times, it is inappropriate.

Leading with parts of the body is a fun way to discover how much our physical body language is allied to our mental self-image and emotional framework. Try to develop personal flexibility when exploring body movement and centring exercises. The next time you are beginning to develop a character, experiment with centring the character in a variety of places. Try different manners of walking. Often, when you have made a conscious decision that a particular style of walking "feels right" for your character, the rest of the physical movement falls easily into place.

These techniques can help you if and/or when you want to make a quick brush-stroke character in an improvisation. They are also very helpful when you have to sustain your character between one rehearsal and the next. Apart from anything else, centring and body language awareness will heighten your own ability to read others in daily situations.

Text and subtext

Having considered how actors need to accurately understand non-verbal communication (body language), it is time to move toward how they must also be able to read clear verbal messages (text and subtext). The **text** is the lines written by the playwright or created in improvisation, the words themselves. The **subtext**, however, is the additional or conflicting meaning behind the words that illuminates the intention of your character. It is revealed through inflection in the voice expressed by the actor (exercises are discussed earlier in Chapter 5).

The difference between text and subtext is illustrated in the following example:

Suppose you are walking down the street and you bump into someone whom you have not seen in years. "Hello," you say. "How are you doing?" Five words form the text. Nevertheless, it is quite possible for that text to be interpreted in many different ways. Here are two contrasted interpretations:

- "Hello. *(Oh no, it's that creep again.)* How are you doing? *(Still the miserable complainer you always were, I expect.)*"
- "Hello. *(Oh gosh, it's her again at last. I'm going weak at the knees).* How are you doing? *(Oh please, let her say she misses me.)*"

It is obvious, especially in such an extreme example, that two such totally different interpretations will lead to well-contrasted vocal subtext and body language. However, any careful reading of a script will confirm that a wide array of interpretations can be found even in seemingly simple dialogue. The context of the dialogue will often affect the actor's subtext interpretation.

The study of 60-30-10 or
Body language 60, Subtext 30, Text 10

This next section is based on information that is available from a number of sociological studies on body language and verbalization conducted in North America over the years. The sociological results generally fall within the approximate percentage range of 60-30-10, but with variations depending on the actual survey. For our purposes in the study of acting, these rounded-off statistics are useful as a tool to help the acting student isolate factors important in communication and put them in perspective.

60%

Body language accounts for 60 percent of our understanding of emotions, our reception of subliminal messages and our grasp of relationships. If you turn down the volume on a television program, you can soon follow the plot and understand relationships between the people in the scene and the emotional content of the moment. Television devices (such as close-ups and panning) help to guide our eye, but the same principle holds true in real-life situations.

The next time you are eating in a restaurant, determine how clearly you understand the relationship between two people at another table, just by discreetly watching how they use their bodies to express themselves:

- their physical alignment
- use of the furniture
- gestures
- facial expressions
- degree of energy and animation
- the space between them
- their method of eating and drinking
- changes (or lack of changes) that occur when the waiter appears
- eye focus and eye contact

- degree of comfort in the surroundings

Further muddying the waters, one culture will often value a certain type of body language while another will attribute different motives to it. This can lead to problems of misinterpretation, because different attitudes to the same body language can exist in the same city. Attitudes are based not just on geography but also on cultural and subcultural values.

For example, in Continental Europe men may be openly physical with each other, sometimes linking arms as they walk down the street. In North America, cultural attitudes are suspicious of such body language and people generally assume there is a sexual connection between the two men.

Other societies have different degrees of "breathing space" between individuals than we normally allow. Permitting someone into your space reflects the degree of intimacy in the relationship. Studies in sociology indicate that we communicate degrees of openness and reception by body positions in a chair. For example, folded arms and crossed legs suggest signals of rejection of closeness. Experienced teachers can read how well their information is being received in a class simply by glancing around the room as they speak.

Additionally, sometimes we project emotional auras we are not feeling and, consequently, others may misinterpret us. For example, if you regularly wear glasses but have momentarily misplaced them, you will generally furrow your brows to help focus your eyes. Someone else may presuppose from your facial expression that you are annoyed or tense and project his or her own insecurities onto you. Psychologists call this "projectering" but teachers will recognize it as the "Oh-no-he-knows-I-didn't-do-my-homework" syndrome. In reality, you could be in the most pleasant possible mood and quite oblivious to the distress you are causing others as you blithely wander around searching for your glasses.

Exercise:

Ask a couple of your classmates to present a scene they have been working on. As soon as they begin, put your fingers in your ears so that you can understand what is happening only through your sense of sight. If their work is good and the body language is fully expressed, you will have some idea of the dramatic or comic nature of the scene, the basic plot outline, and the relationship between the characters. However, if they have not paid enough attention to the movement and energy of the scene — preferring instead to "stand and deliver" lines from the script — then you will be able to help them isolate specifically where their weaker moments occur.

30%

Another 30 percent of our reading of character comes from **subtext** revealed through the inflection or "colour" in the voice. This is a skill some of us learn in childhood. We discover that although an individual appears to be saying one thing, there can be a totally different message being sent in the same words. For example, a parent who tells a child "no" may really be signalling "maybe." This discrepancy between the text and the subtext is implied by the vocal tones. As with body language messages, some individuals may be more skilled than others at reading vocal subtext.

Vocal subtext explains why we can generally understand a reasonable amount of the emotional content of a scene in a foreign language film without necessarily knowing a word of that language. It is also why we tend to distrust the surface meaning of something we are being told when we feel the vocal subtext is telling us something contrary.

Vocal subtext can be more explicitly helpful. Occasionally in discussion, one person will use a word that — to him or her — has a specific meaning. The listener may misunderstand the word or attribute other intentions to the selection of that word. However, the reading of body language and subtext may help to bridge the gap.

Exercise:

Take a scene on which you are currently working and present it to your classmates, but don't use the words of the text. You may use only nonsense words, such as:

- nursery rhymes
- gibberish
- numbers counted backwards
- raw sound

This is a difficult exercise, but if you can bring the emotion of the scene to the nonsense words you are using, you will achieve a stronger sense of the underlying truth of the text. Because the words you're using are meaningless, the subtext must communicate everything contained both in the text and in your interpretation of the emotional content of the scene.

10%

The final 10 percent of our understanding in communication comes from the **text**, the actual words used in speaking. When we say "How are you?" to someone, it is not what he or she says in return to which we pay attention. Responses such as "Fine" or "Okay" tell us very little. Rather, the total package of body language and vocal subtext communicates the intended message.

Yet, when a novice actor first picks up a script, that 10 percent is often the starting and finishing point for attention. "Oh no! Look at all the lines I have to memorize!" Learning the text becomes the principal focus and the actor temporarily forgets about the importance of body language and subtext. Most new actors come to realize in time that blocking, gesture, meaning, and emotions have to be incorporated into their work. But when beginning work, they forget how very necessary body language and subtext are for the actor to develop a truly believable character.

The next time you pick up a fresh script, try to read it with an immediate sensitivity to the intention behind the words. Memorization work is only a fraction of what an actor should do in beginning to approach a scene.

In fact, memorization should start to concern the performer only partway through the rehearsal process. If the preliminary work — characterization, setting, sense memory, images, script analysis, and so much more — has been dealt with thoroughly, the lines will fall into place much more easily. Furthermore, if conscious memorization doesn't begin until after the blocking of the play is set, the actor will discover that remembering lines and cues is reinforced by the blocking action within the scene.

A good actor will not be tied to dull or repetitious line interpretations if inventive and imaginative experimentation has taken place first in early rehearsals.

Chapter Ten
Dramatic Structure and Stage Blocking

A n actor must learn about certain conventions that are specific to the world of theatre. These include an understanding of dramatic and comic writing styles, use of stage area in different types of theatre spaces, actor-audience relationship, and theatre terminology. You have to know how to boot your computer and learn keyboarding skills before you can operate a word processor efficiently. So, too, you must learn about technical components of theatre if you want to take acting seriously. They are the foundation for your craft.

One place to begin involves understanding how playwrights write. It is important that you read the entire play first. This will allow you to see the shape of the play before you begin to analyze its components. Most plays tend to follow a common formula in their structure. There are obvious exceptions to this statement, particularly with the post-World War II absurdist writers. Nevertheless, it is helpful to understand the structure of a "typical" play, because each part of the dramatic structure brings with it its own set of acting challenges.

Introduction, rising action, climax, dénouement

The opening part of any play is known as the **introduction**. It is here that the major characters and basic plot are introduced. Generally, the introduction is the most difficult part of the play to stage due to the tremendous amount of information that must be explained within a very short space of time:

- Where are we?
- When is this happening?
- Who is here?
- What is their relationship?
- Why are they here?
- How did we arrive at this point in the story?
- What is about to happen?

All these questions must be answered in the opening 20 minutes or so of **exposition** before we can get into the complications of the story line. At the same time, the actor must keep the visual picture alive with stage business to avoid the opening moments being "talky."

The next section of a play is called the **rising action**. This is made up of a series of **beats** and **mini-climaxes**. One beat explores a single piece of the jigsaw puzzle of plot, character and conflict, and several beats will build to a mini-climax. Each of these generally ends on a slightly higher emotional note than the previous one, developing and sustaining dramatic or comic tension. After each mini-climax in the rising action, a brief rest period can be created (sometimes by the playwright, sometimes by the director and actors) on the way to building to a strong **climax** to the play.

The climax is the high point of the action. It is here that the basic conflict of the plot is resolved. It generally occurs near the end of the play, and in some cases it happens at the very last moment of the play. Actors involved in the climactic moment of the play must be particularly aware of focus, tension, listening, emotional release, and clarity of action, for all of these contribute to creating a fully developed climax.

Immediately following the climax, the **dénouement** occurs. This is the winding down of the emotional content of the play, and the action is generally much slower than elsewhere in the play. Loose ends of the play are tied up, questions are answered to the satisfaction of the audience, and the final lingering moments of mood and atmosphere can be savoured.

The dénouement usually brings the audience back to an emotional level similar to the opening, but different. The dénouement is heightened and more intense because of the experiences we have undergone during the action of the play, experiences that may bring wisdom, insight, and understanding. We have been transformed.

For actors, the problem of staging the dénouement may be twofold. Sometimes the actor will rush the emotional moments within the dénouement, keeping the same energy level as in the rising action. Alternatively, the actor will get so involved in emotional aspects of the dénouement that the work gets internalized and self-indulgent and, thus, of limited interest to the audience.

Work on one beat at a time in rehearsal, then several in a row that naturally build to a mini-climax, and so forth. This will allow you to understand the conflict within each self-contained section of the play or scene. Breaking memory work into bite-size pieces makes the job less intimidating, so when learning your lines, stick to memorizing one beat at a time. When you are at the stage of running through an entire act of the play, consider the dramatic buildup of each component of the scene.

If this basic structure were to be put into a visual picture, it would resemble the diagram below. (Do remember, however, that many plays do not follow this "formula" yet still remain very effective, workable pieces of theatre.)

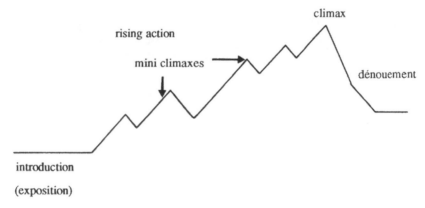

On page 75 of the scene book *Behind the Scenes, Volume One,* there is an absurdist 10-minute two-character play called *The Black Hat* written by Robert Hunter. Because the play is short and self-contained, it is easy to use as an illustration of dramatic structure. Here is an analysis of the structure of plays as applied to *The Black Hat:*

- The introduction runs from the top of the play and continues through Korma's entrance to the point where she puts the hat on Mad's head. We have met the two characters, and we now know where we are in the story line, though we may have many more questions than answers.

- The rising action continues through several mini-climaxes dealing with the balance of power. At each step, Mad gradually gains strength and control while Korma loses her powers over Mad.
- The climax begins with the reading of the poem and finishes with the cacophony of screams and dialogue.
- The dénouement involves the release of tension and several modulations of mood and atmosphere. We return to the opening relationship but we have been altered by the course of events.

The majority of plays follow the same format. By identifying the dramatic structure, an actor can more easily divide the script into beats and work on each one in turn. It makes the work more manageable when focusing on one beat at a time, rather than anticipating what is coming further down the line.

Stage directions

Many novice actors, when first approaching scene study work, pay considerable attention to the stage directions that appear in the text. If the script suggests that their character should take three steps downstage right, then sit on the sofa and pick up a newspaper, inexperienced actors generally do so without apparently questioning it. Blocking patterns that are based on total acceptance of written stage directions often defy logic. Actors get caught up in awkward positions with each other. As a result, many of their moves appear unmotivated.

Stage directions are not necessarily etched in stone. The actor in a scene study class should feel free to accept or reject them according to the needs of all the actors involved in the scene. The stage directions that appear in a script simply indicate the blocking that was used by the original company of actors, under the guidance of the original director, to fill the theatrical space in one specific theatre. A scene that was theatrically effective in one acting space may not work as well when transferred to another space. The typical classroom space, when used for scene study work, creates different demands than the stage of a theatre. Many factors affect staging:

- The selection and placement of furniture, doorways and props will be quite different in a thrust space than on a proscenium stage.

- Complications occur when developing a scene for presentation in a smaller classroom. Existing written stage directions will be thrown out of proportion, and slavish attention to the original stage directions will create numerous blocking problems.
- The stage directions that appear in the script are often not the work of the playwright. They can include numerous additions by the stage manager based on blocking notations in the prompt book from the original professional production.

The purpose of written stage directions is to more clearly suggest the movement of the play so that actors can see the action of the play as they read the script (note how important staging directions are in visualizing Hunter's *The Black Hat* mentioned above). Stage directions clarify certain points that might otherwise be confusing or missed entirely, such as subtle turning points in relationships. Allow the stage directions to help you paint the picture of the play as it unfolds.

Of course, certain stage directions must be followed because the story line demands it. Examples include, "The doorbell rings and she opens the door," "He crosses to turn on the radio," or "He pulls out a gun and shoots the figure behind the curtain." Other stage directions can be accepted in full, in part and revised, or totally rejected without affecting the integrity of the scene on which you are working.

Try to simplify the setting as much as possible for scene study work, and if you can possibly avoid using unnecessary furniture pieces, do so. Remember that the emphasis should be on your acting and not on your interior decorating skills. If a blocking move is indicated in the script, ask yourself what this action might reveal about your character. Some of these questions may include:

- What motivation can you discover from the move?
- Does the move propel the plot forward?
- How can your character be illuminated by this action?
- Does the move enable you to express an emotion?
- Does this move reveal my relationship with another character?
- Does it heighten the dramatic/comic moment?
- Is it a moment when you share something privately with the audience?

When you have altered your set from the floor plan in the back of the script, your blocking moves will also differ. Many specific stage directions can be changed or eliminated and your own interpretive moves can be added instead. Discover the motivation that provided the impetus to the original move, and then incorporate this motivation into your own blocking patterns. It is this freedom that attracts directors to reinterpret classic plays that have been staged hundreds or thousands of times. Bring this freedom of approach to all your scene study work.

Understanding blocking

To **block** a play means to find every moment where your character moves on stage: walks, stands, sits, picks up a newspaper, closes a door, answers a telephone, shakes someone's hand, pours a drink, and so forth. The term **business** is used to describe such physical activity: finding something for your character to do.

Blocking is a matter of bringing life to the scene. It provides the visual pictures that reinforce the sense of character, conflict, and style that have jointly been conceived by everyone working on the show: the playwright, actors, director, and designers. Effective blocking can heighten a moment of comedy or suspense, establish a mood and develop the story line. Bad blocking can destroy a moment, ruin an atmosphere, and confuse or bore the audience.

Many novice actors might assume that it is the director's function to tell them where to move, when to move, and what to do. To some extent, that is true. However, the director has many other responsibilities to assume during rehearsals, so his or her ability to move actors around the stage like a traffic officer may be limited. Some directors keep a firm hand on blocking, but others may allow you some freedom of movement. If you were given that freedom, would you be able to use it effectively and would you enjoy it?

The actor must be completely at home on the stage, regardless of how large it is, its shape, or the distribution of the audience. When an athlete is in an athletic environment, reflexes are all that matter, not technique. The same holds true for the actor. When you thoroughly understand the principles of blocking and you feel able to use your stage without being instructed about movement, you will be free to focus upon the real work of acting.

Blocking brings visual energy to a play. However, the degree of energy and the manner in which stage business is performed must be tempered with awareness that movement for the stage is somewhat different from movement in real life. While there are blocking "rules," rigid adherence may be meaningless. For example, it may be essential in some plays to heighten a dramatic or comic effect by ignoring the old "rule" that you never turn your back on an audience.

Blocking and focus

Focus is essential to blocking. It is the central point of attention in theatre. There are two aspects to the term:

- concentration of the audience's focus (as discussed earlier in the book)
- the actor's focus in the scene

The director is the person responsible for ensuring that the audience's eye is directed to the most effective spot or a particular person for each moment of the play and not, for example, drawn to a misused prop. Inappropriate or drawn-out action will slow down the pace of a scene or upstage other characters. Because an action is stronger than a word, the director must see that every important line is clearly established so that the audience can readily understand it. Lines must be integrated with important physical action.

Every actor, too, should have a good grasp of the principles of audience focus. Such knowledge will help explain why certain moves are more or less effective than others, why some moves must be held for a moment, and why specific reactions must be heightened or made more important. "Make it bigger," the director will say, expecting you to understand what is meant by that term and how to produce the result.

The actor's focus is also known as the **point of concentration**. Part of the purpose of rehearsal time is to allow each actor to discover in every moment of a scene where his or her point of concentration should be placed. This focus can be internal or external:

- An **internal** point of concentration means that the character has retreated into thoughts, images, emotions, time past, time future, plotting strategy, or any other personal mental process.
- An **external** point of concentration takes the actor's attention outward: to another character, to a prop or costume, out to the audience, to part of the set, to a particular technical cue, or to the outside world.

215

Stanislavski, the famous Russian director/teacher, defined the actor's three circles of concentration; these are summarized here. In any play, the actor will regularly hopscotch among all three external areas and the internal area:

1. The first external circle of focus is the most intimate. It involves the actor's position in relationship to the immediate set, furniture, clothing, hand props — everything within the character's reach, even another character.

2. The second circle opens up to incorporate more space. It involves the actor's larger space: more of the set, furniture, props, a larger area defined by light, and any other characters immediately in the scene.

3. The third circle is the largest and involves the entire stage area. This may include the world beyond the stage itself, that is, what is outside the doors and windows of the set. It can have a physical reality, involving things like the weather, time of day, or a back alley leading to the street. The third area can be less tangible, possessing a psychological reality of its own. Imagine a chilling, pervading fear of something unknown but ominous just outside the door, beyond the immediate stage area. An actor can use this awareness to heighten the dramatic or emotional tension in a scene.

Stanislavski believed the actor should try to expand the circle of attention, but should his or her attention begin to waver, the actor should immediately withdraw to a smaller circle of concentration.

In other words, when you hit line problems in rehearsal, try not to break character and ask for a cue from the stage manager. Instead, use this as a rehearsal opportunity to pull your focus back to the first circle of concentration and regroup your thoughts. With practice, you will develop your skill in retaining a character through difficult circumstances. This will only serve to enhance your final performance work.

Breath work will help prevent you from panicking when your concentration wavers. Once your attention returns, you can begin to build your breath to the appropriate emotional level and soon you will feel you have control of your character again. When this is in place once more, begin to open up your focus to the larger world.

The relationship of listening, reacting, and blocking

For an actor to discover the correct point of concentration at every moment in the play, it is critical to listen to what is being said by others at all times. Follow the physical and vocal action of the scene, and react to all such developments in character. Some reactions will naturally be internalized while others will be expressed externally. Your inner responses will bring blocking to life, regardless of whether your character has lines to speak or not. However, no reaction will be believable unless you listen and hear what is being said as if for the first time. You cannot sustain any illusion when acting until you learn to listen.

Listening involves truly hearing what is being said to you, reacting to it, and allowing it to touch you emotionally. Don't fall into the trap of worrying about what your next line is. Listen to your scene partner. Specifically focus only on what is being said to your character.

Listening skills often diminish as rehearsals continue. The more familiar you become with your partner's lines in a scene, the less likely you are to listen carefully to what is being said. Instead, you begin to anticipate what is coming up, to think about your next line instead of paying attention to what is currently being said to you.

The solution to this problem, however, is to listen to what is being said as if you've never heard it before. This becomes more difficult as the actor approaches opening night because there are so many new things to deal with, such as costumes, technical effects, and lighting. One effective way to refresh the cast's attention to the text is to gather them together in a dressing room, turn out the lights, and have them simply speak the lines. Total darkness helps to focus attention only on the words of the play and allows the actors to rediscover the true intention behind the lines. Voices become more flexible under such circumstances, because sound is the only medium the actor has for communicating fully.

Reactions come through good listening skills. An actor can take a reaction to a specific moment and express it in any of Stanislavski's three areas of concentration. Building the intensity of the reaction is simply a matter of degree and well-supported breath energy.

For example, suppose your character and mine are arguing about a bunch of flowers. Perhaps your character insults mine, but the script does not provide me with any scripted response. I am hardly likely to let the situation slip past, so how can I express my reaction to your insult?

My first job is to hear this insult with all the truth of the first time. I can choose to express my reaction strictly within my first area by stiffening physically, perhaps squeezing the arm of my chair or folding my arms. Breath work would help to carry the emotion of the moment to the audience, even though I have no lines in the script.

Having taken time to explore my reaction within the first area, I might decide the reaction is not strong enough. I might choose to extend it into the second area. In this case, I would begin my emotional response within the first area and build my energy level through deepening breath work based on strong, truthful personal images. The energy created might lead to me to cross to another part of the room, for example, and turn my back to you. After a few seconds, I might turn around and give you a telling look. Sounds carried on my breath during these moves would reinforce my meaning to the audience and give intention to my blocking moves.

Remember that the deeper that breath goes into your body, the stronger your emotions will feel to you. The stronger the emotions feel to you, the more clearly and more accurately they will be shared with your fellow actors and projected to your audience.

This is the key that enables you to experience the emotions of your character. It will prevent your movement from being stilted and awkward, or looking "blocked by the director." The moment will "feel right" for you. The stronger your breath work becomes on stage, the more naturally you can express your inner emotions. You are much less likely to feel uncomfortable with your hands or to remain rooted to one spot if you develop energy and emotion through the breath.

Just think back to the time you last experienced a powerfully released emotion in real life. The energy of the emotion was expressed through your breath patterns and it naturally spilled out of you in free movement and emotional release.

However, this reaction still may not be strong enough for the dramatic or comic impact we want in our argument over the flowers. I might want to express my reaction within the third area. In this case, I would go through my reactions in each of the first two areas, then perhaps grab the flowers and toss them out the window into the night air. This could be a casual, understated move or one veering on the melodramatic: it is a matter of choice on the part of the actor and the director. Regardless, breath is the key to carrying the emotional release and the appropriate physical expression to the third area.

It is all really a matter of deciding how big my reaction should be:

1. The first area is intimate, underplayed, and subtle.
2. The second area allows me to express a reaction more fully.

3. The third area is larger than everyday life and generally — but not necessarily — can have a melodramatic or comic quality because it is exaggerated.

Nevertheless, not one of those reactions exists in dialogue. How the actor chooses to react to events in a scene depends on many variables, including the:

- style of the play
- integrity of the text and subtext
- directorial guidance
- other actors in the scene
- dimensions of the playing space
- size of the audience
- actor's instinct

Emotional release and blocking

When an actor's personal tension gets out of control, it can block the character's emotional release. This results in **internalized reactions**.

When that occurs, the actor seeks refuge by either:

1. internalizing all reactions inside the actor's mind
2. expressing reactions only in the first external area

The more internalized your work is, the less clearly it communicates with an audience. It is difficult for the audience to connect with an actor whose emotional commitment fades toward the ends of phrases, and whose physical expression of character is half-hearted.

It is great to discover how to "feel the emotion" of the moment but, if you cannot share this equally with each member of your audience, you are not truly communicating. Internalized reactions may be appropriate for television or film, but not for the stage. In filming technique, the camera picks up detail in close-up shots but cuts away to other angles or visual pictures when the shot risks getting too long or boring. Theatre audiences do not have that option.

The degree of emotional release is dictated by many factors: the nature of the play, the directorial concept, the size and shape of the stage space, the size of the audience, the relationship between the characters in the scene, and the energy of the moment. Some of these factors can vary from one performance to the next, but in theatre, if a reaction doesn't travel to the last row of the theatre, it is self-indulgent.

Actors must constantly examine their work in class, rehearsal and performance so they can develop a solid understanding of what is required to convey emotional release that can fill a variety of theatre spaces. They must remain vigilant that nervous tension does not inhibit the free and appropriate expression of passion and character.

Blocking terminology

There are a few terms you will need to know about blocking. The first two are **stage left** and **stage right**, which are generally shortened to SL and SR in script stage directions. These terms apply to the actor's left and right. (The director has to learn to reverse left and right terminology when watching a rehearsal from the perspective of the audience. Actors rarely have trouble remembering which are SL and SR once it is pointed out that actors are the centres of the stage universe.)

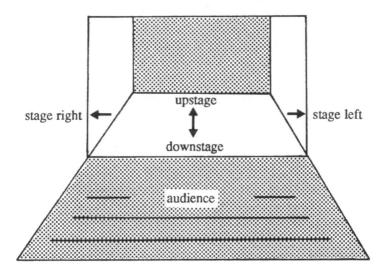

Upstage means that area of the stage farthest away from the audience. So, logically, **downstage** means that part which is closest to the audience (again, these are generally shortened to US and DS in scripts). These two terms come from the type of stage that used to be common in the 18th century. When you understand how the words came about, you won't have any trouble remembering which way to move when a director throws those terms at you.

220

Because the 18th-century audience was seated flat on an auditorium floor with no kind of "rake" (that is, slant or slope) to it, their vision of the play was hampered. So theatre owners raked their stages, sloping them upward toward the back wall of the theatre. This meant that an actor literally walked upstage away from the audience, or moved downstage toward the audience.

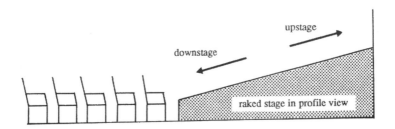

Raked stages and raked stage designs are still occasionally used today but, as you can imagine, they make for problems in movement. For instance, dancers in *Miss Saigon* often incur injuries because of problems dancing on the raked set.

If a director says to **move in**, that means to move toward the centre line of the stage. **Move out** means to move toward the wings of the theatre (that is, the space offstage left and right that is not part of the acting space).

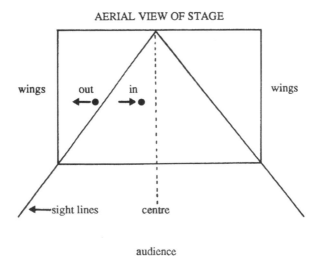

Sight lines refer to the audience's ability to see all areas of the stage clearly. An actor must be aware of the seats farthest off to the sides in the house, in order to acquire a feel for any sight-line problems that may occur in blocking. Otherwise the performer may move too far out, as illustrated above, and not be visible to some of the audience.

If an actor forgets about sight lines, his or her character can be masked or hidden by part of the set or by other characters on the stage. Performers should always be conscious of whether they are being masked, or whether they are themselves inadvertently masking another person. In either instance, the audience is being deprived of the opportunity to see everything clearly. Actors must learn to cheat (or slightly alter) themselves into better positions if they find a masking problem.

When you first move from a rehearsal hall into the theatre, you should explore the set and consider necessary alterations to your blocking caused by sight line problems. This also applies to touring shows where you might present the same show in a variety of theatre spaces. Good blocking always depends on an awareness of sight lines and the actor-audience relationship.

Blocking guidelines:

Guidelines for blocking will change depending upon the type of stage space being used. Three major types of stages will be discussed here. Each of these types of performing spaces makes particular demands on the director, designer, and actor:

1. proscenium stage
2. thrust stage
3. theatre-in-the-round

Several factors govern the blocking of every show. These are matters beyond the control of the actor, but they will affect the actor's use of the stage. For example:

- The ground plan of the furniture and set, which the director and designer are responsible for creating.
- The visual composition of the blocking — especially group scenes — which the director will control during rehearsal.
- The playwright may make certain demands of a character within the dramatic or comic action of the plot.

- Technical requirements that demand you move to or from specific areas. After all, no actor wants to be left sitting in the dark while everyone else on stage is beautifully lit.

Because a director has all this information, he or she may ask you to make certain blocking moves that you may not feel are appropriate for your character at that moment in the scene. This happens to all of us at one time or another. You — the actor — have no option but to do as the director asks.

After a few practices, if you still feel uncomfortable with an imposed blocking move, you have two options:

1. Find a justification for that imposed action within your character so that both the director's needs and the actor's needs are met, or
2. Look for another moment near that point in the script where you can more easily understand why your character would make such a move. (Then hope you can persuade your director that your idea is an improvement to the action of the play.)

From the audience's perspective, objects that are placed together on stage will look closer than they really are. So will groupings of people. Therefore, stage design must allow for breathing space. The extra space is not just for visual purposes, though. It allows freedom of movement within the acting space. Realize that the timing of all blocking moves will have to allow for this extra breathing space.

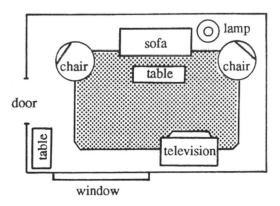

Pictured above is a typical living-room setting. Below is the same type of room transferred to the larger space of a stage setting.

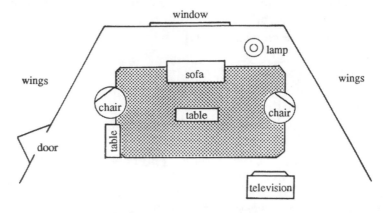

In adapting this living-room setting to the stage, the television set would probably be moved off to stage left against the wall — unless it were to be turned on during the course of the scene. A functioning television set must be placed with its back to the audience or the visual action of the TV program will draw focus away from the actors. In such an instance, the TV would likely be placed flat on the floor (rather than on a sturdy table, as in real life) in order to minimize masking or sight-line problems for the audience in the first rows.

Additionally, a piece of furniture such as a coffee table will not be set as close to a couch as it might naturally be found at home. Consequently, the mere act of reaching for a prop from a coffee table will require your character to cheat into a standby position a line or two before it is necessary to use the prop. Slide to the edge of the couch a moment beforehand to prevent an awkward lurching or grasping movement when reaching for the prop. The rehearsal process will help you find the timing of such moves.

Now it's time to discuss how blocking changes with different types of stage spaces.

The proscenium stage

Let's begin with the typical proscenium arch stage. The proscenium stage is a carry-over from the 19th century and it allows for picture-frame stage design. Curtains generally mask the stage left and stage right wings, as well as any lighting equipment suspended above the stage. A cyclorama (often shortened to "cyc") forms the upstage wall. The cyc is an off-white curtain pulled taut, or an off-white, painted back wall, which can be lit to create the effect of a sky or to heighten an atmosphere by throwing coloured lighting washes over it.

There is rarely even a hint of an extension of the stage floor in front of the curtains (this extension is called an apron). Often the stage edge drops off into an orchestra pit. The term "fourth wall" means that the proscenium arch itself forms the fourth wall of a room setting; this wall has been "removed" to allow the audience to see into the room. The actor on the stage must imagine the décor of the fourth wall and play the action within the confines of the "room."

Elaborate set designs, generally known as box sets, work beautifully with this kind of stage space. Attention can be paid to realism and detail in set dressing, props, lighting, and other technical components. Often a curtain is used to heighten the impact of the first visual moment of such a set design.

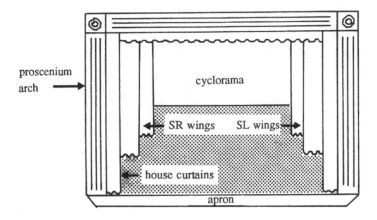

Points to remember when acting on a proscenium stage:

1. The person standing closest to centre stage has the stronger focus. Therefore, if you have an important moment in a scene, you would be wise to play it near the imaginary centre line. If you are not directly involved in the action at the moment, look for a justification to move upstage right or left.

2. Downstage is a stronger area for the actor than upstage because there is immediacy in the connection with the audience. Down centre is the strongest area of all.

3. Use of levels will change these rules because additional height (such as a staircase, landing, or riser) will give an actor a stronger focus. A

good director will try to place an important character on a higher level than other characters, for example, during an essential moment of the scene. Levels can also provide a more interesting visual picture. For instance, three people seated in a row on a bench provide a dull visual picture. But if one person is standing behind, another is seated, and the third is curled up on floor level, the variety provided by the visual picture is more rewarding to the eye.

4. Composition can draw the audience's eye. For example, if one person is isolated on one side of the stage and several are grouped in an area on the opposite side, the isolated individual will have the stronger position because of the contrast provided. Triangular groupings of actors are effective.

5. The audience's eye is drawn to where an actor is looking, to his or her point of concentration. If an actor is looking straight out front, the audience will generally keep its eye on that person. But if the actor turns to look stage right, perhaps focusing on another character, the audience will automatically glance in that direction. In effect, this change of eye direction transfers the focus to the other actor. This is why it is critical that actors know where the focus of the play should be at every moment of the action, and how audience focus can be controlled by ensemble work.

6. If one person is standing upstage and another downstage, direct face-to-face communication between them is difficult. The actor who is downstage will have to turn away from the audience to face the other actor, thereby upstaging him or herself. You can, of course, communicate with your back, but your eyes and face are much more compelling and more easily allow you to share emotional responses with the audience. When people first begin acting, they often get caught awkwardly upstaging themselves

7. If you allow yourself to be pulled away too frequently from your audience, it undermines effective communication. This is especially unforgivable in scene studies or audition monologues when you are addressing an "imagined" person in the scene: you place this invisible person in the strongest position and promptly turn your own back to your audience. Try to keep on the same level as your partner in a scene and, if the other character must move upstage, realign yourself as soon as possible so you don't get trapped in a limiting physical position.

8. Justify the use of all your stage area while remembering that all movement must be believable within the framework of your

character. If your character is timid and is in a strange room, it is unlikely there will be much physical exploration of the space — perhaps the eyes glancing around the room is all that is appropriate in that situation.

Exercises for the proscenium stage:

Place several chairs at random on your rehearsal stage and make sure you know where the fourth wall is. Put three together to make a "couch" and angle this slightly off-centre:

1. Walk back and forth from stage left to stage right, weaving in and out around the furniture and pausing briefly to turn as illustrated below. You will find that the terms "right foot" and "left foot" will only lead you to confusion. Think instead of "upstage foot" and "downstage foot." (Your upstage foot is the one farthest from the audience, and your downstage foot is the one closest to it.) Learn to stop with your upstage foot positioned ahead of you. Then, rotate on the ball of your upstage foot and turn downstage toward your audience to reverse direction. Step off again on your other foot — which has now become your upstage foot. If you keep your eyes focused toward your imaginary audience, you'll find that you never have to break eye contact with them unless you turn the wrong way, in which case you'll also tie your legs in a knot and know instantly that you've messed up the turn.

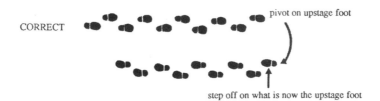

CORRECT — pivot on upstage foot

step off on what is now the upstage foot

FACING DOWNSTAGE TOWARD AUDIENCE

INCORRECT — pivot on downstage foot
(breaks contact with audience)

audience

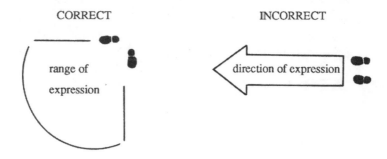

When you are standing onstage, watch the position of your feet. If you have them side by side facing stage right, for example, it will be very hard to "open" your performance out to the audience. On the other hand, if you angle your feet as illustrated below, your body will be much more visible to all members of the audience.

Few things are more frustrating for an audience than to realize that 50 percent of your acting is disappearing offstage right into the wings and, depending on sight lines, less than 50 percent is reaching your audience. We can see only your profile, so we miss half your reactions. We can't see your eyes clearly, so we can't see the real message there. Your voice is being thrown in the wrong direction, so we have to strain to hear. Generally, such trouble can be traced to a problem with the placement of the actor's feet.

2 Walk toward a chair while keeping your eyes on the audience. You'll see the chair out of your peripheral vision. When you reach the chair, don't look to see where you are going to sit. Turn your back to the chair and feel where it touches the back of your leg. Through the sense of touch you will feel when it is safe to sit. This will allow you to avoid lurching, plopping, or bobbing. Rising is just as easy. Make sure you have worked your way to the edge of the chair moments before your cue to rise so that all you need do is stand easily.

3. Watch what happens to your body when you sit on the couch. Because of the angle of the couch, you will find that one side of your body is "opened" more toward the audience and the other is angled away. Notice the difference when:

- you cross your left leg over your right
- you cross your right leg over your left

Do you see how movement in one direction pulls you farther away from your audience, while movement in the other opens you out? This principle applies to many other forms of stage business: greeting someone, accepting a drink, gesturing, picking up a book, embracing another character, or serving a meal. Every action can be performed in a variety of ways, but one method will generally make the action clearer to the audience because the manner in which it is performed opens the action out to the audience.

The most important thing to remember in these (or any other movement exercises on stage) is that you must make them look comfortable, natural, easy. Equipped with the principles mentioned above, you can devise your own assignments in stage business.

For example, create a room setting that uses a large number of props and pieces of furniture. Then develop a scene in which you must justify the existence of every part of your space. Perhaps you are a burglar searching for hidden jewels. Maybe you are in a frantic hurry, trying to find car keys, and you're already 10 minutes late for work. The improvisation should have no dialogue because action and movement should tell us clearly what is happening. Practise every movement so that you achieve maximum clarity of physical action. Every important stage business and emotional reaction must be shared with your audience.

The thrust stage

Let's consider the blocking alterations that become necessary when playing on a thrust stage. This type of stage may have a proscenium arch as well, with the apron projecting beyond the arch as illustrated below.

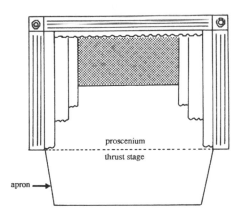

proscenium

thrust stage

apron →

On the other hand, a thrust stage may simply be a stage that projects into the audience, as illustrated below in an aerial view. You will notice how flexible this thrust stage can be in terms of the possible numbers of entrances and exits. That is why this kind of stage is particularly useful in Shakespeare's plays, with their rapid scene changes and large casts. Traffic jams can more easily be avoided. In either case, the audience is seated on three sides of the thrust.

Points to remember when acting on a thrust stage:

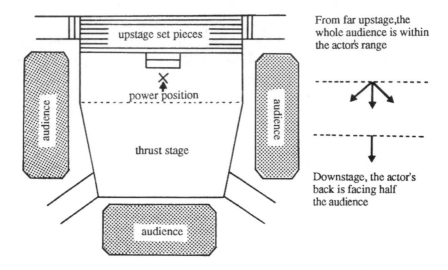

1. Because of sight-line problems, larger elements of the set such as flats, levels, and staircases will be concentrated upstage so as not to hinder the side audience's view across the stage. The actors must create most of the idea of the setting in the downstage areas through sensory work. Considerably more setting details are left to the audience's imagination on a thrust stage than on a proscenium stage.

2. Furniture that is placed downstage on the thrust will likely be low to the stage floor and well spaced. Generally only essential pieces of furniture that are capable of serving a variety of functions will be used, in order to minimize sight-line problems. Set dressing will be kept to a minimum, with one or two well-selected items symbolizing the larger world of the play.

3. The strongest acting area, as indicated on the thrust diagram, is the **power position**. If an actor moves too far down centre, he or she will end up being cut off from full view of some of the audience. Use the power position for your important moments in a scene.

4. This style of theatre works well for costume plays because the detail and movement of costumes provide very strong visual pictures even when viewed from the back. Costume plays demand a lot of movement work if the actors are to look as if they have worn that style of clothing all their lives. (See "Acting in period comedy" in Chapter 17.) In period plays, it is essential to use rehearsal skirts and accessories right from the first rehearsals.

5. Actors will require care in vocal work. They will have to learn to project with clarity to a large number of people to whom their backs are turned. Vocal exercises can be tied into a study of the different blocking principles required for work on a thrust stage.

6. Entrances will take longer, because doorways are placed upstage while the central acting area is downstage. When an actor has a long way to travel on a blocking move, it is a good idea to break the move into two parts. This can be done in many ways: through a slight hesitation, a look around the room, or by incorporating a bit of business with a prop (such as setting down a handbag) or a piece of costume. If there are exits downstage left and right through the audience, however, the flow of the play can actually be faster. One scene can be setting up while the previous one is ending. This is the principle behind Stratford, Ontario's famous thrust stage with its multiplicity of entrances.

7. There can be a widespread sense of intimacy in a thrust space because more of the audience is closer to the action than with the proscenium stage. However, the actor must be aware of the audience's presence and not keep his or her back to them very long. Keep the action moving more frequently than in proscenium acting, especially in the downstage areas. You must not let the visual picture go static or flat. Don't forget about sustaining vocal projection to all members of your audience, wherever they may be seated.

8. Move a line, a word, or a moment by playing out toward more of the audience than in the traditional stand-and-deliver manner. You can do this as you speak your lines or during a reaction to

someone else's line. Cheat your response around 180 degrees instead of merely 90 degrees. This is not a question of making the reactions larger. Rather, it is a matter of learning to open your responses, move them, and share them with as many members of your audience as you can. At Stratford, this is known as the "water sprinkler" technique of speaking.

9. Don't allow yourself to get rooted to furniture. Try to avoid lounging back into a chesterfield or chair. Instead, sit closer to the edge of the furniture and express freedom of action with your torso, head, and limbs. Keep the visual picture alive.

Movement on a thrust stage falls halfway between the principles of moving on a proscenium stage (when the actor is located in the upstage area of the thrust) and the principles of moving in theatre-in-the-round (when the actor is located on the downstage area of the thrust). Exercises for the former are mentioned earlier, and exercises for the latter follow shortly. However, if you are working on a thrust stage, remember:

1. Use the power position.
2. Keep the action moving.
3. Find variation in long entrances and exits.

Theatre-in-the-round

Finally, let's look at acting for theatre-in-the-round. This is particularly common in children's theatre because, with its stripped-down type of staging, it can be performed anywhere: in a park, a classroom, a gymnasium, or a specially designed theatre space. In this kind of theatre, there is immediacy of action, which helps retain children's attention. The farthest member of the audience is likely to be only a few rows away.

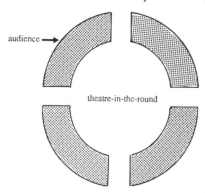

audience →

theatre-in-the-round

Points to remember when acting in theatre-in-the-round:

1. Vocal demands on the actor are heavy. Take care with projection and articulation to make every word clear to each member of the audience.

2. Technical requirements are simplified. Furniture will likely be low-backed (or backless) and the minimum number of furniture pieces will be used. Whatever furniture there is will likely be placed in front of the areas where entrances and exits are made. This minimizes the problem of furniture interfering with the audience's sight lines.

3. No real set pieces are possible in this kind of staging due to sight-line problems. However, levels can be used effectively by building one or two steps up to the stage level all around the playing space. This allows actors to move away from the focus by simply sitting down on the steps, if it is not their moment within the scene.

4. As with thrust staging, movement for theatre-in-the-round serves costume plays well.

5. Lighting and sound are very important for helping to create the atmosphere since set, props and décor are stripped away.

6. With this style of movement, terminology such as "upstage, downstage, stage left and right" will necessarily disappear and be replaced by "in" and "out." When blocking a play in the round, try using a clock as a guide. Fix a point (ideally, the major entrance) as 12 o'clock. Then create three circles: A is the innermost, then B, and the outer ring is C. When taking down blocking notes in a script, an actor can then fix any specific spot on the stage by combining a number from the clock with an A-B-C area.

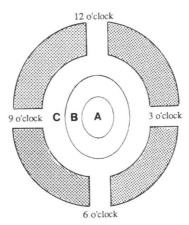

7. Theatre-in-the-round can be a very liberating experience, once you are used to the style of movement required. You must act with your whole body, and this type of staging heightens your awareness of the space behind you. It loosens up the torso and limbs, and develops pronounced freedom of movement.

8. The strongest acting area is the centre of the circle although, because of the immediacy of the audience, there is no really "weak" acting area. What is most important, however, is to keep the action moving. Never become rooted to a spot for more than 20 seconds, don't get caught masking others, and keep the visual picture alive. If you're not needed for long periods of time, find a justification to sit near the edge of the stage, by an exit that extends through the audience.

9. Movement in a scene with two or more people requires a sense of opposition. Two people must mirror each other's blocking moves as much as possible. When one person moves, the other must naturally counterbalance that move. For example, if one person moves to the centre, the other must match the action. Movement to one side of the acting space should be mirrored by movement to the other side. This is the most effective way of keeping masking problems to the minimum, and it creates an easy naturalism to the movement.

10. Try to keep all movement linked to your sense of 360 degrees. In other words, if someone to your left speaks to you, don't turn 90 degrees left to reply. Instead, turn the other 270 degrees to your right. There is a happy medium between playing directly to the other person in the scene with you, and cheating your reactions, lines, and moments out and around to the entire audience.

Exercises for theatre-in-the-round:

1. Create a large circle as your playing space and have everyone in the group stand around the edge of the defined area. Imagine this circular floor is delicately balanced a couple of metres above the ground on a central point, much like a plate being balanced on someone's finger. Choose a leader to start the exercise. The leader "steps" onto the circle but, in order to keep balance in the circle, the person opposite him or her must immediately step onto the circle as well. As the leader moves around the defined space, the follower must mirror every move to keep the illusion

of the balanced plate. If the follower makes a mistake and moves in the wrong direction, the leader must change directions to compensate. In extreme cases, another person along the side of the circle might step in and sustain the balance. From time to time, remove or add others to the exercise. This exercise will help to develop the actor's sensitivity to, and awareness of, others in the visual picture created in theatre-in-the-round.

2. Define a circle again and place a handkerchief on the ground just to the left of the centre. Stand at one side of the circle and fix your attention on a spot across the way. Begin to walk through the circle with a serious intent and a rapid pace. Immediately after you pass to the right of the handkerchief — the idea being that you just spotted something out of the corner of your eye — turn to look at it. Don't turn to your left, however. Spin around as quickly as possible to your right. This action will take you around almost 360 degrees and is, in fact, the technique of staging a double-take in theatre-in-the-round. Practise this with the handkerchief in different places, so that you get experience in spinning in different directions each time.

3. Using the same principle, two actors approach each other from opposite sides of the circle. Just after they pass each other, they recognize each other and spin to greet their friend. This technique allows everyone in theatre-in-the-round to get the full impact of their emotional reactions.

Although a novice actor may feel uncomfortable when first appearing onstage and, indeed, may project discomfort to others, it is only a matter of time until confidence is acquired. With practice, actors develop naturalistic skills in stage movement that will support them in a variety of settings, stages, and scenic designs.

The stage becomes their home.

Chapter Eleven
Getting Into Character

Thinking in character: units and transitions

To understand your character in a play and to make the character come to life, you must identify the thought processes of your character. Breaking down each line that your character says into thought units and transitions can help you. Thought units come from the words of the playwright ,while the actor creates transitions based on personal impulse.

A **thought unit** can be as simple as a single word, or extended throughout many sentences, providing all those sentences deal with the same basic thought. In general, however, a thought unit is a couple of sentences in length. It changes with such things as a shift of subject matter, the discovery of a new emotion, the arrival or departure of another character in the scene, or a shift from one time and/or place to another. In any scene, two or more characters can be involved in a discussion on a single subject and therefore their thought units will be related to each other. If the subject they are discussing changes because each offers differing points of view, each subject change marks the beginning of a new thought unit. Sometimes two characters will share a thought unit. At other times, characters will experience individual thought units that may not overlap with other characters.

A **transition** is the unwritten part. It involves the change or connection between one thought and the next. There are different types of transitions:

1. *Internal:* For example, your character could say something in one thought unit that triggers a childhood memory. Your job as an actor is to create the imaginary childhood memory that will generate the next thought unit. That memory, then, becomes the transition into the next thought unit.

2. *External:* For instance, a sound or lighting cue can provide the thought link-up into the next thought unit. More likely, however, another character's physical action or facial expression in the scene will create external transitions. It is for this reason that no rehearsal is very successful when one of the actors in the scene is absent. Actors depend on other actors to help them learn to listen, discover adjustments of character, and share the connecting energy of the scene.

Transitions often defy analysis. A new thought simply enters the mind: it's just there. Watch your own natural transitions during a given period and you'll see that you frequently hopscotch from one thought or emotion to the next without any apparent logic. More will be said of this later.

Script analysis is the key to discovering characters' thought units and transitions. In some styles of writing, the thought units are clearly identifiable, obvious and easy to understand. However, a good number of them will be difficult to pin down. Break a character's speech into a series of thought units and choose two or three words to describe each thought unit and transition. This will identify the dramatic flow of the scene.

Let's take a look at a specific example in *Behind the Scenes, Volume One* (page 92). It's a scene between Hester and Ruth from *Still Stands the House* by Gwen Pharis Ringwood:

RUTH: You were such a little girl to do so much.
HESTER: After Mother died I did it all.
RUTH: I know, but it was too hard for a child. I don't see how you managed.
HESTER: Father always helped me with the washing.
RUTH: Not many men would stay in from the field to do that.
HESTER: No. (*Her knitting drops to her lap, and for a moment she is lost in the past.*) "We'll have to lean on one another now, Daughter." Those were his words. And that's the way it was. I was beside him until — I never left him.
RUTH (*at Hester's side*): You've never talked of him before.
HESTER (*unconscious of Ruth*): He always liked the snow. (*Her eyes are on

the portrait of her father.) He called it a moving shroud, a winding-sheet that the wind lifts and raises and lets fall again.

RUTH: It is like that.

HESTER: He'd come in and say, "The snow lies deep on the summer fallow, Hester. That means a good crop next year."

RUTH: I know. It's glorious in the fall with the wheat like gold on the hills. No wonder he loved it.

HESTER *(Called out of her dream, she abruptly resumes her knitting.)* There hasn't been much wheat out there these last years.

Here is one way of breaking the above conversation down into units and transitions: unit #1 involves the discussion between Ruth and Hester, as Hester remembers life after Mother died.

RUTH: You were such a little girl to do so much.

HESTER: After Mother died I did it all.

RUTH: I know, but it was too hard for a child. I don't see how you managed.

Then Hester goes into a transition focusing on an image of her father. This transition could be an internal one (specifically, the mental picture of what Father looked like) or an external one (caused by glancing at Father's portrait hanging in the room). Unit #2 deals with Father coping as a widower:

HESTER: Father always helped me with the washing.

RUTH: Not many men would stay in from the field to do that.

HESTER: No. *(Her knitting drops to her lap, and for a moment she is lost in the past.)* "We'll have to lean on one another now, Daughter." Those were his words. And that's the way it was. I was beside him until — I never left him.

RUTH *(at Hester's side)*: You've never talked of him before.

Hester is going into another memory of time past. Her transition here is likely an internal one, probably connected with the manner of her father's death. Some element of Hester's image, such as Father's funeral in mid-winter, should be associated with nature so that Hester's transition into discussing snow can have a logical connection.

You will notice in unit #3 that the stage directions in the script say Hester's eyes are on her father's portrait, and you may feel this provides her transition between the two units. However, as we have discussed earlier, you need not take existing stage directions literally. Use those that you require and ignore the rest. Unit #3 deals with winter:

HESTER *(unconscious of Ruth)*: He always liked the snow. *(Her eyes are on the portrait of her father.)* He called it a moving shroud, a winding-sheet that the wind lifts and raises and lets fall again.
RUTH: It is like that.
HESTER: He'd come in and say, "The snow lies deep on the summer fallow, Hester. That means a good crop next year."
RUTH: I know. It's glorious in the fall with the wheat like gold on the hills. No wonder he loved it.

Ruth's last line hasn't anything to do with winter, but it is an understandable extension of her own thoughts on nature. She is obviously not as keen on the snow as Hester and Father were, so she searches out her own image of the beauty of nature on the farm. The transition between the third and fourth units is instantaneous. It is likely triggered in Hester by a sudden unpleasant image when Ruth says the key word "wheat." The final unit deals with the diminishing productivity of the farm:

HESTER *(Called out of her dream, she abruptly resumes her knitting.)*: There hasn't been much wheat out there these last years.

To summarize this example, the essential unit elements or **spine** of this portion of the scene appear in sequence. (Imagine the spine as two or three words each, one cluster on top of the other like dozens of "vertebrae" in a row. They create the structure that holds the play aloft.) In this example, the spine would read as follows:

- Unit #1: After Mother's death
- Transition: mental picture of Father
- Unit #2: Father coping
- Transition: Father's death/nature
- Unit #3: winter
- Transition: wheat
- Unit #4: barren fields

This is the type of preparatory work that can and ought to be done as homework independently of regular rehearsals, so that you can come to rehearsal equipped with understanding and insight.

In rehearsal, especially in the early stages of working without your script in your hand, avoid rushing transitions. Take your time. Finding transitions is the actor's specific responsibility, and what you discover in script analysis at home may take some time to put into practice on your feet. If you feel pressured in rehearsal you won't concentrate as well, and 90 percent of your homework will not be evident. Furthermore, working something out on paper doesn't mean you have to do it that way in rehearsal. Script analysis is a supportive technique for the actor, not the be-all and end-all. Keep yourself flexible.

An added benefit to learning your scene by units is that if you and your partner "blank out" on one unit, you can often jump ahead to the next. This will keep your scene moving and sustain your characters through momentary line problems.

When you get to a later stage of rehearsal, your transitions will last only a split second rather than the several seconds you explored early in rehearsal. In fact, they will likely be backed up halfway into your cue line. This is all part of working on tightening the pacing of a show.

By working on thought units and transitions, you will be doing detailed text work that will benefit you when it comes time to memorize lines. By that stage, you will know the text intimately. You will also be getting a deeper understanding of characterization, for you will have justified every thought transition and made it work within your interpretation of character.

Transitions are part of what the actor must create in order to make the text truthful. They are the keys to the actor believing every word of the text.

Characterization: fundamental questions to ask

How do you begin to create a whole new character, to sublimate your own personality and make a truly believable person come to life?

The first step is to read the script — not just the scene you are in but the entire text — to see the shape of the total experience, plot, and character development. Read, reread and make lots of notes on what the playwright has given you. Here are just a few questions to ask yourself. Each one can be answered from careful reading of any good script:

1. Who am I?

What is my basic character like? Comb the text for clues. The answer lies in:

- what your character says that reveals important information about him or herself
- what others say about your character (when present and when not)
- how your character reacts to other people and plot developments in the action of the script

Create a biography of your character. Fill in the missing pieces from your creative imagination and careful research. (See chapters 5 and 9 on vocal work and body language for some rehearsal ideas.)

2. Where am I?

What is the country, city, neighbourhood, house, room, or area of the room? The answers to these questions will often change from one scene to the next. Each time your character appears in a different setting, repeat the basic question "Where am I?" Having considered the broader aspects of the setting of the play, think of how differently you have felt in a variety of specific settings: your bedroom, a cathedral, the boss's office, a dark alley, a governmental agency, or the seaside. If you are in a historical play, you will have to research the period for clearer ideas of the setting. At all times, avoid generalizing: be specific.

3. What surrounds me?

What are the animate and inanimate objects near me — the props, people and furniture? What do they mean to me and how do I react to them? We all know people who are careless of things and people who are overly fussy about possessions. Each of us has at least one or two objects that are very precious to us. For example, a woman who is newly engaged may treat her engagement ring with a special significance. When a close relative dies, the mere sight of a familiar object that once belonged to that relative can move us to tears.

As well, other things remind us in a negative or hostile way of a person or situation that we would rather forget. A person who experienced a traumatic event during a thunderstorm may become nervous at the first sign of a storm. An individual who hated school may get a sinking feeling when looking at an old report card. While bestowing emotional meaning on objects is a very important device in character creation, relationships with other people are infinitely more complex, challenging issues for the actor to address.

242

4. What are my given circumstances?

What specific events have happened so far in the play? What events are happening now? How have these events affected me? What is my precise position with regard to other characters in the play? The script will give you the starting point, but discovering the given circumstances for each scene in which your character appears involves research, digging up the past, investigating current events, or projecting into the future. Each scene will have a new set of given circumstances, twists of plot, or dramatic developments while your character was offstage.

You should look at each of your scenes and ask two questions:

- Just before entering, ask, "Where am I coming from and why am I coming into this space on the stage?"
- On exiting, ask, "Where am I going to and why am I leaving?"

Answers to these two questions will illuminate your motivation, provide you with the appropriate energy level for your entrances and exits, reveal something of your character to the audience, and help clarify your relationships with others in the scene.

5. What is my relationship to other characters and plot developments?

This means combing the script for clues from other characters. Don't be tempted to succumb to stereotypes, such as the dumb blonde secretary and the efficient business executive, or the prissy spinster teacher and the smart-aleck student. Such choices are predictable and make for uninteresting theatre. Try to find a fresh and believable way of approaching relationships.

Find the extreme relationship with other characters, because that will give you many more interesting choices to make as an actor. Loving someone is stronger than liking them. Since each of us is a bundle of contradictions, why should it not be so with our characters? Look for opposite qualities and combine them in every possible situation. For example, we may really like a specific person who happens to have irritating habits that bother us. Find as much comedy as possible in a grippingly dramatic scene. Never stop looking for emotional opposites because they will make your acting more real, more textured, and more truthful.

6. What do I want?

What is the main or immediate objective of my character? Your character will have a superobjective in the dramatic plot of the play: one overall goal providing the driving motivation of his or her plot line. A superobjective can generally be summed up in one sentence. For example, the superobjective of Shakespeare's Hamlet can be summed up as "I want to get rid of Claudius and to avenge my father's murder."

However, in each scene there will also be an individual objective that reflects the development of the plot. Individual objectives may be very different, scene by scene, but they fit into the overall superobjective. An individual objective may also be summed up in a sentence. In *Hamlet*, for example, Hamlet's objective in Act II, Scene 2 could be this: to stage a play for Claudius that closely parallels Hamlet's father's murder, thereby to catch Claudius by surprise and reveal his complicity.

7. What is in my way?

What is the obstacle that is creating conflict for me? In real life we sometimes see an obstacle clearly, at other times not at all. An obstacle may be hidden from a character in a scene. However, the actor must always be aware that the obstacle exists and what it is so that he or she can incorporate this insight into the scene.

When the obstacle is a psychological one buried inside us, we may avoid facing it and create other obstacles to suit our purposes. For example, look at this sentence: "I was never good in school because my teachers didn't like me." Perhaps disrupting classes, neglecting homework and making disruptive wisecracks did not endear us to others. However, what caused such behaviour in the first place? From the "older perspective," it is emotionally safer and much easier to place the blame on others rather than examine what caused anti-social behaviour in the first place.

Every good playwright tries to find the right obstacle for each character in each scene. Modern psychological analysis, discussed in more detail in Chapter 14, can be helpful in understanding the nature of internal obstacles within the character you are creating.

8. What do I do to get what I want?

Discovering the answer to this question leads to the physical and verbal action of the play. Action reveals a great deal about our characters: how we get around obstacles can be very telling. Our character may also take the route of inaction, which can also be a dynamic in the development of a play. Refusing to become involved can come from noble or villainous intentions. Action isn't always necessarily the key to character creation.

9. What time is it?

This involves the century, the year, the season, and the time of day. Events in history help to shape our lives and attitudes, whether or not we realize it at the time. Imagine how your character would be affected, say, if you lived in the carefree, roaring 1920s. Contrast this with the same character placed 10 years later in the midst of the Depression. The character would be different 10 years later in the midst of the Second World War. An actor needs to empathize with the time period of the play to gain better insight into the dynamics of historical setting and events. For this reason, actors should constantly strive to learn more about different time periods, social history, and major political events that have shaped our civilization.

Be aware, as well, that some of us are morning people and others are night people. Some of us love the winter, while others feel much more alive on a sunny summer day. Our individual energy levels vary during the day and with the season. These factors can provide the actor with still further character choices.

10. What do I look like?

Often one's physical appearance creates a reaction in others, triggering fear, sympathy, disdain, or envy. We make instant character judgments based on how people look and they do so in return. As mentioned earlier, we are constantly checking people out everywhere: at school, in the supermarket, or at a dance. Yet we get confused and hurt that people categorize us, misjudge us, make presumptions about our character, misunderstand us.

Similarly, each of us probably has a very different self-image, an ideal we would like to present to the world. Sometimes we dress to reflect this; we may dressing differently several times in one day as we play various roles. But there may also be a great discrepancy between our real physical appearance and our self-image. Every one of us can list a number of changes we would like to see reflected in the mirror. Again, the novice actor should avoid stereotypes and search out a detailed physical appearance when creating a character. If there is a designer for the show you are rehearsing, discuss the visual appearance of your character as soon as possible so that you can work toward that knowledge in your creative work in rehearsal.

In the end, you will have read the script a couple of dozen times if you have done the job thoroughly. This kind of meticulous approach will pay dividends ultimately, for it will answer questions about your character that you might otherwise not think to ask. This can only give you more authority within your character, greater creativity in rehearsal, and the assurance that you can cope with unexpected crises in performance.

To help make the character's world come to life, however, more than reading the play is necessary. For example, life in Victorian times (the late 19th century) was very different from life a century later, not just in physical terms but in social, religious, and cultural values. Research is important, for it enables you to visualize the environment and understand the attitudes of your character and others in the play. These topics apply equally well to contemporary theatre and period plays:

- the social setting
- the time period
- political background and issues
- male/female relationships
- the role of religion in society and in the individual
- scientific thought
- recent inventions and technological developments that influence society
- the balance of power in society
- public and personal morality
- topical issues of passing importance
- the message of the playwright's body of work and its connection to your play
- the style of the play

Researching a period play can make the play less academic and remote for you and, therefore, more significant and exciting. The playwright creates the skeletal background of the character in the text itself. Research helps to broaden understanding of the script. However, it is up to the actor to fill in the missing pieces, to create the life experiences of the character, and to make the character really come to life.

The next step:

Now the actor can begin to create an interpretation of the role or character. There are two directions of approach: from the outside in, or from the inside out. Both are useful for an actor to consider and most of the time you will end up using a combination of approaches. More will be said of these techniques in the next chapters. They are complex issues that deserve treatment in depth. However, here is an overview.

External approaches to characterization

The basis of an external approach to characterization is found in the physical appearance of the character. When we are dressed in a new and very expensive outfit that we have been planning to buy for months, our clothing dictates the way we walk, sit, or stand, depending on the restrictions or freedom provided. We have a different way of moving in clothing that is old, well worn, and comfortable. Some people spend a great deal of money on visiting the hairdresser and hate appearing in public with a strand out of place. Try messing their hair during a hug and see how quickly the friendly greeting is replaced by pique. For an actor, making strong choices in visual appearance and finding appropriate rehearsal costumes can be effective in getting "the feel" of a character.

A word of warning here: certain characters should never be rehearsed in blue jeans and running shoes. Perhaps you have seen Dame Edith Evans, the British character actor, in late-night films on television. She used to start creating a character with the shoes. She believed that once she had the right shoes, her character would be "**grounded**" and she insisted on wearing appropriate footwear even at the first read-through stage of rehearsal.

This may seem an unusual approach to us today, given that we in North America have embraced "The Method" in acting for a couple of generations now. Simply put, **Method Acting** is an approach to acting that begins with a total immersion in the inner feelings and emotional life of the character. Subsequently, the actor adds external considerations of movement and voice. However, British stage tradition works the other way around. It begins with externals such as the right costume pieces and props, experimenting with vocal technique in delivery, and being guided by a heightened sense of the stage picture. From there, the actor works backward to find emotional intention and inner verisimilitude.

We in Canada tend to draw from both the American and the British sources, as we do in so many other areas of our culture and customs.

Exercise: Costume prop box

Gather a collection of hats and spread them equally in the four corners of the room. Take turns finding a hat, putting it on, and assuming a character based on the feeling that the hat arouses. Remain in the corner, breathing in and out, until you feel the sense of your character. Then walk toward the centre of the room. Focus on how your character moves.

When you reach the centre of the room, focus on another actor in a different hat. Establish a relationship without saying a word, simply by facial expression, eye contact, and a sound. Complete that moment, then go to another corner and choose a different hat. Repeat the process, trying to establish a distinctive character each time: different breath, dissimilar movement, and fresh relationships with others.

Internal approaches to characterization

An internal approach is one that is based on discovering the mental and emotional complexity of the character you are creating. The actor creates an understanding of that character based on:

- information and facts provided in the script
- elements provided by the actor's imagination

In other words, the actor must have an understanding of human nature and psychology, be prepared to analyze the text of the script line by line, and bring courageous fresh interpretations to rehearsals.

One method of helping find subtext and achieve greater depth of character insight is to create an **inner monologue** for your character. This is the non-stop internal dialogue we have with ourselves from the first thing in the morning to the last thing at night. You certainly have an active one when being reprimanded by an authority figure, for example, or any time your emotions become animated. Inner monologues continue inside each of us as "actors being characters" whether or not we have any lines to say in a scene. It is our private inner-character life that tries to make sense of events unfolding around us. We are constantly observing others, or retreating into ourselves, or thinking and reacting to what others say and do. It leads us to the guts of our character.

Try creating an inner monologue for your character at three stages of rehearsal:

1. just after the first read-through
2. when you have completed the basic blocking of the play
3. a week or so before opening night

Here is an example of an inner monologue created from Sandra Dempsey's play *D'Arcy*, which can be found on page 31 of *Behind the Scenes, Volume One*. The play itself is a one-man show, so the inner monologue must be clearly defined for the actor. There's little else for him to draw upon.

D'ARCY: Ah, it's a shame I wasn't born in a bottle — I'd be improving with age. Why in the name of God they ever delegated such a delicate task to these hands, I'll be dead and buried before I know.

(Mary calls to him from offstage.)

Eh? What's that you're accusing me of? ... No, I wasn't talking to myself — I was talking to no one in particular ...

(He sees her. Pause.)

Mary, you're wearing black ... the middle child ... that'd be young Daniel ... it was the cholera, was it? ... No, no it couldn't be helped. You go on — finish piecing together the shroud. Go on. *(Mary exits.)*

An inner monologue for this excerpt might run as follows (note that Dempsey's script appears below in boldface and the inner monologue appears in normal type):

Ooohhh, that was a lovely song. I always sing so much better when I've had a little nip. **Ah, it's a shame I wasn't born in a bottle.** Wouldn't that be funny, now? Can you see little me squeezed inside this bottle here? Oh! This bottle's almost empty now — oh, wouldn't you know? Well, pickle me in brandy and **I'd be improving with age.** I'm not improving now, though. In fact, I'm in terrible shape. Look how my hands shake....**Why in the name of God they ever delegated such a delicate task to these hands** — I'm such a mess I probably won't live all that long ... oh well (sigh) — **I'll be dead and buried before I know.** Buried. Right there under that bush probably, and I'll be colder than — What? Is that Mary's voice? **Eh?** What did she say? Drunk again? **What's that you're accusing me of?** Don't you have a go at me again, woman, or I'll.... What? Someone out here with me? That's a laugh. I am communing with the spirits. Ha-ha. That's a good one. Spirits. Brandy. What? **No, I wasn't talking to myself**.... I was talking to this bottle. Whoops. Mustn't drop it! Ha-ha. Well, I guess **I was talking to no one in particular**. Particular. What a funny word, particular. Par - tic - tic ... What's that in the shadow? Mary? God, woman, you frightened me ... looking like a — **Mary, you're wearing black.** My God, I don't dare — **the middle child**, the sickly one — well, he was your favourite, not mine ... **that'd be young Daniel** — rest his soul — sweet young Daniel, up with the angels now, I guess ... **it was the cholera, was it?** God protect us all ... if there's one thing that makes my blood run cold it's cholera.... What's she saying now? Stop crying, Mary.... Please, Mary — I can't.... Fault? **No**, it's not your fault, **no**, not your fault and not mine. **It couldn't be helped,** that's all. Here, Mary, stop crying. **You go on** inside and sit by the fire. Find something to do to keep your mind busy. **Finish piecing together the shroud** for young Daniel, poor child. Mary, please go now. Leave me here to mourn. **Go on.**

This is, of course, just a suggestion to illustrate the integration of inner monologue with text. Use your rehearsal time to cultivate your character's personal inner monologue. You will find the richness of the inner monologue develops as the play becomes more polished. When you have it finely tuned, you will be much better equipped to sustain the action of a scene when something goes wrong — if an entrance is late, a prop goes missing, or when lines get flubbed.

Creating emotional truth: "feeling" emotions first:

Authors enable us to see their intention by the use of images in their writing. This is most obvious when a character describes an event earlier in his or her life, and the incident is described vividly and concisely. Images appear in the actor's mind from the playwright's text and are fed by the actor's imagination; at the same time, an emotional response emerges from the actor. The images lead the character to take action, to feel emotion and to deliver the appropriate subtext behind the words of the script. To be successful, the image must be in place before any words are spoken. Images are the key to connecting emotional truth to the actor's text.

Much of our daily thinking involves the use of images and we tend to think in images and thoughts, rather than literal sentences. If you hear someone describing an experience with a dog, you will likely "see" a dog in your own mind. The image you shape will be based on a dog from your own experience, for example a small terrier or toy poodle. If the speaker says something indicating the dog is very large, you may change your image to visualize a larger dog such as a German shepherd or Old English sheepdog.

This points up the discrepancy between what the actor envisages and what the audience receives. The actor's image must be strong enough to serve as an emotional trigger. What is not important is the audience's ability to "see" that image. We need to see the effect of the image on you, not what caused it. For example, an actor may be conjuring up a private erotic image to help make a moment of theatre more truthful and effective. The audience will likely understand the actor's projected signals and find these believable. The audience doesn't need to know what image served the purpose for the actor.

Costumes and props rarely look believable up close, but images can be projected onto these objects, bestowing strong new qualities. Thus, an actor may look at a crown made of Styrofoam — sprayed gold and covered with tatty braid and hideous paste jewels — and transform it into the Royal Crown of England. Cinderella must make her ball gown stunning by endowing the dress with beauty through the emotional response triggered by images.

An image can also be projected onto another actor, enabling one actor to feel emotions that may be very different from the person-to-person relationship existing between the two in real life. Images may also be projected into the theatre directly to the audience, so that an actor's face and eyes will convey the emotional impact of the actor's images to the audience. It is through this method that an actor opens out his or her emotions to the house. An actor needs to be able to use images at any time in any manner to create and sustain belief in the character's inner truth.

Types of images:

Images can be based on one or any combination of:

- a **real** experience that the actor has undergone
- **transferred** experiences from the actor's personal life
- **substituted** imaginary ones based on the phrase, "What if …?"

1. *Real images:*

With real images, the actor draws upon past experience and relives incidents in his or her life to make moments in a scene personal, more real and believable. Some examples of words with real images include: mother, father, new car, teacher, cat, best friend, bedroom, beer, loose change. With few exceptions, all of us can imagine these images because we are, or have been, familiar with them in our own lives. Real images will have different effects on each of us, depending on the nature of our personal experiences. Someone from a happy, close-knit family will have a very much different instinctive reaction to the word "father" than the person whose father was physically and/or emotionally abusive.

2. *Transferred images:*

These images emerge when an actor draws upon past experiences or similar events in his or her life and "hands them over" to a new situation in a script. For example, your character in a play may be describing the death of a parent. If your parents are both alive, you may transfer the image of the death of another relative in order to make the moment in the play more truthful. This person's death provides you with an experience that is similar, related, and appropriate to the impulse of the image.

3. *Substituted images:*

These images open the door beyond real or transferred experiences, to encompass hypothetical, imagined, or supposed situations by substituting "What if …?" If you are playing the role of a murderer, you may substitute powerful moments of rage from your own life experience and ask, "What would have happened if I had taken that anger to the point where I committed murder?"

4. *Composite:*

An image can be made up of two or more separate images — some real, some transferred, and some substituted. For example, your character in the play may be describing the first glimpse of sunrise on a visit to Switzerland. You may have been there yourself (real image). However, if you have not been there, you may have seen a real sunrise in the Rocky

Mountains (transferred image), or you may draw on an imagined idea (substituted image) based on photographs, films and "What if…?"

Your image might include several elements. The Swiss style of architecture can be researched. A bracing day is easy enough for the average Canadian to recall. An actor can approximate the "feel" of sunrise over high mountains — with bone-chilling cold followed by sudden warmth — by moving between sun and shadow beside high buildings. We can transfer or substitute other experiences and use our imaginations to provide the strongest emotional response to the Swiss sunrise. Indeed, the emotional response can be triggered by one or more images completely unrelated to the idea of "sunrise." The emotions will be there if the image is right.

At different times in our lives, we have all devised elaborate fantasies involving very strong emotions, but many of us keep them locked safely inside our subconscious. You can use the strongest ones for your acting to serve as triggers to release emotion. Whatever images you use should remain private and personal. Don't try to explain or share them. You can share them only by using them in your acting. Explaining images merely diminishes their power.

Emotional release

Emotions on stage differ from emotions in real life because they are founded not on the real experiences of the moment, but rather stem from emotional memory — which is a fusion of many elements. The actor can be involved, but there is a "safe distance" built into the recreated emotions. That's not to say they're false. They are just based on a different reality.

Emotions provide the release of a safety valve. They teach us about our relationships and experiences, and they tell us how we're coping with life. They lead us to action, or cause us to retreat through inaction. They can remain buried for weeks, months, decades, until something happens that sets them free. We cannot control our emotions, try as we might. But we can learn to understand the lessons they teach us. We need to understand our emotions because when they dominate us, even for a few seconds, they interfere with our control and our reason.

Emotional release is critical to the development of acting skills. Many of the more advanced exercises in acting classes are deliberately designed to challenge and probe the actor's defences, to break down long-standing barriers, and to elicit honest emotional responses from the individual.

Internalized emotional blocks are the enemy of the honest actor.

The point of breaking down emotional barriers is not to make you "feel good" about yourself, but to help you discover that your character is experiencing the same emotions that you have experienced in life. During the rehearsal process, these discoveries will help you find the truthful physical expression of those emotions. In performance, you will not merely stand on stage rooted to the spot, raging or gushing. You will be able to transform your emotional experience into action.

By the same token, imposing a physical expression of an emotion will often make the emotion itself seem stronger. Uta Hagen, the acclaimed actor and highly successful acting teacher based in New York, says that the mere action of banging a fist on the table can trigger feelings of rage. Physical action unleashes emotional life, and the one fuels the other. It becomes an enriched symbiotic process.

Each of us experiences a wide range of emotions during the average day. Trying to understand what affects us emotionally — and why — is one of the major pastimes of our conscious minds. Our subconscious minds continue to unravel our personal lives in our dreams.

Students often find it difficult to trust themselves when channelling emotion into their acting. The novice actor generally opts for a safe, flat, unemotional delivery that leads to stilted physical action. In particular, young actors can find it difficult to express two specific extremes of emotion: laughter and tears. But if you can get the initial attack of a laugh, you will often find the rest of the laughter feels genuine.

Here is a tip on initiating a laugh: imagine you are standing relaxed and vulnerable when, suddenly, someone beside you attacks as if to punch you in the belly. The sudden contraction of your diaphragm, which happens a split second before the blow strikes your stomach, will give you the initial kick into a laugh. Add vocalized sound to this initial contraction and go on to develop your sense of character within the laugh.

Some actors can turn on a flow of tears at the drop of a hat, yet those same tears will leave the audience unmoved. Why? The answer is simple: too much of one emotion can appear as self-indulgent to an audience. For example, "Boy, did that scene ever feel great. I really cried, I felt those tears!" You (the actor) may have a wonderful time crying, but it may mean nothing to us (the audience). How much more interesting to fight the tears, to refuse to give in to them, to explore other emotions — the opposites or less obvious acting choices that texture the speech. The ability to cry does not mean you are a good actor; it simply means you can keep your images and emotions bubbling near the surface. You must allow us in the audience to cry the tears you are battling.

There are many instances in creative drama exercises where a member of the group or class will appear to become emotionally upset by a specific exercise or experience. This is something that should be viewed by all as a natural and healthy expression and not as a sign of personal weakness or immaturity. (Support your fellow student, for you may be the next to break.)

Bottling up emotions can be frustrating and negative to our freedom of expression. Each of us in our own way must discover the best method for releasing natural emotional responses. To achieve this, the actor generally will focus on a private, personal "release" image — one little aspect of a larger emotional experience that lives deep in your emotional memory. Your image must be specific or you will end up playing "general" emotions. It is impossible to act general feelings. Be specific in your images, be specific in your emotions, and be specific in the actions that express the emotions.

Don't force yourself to use an image or an emotional memory that you yourself have not yet been able to process or deal with in your life. Such a difficult situation will absorb you entirely. That is the realm of the psychotherapist, not the acting class.

Sometimes an emotional reaction can be caused by an exercise that has deep personal significance. Perhaps a particular improvisation releases responses to events, emotions, or images that have not yet been dulled by the passage of time. This situation happens from time to time, and the law of averages suggest that most of us will be caught in due course in such situations. If you have trouble coping with your emotions in any acting situation, remove yourself from the exercise and simply wait until you regain your control. But it's a bit like falling off a bicycle: you have to get right back on again.

Emotional breakthroughs occur when actors are learning their craft, and these happen for a variety of reasons. Sometimes an exercise will elicit a response to a situation that has been buried subconsciously for years. Often the safety of a well-bonded core of performers will allow an actor to come to terms with some unpleasant past experience. Years of frustration can be released in an instant.

Sometimes, too, the subject of an improvisation is simply too close to recent activities. For example, the loss of a meaningful relationship in your personal life can bring a fragile edge to your acting work if the subject of your improvisation deals with the same theme. At other times, the cause can be traced to the joy that comes from experiencing:

- freedom of movement in space
- freedom through release from past guilt
- awareness of your emotional self
- acceptance of your physical self

The result of a breakthrough, however, can have exciting effects on the actor's immediate work. Remember that the study of acting does not progress in steady, measured steps. Rather, it goes along on one level, suddenly shoots ahead to great heights, then regresses to an all-time low. Thus, part of learning to act requires setting aside regular down times when you allow new information and recent experiences to settle into your subconscious.

Above all, acting demands that you not compare your work with anyone else's development. Understand from where you have come, keep fixed on your personal long-term goals, and don't get side-tracked by unnecessary comparisons.

Otherwise, even Sir Laurence Olivier wouldn't have been able to function on stage.

Chapter Twelve
Internal Approaches to Characterization

Getting inside your character's mind through actioning

One effective analytical approach to acting is known as "actioning." It will help you get inside the mind of your character. Actioning involves discovering the specific image and intention behind every line in the text and will help to deepen your understanding of character and motivation.

This technique requires having firm images in place before you speak, allowing images and emotional meaning to grow as the line unfolds. The actor's integrity of feeling can then communicate with others. Experiment. Explore. Leave aside your insecurities. Take risks. Don't rush. Take all the time you need in rehearsal to assemble images and motivations before you begin to speak. Don't feel any pressure of time as you progress from one image to the next, and don't let such pressure be placed on you by your fellow actors.

If you are a freely intuitive actor, you may not need to use the actioning building block at all. On the other hand, it may assist you through a rough part of a scene — now or two years down the road. If you have a cameo role, you may well have time to try this technique thoroughly. Be selective when and where you use it.

When considering actioning, or any other acting-technique exercise, bear in mind the following two pieces of advice:

- You can analyze and theorize as much as you like, but ultimately you must make it your own and be able to express it freely in your acting.
- As Tchaikovsky once said, "Inspiration is a guest who does not like to visit lazy people."

Actioning may be especially useful in a Shakespearean play. It is common for a novice actor to be intimidated by many components of Shakespeare's text: iambic pentameter rhythm, complex meanings, elaborate imagery, archaic language, difficult pronunciation, rules of scansion, and extended lines. Often, the real meaning behind the lines gets entirely forgotten, or the actor ends up merely trying to sound beautiful. However, he or she can get in touch with the intention behind the words through the technique of actioning.

1. Begin by looking for all the images contained within the speech or scene: real, transferred, or substituted. They should be as strong and clear as possible.
2. Then search for the emotion that accompanies the image — your personal reaction, triggered by the image.
3. Now find the "breath" expression of that emotion. The link between emotional life and physical action is breath. It is breath that carries the energy of the moment. Released sound will carry an emotion to the back row of the audience every bit as clearly as the written words of the script. Physical tension and/or relaxation will affect the breath cycle in three major ways:

(a) *It will affect the source of the breath:*

- Does your breath come from deep in the body?
- Is it placed in the chest?
- Is it caught in the throat?

(b) *What is the intensity of the breath?*

- Is it quiet or is it noisy?
- Does it change in nature?
- Is it consistent throughout the full extension of the mental image?

(c) *What is the rhythm of the breath cycle?*

- Is it steady or is it irregular?
- Does a rhythmic pattern emerge?

4. The energy of the breath leads to action. There are two types of action to consider: physical and vocal.

Rediscovering physical and vocal action

Physical action starts inside the mind/body: sometimes you feel hungry first of all in your stomach, and sometimes you initially feel hungry in your mind. Either source can lead to action. Action gradually moves outwards in a natural evolution of physical expression. It may involve some or all of this sequence:

- Your specific mental image leads to certain tension or relaxation in the muscles of your body.
- Your eye focus may shift from one person or object to another.
- There may be a physical realignment of your body — without necessarily getting involved in a blocking move. This might involve slightly readjusting a chair or, if you are standing, perhaps shifting your weight.
- You may expand to include gestures — hand actions, folding your arms, using a prop, adjusting your costume.
- You may make a blocking move — a clear, well-motivated repositioning of the body from one place to another.

Vocal action begins with breath and is tied into physical action:

- Your breath patterns shift with the tension and relaxation of different muscles of the body. This affects the source of the breath, its intensity, and its rhythm as you move from one emotion to another.
- Sound — laughter, gasps, groans, or such noises — may be released as part of inhalation and exhalation.
- Finally the spoken word, as provided by the playwright, emerges.

This is the process that acting should follow. When lines come out before images are firmly in place, before physical and vocal processes are ready, the acting seems hollow, parroted, or forced.

The next step

Images, emotions and breath can all come down to: "I want." We may not immediately believe that everything we do in life can be translated into an easily recognizable "I want," but think about it for a moment.

Take each line in your script and translate it into the pronoun "I" + an active verb. By using an active verb to express your character's intention, you will be providing something forward-looking, a clue to the physical action of your character. Don't express the verb in a passive form. If you need a refresher course in the distinction between an active verb and a passive one, here is a reminder: the active verb shows the subject as "acting," rather than "being acted upon."

> Active: I called the boy.
> Passive: The boy was being called by me.

For an actor, the stronger form of expression uses the active verb form because the active voice identifies the "doer" and places emphasis on the doer's action. In searching for your character's intention, find the verb with the most powerful connotations. Some active forms — like "I think," or "I reflect," or "I wonder" — are quite weak in that they don't hint at much external physical action. Instead, they are introspective and passive. Stick to a verb that implies the strongest possible action and stay away at all costs from weak verb forms.

Learning to express your intention in an active verb form rather than a passive one will enable you to find what your character will "do" rather than what your character wants to "be." In real life, no one wants to be angry or be happy or be anything, in fact. If an actor focuses on being angry or being happy, he or she will be trapped in a generalized emotion that doesn't provide specific, actable intentions. The actor will be trapped in stereotyped activities. This is known in the acting world as "indicating." To delve to the bottom of specific intentions and avoid indicating, the actor must ask specific questions, such as:

- What caused me to become angry?
- Who said what, or did what, to enrage me?
- What incident or comment tickled my sense of humour?
- Why did that particular remark or moment appeal to me?

Many playwrights use adverbs in their stage directions to describe the effect they envisage, rather than the cause. When a writer says in bracketed stage directions, "He enters hurriedly," this doesn't suggest what caused the character to rush onto the stage. The actor must find the cause of the actor's high energy in order to make the moment theatrically effective and avoid indicating a generalized state of being. The same principle can be applied to other given stage directions dealing with any emotion: anger, fear, joy, intimidation, lust, distress, or whatever. Look for the cause of the emotion, not the effect.

Many directors, too, will throw you a line in rehearsal such as, "Be more exhausted in this scene," emphasizing the effect as a shortcut to a desired result. It is up to you, the actor, to discover the cause. Through your imagination, provide the background circumstances that lead your character to the necessary emotional state. Then show us in the audience what created the emotion and how it manifests itself within the framework of your character.

For example, a playwright may create a situation where a character has been drinking heavily because this device permits that character to release thoughts and ideas that might otherwise remain hidden from view. The actions and comments of the drinker will surely create fresh conflict with other people in the scene who, in turn, may or may not be drinking.

In the hands of a novice actor, the character in such a scene will often lurch all over the stage with no sense of control and little insight into what it was that caused his or her character to drink so heavily. An experienced actor will fight against overplaying the effect of the drink because, in fact, when you are drunk, you do not wish to appear drunk. Your desire lies in the opposite way: you wish not to seem to be drunk. You want to show the world you can handle your drink. Instead, ask why your character has had so much to drink. What caused him or her to go this far? This is the insight you ought to bring to your performance.

Here is a tip for actors: to play a balanced sense of inebriation, focus your attention overly strongly on your feet and your eyes as if to say, "See, I'm not drunk. I can control myself." Everything between those two physical points remains loose and disconnected. The two contact points of eyes and feet will provide your movement with tension, in contrast to the looseness elsewhere in your body. This is an example of opposites at work again.

What makes for compelling theatre is the actor who (for example) traces the character's drinking problem back to a source such as "I suffer." Pain, and the source of that pain, provides the motivation for drinking. The character hopes that drink will dull the pain.

The specific choices you make concerning your character's motivation for drink will affect everything to do with your consumption of alcohol. Think of the differences in the manner in which people drink, remembering that social and emotional situations change even within the same evening. Here are some examples that illustrate the contrasting methods of accepting, tasting, and swallowing a drink, as well as a variety of emotional and physical responses to the drink:

- your "first ever" drink
- at a cocktail party where you don't have to worry about driving home
- when you are pressured by your peers, but don't really want a drink
- when you hate the taste of the drink that has been poured for you
- an "end-of-final-exams" in your last year of university
- toasting your new fiancée
- knocking back a fast drink to calm your panicked nerves

This is the challenge for the actor to reveal. This is where unearthing the strongest "I want" will provide the actor with the answers to his or her character's motivation. To ensure exciting, vibrant theatre, everything that every character in any play says and does must be rooted in the strongest possible "I want."

The actioning formula

If the above information could be summarized, condensed, and put into a formula or process, it would read like this:

IMAGES
lead to the
EMOTIONAL RESPONSE
that creates the
BREATH
that gives the character
ENERGY
which leads to
ACTION: PHYSICAL and/or VERBAL
This can be expressed as
"I" + an ACTIVE VERB

How to apply this technique to your script

To use this technique in the creation of a role, begin by looking at each line in the script and reduce it to one pronoun and one action verb. This is the point where most of us discover that our vocabularies are not as extensive and precise as we might wish them to be. However, the use of a dictionary and a thesaurus will greatly assist your work in this type of analysis.

Suppose, for example, we decide that a line can be reduced to "I" plus the active verb "cry." Examine a thesaurus to discover the shadings to the verb "cry." Here are some other types of crying mentioned in the thesaurus:

sob

wail

weep

bawl

whimper

sniffle

snivel

whine

break down

choke up

groan

moan

howl

blubber

Each of these cries has a different placement and type of breath behind it, and its own particular kind of sound which comes from a specific part of the body. Remember: breath has a source, intensity, and rhythm.

A whine, for example, is placed in the head, usually in the pharynx or nasal cavity. It is a long sustained sound and the breath is placed very high in the chest and throat. A moan, on the other hand, is much lower in pitch, is placed in the back of the throat, and is less energetic than a whine — although it is also a sustained sound. A sniffle is placed in the nose, has an erratic staccato rhythm, and can be easily worked between words in a line.

Here is an excerpt from *One Night Stand* by Carol Bolt. Let's see how these lines can be translated into a series of active verbs. The excerpt comes very near the beginning of the play. Daisy has just picked up Rafe in a bar that night, they have returned to her high-rise apartment, and they are alone.

Remember: there are no rights or wrongs in acting, just choices. The action words listed below in italics are simply suggestions designed to illustrate the principle of actioning at work on a text. Depending on whether you choose one action word or another, the images, emotions, physical action, and line interpretation of the same line of text can be strikingly different.

RAFE: I don't work. *(I tease.)*
        I'm looking for work. *(I clarify.)*
        I just got out of prison. *(I startle.)*
DAISY: Why were you in prison? *(I struggle for composure.)*
RAFE: I murdered a girl. *(I intimidate.)*
DAISY: *(backing away)* Now wait a minute. *(I stall.)*
RAFE: What's the matter? *(I push.)*
DAISY: You're kidding, aren't you *(backs away)*? *(I panic.)*
RAFE: You come here and sit beside me ... *(I demand.)*
        Come on ... *(I insist.)*
DAISY: No. *(I repudiate.)*
RAFE: Why are we chasing each other around the room? *(I bellow.)*
        ... Nervous, aren't you? *(I belittle.)*
        Is it because you're a vegetarian? *(I humiliate.)*
        Do health foods make you nervous? *(I crow.)*
DAISY: Who is it you murdered? *(I challenge.)*
RAFE: Is that why you're scared? *(I taunt.)*
DAISY: You told me you murdered a girl. *(I accuse.)*
        Who was she? *(I push..)*
RAFE: Look, I'm sorry. *(I soothe.)*
DAISY: Some fairly beautiful chick you picked up in a bar one night? *(I mock.)*
RAFE: Do you believe me? *(I pursue.)*
DAISY: Stay away from me. *(I warn.)*
RAFE: Look, I'm sorry. *(I follow.)* Daisy ... *(I woo.)*
DAISY: Get out of here, okay? *(I shriek.)*

Having completed this stage of the exercise, extract your own list of action words and line them up on a page like this:

DAISY	RAFE
	I tease
	I clarify
	I startle
I struggle for composure	
	I intimidate
I stall	
	I push
I panic	
	I demand
	I insist
I repudiate	
	I bellow
	I belittle
	I humiliate
	I crow
I challenge	
	I taunt
I accuse	
I push	
	I soothe
I mock	
	I pursue
I warn	
	I follow
	I woo
I shriek	

The next responsibility for the two actors in this scene is to search out an image that each of those active verbs suggests to them. Some images will be easier to discover than others. For example, most of us would not be too hard pressed to come up with an image that would lead to "I intimidate" or "I shriek." However, it is really important that you find a strong image for every action word. The stronger the image, the more easily the emotional response can be found.

Emotions and breath

Once those elements are in place, begin to discover the breath attached to each action word in turn. Rafe's first action phrase is "I tease." Find an imagined situation, or recall a real one from past experience, in which you wanted to tease someone else. Relax on the floor or sit easily in a chair and visualize this situation. Concentrate on your five senses in order to make the situation as real as possible for you.

Focus on this for several moments. Feel the emotions that are being released as you think. Decide what is inside you that might compel you to speak. Simply breathe within the emotion, in and out, over and over. Gradually build the intensity of the breath:

- Where is the source of the breath?
- What is the rhythm?
- Does this change as the breath develops, or as the image becomes clearer/less clear?

Find the physical action:

- What inner tension or relaxation of the muscles is occurring in your body?
- Where are your eyes focused?
- What happens to the alignment of your body as emotion intensifies?
- What does it make you want to do?

Let the physical action break out in a gesture and — if the emotion is strong enough — discover the right blocking move to accompany your image for "I tease." Now let the emotions build to a sound. Sustain this for a full breath, then let it build on the next breath. Try to express as much as you can without actually saying specific words. Finally try to put it all together step by step and, at the very last moment, speak the words as written: "I don't work." Having done that, repeat the process for the second action word, "I clarify."

image
emotions
breath
physical action
sound

Build everything until you must say, "I'm just looking for work." Add the third building block, the action word "I startle." Follow the same steps until you reach the point of exploding into the line, "I just got out of prison."

At this point, you might try going back to put all three of these together. The first time you do so, try it in the following manner. Take one big, deep breath in and out for "I tease." Then allow yourself to release the emotion and have a neutral breath cycle. When that is complete, proceed to the next breath cycle in and out for "I clarify." Again, breathe a neutral cycle before proceeding to the third one, "I startle."

Repeat the sequence of three images and breath cycles separated by a neutral breath, but this time allow each exhalation to explode into the lines that Rafe speaks. The final time, omit the neutral breath between each line. Just make sure you follow each image in the sequence.

When to use technique

To many people, this painstaking process seems an unnecessary amount of analysis and paperwork. Objectives and superobjectives are easier to deal with and they require less work. However, you may find it difficult to grasp a particular objective in one scene. You may discover that by choosing a dozen action words contained in the objective, you find the key to understanding the scene.

Some performers are intuitive in their acting and need little time to grasp the complexity of their character. Most of us become more intuitive as our acting skills mature and develop. But even the most "natural" actors may need some help with certain roles or specific moments in a particularly difficult script.

When to let go of technique

Here comes the surprise. Having done work at home with your dictionary, thesaurus, and actor's journal, you will probably not use many of your analytical discoveries in rehearsal. Be prepared to let go of these when you are up on your feet rehearsing.

Script analysis is just the starting point for insight and understanding. It requires that the actor work in isolation. But the process of acting is not a private activity. You must be willing to give and take in rehearsal, to feed off the new ideas and situations that your co-actors and director bring to the rehearsal. "Acting is reacting" is a commonly heard phrase, one that will drive the action of the play. Keep trying new interpretations, for you will only have scratched the surface of a character in the first few hours or days of rehearsal. Much more insight can be discovered through constant experimentation, individually and collectively.

You cannot bring your paperwork to rehearsal and simply attempt to recreate what you have written. Acting requires that you be totally involved in the moment — not in last night's moment, or last week's moment, trying to imitate on your feet the work you did at your desk. However, you will likely discover some interesting points for yourself when you employ actioning technique.

1. The deeper within your body that you breathe, the stronger and more personal your emotions will feel. In rehearsal and performance, when you don't believe what you are saying you will discover that you have not placed your breath deeply enough. What is happening is that your head is doing all the work and your body isn't involved.

2. In most scene study work, students don't have a director to help them. The actors may have no sense of where to begin to bring the scene to life. If you follow each of these steps in turn and practise in a space that is loosely set up to resemble the floor plan of your set, you will discover that you can block the scene yourself.

   You'll find that you don't necessarily need someone to tell you that you should stand by the doorway for this line, or sit on the couch for that one. You will intuitively know where to move, when to move, why to move, and how to physically express your character's motivation. This comes from a strengthened connection with the emotional life of your character.

3. You will be able to take direction more easily. Sometimes when a director suggests that you make a particular move in blocking, it will feel alien to you. It will feel as if the movement is externally imposed rather than evolving from inside your character. If you try to marry the director's suggestions with your own internal process, you can make the director's blocking suggestion work for you.

4. You will gain deeper understanding of the text and your character in rehearsal. Many of us are likely to be cast at one time or another in a role for which we have no immediate feeling or understanding. Perhaps the character is totally alien to our experience. For example, if the character has a totally different sexual orientation from our own, that element alone creates barriers capable of stopping many novice actors cold in their tracks.

Sometimes the language of the script hinders your understanding of the character. Almost everyone feels this when first approaching Shakespeare's text. Yet actioning works as well for Hamlet and Ophelia as for Rafe and Daisy. Actioning can get behind the words to the feelings, and put you in touch with images and emotions from your own experience — past, present, or imagined — enabling you to marry your emotions with those of your character.

Emotions are the universal threads that make up the fabric of our theatrical worlds. We share the same emotions that have been experienced by every person in history and in literature. In a well-written play, the answers are always there in the text — if you take the time to look deeply enough.

Chapter Thirteen
External Approaches to Characterization

Flexibility and imagination

There are exercises in acting technique that can help you see your character from a different perspective than script analysis may provide. These exercises are imposed in the same way that wearing a funny hat will make you feel silly, or getting dressed in your best finery will create a sense of confidence and power inside you. External character work may sometimes baffle you in its initial stages, but in time may enable you to bring fresh, imaginative ideas to your work.

Before we begin, let's look at some of the ways in which we approach problem solving, both in life and in acting. To illustrate, imagine you have an ordinary red brick sitting in front of you. List on a page all the different things that you might use it for. For example:

- building a wall
- propping open a door
- breaking a window
- hammering a nail
- as a paperweight

If you extend your imagination, you may find that some unusual or eccentric ideas pop up on your list. Things like:

- grinding it to a powder and poisoning the cat
- spray-painting it gold and entering it in a modern art exhibit
- decorating it with red sequins and white ribbon to wear at a Canada Day parade
- putting it in your knapsack and taking it for a bicycle ride

These examples illustrate two types of thinking and problem solving: convergent and divergent.

1. To converge means that two or more points come together and meet.
2. To diverge means to differ, deviate, go in different directions.

Convergent thinking is problem solving that focuses on commonly accepted methods of reasoning and deduction. It zeroes in on an expected result and generally follows logical thought patterns to reach a conclusion. It is intelligent and reasoned. **Divergent thinking**, on the other hand, may seem to branch out in all different directions at the same time. It often appears highly improbable, but it also has an inner, consistent logic of its own. Divergent thinking is, in fact, the source of much creativity and can lead us to think unconventionally in many phases of theatre work: writing, directing, designing, performing. We can learn to think in metaphors and analogies either as the result of conventional thinking or unconventional thinking.

The key to creativity in theatre, however, is to keep all your thinking patterns as open as possible. Never accept anything at face value and always look for an unexpected interpretation of a word, a phrase, or an entire character, no matter how bizarre it may seem at first glance. Ask yourself, "Is there another roundabout road that may help me discover the action of the play?"

Divergent thinking is one of the major components of the school of absurdist theatre, a great deal of political satire, and the bizarre view of life as expressed in the Monty Python television series. It can lead to the juxtaposition of outlandish characters in real/unreal situations, or the total inversion of social conventions.

Writers of absurd plays feel that, since the world has been thrown into turmoil with the arrival of the nuclear age, theatre should seem just as pointless and disjointed as life. The scripts of Eugene Ionesco and Samuel Beckett may initially appear confusing to someone who has been exposed only to traditional, realistic theatre. But these plays have a logic of their own which you can discover in time. For example, Beckett's *Waiting for Godot* creates a situation where two characters wait in vain on an almost bare stage for Godot to appear; they are waiting for action to happen. The seemingly "inactivity" of waiting defies the theatrical convention that "acting demands action." Many plays being written today contain some degree of unconventional thought.

Some of these plays address domestic conflict. In the hit play *Trafford Tanzi*, playwright Claire Luckham took the idea of the battle of the sexes and interpreted the plot using the metaphor of a wrestling match. The play is set in a wrestling ring and each character is interpreted in terms of the world of wrestling. The actors have to train as wrestlers, and get thrown violently about the ring every night in performance. The play has a referee and gongs that signal the ends of rounds. *Trafford Tanzi* involves the same type of audience participation that occurs at a wrestling match.

This novel idea created immense physical demands and dangers for the performers, but it generated interest among theatregoers everywhere. The script has been given many productions throughout the English-speaking world. It seems that the allegory of the wrestling ring works in dramatic terms to offer a fresh look at a well-worn subject.

Years ago, British director Peter Brook took Shakespeare's *A Midsummer Night's Dream* and interpreted the entire production as a circus, complete with trapezes, gymnastic stunts, and all the trappings of the circus world. The characters of the play lived in a "convergent" manner, that is, in keeping with expected circus behaviour. But the context of the play was the result of non-traditional thinking. Brook stripped the lush dream-world of the woods and set the play on a bare, white-and-black stage. From the moment Titania and Oberon made their entrances on bright, primary-coloured feather trapezes, the audience knew it was in for an exciting and imaginative evening of theatre. The production was a stunning international success and is still spoken of in awe by those who were fortunate enough to see it.

Applying imagination in convergent-thinking situations

Pouring and consuming a drink is a simple action that we rarely think about in everyday situations. But like every physical action on stage, it should be clearly thought out and well-motivated if it is to reveal some aspect of character to an audience in a realistic, conventional scene. Get a stack of disposable cups and have everyone in the room imagine they are to pour a drink. Physical action can and should reveal a wide variety of emotion and motivation.

- Try the exercise with many different types of drink in the cup.
- Pretend you're parched and have been without water all day.
- Pretend the cup is made of lead crystal, then institutional crockery, delicate china, tin, or plastic.
- Sometimes it's filthy, or someone has left a smudge of lipstick on the side.
- Whether you are alone or not will affect your use of the cup.

What changes occur in your use of the cup with each alteration of these elements? Does your own sense of character — who you are, where you are, what is going on, why you are drinking, how you are dressed — change with alterations? Your creative imagination will endow the disposable cup with endless variations. Experimentation is the key to creative action.

Here is an exercise that begins with convergent thinking but may lead to more imaginative use of a prop. Even convergent thinking, with its conventional approach to the use of a prop, can free up the imagination and help you discover fresh ideas to bring to rehearsal.

Exercise: 25 ways to use a chair

Place some chairs in a large circle and let everyone take a seat. Each person thinks of a character type. Freeze in an attitude and physical position typical of such a person. Then, using just your head, look around the room and "read" the body language of everyone else in turn. See what assumptions you make about each character: age, mood, social background, occupation, personality, and so forth.

Then everyone gets up and rearranges him or herself in a different position in the chair. Repeat the freeze. Repeat the process of assessing other characters in the circle. Your assumptions regarding some people will change because of their rearranged body language. Continue this exercise until everyone has struck 25 different poses with his or her chair.

As the exercise progresses and you begin to run out of conventional expectations in using your chair, your creativity takes over. The more imaginative, unconventional, and divergent you become with your use of the chair, the freer your thinking patterns will be. For example, initially you will likely sit on the chair in various positions. Later, you might end up draping the leg of the chair over your back (pretending it is a school knapsack), or begin to speak to it as if it were a person.

Repeat the exercise sequence, but this time use a hand prop or a costume piece.

Scene study exercises for divergent thinking:

The following exercises can be applied in rehearsal once you are familiar with your character, the conflict, the plot, and the dramatic or comic structure of the scene. These exercises work equally well with scenes or monologues, though you may find some of them difficult depending on the nature of the material you are using.

The first couple of exercises are warm-ups:

1. Begin by acting out the scene without using dialogue — simply through body language, facial mobility, gesture, and the release of basic sounds. Allow only a few sounds to be used — and then only at strong emotional points in the scene. This exercise forces you to use your physical self more than you have probably done up to that point in rehearsal. Breath is taken deeper into the body, so the connection between deep body breathing and emotions can be reaffirmed. Basic sounds provide the only method of vocalizing emotion in the scene.

2. Repeat the scene, but vocalize your emotions using gibberish or nonsensical language. When you can no longer speak the text the playwright has provided, you must try much harder to discover an emotional element in alien words. If gibberish is hard, try repeating the first line from a nursery rhyme. Read definitions from physics textbooks. Read newspaper articles backward to obscure the meaning. Read an instruction manual on changing sparkplugs — anything, so long as the material is totally removed from the text of the scene in rehearsal.

Now for the tougher exercises:

3. Repeat the first exercise above, but this time the size of the cast is doubled. Each actor in the scene is assigned a "twin," who acts as an alter ego. The twin speaks the lines he or she feels are necessary to the scene — and only those lines, sparingly and carefully — as the actor is going through the physical movement of the scene. Dialogue is not delivered in the manner of a narrator explaining

what is happening in the scene. Rather, it is spoken as the character experiencing the scene and using whatever lines come from that action. The twin and the actor are two halves of a whole. The twin's lines must come from the emotional life that the actor is providing. If the twin has nothing to say during the scene, the actor is getting immediate feedback that he or she is not releasing sufficient emotion to guide or prompt the twin to speak. The lines spoken by the twin may not be remotely close to those that the playwright wrote, but this point is not important to the exercise. For a really interesting twist, try using someone of the opposite sex as the twin. This is reminiscent of the device of cross-gender casting that was used with devastating effect by Caryl Churchill in *Cloud Nine,* a play that offers a fresh look at role-playing in historical and contemporary social conventions.

4. Translate the scene into a melodramatic bad opera. All lines must be sung in a grandiose operatic style, gestures should be extravagantly larger than life, emotions should be overblown and all sounds should be sustained. Note the word "sound," not music. This is not an exercise in singing, for there is no musical score. So it doesn't matter whether people think they sound out of pitch or not, as long as they keep "singing" in a confident and sustained manner. Encourage the actors to repeat words and phrases, as so often happens in real opera. They should strive to find strong emotional moments between characters, and overplay them outrageously. They should hurl themselves around the rehearsal space with great freedom. This is a very good warm-up exercise to make acting "larger," or help open performances up to fill large theatre spaces. It also reminds the actors of emotional relationships and it identifies strong moments of conflict.

5. Now that you have had a stab at an operatic career, how about trying a balletic one? You will likely need to spread out your rehearsal space in this assignment, for the extra extension to the actors' physical body line requires a greater area. Presenting a scene as a ballet automatically removes the dialogue from the actors once more; it also changes the type of communication between the actors in the scene. The exercise demands actors translate objectives into fluid movement with clear intentions and simple action.

6. Do the scene as a radio play, with the lines being delivered behind your audience so that they cannot see what is unfolding. They must visualize the action. This exercise places a greater

awareness on the vocal delivery of the lines. You will likely find you have to work harder, to point or emphasize certain things a little more carefully, when you can no longer rely on the visual picture to reinforce the meaning of the text.

7. Choose a famous character or personality from the entertainment world whom you could vaguely imagine being cast in the specific role you are creating. Take a few minutes to think of the physical appearance of that individual, his or her manner of walking, as well as speech patterns and whatever slang phrases or idiosyncrasies are associated with that person. Perform the scene imitating your famous character playing that role.

8. Try performing your scene in cross style. This means that you attempt to present your scene in the manner or style of a well-known film or play. Do your scene from *Leaving Home* as if it were *Gone with the Wind*. Present *Canadian Gothic* as if it were an episode from a current television situation comedy.

These few examples of a divergent approach to your acting are designed to keep you from becoming rooted in one approach to your character, and to extend your physical, vocal and creative abilities.

Acting to music

Music can have a strong influence on our emotions, although we may often be unaware that it is affecting us. One way to keep flexible and divergent in your acting work is to think about using underscoring music in rehearsal.

Sometimes you will encounter a scene that seems to flit along like a piece of Scarlatti's harpsichord music; at other times a scene will seem Wagnerian in its mood; and another time the scene will have the relentless impulse that reminds you of hard rock music. Some scenes are difficult to imagine without music. For example, the famous Act 1 meeting between Elyot and Amanda in Noel Coward's *Private Lives* is impossible to imagine without the haunting theme music that Coward wrote especially for the scene: "Someday I'll Find You."

Exercise: Underscoring

Find three contrasted pieces of music and rehearse your current scene or monologue with underscoring from each of them in turn. Classical music generally works best because you are less likely to become trapped in a continuum of rhythm. But within that framework, the diversity of style of composers is immense. You may find that the rhythm of your work changes depending upon the tempo or mood of the music. On the other hand, you may find the process interferes with your concentration (which is all the more reason to use this device in rehearsal).

Look at the scene between Beattie and George from Warren Graves's *The Hand That Cradles the Rock* on page 36 in *Behind the Scenes, Volume Two:*

- Read it aloud without any music, just to get a sense of the content of the scene and the style of the writing.
- Then play the opening moments of "The William Tell Overture" and see what changes occur as you reread the scene.
- Now repeat the exercise, but using the muted five-tone Chinese bells of "Tintinnabulation" or something equally mellow and distant.
- Finally, try the scene with underscoring from Gustav Holst's "The Planets." This piece of music is composed of seven movements — some warlike, some delicate — each one of which can generate a different emotional response.

You may discover that the rhythm and energy of the scene is very difficult to sustain, but you will probably find a moment or two where the music actually helps a certain point.

Metaphors in character work

There are other ways of keeping your thinking as imaginative as possible when working on a scene. The basic rule is this: don't present the scene as written. Play with it and experiment, no matter how bizarre or silly the exercise might be. You may discover something important that will help you when you return to work seriously on the scene.

The next exercise, "If I were a ... ," will provide further ideas for the interpretation of character, because it helps you think in metaphors. The exercise develops from one of the familiar cartoon stereotypes of dog owners: namely, specific breeds of dogs bear an uncanny resemblance to their owners. So it often seems that shaggy-haired dog owners have shaggy-haired sheepdogs, elegant women of fashion have elegant Afghans, cute perky people have cute perky poodles, and so forth.

Looking for similarities between animals and people has long been a favourite human pastime. In some of the sketches of contemporaries who modelled for him, the artist Leonardo da Vinci demonstrated keen insight and a real genius in ascribing animal characteristics to the human face.

The use of metaphorical imagery as illustrated in this next exercise can be of great help to an actor. Occasionally words fail us and we resort to describing someone or something in figurative terms, comparing him/her/it with something seemingly quite dissimilar. We say, for example, that someone is very country and western, while another person is described as a whirlwind. In both instances, we have a clear idea of the personality types. If we say that someone is like a Brahms lullaby, anyone with a passing knowledge of music will have an immediate grasp of the type of person being described.

Often, speaking in metaphors and similes like this can provide a more dramatic way of expressing ourselves.

Exercise: If I were a ...

This exercise can be fun for discovering refreshing and unusual approaches to creating a character. It can also help you find a new physical expression for your character or identify a rhythm on which to base that character. To begin, take a piece of paper and a pencil and at the top of the page, write the following line:

If I were a_____, I would be a_____.

Under the first blank, write the following list of categories:
1. wild animal
2. automobile
3. household appliance
4. article of clothing
5. house pet
6. flower
7. office equipment or industrial machine
8. bird
9. song
10. kitchen cooking implement
11. colour
12. drink
13. city/country

279

14. food
15. sport
16. musical instrument

Choose a specific character from a major play or a well-known film, or someone from a television program. With this individual firmly in mind, begin to fill in each of the blanks in the second column. But don't stop at filling in the blank. You must also be prepared verbally to justify each selection or description in your list.

When you read your list aloud to the rest of the group, identify only whether you are describing a male or female and whether that character is from a play, film, or television program. Despite these restrictions, it is remarkable how often people can correctly identify the character you have selected for the exercise.

It is sometimes helpful to take a well-known example to illustrate the exercise. For example, let's look at Juliet in Shakespeare's tragedy *Romeo and Juliet.* The following choices are a matter of interpretation, and each actor approaching the role of Juliet will bring her own ideas to the character. But for the sake of illustration, here are some suggestions with a justification for each choice:

1. If Juliet were a wild animal, she might be a gazelle: something rare and exotic, high-strung, delicate yet strong, fast and very beautiful.
2. If she were an automobile, she might be a Ferrari: Italian, maybe with a rich burgundy paint job, black leather interior, elegant and exotic, capable of rapid high speed.
3. If she were a household appliance, she could be a convection oven, whirring with energy and capable of becoming very hot much faster than an ordinary oven.
4. If she were an article of clothing, she might be a delicate ivory-coloured lace shawl, or perhaps a flowing nightgown adorned with ribbons and flowers, suggesting a sense of something romantic, fragile, timeless, and lovely.

We might discover that colours in a similar range repeat themselves in many of the images in our list. (Dominant colours of red, white, and black can be found throughout the script of *Romeo and Juliet*.) Burgundy — mentioned above — is associated with passion, blood, and wealth. Or we may find many images have white or off-white shades connected to them, because white is the symbol of purity. Elements of speed and impetuous action, so vital to the story line, are reinforced in many of the selections. A sense of privileged class, beauty, innocence, passion, and energy will likely appear several times each in the exercise list.

One thing to remember is that such descriptions must be made from the actor's perception of the character he or she is creating. It should not be viewed as the character in the play doing a self-assessment. If you are using a character from a television sitcom, make sure it is the actual character portrayed each week that you are describing, not the actor who plays the role.

This is a simple exercise, but it can be helpful in generating group discussions in the early stages of rehearsal. Share your ideas within the cast or group. Often, when an actor has a problem finding the strongest possible word or song or animal, another cast member will have no trouble coming up with the ideal descriptive word.

Let's take a look at an example from a scene on page 45 in *Behind the Scenes, Volume One*. In *Leaving Home* by David French, Jacob is the towering father of a transplanted Newfoundland family. He uses every trick to manipulate and control the members of his family, ultimately alienating those he loves. He is intensely complex on the one hand, yet capable of great love at times. Even if you do not know the play or character, simply reading the following 16 points will give you a good idea of Jacob's fundamental nature:

1. If Jacob were a wild animal, he would be a lion. He roars down others and relies on brute force and the intimidation of strength to keep control. He travels alone through life, save for a mate and two cubs.

2. If Jacob were an automobile, he would probably be something sensible like a pickup truck: no pretensions, sturdy, a bit battle-worn and rusty around the edges, but reliable.

3. If he were a household appliance, he would be a washing machine. He churns things up all the time on a daily basis. He is solid and straightforward in his approach to life.

4. If Jacob were an article of clothing, he would be an old, plain navy wool roll-neck sweater, with patched elbows and particularly baggy around the waist. There would be something comfortable and yet sad about it.

5. If he were a house pet, he would be a tomcat of indeterminate age. He would actually live in the barn and put in only an

occasional indoor appearance — at his convenience. His ragged ears would provide evidence of many midnight scraps.

6. If Jacob were a flower, he would be something very sturdy and serviceable like a brown chrysanthemum. Indeed, Jacob might never rise above being a dandelion. He would certainly not be perfumed, delicate or tall.

7. If he were a piece of machinery, he would be found in a factory, not an office. He might be an oversized machine used in processing or manufacturing, one that repeats its cycle endlessly and works steadily through three shifts a day.

8. If Jacob were a bird, he would be turkey (and the word is not used in its current pejorative or slang meaning here). Turkeys generally are overweight, can barely fly and tend toward unpleasant dispositions. They lack the beauty, sociability and songbird attractions associated with most varieties of birds.

9. The category of song is, in fact, an easy one to decide on if you have read the entire play. Jacob's song is the traditional Newfoundland number "I'se the b'y that builds the boat."

10. If he were a kitchen implement, he'd be a plain wooden spoon that has seen a lot of use. Nothing modern, nothing mechanical, yet something that can pack a wallop.

11. Jacob's colour is dark and earthy: probably brown, although the navy blue of the sweater could be repeated here.

12. If Jacob were a drink, he would be draft beer.

13. For the category of city or country, Jacob would be an outport in Newfoundland, a fishing village that has clung tenaciously to the coast for hundreds of years with barely a sense of the passing of time.

14. If Jacob were a food, he would undoubtedly be one of the staples of the Newfoundland diet: cod and brewis, heaped upon the plate in generous amounts.

15. If he were a sport, he would be boxing — antagonistic, lashing out at others with unexpected violence. Boxing is an individual sport rather than a team sport, and Jacob is headstrong and independent.

16. If Jacob were a musical instrument, he would probably be a pair of spoons being played on the knee of an old codger at a tavern.

This exercise can give you insight into many aspects of your new character and help you feel more comfortable in the role. For example, if you find the right article of clothing that symbolizes your character, it could become part of your costume in a specific scene. The exercise might guide you to a piece of music that your character sings when entering a scene. Necessarily, you will come to know your character thoroughly because you are required to justify each example. In the process of applying this exercise, use the strongest words that define your character.

The animal persona

This subject continues along the theme of the previous exercise. It is a more complex level of work, however, with more physical demands being placed on the actor.

We all know someone whose appearance, movement, vocal patterns or habits remind us of an animal or bird of some type. Perhaps it's the "pack rat" type of person who squirrels everything away. Maybe it's a person who moves in a sensual, feline manner. Or maybe it's an excitable impish child whose family even teasingly nicknames him the "little monkey." Just think of the words from the animal kingdom that we use to describe other people and their actions. Here are a few to illustrate the point:

- They were all in a flap.
- Like a bear with a sore head.
- He's a real toad.
- Listen to them squawk.
- Slimy as a snake.
- I'm such a silly goose.
- He behaved just like a cat among the pigeons.

Our language is rich with substitutions, similes, and nicknames derived from the animal world.

Sometimes the animal persona is strongly written into a script. For example, it is difficult to think of the character of Maggie in Tennessee Williams's *Cat on a Hot Tin Roof* without considering the many parallels between Maggie and a cat in heat. Feline, sensual movement, her seductive preening at the dressing table, her relationship with Brick: all these must be examined with a strong sense of the animal persona. To do otherwise would be unfaithful to the integrity of the character as written by Williams.

Every good British pantomime has at least one animal in it. Think of James Barrie's *Peter Pan*. What would it be without Nana, the family dog? Consider shows such as the modern smash hit *Cats,* based on T. S. Eliot's poetry. In the 16th century, we have *Volpone (The Fox)* by Ben Jonson. Then there is the modern political satire *The Insect Play* by the Brothers Capek.

These plays — to name just a few — were all written in different time periods, in different styles, and dealt with widely different subject matter. Yet each of them uses animals, each in its own way, for specific theatrical purposes in creating the story line.

Exercise: Animal persona

In this exercise, the actor experiences some improvised situations while pretending to be an animal or bird, then extracts from that process whatever physical elements may be useful in character work. Animals experience life through the five senses, which is the key to animal persona work for the actor. Not only will centres of movement, weight, and power be discovered, but also rhythms and tempos will be found. Vocal sounds, speech patterns, and instinctive attitudes to others will be experienced.

Both parts of this improvisation should contain whatever sounds or noises feel right, but each individual must focus only on his or her body and surroundings.

To prepare for this exercise, make sure the floor is clean. Remove your shoes (and any loose or noisy accessories such as bangle jewellery), and take a comfortable position on the floor. Turn off all overhead lights if possible.

> *Part one:* Begin by creating a situation where you and the entire group are sleeping. When each of you awakens, you will do so as a bear. Working individually and involved only in your own five senses, emerge from sleep as if from a winter's hibernation. Enjoy the feeling of the sun. Look around. Go searching for some food. After discovering the food and eating sufficiently, doze off with a sense of contentment in the midday sun. This should take between two and four minutes to complete.
>
> *Part two:* Repeat the situation, but translate it into human terms. Awaken as a human being lying on the living-room couch, but a human being with bear-like qualities. Stretch a bit, look around, and go to the kitchen to find something to eat. Having found some food, lie on the sofa in front of the television and eventually doze off again. This should last between two and four minutes.

- What did you discover in exploring the world through senses and instinct?

- Did you rely on thought?
- What were the similarities and the differences between the two stages of the exercise?
- How was your outlook on your world altered, both as the animal and as the animal persona?
- What did you eat?
- How did you move?
- What did you want at each stage of the improvisation?

Repeat the exercise two or three times with other creatures, such as:

- cat
- snake
- butterfly
- raccoon
- guard dog
- ostrich
- chicken
- cocker-spaniel puppy
- giraffe
- swan
- squirrel
... and so forth

This exercise will enable you to extract an understanding of the physical sensations of the animal that you have chosen. Insight and understanding will be found through discovering the rhythm of the creature, its breath cycle, centre, energy level, and mannerisms.

Your perceptions and level of awareness will change from one animal to the next depending on your personal understanding of the animal: the different types of food that each one eats, contrasted eating habits, differing methods of bedding down for a nap, and so forth.

Less obviously, you will discover altered impressions of the world and altered self-images. This can be very useful in getting actors outside their own central universes and personal perceptions of the world.

Exercise: Group animal personae

The purpose of this next stage is to create two or more contrasting animal personae, to see how strongly this technique will heighten the contrast of characters when transferred to human terms. Once again, remove your shoes and loose jewellery before beginning work. Choose two or three partners for this exercise. Each member of the group then selects a different (and well-contrasted) animal or bird. Sounds can be incorporated if helpful.

Each group then creates a situation where the two or three animals meet, such as:

- an escape at the zoo
- a crisis in the barnyard
- a meeting at the water hole
- stalking for fun and/or food

Repeat the first stage of the previous exercise, first coming to life as animals and then interrelating in a manner that is as true to life as possible.

On finishing this stage of the exercise, create the human situation in which each person retains his or her own animal persona. The setting here will change to:

- shopping at a department store in the Christmas rush
- the first day at a new school
- newcomers gathering for a social club picnic
- gossiping at the office water cooler

Conflict will be built into the situation through the contrasted animal personae, as will a variety of vocal patterns, centres, energies, habits, rhythms, and characterizations.

At times, it takes a great deal of searching to find the exact animal persona to use in creating a character. Avoid modelling your work on your pet dog or cat, because you will inevitably bring a pre-existing emotional connection to the exercise.

Observation is the key to success in animal persona work. This gives you a good excuse to visit a zoo and/or read up on the animal you have chosen. If possible, observe your animal in its natural habitat and going about its daily functions. Don't merely rely on generalized knowledge and vague past memories, or your work will be generalized and vague.

During the rehearsal of a play, if you are worried that your character seems too "similar" to another character in the play, animal persona work can provide the basis for studies in contrast. This technique is very helpful in improvisation work and ensemble creations, too.

It can also be a lot of fun.

Chapter Fourteen
Psychology and Acting

Digging deeper into characterization

M odern psychology provides another important "internal" approach to character work in acting. The interior psychology of a character must be plausible, believable and well thought out by the writer, director, and actor. When an author doesn't provide solid psychological clues, the director and actor have to work harder to bring the fullness of the character to life.

This chapter deals with psychology applied to the actor's craft and is distilled from the writings of a number of psychologists. Their work in this century has had a profound effect on humankind in general. As a teacher of acting, I do not profess to be an expert in their field and it is not my intention to validate their theories. Rather, I present them as another tool for the actor to consider when developing a character. Knowing these theories may help you enrich the interpretive work and emotional texture of your acting (refer to Chapter 11, "Characterization: fundamental questions to ask"). In addition, they can provide you will concrete approaches to improvisation work.

Acting can almost be described as another form of applied psychology. The work of Sigmund Freud, Carl Jung, Alfred Adler and a host of other researchers and writers can help to give the actor fresh viewpoints, provide stimulating new ideas, or present yet another way of approaching character work — as well as giving deeper insight into the actor's own psychological make-up.

Thinking with the left brain and right brain

One area of cognitive research in personality functions comes from recent developments in the study of the brain, which have begun to explain the mysteries of mental processes and activities:

- The **left side** of the brain governs words, text, and the sequence of time. It allows us to identify and evaluate events.
- The **right side** of the brain governs sounds, interpretive meanings, context, and subtext. It gives us an awareness of space and allows us to interact with what surrounds us.

An understanding of this dual nature of the brain can be useful to the acting student. For one thing, it provides a method of understanding acting development and performance skills. Sometimes we respond well to one type of exercise, but not to another. Why? Perhaps we tend to rely a little bit more heavily on one type of brain activity over the other. Certain acting exercises may be viewed as left-brain stimulants, while other exercises can be considered catalysts for right-brain activity. Naturally, a synthesis of both activities occurs in almost every one of us.

The fully trained actor must develop the mental functions of both sides of the brain rather than relying too heavily on one side over the other. Additionally, an understanding of the dual nature of brain activity makes it easier to explain why particular exercises can be very difficult for one actor but not for another. Here is an exercise that illustrates the distinction between the functions of both sides of the brain and reinforces our understanding of how both elements are necessary to good acting.

First, choose a scene that you and your partner have been working on for a time. Demonstrate it in front of others and ask them to watch carefully to see how much they can conclude from your work. Urge your audience particularly to look at the relationship of your characters, the emotional levels in the scene, and its overall dramatic power. Ask them to remember their impressions clearly, for you will be presenting the scene again. Your audience must remember the first viewing clearly for comparison purposes.

Then run through the two steps below, looking first of all at an exercise that stimulates more left-brain activity than right:

1. *Left-brain exercise:*

Because the left half of the brain governs the literal meaning of words, it would take a very long time to perform the following exercise using an entire scene. Instead, just take a portion of your scene. This exercise will slow down the pace of the scene to a complete crawl, so make sure you and your partner work on an excerpt with a lot of give and take in the dialogue — rather than individual extended monologues.

From now on, forget about the meaning of the text as a whole and work on each isolated word in turn — without rushing any moment. Before you say each word in the sentence, focus on an image for that word. Don't say the word until you know its full meaning. When considering sensory words, a literal image can be easily created. But you must force yourself to think about every single word in the line, even "the" and "of." Each word will be sustained for one full breath cycle (much like the "Row, row, row" exercise in Chapter 5).

By isolating each word from the others around it, you will break up the context of the dialogue. The original intention of the author will be lost completely and the words themselves can be treated as totally separate items, each with an independent existence. Even in a scene of high comedy, the humour will no longer be evident.

Here is an excerpt from Margaret Hollingsworth's play *Ever Loving*. The scene, which appears on page 70 of *Behind the Scenes, Volume One*, takes place between Ruth and Diana on the train while they are en route from Britain to join their Canadian husbands. It is their first glimpse of the vastness of Canada. First, read the scene normally with a partner, then approach the script with a view to applying the above left-brain exercise.

DIANA: Fir trees.
RUTH: Aye. And do you know they're full of bears. Dave told me. I wonder what the cows eat? It's all trees.
DIANA: Lovely colours. They must be maples... See ... those red ones. That's their national tree.
RUTH: National tree? *(thinks)* We've got the thistle.
DIANA: They call autumn "fall."
RUTH: It feels ... different. Creepy. Foreign. *(pauses, has no word to express her feelings)* Big.
DIANA: Don't look at it.
RUTH: I can't help it.

DIANA: Well, don't.
RUTH: Don't shout at me.

Now try an exercise that makes heavier demands on right-brain activity than left. The simplest way to minimize the literal meaning of the words is to remove the words altogether from the scene:

2. *Right-brain exercise:*

Using the same excerpt, remove all the words contained in the lines and communicate the real meaning of each line to your partner simply through sound. Remove all the consonants contained in the text and allow yourself to express emotion and subtext only through colouring the voice on the vowel sounds.

Since the text is no longer able to assist you, emotional release will have to be exaggerated in this exercise. Allow your body to express itself more freely. Read your partner to see what you can get from his or her sounds, body language, and emotional release. Let this stimulate an even greater response from you.

In the scene from *Ever Loving,* for example, the characters experience a number of emotions. An actor must decide on:

- the relationship between them, having travelled in close quarters for three weeks
- their apprehension of — and anticipation at — meeting their men again
- their sadness at leaving everything familiar back in Britain
- their insecurities and inner doubts about this major change in their lives
- their loneliness
- their genuine emotional reactions to the unfamiliar landscape they are watching through the train window

Isolate these emotions. Put them in sequence and then release them as fully and freely as you can. Use your body, gestures, and facial reactions to support your work. Because of the strong tensions between the two women and their deep internal insecurities, the degree of emotional release in this exercise can be a bit frightening to the uninitiated.

Now that you have completed both steps of the exercise, repeat the scene yet another time — as originally written and in its entirety — with your partner. Ask your audience to indicate what kinds of changes they have witnessed this time, in comparison with your earlier presentations.

If you are like most people in the early stages of acting training, the second step of the exercise will prove to be very difficult. We tend to bottle up so many emotional responses throughout our everyday lives that it can be difficult to break out of a pattern of restraint. But removal of the literal meanings of words forces the actors in this exercise to focus on the real intent behind those words.

Connecting Freud with acting

While the whole range of Freudian and Jungian theories of psychology are better dealt with in their textbooks, it is appropriate to review some of their popular assumptions in relation to acting. One internal approach to characterization involves applying the psychological approaches, vocabulary and techniques of **Sigmund Freud** (1856–1939) to the text of a script. It has proven to be effective with actors searching for character motivation, and can provide insight into why various combinations of characters are almost doomed to continuous conflict within the plot development of a play.

Freud is deemed to be the grandfather of modern psychology. His concepts of the **id**, the **ego**, and the **superego** — three interwoven but distinct aspects of the human personality that exist continuously within each of us — make it easier to understand the complex nature of the human spirit.

The id:

Freud defined "id" as that part of the personality that is spontaneous and instant. It is the closest element to our true natures. The id is seen most easily in a young baby: everything in its life is "me-oriented." During the socialization processes of childhood, the ego and the superego start to form and the id becomes less visible.

The id does not think; it only wishes or acts. It encompasses:

- our immediate reactions to sensory stimulation
- what is said or done to us
- our physical surroundings
- our basic animal drives

Freud believed it to be the most obscure part of our personality. It is associated with instant gratification of pleasure and the avoidance of pain (he called this the "pleasure principle"). Much of what we know of the id comes from the study of dreams and neuroses.

One example of the id at work can be seen if you are sitting in a darkened room and another person enters, suddenly turning on a bright light. Your id reacts spontaneously, resulting in wishing or action. Your id can react simply by wishing that the light be turned off. On the other hand, the intrusion of light can lead to action. Action can be either physical — such as squinting your eyes or turning your head away — and/or verbal, leading you to ask or demand that the light be turned off.

For the actor, focusing on the id can offer a new perspective on the understanding of a character. What your character in a play regards as pleasing or worthy of pursuit can often be at odds with your own personal, natural inclinations. How and why we "choose" to react to situations can be used by actors to convey aspects of personality that may only be hinted at in the text of the play itself. Choices are limited only by the actor's imagination and understanding of the script.

The ego:

Freud defines the "ego" as the reality principle; it is the aspect of the character that allows it to function in the real world. In the well-adjusted personality, Freud believed, the ego controls or governs the id and the superego, much as if it were the "executive" of the personality.

Freudian psychology says that the ego is what allows us to tolerate uncomfortable situations by thinking the problem through rationally. It depends on reasoning to help us put up with unpleasant but temporary situations. The ego involves an awareness of the real world and the use of memory. Thus, the ego allows us to tolerate the sudden intrusion of bright light in a darkened room, for we can rationalize its necessity or usefulness.

It is the ego that says, "I want to be a doctor and even though I don't like chemistry, I'm going to need it to get into medical school. So I have no choice but to buckle down and learn this chemistry."

The ego is constantly assessing our idea of "self." This understanding begins to form in a baby once it realizes there are other children in the house who place demands on the parents' time. Things become more complex when the young child goes out into the neighbourhood. Our concept of self continues to alter through life as we become increasingly aware of the complexities of the global community and the dilemmas that each of us face every day of our lives.

For the actor, discovering the nature of your character's ego using Freudian analysis may be a tremendous challenge. In some scripts there will be a few instances where the action of the character's ego is clear. For the most part, the actor must create the ego that drives the character. You must discover links between thoughts; if the links are not there, you must create them.

The superego:

Freud said the "superego" is the moral or judicial part of the personality, that which strives for a sense of the ideal. It is formed by pleasant and unpleasant influences on us in childhood from parental or authority figures, and can affect our behaviour. Consider:

- "Big boys don't cry!"
- "Don't giggle in church!"
- "Clean up your room!"

These comments are based on the promise of reward and/or the threat of punishment:

- **Reward**: "You're Daddy's best girl!"
- **Punishment**: "Don't come out of your room until your homework is done!"

Eventually, the external influences on us that form our superego become internalized. We develop our own methods of living up to (or rejecting) our rewards and punishments, according to Freud. This is where guilt — that most universal, destructive, and long-lasting of all emotions — comes into full prominence. It can affect our behaviour and the choices we make in life.

We become overly fussy people who cannot sit down and relax after dinner until the dishes are all washed. Maybe we turn into workaholics, incapable of spending time with our families because of a driving ambition rooted in childhood experiences. Perhaps we become people who tell a little white lie, then over-berate ourselves for weeks thereafter.

Formation of the superego includes influences of education, religion, and peer-group pressure. Whether called Freud's "superego" or some other term, what most of us struggle with throughout life is learning to balance expectations. We develop methods of role-playing in different daily circumstances in order to accommodate those various opinions.

At different times in the same day, we may have to function as:

self	self
son	daughter
husband	wife
teacher	lawyer
best friend	club manager
grandson	godmother
uncle	aunt
choir member	bridge partner
neighbour	mother

Each of these roles demands a specific kind of adjustment in our role-playing within relationships. In turn, this may affect our physical appearance, body language and speech habits (both in our choice of words and in our manner of delivery). It may affect our self-perception and our response to other people's behaviour.

The maxim "one man's freedom fighter is another man's terrorist" conveys a sense of the conflicting demands made of us. It means that we often have one external source in our lives saying to us "this is wrong" and another equally powerful influence saying to us "this is right." Any two people will judge your actions and statements from different perspectives based on their own experiences and beliefs.

Freud said that the superego allows us to regulate impulses, such as aggression and sexuality, in socially acceptable ways, by reinforcing or rebuking the ego that controls our actions.

For an actor, your character's superego (like the ego) must be based on information that can be extracted from the script. Then you must create an entire "other world" for your character:

- Decide on your character's relationship with his or her parents.
- Visualize some childhood incidents that affected the emotional development of your character.
- What effect did religion and education have on the formation of your character in the play?
- What internal conflicts can be found in your character?
- What caused those conflicts?
- What is your character's deepest secret? (This may have nothing

directly to do with his or her function in the play.)

- What triggers guilt in your character and why?

In life, we know that when the superego is taken to extremes, physical effects like headaches, ulcers, and other interesting sublimated traits can appear. These can be useful in creating a character. For the actor, repression of an earlier trauma — taking a memory out of the conscious mind and putting it into the subconscious — produces a barrier of anxiety.

Remember that the names id, ego, and superego are simply methods of designating different functions within us, according to Freud. He believed them to be totally intertwined: the ego is formed out of the id, while the superego is formed out of the ego. When problems occur in this evolution, the ego can deal with it by various means, such as refusing to think about it, worrying about it to the state of creating a neurosis, or projecting problems of its own making onto other people.

This is a very brief summation of Freud's work. You might like to review these illustrations showing id, ego, and superego at work.

Example #1: You are walking down the street, and you see a $20 bill lying on the sidewalk. You reach over to pick it up. What do you do with it then? In simple Freudian terms, it is the id that gives the first, spontaneous reaction to spotting the $20 bill: the reaction to sensory stimuli. The ego then says, "Hey, $20! Fantastic!" and causes you to lean over and pick it up.

Depending upon your own sense of personal morality, you may choose to pocket the money, or look around for someone who may have dropped it, or decide to turn it over to a charity. The superego would be busy at work here. It would be this factor that would probably make you look around to see who witnessed you pick up the money.

This simple example, like any improvisation situation, can be given dramatically different treatments by incorporating other influences into the action. For example, your reaction could be very different if you were taking your six-year-old nephew for a walk when you discovered the money. You might choose to "set a good example" for the child, and search out a police officer in order to hand the money in to "Lost & Found." (This action, according to Freud, would in turn be helping to form the child's superego.)

Your reaction to finding the money could be different again if you were with a group of your friends, broke and hungry, with all of you keen to share a pizza. The presence of another person can modify our behaviour because of the expectations of our role-playing with that individual.

Example #2: You walk into a party with a date. The party is in full swing when suddenly you see the Vision of your Dreams across the room. All your hormones stand up and say "Whoopeee!" That would be the id at work: releasing spontaneous and uncontrollable chemistry that complicates existing personal relationships.

   The ego would be the part of you that deals with the dilemma of how to meet your Vision — without appearing to come on too strongly — and how to cope with the another problem: having arrived at the party with a date. The superego would be the part of you that wonders what others (the two individuals involved, your friends, and the rest of the partygoers) will think of you if you dump your date and begin to make a move on the Vision.

Once again, the drama of the situation can be altered by an awareness of other relationships: suppose your date is your boss's favourite offspring. Perhaps you are not emotionally involved with your date, but you realize that, if you cause unpleasantness, you may jeopardize relationships in your career.

Using Freudian theories in acting technique

In theatre, the battle between the id, ego, and superego can sometimes be applied clearly to a script. Characters could be said to contain all three elements — like us — but may be dominated by one of these functions. You could have an id-dominated character in conflict with a superego-dominated character. You can presume that they will rarely manage to communicate on the same wavelength, intensifying any conflict between them.

   Similarly, you could call a well-adjusted character ego-dominated. As the plot develops, the superego or id may increasingly dominate him or her. Generally, this kind of growth or disintegration of character opens the way to interesting personality changes during the course of the play. The Freudian approach may provide a wealth of interesting acting choices for the performer.

   An understanding of the three Freudian functions can lead to dynamic discussions about characters and relationships in scene study work. Freudian psychology can be a practical tool in setting up improvisation sequences. It provides a method of establishing three different strongly contrasted character types in an improvisation, by giving each individual a different dominant.

As an actor, then, your job involves finding in rehearsal the most effective dramatic or comic moments that reveal the inner conflict of your character. In performance, it is important that you share these conflicts — not necessarily with other characters, but with the people in the audience, who need to understand what makes your character tick.

Remember that the most effective moments in theatre often involve the use of opposites: contrast in emotions, characters, or energy. It is with this sense of opposites in mind that Freud's theory of the id, ego, and superego can be very effective in unspoken moments. The sudden shift from one part of the personality to another — from superego to id and then back again, for example — can create heightened dramatic or comic moments.

Improvisation situations based on Freudian theories:

1. Three girls — each with a different id, ego, or superego dominant — enter a darkened nightclub that is about to present a risqué male strip show. Trace their various reactions during the episode. There will likely be a strong contrast between all three characters when each girl is focusing solely on one dominant. What happens when you add the sudden appearance of a fourth person whom no one expected to encounter there?

    Repeat the improvisation three more times. Have each actor try approaching her character through a different dominant on the next two presentations. Finally, each actor should integrate all three aspects of the personality, enabling her to make her character complex, real, and believable. Her character will experience the inner struggle triggered by such an emotional situation. She will no longer be a one-dimensional character but a fully textured and complex person.

2. An id-dominant applicant enters an office looking for work and is met by a superego-dominant secretary. He or she is eventually ushered in to meet an ego-dominant boss. Reverse the dominants twice and repeat the exercise in order to explore how each character alters in his or her attitude toward the other. Blend all three aspects of the personality in a fourth and final presentation, striving for believable complexity of character.

3. A teenager breaks the news to her parents that she is expecting a baby and wants to keep the child. Allow each of the characters to

express all three aspects of the personality in discussing the problem, but see which dominant ends up strongest in coping with this emotional crisis.

Applying Freudian theories to scripts:

This technique obviously works best in those kinds of plays that can be described as psychological studies. On page 54 of *Behind the Scenes, Volume One*, for example, take a look at the excerpt from Ted Galay's play *After Baba's Funeral.* This play provides an interesting study of complex family relationships and an understanding of the psychological effects of one person's behaviour on another individual.

Netty, mourning the death of her mother, is reminiscing with her friend Minnie about her early family life on the prairies. We get a vivid insight into Netty's childhood background and environment. Her son, Ronnie, who has returned home from British Columbia for the funeral, has rejected the traditional values of the immigrant farming community and created his own life away from his family roots. His parents have trouble accepting this independence. Tension is created by this conflict.

Ronnie and Netty exchange terse words and Ronnie points out that his mother has told the same story twice already. Netty dumps another guilt trip onto Ronnie, saying:

NETTY: So what if I have. It's so hard to listen to me? *(Pause)* Never mind. You'll go Sunday, you won't have to listen to me anymore. *(Turns to Minnie)* You look forward to your kids coming home and they treat you like dirt.

Many of us can identify with the conflict in this situation (knowing how difficult it can be to get rid of unsought Freudian "guilt" created by others) and can use Freud to help understand the characters and their motivation in this scene.

In the classic Henrik Ibsen play *Hedda Gabler,* the characters can be identified as being dominated by one of the three Freudian factors:

- Hedda is id-dominated — impulsive, irrational, focused only on her own needs and ready to scream with frustration that she has no control over the events of her life. She is a 20th-century woman trapped in a 19th-century situation. "How mortally bored I have been!" she says in describing her six-month honeymoon.

- George Tesman, her husband is superego-dominated — very aware that others will envy him because he has married the most prestigious lady in town. He spends money he has not yet earned to keep her in style. His concern of what relatives and neighbours will think of Hedda's increasingly irrational behaviour causes him mounting anguish as the plot unfolds.
- Aunt Juliana Tesman, who raised George, is dominated by superego — she goes into debt and overlooks many deliberately rude actions by Hedda (most notably the bonnet business in the first scene) out of deference to Hedda's superior social standing.
- Thea Elvsted, Hedda's friend, is ego-dominated — she is able to function in the real world, difficult as that may be for her at times. Thea is one of the few people in the play capable of making a decision and acting on it. She believes in her own ability, has the courage of her convictions, and finds the power to carry on despite adversity.
- Judge Brack also is ego-dominated — he is able to work out the strategy that he feels will eventually drive Hedda into his arms. But because he expects the same process of response from her, he fails in his ultimate objective. His last line of the play, famous for the irony it contains, is "Good God! — people don't do such things."
- Eilert Lövborg, Hedda's former lover and an equally untamed creature, is id-dominated — a romantic, dramatic figure who lives life to the maximum, with all its excesses. When the one great piece of writing he has created is lost, his reactions are wild and passionate, springing from the id.
- Even the modest role of Berta, the Tesman's servant, is superego-dominated — "I'm mortally afraid I shan't be able to suit the young mistress."

Of course, each character contains elements of all three aspects of personality, but each is governed by one dominant quality. To summarize the character dominants in this play, then, we have the following categories of Freudian personalities:

Id	*Ego*	*Superego*
Hedda Gabler	Thea Elvsted	George Tesman
Eilert Lövborg	Judge Brack	Aunt Juliana
		Berta

It is not mere coincidence that, within the play, the same dominant types agree:

- Hedda and Eilert had a long-standing relationship that fell apart only because of her sense of social convention — a force with which Hedda did not agree, but which overwhelmed her own instincts.
- Thea and Brack are the only two people who have a grip on reality and can function well in any situation. They are the survivors.
- Tesman, Aunt Juliana, and Berta have lived together over several decades. They can understand each other, not just through the familiarity that time brings to relationships, but also because they are responsive to their superegos.

It is no surprise that when id or superego dominants cross over to deal with each other, they are doomed to miscommunication and failure. Only the ego dominants end up coping by the end of the tragedy.

This Freudian summation of *Hedda Gabler* underlines how an understanding of psychology can enlighten your comprehension of a script, deepening your insight into the relationships between characters. When you are working on a text that is "psychologically thin," knowledge of some psychological theories can be useful.

Connecting Jung with acting

Another method of applied psychology is based on the writing of **Carl Jung** (1875–1961), the noted Swiss dream analyst. Jung divided our mental functions into four categories or **modes**:

- thinking
- feeling
- sensing
- intuitive

The last of these is important in improvisation, as you learn to trust your instincts. However, it is the first three modes — **thinking, feeling and sensing** — that the following section will deal with in greater depth.

Jung believed that each of us tends to be either introverted or extroverted in our view of life:

- An **extrovert** is one who is quite outward-looking, oriented to the objective outside world, concerned with people, ideas, social and political events, and the physical world.
- An **introvert** is an inward-looking individual who is preoccupied with seeing everything in subjective or personal terms. Often this private world is not even accessible to our own conscious mind, but can be understood only through analysis or dreams.

Jung, in fact, delved into the study of dreams in some depth. But creating a "dream life" for your character is an element that — for the actor — is not "playable."

We all have situations in life in which we become extroverts and other situations where the opposite is true. Because we generally appear as one type or the other in daily life, on those occasions when an introvert suddenly becomes energetic and outgoing (or an extrovert suddenly clams up), interesting character revelations can appear. Conflict between the three modes, as well as between the introvert and extrovert parts of our personalities, provides the very essence of theatre. Our personalities, neuroses, creativity, and psychoses emerge from these tensions. Thus, an understanding of the role of conflict and opposition within the personality can be very useful for an actor when developing a fully realized character.

The thinking mode:

Jung believed the "thinking-dominant" individual is ruled by focused thought. Everything is seen in terms of logic. He or she is drawn to numbers, patterns, sequences, and ideas. This personality type will react to any given situation with an immediate, detailed analysis of all the implications and ramifications of the circumstances. Such an individual will readily devise a strategy favourable to his or her purposes, and is generally good with money matters, scientific study, or theoretical pursuits.

Because of this predisposition to intellectual thought, matters such as emotions and the senses play a limited role in his or her life. Thinking-dominants often appear to be living in the future: worrying about the next stage of a problem, looking down the road, trying to anticipate what's coming next, or projecting strategy on a giant mental chessboard.

The feeling mode:

According to Jung, the "feeling-dominant" person is governed by his or her emotions. Everything is seen in terms of what it means emotionally. If something is pleasant, it makes that individual feel good. If it is ugly or distasteful, it leads to negative feelings. Every situation in life is evaluated in terms of what it means emotionally to that individual.

Understanding factors that cause different emotional responses is a tricky area and often the secret lies in our subconscious past. The feeling of disliking a certain individual on sight may not stand up to rational thought processes. Yet, that person may remind you subconsciously of someone who was cruel to you when you were a child, or perhaps a character in a horror film that terrified you years ago.

The "emotional baggage" you carry with you from those experiences throughout life makes you project similar emotional reactions onto other individuals. Because feeling-mode types see life in very personal and subjective terms, they can be susceptible to mood swings. These moods often seem to defy logic from other people's viewpoint. Because so much of their reaction is based on personal life experience, Jung described them as past-oriented. They rarely are aware of their immediate situation, let alone the future, he maintained.

The sensing mode:

Jung said that the "sensing-mode" dominant lives very much in the present and is caught up in the five senses of sight, sound, touch, taste, and smell. Our reactions to most given situations, he said, are based on how these five elements respond to sensory stimulation. Sensory awareness is not just the result of external factors. It can be rooted in the individual's physical well-being. Sensory awareness is not logical or rational and, therefore, often defies traditional thought processes, according to Jung.

Sensing-dominants are very aware of physical surroundings, colours, texture, warmth or cold, physical pain, atmosphere, aesthetics, hunger and thirst, physical exhaustion, the comfort of a chair, and so forth. Jung believed they can often be pleasure-loving sensualists who tend to view life only in terms of the immediate situation.

According to Jung, each of us possesses elements of all these modes, but we are dominated by one. That specific mode rules the personality. Let us combine some Jungian dominants to see what kind of improvisation situations actors might explore. Remember that the combination of

Jungian opposite types will make for stronger theatre because conflict will be inevitable.

Using Jungian theories in acting technique:

Jung's theories are particularly applicable to improvisational characters and situations. For example, thinking-dominant person (A) is having a serious conversation with a feeling-dominant character, (B). Conflict emerges if:

- (A) is expecting (B) to understand his or her rational arguments.
- (B) is hurt that (A) doesn't understand his or her emotional make-up.

If a sensing-dominant (C) is being interviewed for a job by a feeling-dominant (D), conflict appears as:

- (D) makes an immediate emotional assessment of whether or not he or she likes (C).
- (C) is more impressed — favourably or otherwise — by the surroundings, atmosphere and climate control than by actual salary considerations.

Imagine the three personality types each being given $500 to buy some new clothes:

- The thinking-dominant will immediately scan the newspaper ads in an efficient manner, comparison shopping and searching out a deal. A trip to the other side of town to find a bargain will seem perfectly logical and worthwhile. The final outfit may not be the most fashionable but it will represent good value for money.
- The sensing-dominant will immediately go visit a store which provides a soothing environment — beautifully decorated with effective displays and equipped with attentive sales staff — and begin to search for the right fabric, the right texture, the right colour, and the right outfit to make him or her feel glamorous. Price really is of little importance
- The feeling-dominant, governed by emotions, will likely respond quite differently. He or she may boycott a particular shop because of the way a sales clerk behaved years earlier. On the other hand, the feeling-dominant will likely be influenced in decision-making

by past experiences and end up choosing something that seems familiar and "me."

Using Jungian interpretations of a sales situation, we can see how a smooth sales clerk will size up a customer and automatically respond on the same wavelength. For example, if a sales clerk recognizes a customer is looking for value, that will be the major thrust of the sales pitch. If, however, the customer is seen to be looking for clothes that appeal to the senses, discussions of colour and line will be important in closing the deal. If the sales clerk determines that emotions might help sell the product, the clerk will try to form some type of personal bond with the customer — talking about the weather, discussing general or common subjects.

Certainly, if there are two individuals who relate to each other on the same wavelength, they are more likely to understand each other and to follow the other's thought patterns — but there is no guarantee of this. Some people just do not work well with people who are too similar to their own personality type. If two individuals are approaching the same situation from opposite types of perception and understanding, conflict is even more likely to occur, according to Jung.

Jungian observations could provide rich personal or professional insights in life situations, improvisation, or in script work.

Improvisation exercises based on Jungian theories:

Choose some acting partners, and establish simple situations such as those mentioned above applying Freud's work to improvization. Instead of using id, ego, and superego as dominants, substitute in their place thinking, feeling, and sensing modes. Then allocate one or other of the dominant modes to each character and see what happens when Jungian psychology is applied to help create the conflict in the relationship. Remember to explore each of the dominants in turn so that you may experience and understand changes in attitudes and character that occur from each new perspective.

Applying Jungian theories to scripts:

Let's look first at a fairly well known play and discuss the application of these Jungian modes to the three principal characters. The play is *A Streetcar Named Desire* by Tennessee Williams, and the three characters are Stanley Kowalski; his wife, Stella; and her sister, Blanche du Bois.

Although each of the characters is discussed below from the point of view of a dominant mode, such over-simplification is designed only to illustrate a brief application of Jungian psychology. It would be a mistake for any actor to approach one of these roles using only one dominant mode while ignoring the other modes in the character's personality.

None of us is that simple. We flip from one "dominant" to another in daily situations, often within seconds. For example, you may be sitting in a theatre arts classroom at the moment, reading this section in your text. You are using your thinking mode to understand what you are reading. Suddenly, your stomach rumbles and you become aware of feeling hungry — that's your sensing mode at work. Perhaps the chair you're sitting on is too hard and you realize you're not comfortable. Maybe a draft blows through the room. This is more sensing mode at work. Then someone nearby interrupts your thoughts and, because you have an existing relationship with that person, you react emotionally — positively or negatively — to their comments or actions. Now your feeling mode is taking over.

Each of these changes in mode can come spontaneously from inside us or they may be the result of external stimuli. If such changes can happen to you in a few seconds, don't expect your character to remain governed by just one mode for a two-hour performance.

Let us say, in Jungian terms, that Stanley is a sensing-dominant who lives in the immediacy of the moment. When he is hungry, he demands food. When he is thirsty, he grabs a beer. He sees his existence in terms of his own needs, not those of others, and he lacks an awareness of the effect of his actions. It's all "me, me, me" — sight, sound, touch, taste, smell — and he is slow to understand how other people function.

However, Stanley has his moments when other modes begin to work. His research into Blanche's past illustrates that he can use a thinking mode when he needs to. But the overall nature of his character springs from a sensing mode.

Blanche, on the other hand, is feeling-dominant. She lives in time past and relishes her memories of more gracious living. These thoughts, and the feelings they arouse in her, are more pleasant than her present surroundings and her bleak future. The present and future hold no attraction for Blanche. Because a great deal of her immediate past is unpleasant, she has rejected and sublimated it, substituting instead a world increasingly full of fantasy. She is a "feeling introvert" who is on a downhill slide, escaping from reality.

Jung might say that Stella is the thinking-dominant person because she holds everything together. She has a better understanding both of Stanley and Blanche than they do of themselves. She can cope with the realities of her life because she can rationalize what she is getting out of life, balanced against what it is costing her. She will survive.

There is a complex character study in a scene from John Murrell's *Waiting for the Parade* on page 77 of *Behind the Scenes, Volume Two*. Using a Jungian focus, we could say that Catherine is a sensualist. She is aware of her own physicality and sensuality, and she speaks in words of strong imagery. Here she is reminiscing about her relationship with her husband, Billy, who has gone away to war. Yet, she intersperses these memories with fantasies of Jim, the man at the plant where she works. Between her two longest monologues about Billy, Catherine says, "I nearly didn't say 'No!' Yesterday afternoon. To Jim!"

With your own background and/or personal standards of behaviour, you may have trouble understanding Catherine's apparent lack of fidelity. Certainly in the same scene Margaret has trouble understanding her friend's statement. In response to Catherine's admission, Margaret says, "Well, I think that's terrible!"

If you yourself are a thinking-dominant or a feeling-dominant, you might not be able to relate to the sensing-dominant Catherine. But because she lives in the present, Catherine is able to love Billy while not necessarily remaining faithful to him while he is away at war. A useful key to developing Catherine's character in rehearsal is to use a Jungian focus on the five senses in Catherine's life to discover an important key to how she functions from day to day.

Understanding yourself/understanding your character:

It could be interesting to analyze your own personality using the Jungian analysis. Each of us has varying amounts of all modes within our personalities. We can flip from one to another with startling rapidity. Think how often we get into a disagreement, which becomes an argument, which develops into a full-fledged fight. When you later reflect on what happened, you will probably discover that your thinking mode got confused with your feeling mode.

Because emotional responses do not follow the same logic as do intellectual thoughts, we end up confusing the whole discussion with a lot of unrelated issues. Additionally, we are extroverts in certain circumstances and introverts in others, and we often do things without realizing why. Sometime, it can take years of self-analysis before we understand the reasons behind certain decisions, or understand events long since buried in the past.

When you are beginning to create a new character, it can be helpful if you have a clear understanding of your own personal dominant mode: whether you are thinking-, feeling-, or sensing-dominant. Your challenge, then, is to approach your character from a different mode.

If you are a thinking-dominant, try to create your character from a sensing mode based on a very physical foundation. Scour the script to find instances where you can incorporate sensory work and awareness of your physical surroundings. Find the right costume and accessories. Take an external approach to creating the character.

If you want to develop a feeling-dominance, project images onto other actors and props:

- Free up your emotional responses to those images.
- Allow yourself to luxuriate within the appropriate emotional moments in the action of the play.
- Develop sensitivity to the mercurial opposites of emotions.

Should you want to approach the creation of a character with a thinking-dominant mode, you must do a great deal of script analysis. Carefully search out the reason for your character getting from Thought One to Thought Two on every page of the script. Look into your relationship with each individual and consider how every twist of plot affects that relationship. Be analytical. Devise a diagrammatic approach to character development for, after all, that is what your character would do, isn't it?

Not every play will provide you with clearly identifiable Jungian modes, but the technique remains an interesting approach to keep in mind with every new script you address. It can also be very helpful to keep in mind when you are searching for a "handle" on a character in an improvisation.

Connecting transactional analysis with acting

There is another method of psychological analysis, based on the work of Eric Berne, that the actor may find helpful in taking an internal approach to creating a character. It is known as transactional analysis, or TA, and the technique can provide still another way of understanding a role and the complex relationships between characters in a script. Unlike Freudianism, which looks at personality as isolated in the individual, TA looks at personality as a dynamic of the interaction between people — hence, "transactional."

TA deals with the behavioural role-playing that we do in everyday life: the things we say and do to one another. It identifies the types of role-playing we employ during the course of our lives and the way we move from one mode to another. Other people's reactions to us have the power to affect us emotionally and, in turn, affect our assumed roles. We flip in and out of many different roles during the course of a single day, let alone during the course of our lives.

In comprehending others in the world around us, in understanding the diversity of reactions to what we say and do, we continually analyze other people: their physical body language, mannerisms, vocal intonation, facial expressions, and a host of such observations. Watch what happens inside you when you are walking down a busy corridor at school or when you are at a shopping mall. We take what we "read" and interpret it in the framework of what we already know of the world. Like non-stop computers, we feed the information into our brains and, consciously or subconsciously, come up with a revision to our existing knowledge and experience of life.

For example, TA explains that when people listen to stories, they take what happens in the tale and interpret it within a personal understanding based on their own experience. What you say stirs up images, emotions, and memories in others' minds so that they often end up thinking of their own experiences, rather than listening to what you are actually saying for the balance of your story.

Teachers often comment that 35 different students will hear the same lesson in 35 different ways. In saying this, such teachers are interpreting class behaviour using TA. Actors should also be aware of this fact, for it reinforces the need for absolute clarity of intention:

- in every word of the text
- in every physical action on stage

Because of its analysis of role-playing in life, TA may help us understand ourselves, which is a critical first step for an actor. However, the principles of TA can also be applied in acting to give you yet another way to approach improvised characters and script analysis.

*The **analysis** part of TA:*

According to Berne, in TA there are three parts to the personality, known as the:

- child
- adult
- parent

The terms do not relate to the age of a person, for each of us may play the role of child, adult, or parent at any time. The ability to play these roles appears in childhood and continues throughout life, says Berne.

The term ego, which was discussed earlier in Freudian psychology, also appears in TA. It might be a good idea to reread that earlier section to become reacquainted with the emergence of the ego in the personality:

- The **child-ego** state incorporates the same kinds of natural impulses that we felt when we were children. It's the part of you that says: "Let's go play with my new toy," or "Wow, can I get behind the wheel of your car for a spin around the block?" or "You're nice to be with."
- The **adult-ego** state involves our ability to gather and assess information on a daily basis without emotional factors getting in the way. It is objective and organized. For example, the adult-ego state says: "What time should I be here for rehearsal?" or "Well, I'm going to have to do this eventually. I might as well get it over with now."
- The **parent-ego** state involves the behavioural patterns — feelings, thoughts and action — that we observed in our own parental authority figures. Often these patterns emerge as critical or negative ones, though they can be nurturing. The parent-ego state says: "Do not interrupt when I am talking," or "I cannot believe the trash those kids listen to on the radio today," or "Forget the calories in that piece of cake. Don't you think you should keep your energy up?"

Berne says the child-ego state is the first to appear in an infant, as the pleasure principle is seen at work very early on. Next, the parent-ego state appears with the child imitating its parent figures as it plays, pretending to be Mummy or Daddy. Then the adult-ego state develops as the child understands the larger world and relates things to his or her own experience.

In a well-developed personality, the adult-ego state becomes the executive part of the character. All three parts are well integrated, but the adult-ego state dismisses (when necessary) the red herrings of the child- and parent-ego states. Although all three states exist in each of us, says Berne, one of them tends to dominate our personality and approach to life.

*The **transaction** part of TA:*

The transaction element of TA, according to Berne, is the sending of a message and its reception by another person. This message may not be verbal, but rather dependent on gestures, body language, or facial expressions. If it is verbal as well as visual, there may be a discrepancy between the text and the subtext of the message.

Berne says an **open transaction** is one where the reaction to the message is appropriate, natural, and straightforward. Here is an example of an open transaction from one child-ego state to another:

- "Wow, can I get behind the wheel of your car for a spin around the block?"
- "Hey, great! Why don't we take it over to your brother's place and he can come with us."

Here is an instance of open adult-to-adult communication:

- "What time should I be here for rehearsal?"
- "Don't bother to come till 8:30. By then I'll have finished with the first scene, so we can pick up where you enter in Scene 2."

One parent-ego state to another might react with an expected open response like this:

- "I can't believe the trash those kids listen to on the radio today."
- "And the way they dress nowadays is frightful. Whatever happened to the idea of looking neat and tidy?"

An open transaction does not necessarily mean that one ego state is talking to a matching ego state. Expected responses can cross between either of the other two ego states and still be considered open because the comments are expected, natural and logical to both parties in transactional analysis theory. For example, consider these responses to: "Wow, can I get behind the wheel of your car for a spin around the block?":

- An adult-ego state may say, "Sorry, the insurance won't cover you. Do you want me to take you for a drive?"

- The parent-ego state may respond, "No, it's too muddy. I just washed the car and I don't want you getting it splattered."

If the initial questioner was expecting such a result, communication between the two is considered to be open.

According to Berne, a **crossed transaction** is the root of most of our arguments and stress in life. It arises from a situation where the answer to the original message is not the one that the sender anticipated receiving, or oftentimes particularly wanted to hear:

- "Wow, can I get behind the wheel of your car for a spin around the block?" says the child-ego state, expecting to be responded to in a similar child-ego positive manner.
- Suddenly from left field comes a parent-ego response: "You're a terrible driver. Don't think I'd be so silly as to let you have the keys."

  What is the result? Hurt feelings, confusion, a possible argument, or perhaps the beginning of a long-term grudge.
- "What time should I be here for rehearsal?" Here, the adult-ego state is expecting a similar adult-ego response.
- If met with a child-ego response, we hear: "Why bother? No one's going to come see our dumb old play anyway."

Again, the result is hurt feelings and confusion. The next several minutes are wasted trying to justify the time spent rehearsing the show.

- "I can't believe the trash those kids listen to on the radio today."
- Fully expecting a supportive response, the parent-ego state is met with an adult-ego response such as, "Oh, I don't know. I think there's an interesting focus on issues today and modern technologies are creating entirely new combinations of sounds."

The parent-ego state sniffs an indignant "harumph" to this unexpected response and an air of tension is created between the two individuals.

These are some examples of crossed transactions between two ego states. Many of our arguments follow repetitive patterns that result from crossed transactions. Think of your own situation. Consider how frequently you can predict that specific conditions will develop into out-and-out conflict between certain members of your family or your circle of friends, following a very well-worn path of crossed transactions.

The next time you are caught in an argument, employ the TA approach and determine which ego state is dominating your partner. If you respond from the same perspective (child/child, adult/adult, or parent/parent), the chances are you will reach an understanding more quickly by improving communication and minimizing the duration of the argument.

Psychological scripts

TA analyzes the **psychological scripts** that each of us follow in our lives: the programmed responses that date back to our parents' expectations of us and our childhood role-playing. An understanding of TA psychological scripts can be particularly helpful in acting, bringing fresh insight to improvisational choices and character work. Script application involves several factors:

- cultural elements (ethnic, nationality)
- a variety of subcultures (religion, regional geography, and peer groups)
- family scripts (long-held traditions and expectations)
- individual psychological ones based on one's early life experiences

The answers to "Who am I?" and "Why am I here?" can be found from these four elements of TA.

According to TA, scripting messages are put into words that send powerful messages to the child:

- "You're just the cleverest little one! You're going to become a brilliant scientist one day."
- "Shut up and stop bugging me. You're nothing but a pain, so leave me alone."

In either case, the child will be strongly influenced by these messages.

Messages come originally from our parents and immediate family. In time, other messages come from our extended family, friends, teachers, classmates, and various adults who coach our extra-curricular sports and activities. Each person will send supportive or contradictory messages that affect our existing image of self. Also to be considered are the values that our religious, educational, ethnic, and cultural systems hold dear or denigrate. You just have to pick up a newspaper and read about the latest civil wars or examples of ethnic cleansing to understand the strength such messages carry in many civilizations.

The child learns to select or manipulate others to create a "cast of characters" to use in following his or her "life script." This accounts for why some people are constantly attracted to certain types of people or situations. We create self-fulfilling prophecies through increasingly sophisticated role-playing. But we each have the capacity to change our "expected" role. Once we know what makes us tick, we have the potential to change our behaviour.

Applying transactional analysis theories to acting:

TA can be applied both to improvised situations and to script analysis. Here are some ideas for discussion and application:

Improvisation exercises based on transactional analysis:

1. Devise a scenario for three people that deals with a teenager being encouraged by friends to take his or her first drink. The central character is to perform the scene initially from a child-ego state, one of the friends from a parent-ego state, and the second friend from an adult-ego state. Repeat the exercise twice more, changing the ego states around until each person has approached the same character from all three ego states.

   You will discover that the relationships and conflict will be substantially different from one improvisation to another, merely because there is a consistency of thought when playing a single-minded ego state. Sustaining a character's outlook in an improvisation may become easier for the actor, because TA provides an identifiable central focus for character work.

   Repeat the improvisation a final time, allowing each character to move from one ego state to the other and back again, as we do in real life. This will texture the performances, making the characters more believable, human, and vulnerable. It is likely that one character may be dominated for much of the action by one particular ego state. In this last step, do not sustain any particular ego state. Just let the exercise unfold.

2. Put three groups of three actors each in the following situation, with each group presenting its scene in the same setting. Avoid stereotyping or obvious choices in this exercise. Here is the

situation: a customer is returning merchandise because it is of poor quality. The newly hired sales clerk is trying to deal with the matter but the supervisor overhears and becomes involved:

- Group 1: the customer is adult-ego state, the sales clerk is child-ego state, and the supervisor is parent-ego state.
- Group 2: the customer is child-ego state, the sales clerk is parent-ego state, and the supervisor is adult-ego state.
- Group 3: the customer is parent-ego state, the sales clerk is adult-ego state, and the supervisor is child-ego state.

3. Create an improvisation from these suggestions using one partner. Apply your understanding of Freud, Jung, and transactional analysis as you try to find real, believable, and unique interpretations for your characters in the following relationships. Be aware that the situations and characters suggested below are fraught with stereotypes, so avoid falling into obvious traps:

- a customer and cashier at the supermarket checkout
- a husband and wife discussing finances
- two young teenage girls planning their futures
- a motorcyclist and a traffic officer
- a boss and secretary dealing with a work problem
- an environmental protester and the head of the workers' union
- a panhandler and a passerby
- a teacher and a student discussing an assignment
- a truck driver and a motorist after a minor accident
- two friends deciding whether or not to crash a party
- a loans officer and an applicant
- a photographer dealing with the bride-to-be
- a prominent politician and the investigative reporter
- a doctor and a terminally ill patient
- the intellectual leader in the class and the slow learner
- an older couple planning their retirement
- an athlete talking with an actor
- an applicant for part-time work at a gas bar

Examples of script work using TA: Perhaps one of the easiest scripts to which you can apply transactional analysis is John Patrick's play *The*

Curious Savage. The residents of "The Cloisters" are all representative of the child-ego state, the medical staff who run the institution are clearly examples of the adult-ego state, while Mrs. Savage's avaricious family members neatly fit the description of parent-ego states. The comic impetus of the plot occurs when these three ego states come into conflict. Yet, because the characters so rigidly fit their ego states, the entire play takes on a predictability (you know it's going to have a happy ending) and is filled with sentimental clichés.

In *Behind the Scenes, Volume One,* the excerpt from *A Wife in the Hand* by Jack Crisp on page 17 demonstrates the concept of TA. It is interesting to discover throughout the play which character ego states remain fixed, which are in a constant state of flux, and what causes them to change. Such a discovery will give you an immediate clue to creating the characters.

At the beginning of the scene, Valerie is speaking from the child-ego state as she says, "Good morning, this is your hostess, Valerie Scott. On behalf of Captain Bligh and the crew, I'd like to welcome you all aboard."

James responds with a parent-ego state, "Alright, alright ... very funny...." A couple of lines further, when she has had time to become even more annoyed with James, Valerie gets sarcastic and speaks back to James from a parent-ego state. Bitingly, she asks whether James's pregnant daughter is married. James then shifts from the parent role to the adult-ego state with, "That wasn't very nice."

The relationship between these two characters gets off to a rocky start because they don't communicate in an open adult-to-adult manner until after James apologizes. At that point they agree to tackle their problem sensibly. In the opening minute of the scene, however, they are demonstrating crossed transactions one after the other. Actors rehearsing this scene should be aware of the source of such conflict.

These methods of applied psychology — Freudian, Jungian, and Bernean — are included in this acting book for two major purposes:

1. Self-comprehension is the single most important initial step for a serious actor. Perhaps one of these techniques has helped you to understand more about yourself or others in your family, classroom, or theatre group. Maybe you have gained some insight into how your mind works. Possibly you can reconsider the dynamics of some relationships or free yourself from the

ghosts of the past so that you may more easily deal with the demands of the task at hand.

The process is a slow one, a never-ending one, and a creative one, but essential to anyone who strives for integrity and growth in acting. The more you learn about yourself, the more easily you will be able to work with others — your director, fellow actors, and technical crew. If you can discover how you function as an individual, and if you can begin to acquire insight into the workings of your colleagues, the chances are that the creative process of rehearsing a scene or a production will be more harmonious and exciting.

2. It follows that the more understanding you have of how the human spirit functions, the more insight you will bring to your character development. The resulting character will be dramatically different from your own personality. You can stretch yourself within your acting work, take on challenging roles, and avoid the problem of playing "safe" characters. Typecasting is more common in film and television than theatre, but there are still sufficient examples in stage work of actors who remain locked within a limited range of characters.

We all know of film actors who spend their entire careers merely playing variations of the same basic character type:

- the actor who always plays the "good guy"
- the ingenue who portrays the eternal, chaste teenager
- the character actor who appears as the friendly neighbour
- the actor who is always cast as the psychotic murderer

This predictability can be as frustrating for the audience member as it must be for the actor involved.

But we also know of actors who are constantly looking for challenging new roles: characters of wide-ranging types, situations, and conflict. Such actors take chances, and can achieve greatness in their work. They go beyond merely entertaining people to inspiring an audience with their vision.

Chapter Fifteen
Stimulating New Ideas in Acting

Mask work

This chapter deals with the devices of masks and rhythm as aids to creating a character. The use of masks in early acting work has long been recognized as a valuable technique in freeing up the expressive use of the body. When you can no longer rely on your voice or facial reaction to carry the emotion of the moment, new demands are placed on the ability of the entire body to communicate the message.

Mask work gets the actor away from television acting (where the face and eyes do most of the work) or overly internalizing thoughts and emotions, which is common to novice actors. It not only teaches you to use the body in free and expressive movement, but develops your ability to read body-language messages in others.

There are two main styles of mask, each of which is available in full- or half-mask versions:

1. The neutral mask is devoid of expression and is generally painted flat white.
2. Character masks have exaggerated features and are often decorated with hair and strong colours to look like character "types."

Exercises are given below for individual and group mask work. These will work equally well with neutral masks or character masks and, if you are fortunate enough to have access to both styles of mask, you may find it interesting to try repeating one exercise using both.

Half-masks allow greater freedom of sound and speech and are best illustrated by the comic masks of *commedia dell'arte*, the travelling comedians of Renaissance Europe. Character masks can be useful in illustrating how we prejudge character types, relationships, and intentions by the way we "read" others. Mask exercises can be followed by discussion about how we correctly or incorrectly read the body language and facial expression of others.

Preparation for mask work:

- It is important that one wall of the room be mirrored so that performers can get an instant impression of their work. This will allow individuals to see if, how, and where they carry tension and how fluid their movement is. Clarity of action, alignment problems and centring exercises can be observed and corrections can be made easily by each individual.
- Actors should have bare feet and wear dark, neutral clothing so their own sense of self can disappear as much as possible.
- There is a custom in mask work that the actor must treat the mask with great respect; performers should follow this etiquette:

  - The actor begins by studying the face of the mask to let it "speak" to him or her. When ready to put it on, hold it by the edge, then slip it on. Look at your reflection in the mirror for a few moments of quiet thought.
  - When the exercise, rehearsal, or performance is over, return the mask to its proper location and place it face up.
  - Never place a mask face down, and never play around disrespectfully with your mask or anyone else's.

Building masks

Supplies include:

- Vaseline
- surgical gauze
- scissors
- water

- hair dryer
- elastic bands or ribbons
- small ice pick or skewer
- white latex paint and brush (for neutral masks)
- coloured paint (for character masks)
- various craft supplies (for character masks)

The process:

Creating masks works best by when the group is divided into pairs. One person builds the mask on the face of the other person, who is lying on the floor. Cover the subject's face first with Vaseline first, to protect the skin.

Use two-inch-wide surgical gauze, such as that made by Johnson & Johnson for creating plaster bandages, and cut into suitable lengths as required. Wet each strip in turn and place it on the subject's face, gradually building up the mask to accommodate individual contours of the face. Smaller contoured pieces can easily be cut to provide a good fit around the eyes, nose and mouth. In building a neutral mask, it is important to keep the mask as expressionless as possible. If you are making a character mask, you will want to build up part of the face to form, for example, an exaggerated nose, chin, brow ridge, or cheekbones.

When the mask is finished, dry it with a hair dryer. Remove it from the subject's face so that the inside may be dried as well. Using the small ice pick or skewer, make two small holes on either side of the mask near the temples, then insert the elastic bands (or ribbons if you prefer). Once the mask is thoroughly dried, apply two coats of white latex paint to smooth out the finished neutral mask. Character masks — as discussed later — can be decorated more elaborately using various craft supplies.

Half-masks and character masks (such as the type used at Halloween) can be built in the same manner as neutral masks, but they must be more elaborately painted using a variety of colours, textures, facial hair, and the like. They can also be made out of cardboard, wool, poster paint, and other ingredients commonly found in the home. In fact, imagination can be released if each student is assigned the task of building a character mask at home. Add details to embellish characterization, such as:

- exaggerated noses
- expressive eyebrows
- stringy moustaches

- extravagant beards
- strong facial expressions

Neutral and character mask exercises

Individual mask exercise #1:

Choose an emotion from the following list:

- insecurity
- gratitude
- pensiveness
- grief
- fear
- joy
- regret
- guilt
- elation
- innocence
- anguish
- envy
- love
- disgust
- anger
- wonder
- astonishment
- irritation
- amusement
- lust

Then express that emotion:

(a) in a pose
(b) in motion
(c) in an opening pose + transitional motion + finishing pose

Choose another emotion and repeat the exercise. The two emotions you have used may have no logical connection, but search out a situation in which the two emotions can conceivably be linked. Having decided upon the situation, repeat the three stages of the exercise:

(a) in an opening pose reflecting the first emotion

(b) in a motion of transition between the first and second emotion

(c) in a pose reflecting the second emotion

Repeat the exercise using two new emotions — first individually, then paired — just as before. Now think of a situation in which all four emotions you have selected can be integrated into a plot (but not necessarily in the order you selected). Experiment with the sequence of the emotions until you have created a story. Put yourself into an imagined situation in which the four emotions emerge, each in turn, to illustrate the dramatic story line. Incorporate a sense of setting and character while keeping in mind the principle of beginning, middle, and end at each stage of the story line.

Individual mask exercise #2:

Take a nursery rhyme, limerick, or poem and try to recount the story line using only gesture, body language, movement, and mime. Act out all the characters in the poem.

Individual mask exercise #3:

Choose a domestic situation from the following list of actions:

- peeling vegetables
- washing the car
- dusting the living room
- fixing an electric plug
- washing the dishes
- weeding the garden
- cleaning the floor
- working on a temperamental computer
- baking a cake
- shovelling snow
- arranging a bowl of flowers
- raking leaves
- making a bed
- ironing
- doing up the garbage
- grooming a dog or cat

- washing windows
- polishing shoes

Once you have decided on the situation, choose a character type. Now imagine your character in the situation, but make sure there is some plot development to the story. Don't simply repeat an action over and over, but make sure there is an emotional development within the story. Work out the series of actions that you intend to complete, making sure that the story has a beginning, middle, and end. Decide on your character and perform the actions. Gauge your work in the mirror:

- Was each physical and emotional element clear?
- Was the quality of the mime precise?
- Did you achieve emotional change within the story?

Repeat the actions but with different choices of character, emotion and environment:

(a) as a child, then as an adult, finally as a grandparent
(b) in a different mood: grumpy, whimsical, bored, determined, and so forth
(c) in someone else's home: a new friend's home, your boss's home, a spooky house

Group mask exercise #1:

This is an exercise in using your body in reaction. It encourages action first, with thought occurring secondarily. It is designed to help actors make bolder physical choices while being more spontaneous and less judgmental. To begin, form a group of four. The first person strikes a pose, then mentally answers the following questions:

- Where are you?
- What do you feel?
- What is your body telling you?

Five seconds later, a second person strikes another pose in the strongest possible reaction to the first one, and asks him or herself the same questions. A third person then joins in, then a fourth — always asking the questions after striking a pose.

Now the first person strikes another pose in reaction to that created by the fourth person. Each actor repeats the same mental questions after each person strikes each pose. Continue for two minutes with one fresh action every five seconds in sequence. You must accept what each person in turn brings to the story to build the improvization.

Group mask exercise #2:

This is an exercise using emotion within movement. Divide the group into four sections and place one section at each corner of the room. Each person wears a neutral mask and crosses in turn from one corner to the opposite. Use feeling and emotion in the crossover and express it through rhythm, body alignment, tempo, and breath. Either create your own feeling or have the leader call out a word from the list of emotions above (see individual mask exercise #1 above). Each individual must carry that emotion but may choose during the crossover to react emotionally to messages received from others. Keep the crossovers coming quickly and overlapping. Don't think first; just do it.

Variation: Try this exercise to music. Especially good are the slow, melodic sections of the "Hooked on Classics" series of CDs. They change emotion and mood every few bars while retaining continuity of rhythm. The rapidly changing melodies and styles will assist in developing the sense of "doing" rather than "thinking" of what to do. Allow emotion to come from the music, rather than selecting and imposing an emotion on the music.

Variation: Have each person circle another person at the midpoint of the crossover and allow the emotions of the moment to be altered or heightened. Use pronounced breath work and sounds while circling to assist in communicating emotions.

Group mask exercise #3:

This is an exercise for pairs and deals with "I want." It involves sending an "I want" message from person A to person B, the reception of that message, and the return of a responding message from person B to person A.

The theory of "I want" is based on the belief that everything we do in life, no matter how apparently trivial, is based on a deeply rooted need that we feel. This need can be a positive one or a negative one, it can be internalized or subconscious, or it can involve others. It can be aggressive or passive, but it provides the basis of everything we choose to do (or not do) in life.

Begin by saying to yourself "I want to ..." (avoid "feeling" statements because these lead to general conditions, not actions). Choose a strong and personal "want" so that you may find a motivation that is deeply rooted, for example:

- I want some money.
- I want to punch you out.
- I want some information.
- I want to be noticed.
- I want a hug.

These are simply some suggestions from the thousands of wants we all experience during a typical week.

The first person strikes a pose that directs an "I want" demand to another actor, thereby creating immediate conflict. The second person responds with his or her strongly felt want. Both these "I want" movements are done in a count of 10 and end in a freeze. The first person then reacts on a second 10-count according to what message he or she received from the second person. Find the new "I want." Don't think about what you're doing; simply respond. After all, you don't know what message you are going to be sent so you cannot "plan" a reaction. You must go with your immediate instincts.

Repeat the exercise in such a fashion several times over, back and forth like a tennis match — although for a beginner it is better simply to stick to "action one" and "reaction two" until you are thoroughly comfortable with the concept.

Variation: Send one person to the middle of the room to begin the exercise, then allow whichever participant is feeling the strongest "I want" to enter the centre and respond. The exercise continues, with people taking over at random according to how strongly they feel a responsive emotional need to move to the centre of the room. With this alteration, the rigidity of the 10-count is gone. But do not allow anyone to enter before the current action is appropriately completed. For that reason, it is wise to have a circle leader who must give a quick nod to the next participant.

Group mask exercise #4:

This is an exercise in space awareness, use of levels, and opposites. It works well with groups of 10 or so.

Have five individuals establish themselves in a freeze, making sure that they are connected one with the other by the sense of touch along a line. One person's hand can contact with another person's foot, or whatever, as long as there is a linear continuity to the five individuals. Collectively, they should try to occupy as much space as possible in the room freely and imaginatively. Use all levels and all space.

Now the second five actors are to work themselves in and among the original five, making sure they do not make physical contact with the original five. However, there must be the same light physical contact, one with the other down their line, in order to create their own linear continuity. Their poses should reflect a sense of opposition or reaction to the original pose nearest each of them.

Once they are in place, the first five break out of their pose. Now they must entwine themselves among the second freeze, incorporating yet another use of space and levels. This exercise is repeated several times over.

Variations: These can include:

- use of music
- change of time frame (slow motion or double-time)
- imposition of an emotion, which each group must explore in establishing its freeze

Group mask exercise #5:

Take three actors and give each a character mask. Place each actor in a pose using a variety of positions and levels, ensuring that the tableau has a unity. Ask each person watching to decide:

- What is happening in the tableau (or what has just happened)?
- What are the relationships?
- Who is the dominant character?

Keeping the actors in the same pose, change the masks around. Ask those watching once again to decide on the characters, their relationship, and what has just happened or is about to happen. Repeat this yet again so that each of the three masks has been viewed in three different positions. Each time, repeat the series of questions.

It will be observed that the three resulting stories are entirely different. At one time, a certain facial expression may appear to have a benign gentleness, yet in a different position or angle it will take on a threatening quality.

Group mask exercise #6:

Using a variety of neutral or character masks — three, for the sake of argument — establish an opening tableau with three actors. Make sure that each person in the picture has a specific point of focus. Take a few moments to work out a sequence of changes that will occur in response to a series of counted numbers. On the first count, for instance, Character A may stand and turn. On count two, Character B may look down. On count three, Character C may turn her back and slump while — at the same moment — Character B looks up.

A leader can plan these moves. Alternatively, the moves can result from the leader simply calling out the count and a letter, which brings that individual out of the tableau to respond: One-A, Two-B, Three-C and B, and so forth. Generally, a dozen such changes will suffice. Now run the sequence to a slow and steady count, allowing members of the audience enough time to create their own story to match the sequence of action unfolding in front of them.

Next, move the characters into different positions. The masked actor who was playing Character A may now become Character B and will perform each of the functions assigned to Character B. Re-explain each action for the entire dozen counts, making sure that everyone understands his or her new movement.

Here is an example of opening positions and sequence of action:

Starting positions:		A	sitting, eyes cast downward
		B	standing, looking ahead
		C	standing at doorway ready to enter
Action:	On one	C	enters
	On two	A	looks up
	On three	A	looks away
	On four	B	turns in
	On five	C	sits
	On six	A	crosses to door

On seven   B   turns
On eight   C   looks to A

When these moves are repeated three times through, the result will be that three entirely different "stories" have been created for the audience. Try the exercise with differing combinations of males and females and you will discover that those who are watching will receive strikingly contrasted messages.

The interesting thing about this exercise is that it is more for the benefit of the audience than the performers, who cannot see each other clearly. Nevertheless, the audience will have no trouble reading body language and relationships, and creating stories to match the unfolding action. These stories will change if character masks are used and then exchanged between actors from one sequence to the next.

Connecting mask work with acting

Mask work can be a wonderfully freeing device for the novice performer. It releases you from the restrictions of dialogue and opens up the world of emotions and physical expression.

The next logical step in mask work is to apply the use of the neutral mask to scene study work. Once the initial blocking and character work have been done in rehearsal, run the scene with everyone wearing his or her neutral mask. This will force actors to look beyond the words and to speak the message with their bodies instead. (If neutral masks are not available, have the actors sustain a totally blank facial expression.) Set the scene so that it is played in front of mirrors, if possible, thereby enabling the actors to get feedback on body-language messages.

The actors must communicate everything that their characters are thinking, feeling and experiencing without saying a word. They should live the action of the play in every way, except vocally (neither should they mouth the words). The actors can go through their lines in sequence in their minds, relying on blocking and emotional messages to keep them together at the same moment in the play. They must focus on their communication with each other, so that they can establish the dramatic build of tension without relying on the text.

Blocking, body language and gestures are very helpful in this exercise. Another important element that will enable the actors in the scene to remain together throughout the scene is breath work.

This exercise can help release emotions and get actors back in touch with their own characters as well as other characters in the scene. Equally important, it can stop the kind of anticipating that occurs shortly before a play is ready to open, when actors know the script so thoroughly that they react to a line that has not yet been spoken. Incorporating masks into scene work can enable actors to discover new levels of body awareness, fresh insight into character and relationships, and true freedom of physical expression.

Rhythm

After mentioning rhythm as part of exercises, it might be helpful to look at the concept of rhythm by itself. **Rhythm**, whether an accent, beat, or rising and falling stress, suggests patterns of movement.

Sometimes it is difficult to help the performer discover what is meant by the rhythm of a character. A certain level of work is required before we can understand what rhythm means, learn how to discover it in the script, then apply it to a scene. There are so many other things upon which the aspiring actor must focus at first that this problem hardly seems surprising. Occasionally the rhythm of speech of a particular character will catch your eye as you are reading a script. The lilt and melody of the language almost rise off the page as you skim the script.

In the latter stages of rehearsal of a scene or play, however, an actor may often find the character's own distinguishing rhythm begins to emerge and is reflected in the manner of expressing emotion and thought through movement and speaking.

Generally rhythm is an area that is best discovered in rehearsal, because it often develops through the ensemble nature of the rehearsal process. It is affected by factors such as pace and picking up of cues, natural pauses between the beats of a scene, and the energies of the characters in the scene.

You can impose a rhythm on your character, much as do a couple of the following exercises, but normally the rhythm of a character or a scene will develop as you repeat scenes over and over again. Rhythm exercises can be adapted from the beginning-middle-end exercises mentioned earlier in Chapter 8. Use a metronome to establish a fixed beat. Allocate a fixed count to the group.

For example, the first time through a beginning-middle-end exercise, impose four counts for the beginning action, four counts for the transition, and four counts for the end action. The next time, impose four counts for the beginning, three for the transition, two for the end action. See what differences can be observed between these two rhythms.

There are many variations that can be based on this idea. It is essential, of course, that each person begin on the split second of the metronome count, otherwise the overall group rhythm will be lost.

Here are further exercises that deal with the subject.

Exercise: Rhythm in action

Divide the group into pairs and give one actor in each pair a beat such as this one:

- strong beat
- strong beat
- pause
- weak beat

The other person works from a different beat, for example:

- strong beat
- weak beat
- pause

The pauses are very important to permit a breathing space. It is also helpful if the rhythms are handled very slowly at first, to allow thinking time.

1. Initially working individually, discover a walk that allows you to sustain this rhythm without fail. You may include the use of a cane or other such prop to fill a beat or, indeed, a sound may be substituted for a beat. Once both actors have discovered their own walking rhythms, incorporate the two contrasted rhythms together in a non-verbal improvisation. It is easier at first if the situation allows one actor to have a turn, then the other, rather than working with overlapping beats. Later, when you are more comfortable with this exercise, complications can be more easily added.

Variation: Assign two musicians to each improvisation (each musician being matched up with an actor). The sole purpose of the musician is to beat out a consistent rhythm with a simple percussion instrument.

2. Once you have completed the walking rhythm stage, both actors

combine their two rhythms within an improvised situation. The characters and situation should emerge from the rhythm, rather than being imposed. Dialogue may be added now but it, too, must exactly fit the imposed rhythm. You may end by fracturing the rhythm of speech to make it fit, but have you noticed how frequently we break our rhythms of speech in normal, daily conversation?

All the components of a good improvisation should be maintained: character contrast, conflict, beginning-middle-end, and so on. It is easier if speech and movement are two separate activities, for if they overlap within the improvisation, sometimes a certain amount of temporary confusion results.

Variation: Reverse the order. Let the student find the character first, then discover a rhythm that will reflect and support the character.

Exercise: Vocal rhythm

Read the following excerpt to see if there is a natural rhythm to the lines:

A: Hello.
B: How are you?
A: Just fine.
B: Real nice day.
A: Not bad.
B: What can I do for you?
A: Well, now.... See this? If I could mail this right away, would it be there within two days?
B: The second of April? I'm sure that it will ....
A: I hope it won't cost very much. You see, I'm really broke today.
B: A dollar and ten.
A: Oh yes. Right here.
B: In pennies and nickels?
A: Well, cash is cash.
B: I think if you're lucky it might just get there. In fact, if we hurry you'll catch the last mail.
A: That's great. Well done.
B: Not at all. Twenty-one, twenty-two, twenty-three, twenty-four ....

In the following example, rhythm is not found within the text, but is imposed from without, through structured pauses:

A: Honey?
B: Hmm?
A: Honey?
B: What?
A: Are you busy?
B: Well, I was.
A: Can you give me a hand with this?
B: Well, can't you see that I ...
A: Honey?
B: Hmm?
A: Now.
B: Sure.

Try the following variations, which allow the student actor to hear the effects of different imposed vocal rhythms on a scene:

(a) Add a pause of a three-count after every line.
(b) Allow no pause whatsoever, but keep the pace as tight as possible with lines almost overlapping.
(c) Insert a five-second count at the end of the first line,
a four-second count at the end of the second line,
a three-second count at the end of the third line,
a two-second count at the end of the fourth line,
a one-second count at the end of the fifth line, and
no pauses thereafter.

Have someone beat out the pauses lightly during a first read-through, then try it without audible beats.

Exercise: Finding the tempo of a scene

Once you reach a certain comfort level in rehearsal on a scene — when everyone is off book and blocking has been established — it is useful to devote some rehearsal time to experimenting with rhythm. This is a good exercise to tackle when you are at the stage of rehearsal where actors are hesitating before picking up their cues from each other. There is often an unspoken "pause, two, three" between lines and the scene is lacking dynamic energy.

In this exercise, however, you may need to pick up scripts again, because lines can often disappear when you begin practising this technique of overlapping delivery.

Run through the scene with everyone speaking at the normal rate of delivery that they have been accustomed to. However, do not allow any pauses between cue lines. When one actor is four or five words from the end of his or her line, the second actor (having already inhaled a huge breath) should begin to speak. Jump right on top of the first actor's line regardless of whether you cut off a key word or trample on an expected laugh line. This pattern continues line after line, so there are no pauses in the entire scene.

There is often a temptation to pick up the rate of speech and chop short the vowel content of the words, but don't let that happen. This is strictly an exercise in getting rid of every pause.

You will notice this brings an increased energy to the scene. You may also discover occasional moments where overlapping dialogue is actually appropriate. For instance, when two characters are fighting, or when there is a rapid exchange of short lines, overlapping dialogue can be very effective. Audiences can actually make out what both characters are saying.

Now you can repeat the scene, allowing the actors to replace some of the pauses but encouraging them to retain as much overlapping dialogue as possible. This exercise is yet another example of taking an acting exercise to one extreme in order to make discoveries. Subsequent rehearsal time will allow the pendulum to swing back to a happy medium. The natural tempo of the scene will begin to emerge.

William Shakespeare was a master of the rhythmic line. The iambic pentameter rhythm, with its subtle variations in his later plays, reminds one of the origins of the old theatrical expression of "going to listen to a play." Sometimes the use of dialect adds rhythm to the lines, as discussed in an earlier chapter on accents and dialects. The more truthfully a dialect is written into a script, the more easily the sense of rhythm can be felt.

If a truly well-orchestrated scene is to emerge from rehearsal, the actors and director require an ear for the rhythms that the playwright intended. Then the performers must pick up cues with split-second timing and allow pauses to be held where necessary.

Try some rhythm exercises with excerpts from scenes and monologues on which you are currently working. See whether you can discover a natural rhythm in the writing. Perhaps an imposed rhythm will add another element to your work. Rhythm in theatre production is a complex issue, and finding the rhythm of a character in a scene can take hours more work than these exercises might indicate.

Chapter Sixteen
Stage Fighting

S tage fighting is an aspect of staging that actors occasionally must deal with. Some plays require simple physical action — such as face slaps, fainting, or other stage business — that actors should learn how to deal with safely and effectively. Other plays, such as Claire Luckham's *Trafford Tanzi*, which is set in a wrestling ring, make tremendous physical demands on actors.

Safety

No matter how easy the stage stunt appears to be, the margin for accident demands that any stage fight be carefully thought out, choreographed, and rehearsed. The overriding concern in staging physical business is safety, and the most important factor in ensuring safety is establishing and sustaining eye contact. It goes without saying that you should dress properly for such physical activity, removing jewellery, combs from pockets, and so on.

A full-length fight is choreographed by piecing together many individual steps in the same way that comic "shtick" may be pieced together in visual comedy to create sight gags. Each stage is rehearsed clearly and with maximum control. If you are involved in a stage fight, you must practise it with the ensemble both in rehearsal and prior to every performance during the run of the show in order to maintain precision and safety. A reliable fight captain may help to keep the integrity and safety of the fight at these rehearsals.

When you rehearse an extended fight, never anticipate the next action or you run the risk of rushing one of the choreographed moments. Fights must live in the present, not in the future. Make sure, too, that you keep a dual awareness at all times of you (the actor) and your character. Each will have different intentions in a stage fight. A character may be living in a volatile emotional state but the actor must remain cool and controlled, while keeping the pitch of the action at a believable energy level.

Principles of fight choreography

Bear these principles mind in any stunt rehearsal:

1. For safety's sake, rehearse the stunt in **slow motion** to allow everyone involved to have sufficient time to think about each stage of the action, including: body weight, relationship to other people, blocking within the stage setting, potential costume problems, positions of feet and arms, and eye contact. Early rehearsals will proceed more slowly than normal until every physical action is clear and consistent.

2. Every stage stunt must have a built-in safety **control**. For example, in a punch, the aggressor will put a hand on the victim's shoulder to maintain a precise physical sense of the distance between the two of them.

3. Stage stunts should be broken down into individual steps and a series of **counts**.

4. Every piece of stage fighting involves a **transfer of energy** and tension from one character to another. In real life, however, when an aggressor strangles a victim, tension is created by the strangling action of the aggressor's tightening hands and the struggle by the victim to release the strangle. Transfer of energy is from the aggressor to the victim. In stage fighting, energy transfer is reversed so that it moves *from the victim to the aggressor*. Tension exists but the audience is unaware that the *victim* who is being strangled is really in control and doing the strenuous work.

5. Every good stage stunt includes **sound effects** which, when accompanied by effective staging of the physical action, will do much to make the fight realistic.

Basic stage stunts

Actors should become familiar with these common stage-fighting stunts. (Note: The exercises are designed using left- and right-hand terminology; left-handed people should reverse all directions. For simplicity in writing, the male pronoun is used throughout.)

Strangle:

To begin, the aggressor places his hands around the neck of the victim and the victim places his hands on the aggressor's wrists. Instead of the aggressor squeezing the victim's neck as in the normal strangling action, the aggressor uses all his strength to try and remove his hands from that position. It is the victim who tries to hold the aggressor's hands in place. The victim always has control, then, of any pressure on his neck.

This reversal of the expected physical action keeps the physical tension of strangling. If the aggressor moves (for example, lowers the victim back onto the floor as if winning the fight), the contact between the two through their hands/wrists allows this movement to be executed with control and safety. This contact point also makes it easy for the victim to use the rest of his body in the struggle.

This strangle will work from a standing or sitting position, as well as from a front or back placement of the aggressor. All that remains to be added, then, are the sound effects.

Slap:

There are several ways of staging a slap. To heighten its suddenness, the aggressor should partially turn the victim around to face him prior to the slap.

To begin the action of the slap, have the aggressor hold his left hand up to the victim's face as if cupping it in preparation to slap with his right hand. The aggressor's left hand on the victim's face provides the element of safety and control because the aggressor can accurately gauge his hands in this position.

The aggressor pulls back with his right hand, ready to strike. This action should be fast and sharp to create the sense of energy. The further back the aggressor pulls his right hand, the stronger the forward striking action will appear to be. However, as the aggressor begins the forward action, he can afford to take the movement a bit slower for safety's sake.

Energy has already been created in the previous "pulling back" move, and the audience's eye is drawn to this strong move.

At the last moment, when the attacking right hand approaches the victim's face, the aggressor pulls his left hand out from holding the victim's face and slaps it with his right hand. He continues the motion around, managing to bury both his hands behind his body as he turns. The slap must be set up so that the audience does not see the contact point between the aggressor's two hands.

The aggressor supplies the energy up to the point of the slap but, at that moment, the responsibility for continuing the energy transfers to the victim. The victim should suddenly and strongly jerk his head (following the logical direction of the momentum, of course), thereby providing the sense of contact and impact.

The stronger the victim's head action and subsequent movement, the more likely it is that the audience's eye will transfer away from the aggressor. The victim brings a hand to his face in anguish as he is "knocked back" by the impact. He also adds a series of cries and moans to match the energy of the slap.

Remember: the victim must appropriately complete the momentum of the slap based upon the energy of the impact — and this impact will vary to a certain degree each time. Consequently, total communication between the two actors is critical.

Stomach punch:

In this exercise, control is established by the aggressor placing his left hand on the victim's shoulder to retain an awareness of the space between the two of them.

The aggressor pulls back with his right hand, again with a strong movement to create tension, and begins the forward attacking movement. The aggressor, however, pulls his punch and stops abruptly just before he is about to make contact with the victim.

Once again, it is the victim who must pick up the energy and continue momentum of the move. The stronger his action is, the faster it grabs the audience's eye away from the aggressor. The victim doubles up and rises upward slightly as if being lifted off his feet. At the same split second, he makes the sound of expelling air from the impact, then brings his two hands to his middle as if clutching himself in pain. The aggressor's left hand remains on the victim's neck, near the shoulder, to control the action.

In reality, the victim's hands grab the aggressor's right fist and hold it to his own body. This prevents the audience from seeing a space appear between the aggressor's fist and the victim's stomach — for that would break the illusion for the onlookers.

Karate chop:

The karate chop works well as a follow-up to the doubled-over position resulting from the stomach punch. The aggressor pulls his right hand out from the victim's belly while the victim remains conveniently moaning in a "readied" position. The aggressor's left hand remains placed on the victim's shoulder/neck in preparation for subsequent moves.

There is a reversal of energy in the karate chop action, too. Instead of the normal energy of such a move, the aggressor pulls back fast and violently, but he slows the forward chopping action itself. The aggressor pulls his punch. In fact, he does not touch the victim.

Instead, the aggressor brings his attacking right hand down and contacts with his own left hand, while the victim once more takes over the energy of the fight. The victim collapses to the floor on his hands and knees in a strong, loud, vocalized action.

Kneed in the face (while doubled over):

This move can also follow from the stomach punch. It looks as if the victim is getting his face smashed in after he has doubled over in pain from the stomach punch.

With the victim still doubled over, the aggressor pulls his right hand out from the victim's stomach and rears up. He keeps his left hand on the victim's back to sustain the element of control. The aggressor lifts his right knee back, then brings it forward to contact with the victim's right shoulder. This should be staged in such a way that the audience doesn't clearly see that the contact point is the shoulder, not the face.

Once the contact is made with the shoulder, the victim suddenly and sharply flings his head back, creating the illusion that the aggressor's knee landed right in his face. Embellish this moment with various sound effects. The victim brings his hands up to cover his nose or jaw, and he continues the momentum of the action.

Hair pull:

This can be an effective piece of physical action. Again, it is based upon reversal of functions. The aggressor simply places his hand on top of the victim's head. No attempt is made to grab any hair, for the aggressor merely fans his fingers out on the victim's head. The victim grabs the aggressor's wrist with both hands to hold the aggressor's hand firmly in place, and the victim does the rest of the work.

This includes jumping up and down as if in agony, running around the room, or perhaps sinking to his knees. Sound effects are critical and will ensure the hair-pulling action does not take on unintentional comic overtones.

A variation on this begins with the victim lying on the ground. The aggressor simply places his hand under the victim's head. His sole job is to support the victim's head. The victim grabs the aggressor's wrists again, arches his back so that only his feet touch the floor, begins to scream and pushes himself toward the aggressor with his heels digging into the floor. The aggressor backs away, and the resulting impact — especially with the addition of sound effects — is that the victim is being dragged along the ground by his hair.

Eye gouge:

This exercise must be rehearsed carefully and in slow motion. It begins with the victim turning his back to the audience. Instead of two fingers being poked into the eyes, the aggressor's fingers are placed (not thrust) high up on the victim's forehead.

Once again, the victim holds the aggressor's fingers in place as the aggressor tries to remove them. This has a twofold function: to provide the tension in the move and to disguise the fact that his eyes are not, in fact, being gouged. This action is made believable through a combination of factors including the careful positioning of both bodies in relationship to the audience, sound effects, and the victim's reactive movements.

Another method is for the aggressor to grab the victim in a headlock with his left arm, pulling his right hand back so the audience can see clearly that the aggressor is preparing to gouge the victim's eyes with two fingers. The aggressor then buries his two fingers between the victim's face and the aggressor's body. Sound effects are critical in completing this action. Planting the idea of gouging eyes in the minds of the audience by using the power of suggestion is sufficient to make the average audience member cringe in agony.

Ear pull:

The aggressor sets his hands over the victim's ears. The victim grabs the aggressor's wrists. They reverse natural functions: the victim holding the aggressor's hands there and the aggressor trying to pull his hands back. The victim does all the work — providing the screams and kicks, jumping up and down like a jack-in-the-box, and so forth. This can be played painfully or comically, depending upon the circumstances and the victim's actions.

Faint:

The faint can be adapted easily into numerous variations, such as being shot, suffering a heart attack, or other grisly deaths. Remember that a faint begins in the head with dizziness, but violent deaths have a specific bodily contact point that will provide the initial action.

In any event, the actions involved in losing consciousness can be broken down easily into steps or counts. These should be rehearsed in slow motion. When you are practising this action, remember to keep a large free space around you until you become experienced enough to predict where you will fall.

1. The head falls forward and to the side.
2. The shoulders slump following the same direction as the head motion, with one shoulder dropping before the other. This will begin a corkscrew-like action that the rest of the movement will follow.
3. The torso begins to turn following the same direction.
4. The knees buckle as the corkscrew action continues.
5. The victim twists around and falls onto the side of the calf.
6. The body falls back onto one buttock, which absorbs the impact.
7. The torso falls back, landing on the shoulder.
8. The head is set down on the floor (a critical point for total safety control).
9. All the remaining tension in the body is released, along with breath and sound.

Paired body roll:

This is an effective type of stage struggle. However, it must be rehearsed on gym mats. Two people intertwine themselves as follows: each person tightly squeezes one of his partner's legs between his own two legs. This clinching action will keep all four legs from flailing about and injuring someone. Their hands are placed as if they are strangling each other. In fact, each person is responsible for protecting his partner's head from danger. Elbows are kept tucked in and bodies are kept tight together as the roll begins.

There is a momentum to the roll. The person on top (the aggressor) begins the rolling action, because the victim underneath is relatively powerless at the moment. When the positions are reversed and the action appears to be stopping, the victim (now on top) gives the pull that continues the roll. So the action continues, roll-tug-roll-tug. Stop and reverse directions for variation and accompany the action with lots of loud screams. Remember at all times:

- Keep elbows and legs tucked in.
- Protect each other's head.

Bear-hug grip from behind:

Everyone is familiar with this basic action. To break the grip, the victim who is being gripped takes the initiative through an elbowing action to the aggressor's stomach. The action of the victim drawing up is important, for it establishes the energy. Sound effects will heighten the tension of the moment. The victim pulls his punch, however, just as his elbow reaches the aggressor's midriff.

The aggressor is the one who takes over now, with a violent physical reaction and sound effect. With a different sound effect and action, the same movement by the victim can suggest that the elbow landed in the groin rather than the stomach.

Groin kick:

This exercise follows nicely from the karate chop, for the victim can easily fall into the correct position from the karate chop in preparation for the groin kick. He falls flat on the floor on his stomach, arms extended above his head — well out of the way of the action — with his right knee bent so that his right leg is extended away from the body.

The aggressor stands near the extended right leg, draws his right foot back and swings as if aiming for the victim's groin. However, his toe actually contacts with the victim's mid-thigh. The aggressor cuts the momentum of the kick to ensure that the lightest possible physical contact is made. (It's better in this exercise to be closer to the "knee end" of the thigh than otherwise!)

Once more, the victim takes over the physical energy by doubling up in a violent spasm, rolling onto his back and screaming in agony. Because his arms were positioned well away from his groin, the action of bringing his hands down into his groin area will be doubly effective due to the extra distance involved. If there is a sufficiently strong reaction from the victim, the audience is unlikely to see that the contact occurred some distance away from the actual groin area.

Body roll:

The basic body-roll position, which can be adapted as a wide number of flips and rolls, is similar to a somersault. It should, of course, be practised only on gym mats.

In a normal somersault, both hands are placed on the ground and the body rotates over in a 360-degree turn. In stage fighting, however, the actor learns to roll, initially placing only one hand on the mat as he moves into the roll. Then he progresses to the stage where he uses no hands at all, but rather lands on one shoulder as he moves through the roll.

In a staged body roll, he can alter this action. For example, to create the effect of being knocked unconscious, he can begin the body roll but suddenly collapse on the mat instead of continuing the roll. There are many such possible variations.

There are innumerable ways of piecing these simple components together to stage a real, believable fight. Within the outline of the fight, remember to keep characterization foremost in mind: "Would my character fight in this manner?" Remember, too, the principles of comic and dramatic action. "Can my character get an extra laugh by doing something which is strongly out of character?"

Additional ideas for stage stunts appear in the following chapter, but they are comic in nature and based on principles of comic "shtick." Regardless of whether one is acting in broad comedy or realistic drama, stage business is based on these principles of stage fighting:

- slow motion

- safety control
- choreographed beats
- transfer of energy
- sound effects

Embellishing fight choreography

Don't overlook other devices that can be a lot of fun to incorporate within fights. Bearing in mind the principle of transferring energy from one person to another, why not try transferring the energy from one person to an object or group of objects?

Within the choreography of the fight, throw unbreakable objects around the stage area. Make one action substitute for several. For example, place a pile of loosely arranged newspapers that can be hurled about to litter the stage in one single action. Try a pile of magazines, but slice every 10th page with a razor blade so that when the magazine gets thrown, pages fly everywhere. Use pillows. They're safe, provide lots of potentially comic moments in staging and — just for fun — you can always slit one or two so feathers will fly about the stage.

While some of these choices are directorial in origin, you will likely add others as you explore the external physical action of your character.

Chapter Seventeen
Comedy and Style

This chapter deals with physical aspects of the creation of character. The emphasis now is on external approaches to acting. These techniques are useful both in comedy and drama, although most of what follows here refers specifically to comedy. The external visual look of the show is the realm of the director, providing a means through which he or she creates the overall style and pictorial cohesion of the show.

Many forms of comedy must have a strongly developed external appearance. However, all comedy must be founded on the internal truth of the character or your work will be unbelievable.

Warm-up games for visual comedy

1. *Basketball toss:*

Define a large square or rectangular space to contain the participants. Within this restricted area, toss a basketball in the air. Everyone must help to keep the ball in the air, never letting it touch the floor or go outside the confined space. Once this is working smoothly, add some complications such as:

- continuous counting
- making a sound each time you hit the basketball

- naming the person who just sent you the ball and the one you are aiming it toward

2. Guard and Target:

Place two people in the middle of a circle of people. One is to be the guard, and the other the target. Circulate a basketball around the space, with each individual in the circle trying to hit the target. The guard's job, obviously, is to prevent the target from being hit.

Once the target is hit, there is an immediate change of roles. The guard now becomes the new target, the person who successfully hit the target becomes the new guard, and the former target joins the others in the circle. This shift of roles must be instantaneous. If you don't keep your wits about you, you won't last long in your new function — a split-second hesitation can bring about another immediate change of roles. Another piece of advice: don't let the circle change shape with the energy of the exercise.

3. Costume race:

Collect old, random clothing pieces from the dregs of the costume room and set them in two piles. Divide the group into two teams and organize them in lines. Number the first three people of each team as 1-2-3. The second person in each line must dress the first person from the costume oddments. Once dressed, the first person must dash to the end of the room and back again, whereupon the third person in the line undresses the runner.

The first person then goes to the end of the line. As the next person moves into position in the line, a new set 1-2-3 is created. They each assume the functions of the revised number they now hold. The game continues until every member of one team has completed the action of dressing and undressing. For a variation, create an obstacle race for the costumed runners including such things as somersaults at specific points or various slapstick pieces of business.

The theory of visual comedy

Many things make people laugh and, of course, what one person finds amusing may not even make another person smile. Every actor knows how often in performance an expected laugh doesn't materialize. Similarly, a laugh sometimes occurs in the most unexpected places, leaving the actor wondering, "What happened?"

However, there are ways of creating a stage situation that will make an incident funnier, thereby increasing your chances of a good audience reaction. Consider a typical slapstick situation: a character slips on a banana peel and falls on his rear end. If the actor takes the reaction one way, it can evoke winces of pain from the audience. However, if the actor's reaction develops in a different way, it can create a highly amusing comic sight gag. Sometimes developing elements of pomposity in the character, making him or her overblown and deserving of humiliation, can heighten the laughter. In this case, the actor must search out bits of business and mannerisms that emphasize the grandeur of the character.

Four major factors provide the foundation for all comic farce:

Discomfort: An audience will accept seeing actors experience a certain amount of physical discomfort in comedy and farce. For example, the kick in the rear end creates the appearance of physical discomfort in the actor. But it is an acceptable degree of discomfort, and we in the audience don't worry on behalf of the actor. If the actor takes the physical action beyond the point of acceptable discomfort, the audience becomes uneasy that an actor could be hurt by the business. This worry dissociates us from the actor and diminishes the comedy. We stop believing in the character and begin worrying for the actor.

Distortion: There is a distortion to the action, making it different — but not blown out of shape. As a result, some actions become larger, while others are slower.

Distance: The audience has an emotional distance from the actors, which gives the audience a feeling of safety. The actor should look for things to make the physical action appear emotionally distant from the audience. Distance minimizes our emotional involvement: witness the way we can laugh at the antics of the Three Stooges, despite the extravagantly violent forms of physical action in all their films.

Dynamics: The dynamics of action in farce involve fast rhythms. Action should be short, sharp, and quick. Comic action must, in fact, be more clear-cut than the action in regular drama. The next time you develop a funny piece of visual comic business in acting class, try running it again at half-speed for the rest of the class. You will quickly discover that drawing a comic moment out too long kills the humour in almost every instance.

Elements of action in visual comedy

Here are some things to keep in mind when developing physical comedy in rehearsal. Although some of these may appear to be the realm of the playwright, imaginative actors and directors can find ways during the rehearsal process to work them into the action of a play.

1. Surprise:

Bear in mind how powerful the element of surprise can be when you are rehearsing visual comedy. Look for moments where you can fool your audience by doing the opposite of what they might expect your character to do. Unexpected events may happen at one of the following stages of action:

- the set-up
- the expectation of the action
- anticipated but unfulfilled reaction

It is often funnier if characters in the scene are unaware of the comic event that has just occurred under their noses.

2. Timing:

Know when to use the comic invention and when to leave it alone. Trust your intuitive instincts and learn from your experiences on stage. Each time you perform some comic business, you should later analyze what worked, what didn't work, and why. Such analysis will help you out the next time your sense of timing is put to the test.

3. Repetition:

"Three" is the magic number for repeating an action on stage. Fewer than three times doesn't give enough time for the set-up, while more than three times overdoes it, thereby diminishing the audience's reaction.

4. Reversals:

An example of a reversal can be found in a chase scene where the pursuer runs offstage chasing the victim, and then three seconds later runs back onstage being chased by the victim. Such a device can create very funny visual moments. It works well in bedroom farce and "in-one-door-and-out-the-other" situations.

5. Mistaken identities:

Most of us have experienced situations in real life in which we were mistaken for someone else — sometimes with embarrassing results. This comic device was well understood by Roman playwrights; and by Shakespeare, who based more than one play on this principle. The tradition continues today in theatre, film and television.

6. Opposites:

Character contrast can lead to comic action. This is the principle behind the visual comedy of American clowning technique using Joey, the manipulator; and Auguste, the fall guy. (European clowning tends more toward the Pierrot type: classical, sad, and romantic.) Shrewd Joey says to Auguste, "Hey, why don't you go over there and kick that fellow for me?" Auguste, a bit of a dolt but always willing to please, says, "Oh, uh. Ya. Uh. Okay" — does so, and immediately gets thumped. Joey remains untouched by the physical action, illustrating character opposites in comedy.

7. Disguises:

Shakespeare used cross-dressing to create great situation comic effect. More recently, in the play *Charley's Aunt* by Brandon Thomas, the sudden appearance of a university undergraduate disguised as an elderly lady creates both visual comedy and situation comedy. The less real the disguise is, the more amusing it appears to the audience: think of the man with a moustache who is disguised as a woman. We may suffer for the person in disguise, but the lack of believability provides the audience with the necessary emotional distance.

8. Hiding:

The sight of people hiding from one another onstage can be used to create low-comedy effects, especially when coupled with some of the above principles. Different types of mirroring action can add additional comic elements to such business and should be explored as part of the rehearsal process. (Refer to Chapter 9 for exercises in simultaneous mirroring, opposition mirroring, and delayed mirroring.)

9. Blocking:

When you are rehearsing comic business, remember that symmetrical blocking onstage creates a very formal appearance. Because such symmetry looks unnatural, it automatically looks funny. Think of an instance where one person is fighting another back and forth across the stage in a very stylized way. There may be lots of "John L. Sullivan style," but there is no real physical contact. When action is given an exact duplication or mirroring effect, the comedy is heightened.

Acting in comedy and farce

Sincerity and seriousness is critical in acting in comedy, farce, and slapstick. The character you are playing must never see the humour in the situation, for this will weaken the audience's enjoyment of the comedy. Remember how dismal a joke can be when the teller of the tale enjoys it more than the audience does?

Keep the movement clean. Members of the audience have only one opportunity to see and hear everything, so they must see each action clearly and crisply. Sounds and noises made by the actor can sometimes be more effective if they are the opposite of what is expected — for example, a chuckle when hit in the groin.

Despite the temptation, don't over-use the device of visual sight gags. Remember how effective the element of surprise can be when, for instance, red bloomers are suddenly discovered under an otherwise sober and sedate costume.

Acting in period comedy

Period comedy poses another level of challenge for actors. The plays can be witty parodies of social custom and character type, such as found in

Oscar Wilde's incomparable *The Importance of Being Earnest* — which has sometimes been described as the most perfect comedy of manners in the English language and is a must-read for all young actors. Other times, comedy can be very physical — based on slapstick, visual stunts, and broad brush strokes of character work such as is found in plays of the *commedia dell'arte* style.

Whether the comedy is based on language and wit, or whether humour emerges from physical action, the actor cannot begin to rehearse a character in a period play without a completely thorough understanding of his or her costume. In fact, period comedies are sometimes called "costume plays."

Just as our clothing today restricts or frees up certain physical movement, so too did clothing worn by people who lived in time past. For example, when a woman today wears high-heeled shoes, she must learn to walk differently than if she were wearing sandals. Her sense of balance and movement will be affected from the ground up. In fact, even the way she sits and crosses her legs might be different. Men, too, find there is a different way of moving when wearing a suit, shirt, and tie than when wearing a tracksuit and running shoes.

When developing a character in a period play, the actor must research every part of his or her costume, because this will affect all movement. For a period play from the late 18th century, such as those by Oliver Goldsmith or Richard Brinsley Sheridan, it can be helpful to research costumes from the period and imagine you are wearing them. These plays share themes of the pursuit of love and/or sexual flirtation, social convention and status, love versus marriage, youth versus age, and the sophistication of city life versus the simplicity of rustic country life. Consequently, costuming is the very foundation to success in developing comic characterization.

Study paintings by artists of the time and find the common features shared by all fashions (within the status level of the character you are portraying) of a given decade. For women, these will include:

- heavy fabrics with lots of material in the skirt, with very rich fabrics for high-status or privileged persons
- a very tightly drawn waist
- low-cut neckline
- tight sleeves to the elbow, perhaps decorated with lace trim
- shoes with medium-high, contoured heels
- elaborate hairstyles and accessories, or a simple housemaid's cap, depending on status
- hand props such as fans

Men will find their appearance includes (depending on the character's social position):

- coats that come to near-knee level and are made with heavy fabric
- large jacket sleeves that reveal the shirt cuffs
- fancy treatment of the shirt at neck and cuff
- waistcoats made of rich material
- breeches and stockings
- shoes with slightly raised heels
- periwigs, or long hair tied back with a ribbon
- large hats with plumes
- perhaps a sword and scabbard, or a walking stick (depending on the character being portrayed)

These are sweeping generalizations, but illustrate the following steps. Imagine yourself getting dressed (with some assistance from your imaginary servant) layer by layer in a period costume. Take your time with each item and allow yourself to adjust your physical position with each step. Feel the fabrics, consider how each item in turn restricts your movement, and see how this affects your "sense of self." Once you are finished, feel how the layers of costume and accessories affect your alignment as you stand, sit, and walk.

Women will discover a number of things right away:

- Freedom of movement is limited, automatically placing more awareness on the parts of the body that can, in fact, express action: the hands, the eyes, and the voice.
- You must move gracefully to keep the skirts in order.
- The head must be held erect so the hairstyle doesn't become disarranged.
- You cannot slump in a chair because corsets were bound tightly, so you must hold yourself erect and lean an elbow on the back of the chair for support.
- A hand that is holding a fan automatically has increased elegance of line.
- Attention is drawn to the bosom through the low-cut neckline, which can be a clue for developing character.
- Gestures and the musicality of vocal inflection will embellish the character.
- Greeting another person must be done carefully, with just a

slight curtsy, because anything more elaborate will be awkward.

Men, too, will find their movement is affected:

- The formal cut of the coat provides a stiff look to the upper torso.
- Alignment is different when wearing shoes with a slightly raised heel.
- Removing a hat requires large movement because of the size of the sleeve, the proportion of the hat, and the stiffness of the jacket fabric.
- You must be careful when sitting because of the sword (even if your character isn't wearing one, his customary movement will have been shaped by regular wearing of a sword) so you must sit slightly off to one side of a chair.
- You cannot lean forward when bowing to a lady or your wig might slip, so you must lean back onto your rear leg while extending your forward leg as you bow. (Don't forget to remove your hat as a sign of respect.)

These are just a few, generalized matters that an actor must consider in developing a character in rehearsal. Actors in a period costume play will rapidly learn to embellish entrances and exits to show off their costumes. Instead of straight lines for blocking moves, try to use semi-circular moves that are true to the nature of your character. The key is to use "figures-of-eight" in all blocking moves and gestures. The elaborate social manners of the period will allow you considerable opportunity for embellished movement. For example, gentlemen always rose when a lady entered or left the room (we tend to be more casual in this century) and greetings provide further opportunity for social "business."

There are many rituals, too, that can provide period charm in such plays. For instance, there was a whole language of fans in the 18th century. Ladies used fans for almost everything except actually fanning themselves. Fans can express a variety of emotions — ranging from irritation, to contempt, to flirtation. Gentlemen in time past had an entire ritual surround the taking of snuff (which was carried in little snuffboxes tucked in a waistcoat). Actors must research the purpose and use of these accessories.

Wearing rehearsal costumes (long skirts, appropriate footwear, and so forth) right from the first blocking rehearsal is the secret to becoming comfortable with period movement over time. You will also discover the potential for comedy as you rehearse with your costume. By the time you approach opening night, you will be able to convince the audience that you have worn such elaborate clothing all your life.

Which, in fact, is what your character has been doing.

Comic "shtick"

This term is often used in a derogatory manner, implying the lowest of low comedy, such as the "finger-in-the-eye" type of stage business. Nevertheless, every actor should have a clear understanding of the principles behind comic shtick and should feel free to use it when it is appropriate. Please note that the precautions for stage fighting in Chapter 16 are equally important when rehearsing comic shtick. The pieces of business suggested in that chapter, such as hair pulling, can be adjusted to suit the needs of comedy.

When the action is real, tension is much stronger on the part of both the aggressor and the victim. Believability is the key to all movement. However, some bits of comic shtick are very simple pieces of action. Here are a couple of specific examples:

Kick in the pants:

There are two stages to the action:

- the reaction (arch the back on impact for maximum effect)
- the collapse

A rigid fall works best in comedy.

Stage bite:

Have a good windup to this action, then bite your own hand (not the victim's) and wriggle your head as you make loud noises. The victim merely screams.

Other pieces of comic shtick are more complex and involve integrated action. Systematically, build two or more moves along the lines of those listed above, making sure that each move in the sequence is clear, controlled, and distinct. If two actors perform the same series of comic business simultaneously, the synchronized result can be very amusing. This is illustrated when, for example, two attackers approach a victim with identical moves, but the victim knocks them both flat with a mirrored punch.

The domino effect is the most difficult type of comic shtick business to stage. The variations are endless, however. For example:

- A and C are fighting B.
- A hits B, who is being held by C.
- B falls into C and sends him or her flying.

Never underestimate the comic value of sound effects. Several types of sound effects can intensify the comedy of the moment:

1. The actor's voice.
2. The sound of the props used within the action.
3. Mechanical sounds such as a squeaky toy, a slide whistle, or percussion instruments like drums, triangles, and bells of all types.
4. The traditional **slapstick** is an ancient theatrical device and is easy to make. It requires two pieces of wood and some leather. The sound effect is produced by suddenly flicking the device: the slap is created by the two pieces of wood hitting each other. This trick can be used with great success in the particular type of low comedy to which the device has lent its name.

Chases are a lot of fun to rehearse, but they are deceptively energetic. The key is to keep the rhythms short and sharp. Use physical tension and condense the action. A very good device is to incorporate reversals and opposites. For example:

- A chases B three times around a chair.
- B sits down while A continues the chase.
- Then B gets up and starts chasing A.

Consequently, we have the reversal of the original business. Don't forget to add other comic elements, such as the moment of realization, reversal of the action, sound effects, and screams.

Cartoon acting

This is a term often used to describe a very visual type of comedy. If you think of a cartoon strip, the characters you see there exist in two dimensions: height and width. There is no sense of depth other than the thickness of the newsprint.

If you imagine the cartoon transposed to the stage, you will envisage a style of acting where people exist in height and width, but with little sense of depth in the playing space. The result means, for example, that two or three actors in a scene will appear in a line rather than being randomly placed around the set.

It also means that the actors try to restrict their physical actions to two dimensions. Rather than turning partially to the front to play a specific reaction, as in a realistic style of acting, they will try to use 90-degree turns. Acting with the 90-degree turn requires that you either:

- first face the audience, then turn your head 90 degrees toward other actors on the side, or
- first face the other actors beside you on stage, then turn your head 90 degrees out toward the audience to express your reaction.

Like anything in life or in theatre, if you rely on 90-degree turns too frequently in a production, they will lose their comic effectiveness because they work against or remove the unpredictability that is essential to comedy.

Nevertheless, this is a good warm-up exercise to use before beginning to work on very visual or exaggerated forms of comedy — whether in a script work or in an improvisation. It heightens the actor's own sense of the proportions of his or her body in space and, therefore, helps to get away from realistic or naturalistic acting modes.

Because the following cartoon-style exercise is based on exaggeration, it's easier to express less extreme comic reactions afterwards without feeling as self-conscious as you might otherwise be. If you take theatre exercises — those requiring over-exaggeration of articulation, physical extension or vocal projection — beyond the point of reality, you will feel more comfortable when you return to the more realistic level required for the style of your play and the physical space of your theatre.

Cartoon-style exercise:

1. Stand several people in a straight line with toes lined up along an imaginary line (Line A). Draw a second invisible line (Line B) one giant step in front of everyone. Each stage of this exercise begins with the subject standing on Line A, moving to Line B, and returning to Line A.
2. Initially, each of you in sequence takes one giant step forward

from Line A onto Line B. While standing on Line B, say your name loudly and step back immediately onto Line A, keeping a military precision to the evenness of the line. Try this stage of the exercise a couple of times until everyone moves quickly and precisely in succession, with rapid-fire sharpness to the physical action and the vocal energy. Don't allow sloppiness to creep into the exercise when the speed is increased.

3. The next time through, you must each say your name again but preceded by a strong pose or gesture. For variety's sake, no one may strike a pose using the same physical level (high, middle, or low) as the predecessor. Once again, precision and speed are important.

4. Add another component: gesture, name, and a second gesture.

5. Now that everyone has the idea, begin to complicate the exercise. Variations may include using words or phrases — either made up on the spot or lines taken from a text.

6. Additionally, you may build a story with each person in turn striking a pose then adding a sentence that logically develops the plot. Continuity is important, but so is finding the most effective pose or gesture to support the added line — and doing so as quickly as possible.

7. Now add the element of the 90-degree turn — either before or after the gesture, name, second gesture, word, phrase, or sentence. Experiment with the 90-degree turn preceding speech, simultaneously with speech, or following speech.

This action of the 90-degree turn brings the actor out of contact with other people in the scene. The actor's head turn and facial reaction are projected directly to the audience. A 45-degree turn is too subtle. The action will be broad enough only if the angle of the turn is equally broad: a solid 90 degrees.

Watch for this technique in the British *Carry On* series of films, where subtlety is thrown out the window. These films use the degree of comic exaggeration that is part of the tradition in London's commercial West End stage farces. Head turns are accompanied by strong facial reactions and extended vocal sounds to point an emotional response, such as anguish.

In applying the 90-degree turn technique to a rehearsal, actors must be very aware of:

- their body angle
- their physical relationship to other actors in the scene

- the placement of the audience
- at which specific point in the play the 90-degree turn will be most effective
- a clear separation of line delivery from the turning action

It doesn't matter particularly in which order the line and action occur — look first, then speak, or speak first, then look — for such choices vary according to the actual dialogue of the script, the blocking, and the rhythm of the scene. But as long as the two elements (the line and the turning action) don't overlap, the principle will work.

This does not mean that you separate the spoken word from the physical action on every line, or even the majority of lines. That would lead to boring predictability in performance. Save the 90-degree turn for those special comic moments when you want to find the best possible audience reaction.

The 90-degree turn is particularly useful when you want to make a comic moment more elaborate. Embellishment is important in visual comedy. Remember this when you block entrances and exits and never throw away a chance for developing a comic action. For example, begin by asking yourself a series of internal questions and then send each message to a specific point: to the character in the scene who asked you the question, to the audience, to yourself:

- "Did I just hear you say that?"
- "Did he just say that?"
- "I can't believe he just said that!"

Experiment with the sequence of these thoughts and your point of concentration before, during, and after each line.

This group exercise will help develop your sense of the 90-degree turn.

Exercise: Two-dimensional stories

1. Divide the class into groups of seven or eight people. Allow each group to work in as much privacy as possible so that when each final scene is presented, it will come as a surprise to the others.
2. Each group is to choose a well-known fairy tale, or children's story, then isolate seven incidents from the story. Each incident, which is called a "frame," should tell one of the major plot developments in the story line.

3. Every person in the group must be used in the portrayal of all seven frames. If there are only three characters, for example, in a particular frame, the others in the group must be worked into the frame as inanimate objects: trees, furniture, doorways, chairs, and so forth.

4. One person may play the same character throughout the seven frames of the story, or several people may each take their turn — the continuity of character being portrayed, for example, by a hat. Most people will generally end up playing a variety of roles within the plot.

5. A frame should be considered as close to a tableau as possible. There should be a real attempt to minimize and simplify all movement, to indicate in one or two moves what might in reality require more action.

6. As much as possible, all physical positions and all movement within each frame should be done in a linear, two-dimensional style. If you were to imagine the participants in each frame being compressed between two giant pieces of Plexiglas, you would find it easier to envisage the restrictions placed on their physical positions. When someone breaks out of the tableau to move, a 90-degree turn may be permitted. Be very sparing regarding when and where this is used.

7. In presentation, the group lines up along an imaginary straight line (Line A again). The leader of the group begins the action by a finger snap. On this cue, everyone takes a giant step forward onto the imaginary Line B, then immediately rushes into position for the first tableau or frame, extending along Line B.

8. Once everyone is frozen, whatever limited action is necessary may begin. The frame ends with a freeze. Another finger snap breaks the freeze and sends everyone back into the line with speedy military precision. The second frame and all subsequent ones follow the same disciplines in presentation

This exercise creates fun in rehearsal and presentation, especially when two groups have unknowingly chosen the same story. After each presentation has been identified, discuss whether or not any refinements are possible in the two-dimensional use of bodies, or whether the physical action can be simplified still further while remaining clear.

Clarity is the key to successful visual comedy.

Style in acting

Sir John Gielgud once described style as "knowing the kind of play you are in." Sometimes actors will play a light "comedy of manners" in too broad a manner, bringing farcical elements into a type of writing where exaggerated physical action is inappropriate.

The following vocal-interpretation exercise is interesting because it requires using the different principles underlying major styles of theatre with the same ambiguous dialogue. Some of the styles explore the different types of comedy, but others deal with more dramatic genres.

Divide the class into several groups of three. Everyone works with the same dialogue below, with only a minor variation allowed. If only two people are used, because of odd numbers of participants, reallocate the dialogue so that it is evenly distributed between A and B.

Dialogue for three characters:

A: What is it?
B: I don't know.
C: What is it?
A: What?
B: It can't be.
C: It isn't.
A: It is.
B: Really. Oh.
C: Is it?
A: It is.
B: Oh.
C: Oh no.
A: It is.
B: No.
C: Oh.
(optional last line by one person)

Whether the scene is treated as a drama, comedy of manners, farce, tragedy, or any one of a number of other acting styles will depend on how the lines are spoken. Inflection in the voice, pause, pace, pitch, volume, energy, noises, sounds, and rate of delivery must reflect the emotional content the actors are aiming for.

Briefly discuss the contrasting aspects of style from the following list of genres. Each group chooses one of these and interprets the dialogue according to the demands of the style. You will discover that a wide range of situations, conflicts, characters, and emotions can spring from the same source. Let your imaginations soar when you approach the text, so that you don't choose an obvious or expected situation or character type. Be divergent in your thinking. Above all, this is an exercise in vocal interpretation:

- **comedy of manners:** in the witty style of Oscar Wilde or Noel Coward
- **tragedy:** following the style of Greek theatre
- **melodrama:** with emphasis on overblown emotions
- **farce:** developing broad physical action and comic timing
- **Theatre of the Absurd:** inverting all the "normal" rules of theatre
- **drama:** conflict, character and believability are important
- **futuristic:** abstract or surrealistic elements can be explored
- **realism:** as true to life as possible
- **soap opera:** making meaningful moments whenever possible
- **children's theatre:** earnest and energetic, strongly articulated
- **romanticism:** exaggerated realism with embellishment of action
- **thriller:** enhanced suspense and tension

Each group then creates a scene with real characters, clear blocking and many unspoken moments to make this simple dialogue fit within the principles of its chosen style. Remember that each scene must have a beginning, middle, and end.

When the time comes to present the improvisations, don't identify each assigned style to the audience before the scene. Instead, let the results illustrate it. Ask your audience to tell you what style you were exploring. This will let you know immediately how successful you have been in dealing with the elements of style in acting.

Chapter Eighteen
Today's Influences on Acting

Because both video and television work incorporate sound recording, this chapter introduces you to a common element in drama and media: sounds and music.

The modern stage musical and the medium of television place specific demands on the actor. Each medium requires an understanding of the nature of art and technology and how acting is thus affected. For example, in a musical it is important that an actor understand why a song is placed in the middle of a scene and how acting ties into the heart of the song. With television, actors should be aware that the reality of acting on television is very different from that in live theatre, although there are similarities in the process of creating character. There are also important differences in the process of auditioning for stage work and for television and film.

The function of songs in plays and musicals

During the past couple of decades, music has played an increasingly important role in theatrical presentation. Musicals have long been popular as a form of entertainment, but the use of music in other styles and forms of theatre has grown substantially in recent years. Despite the considerable expense and risks faced in staging a musical, or the competitive threat posed by music and variety shows on our 500-channel universe, the Broadway musical remains a popular form of entertainment.

Audience time for listening to music has increased with the introduction of Muzak in shopping malls and sophisticated sound systems for personal time. We may hear a Broadway musical in our living room long before we get to see it in the theatre. The quality of technology and the quantity of musical output have been growing at such a pace that audiences, theatre directors, and performers have a broader knowledge of music than in previous generations. Developments in computer technology are accelerating that growth immeasurably.

Music has a greater presence in contemporary drama than in the past. Most professional actors now realize that singing skills are as important as acting skills if they hope to be employed as frequently as possible in theatre. Actors are learning that singing is simply another form enabling the expression of emotion. For this reason, actors should know something about the function of songs in theatre.

Songs have two basic purposes in a musical:

1. They can serve to reveal the inner mood and thoughts of a character. Those thoughts and emotions that a character cannot express verbally to another character are the thoughts and emotions that must be sung. The song emerges from the character's soul. A character will speak in prose in the script of the play, but speaks more poetically in the text of the song, and likely reveals the true self through the lyrics of the song.

    Songs reveal the inner moods of characters and, in turn, establish the external acting mood for a scene or a special moment in a musical. In this sense, songs are like soliloquies in plays. In fact, the general rule in musical-theatre writing is that if a thought or feeling is important enough to warrant 10 or 20 lines of prose, it should really be turned into a song.

2. The second major function of a song is purely dramatic. Singing is more emotionally powerful than speaking. At moments of high emotional intensity, at crisis points when important decisions must be made, or when a conflict between characters comes to a head, songs are used to increase the emotional force of the action.

On page 19 in the scene book *Behind the Scenes, Volume Two*, there is an excerpt from Christopher Covert and Barbara Spence Potter's Dora Award-winning musical, *Colette — the Colours of Love*, in which two songs appear. The first song, "Turn Out the Light," is really a bridge between Scene 2 and this scene. At the end of Scene 2, Colette appears on stage in a music hall and defiantly bares her breast in public. She tells the world it must take her just as she is — a risky act in 1910. Colette appears to be brash and confident; in reality, she is lonely and confused. Her life seems to lack focus and her attempt to fill it up with the love of a man has proved to be disastrous. So she sings:

> Rounding the corner and taking
> The key in your hand.
> Think on the evening you've come from
> And wasn't it grand?
> Music and faces and you held
> The world in your hand
> As you stood in the light.
> Turning the handle you smile
> As you come through the door.
> Pick up the papers and letters
> That lie on the floor.
> Look for the cat on the stairs,
> He'll be there as before,
> As you turn out the light.
> Take in the laundry tomorrow
> Remember to order some milk for the cat.
> What is this feeling that's so much like sorrow?
> It's late and I don't want to think about that.
> So just turn out the light.

WOMAN: *(off, sings)* Turn out the light.
Turn out the light.

COLETTE: Turning and turning the memories
Seem to be spinning around in my brain.
Wasn't it something he did?
Or is there the faint possibility
I was to blame?
Waiting and waiting for someone
But nobody came.
Lost in a memory of longing
That hadn't a name.

WOMAN: *(off)* Didn't you want to be happy?

COLETTE: Of course, but the same way
I'd rather be right,

And stand in the light.
Tired of fighting and being alive.
Finding now that the way to survive
Is to turn out the light.
Turn out the light.
Turn out the light.

WOMAN: *(off)* Didn't you think he might ask you to stay?
Turn out the light.

COLETTE: Didn't occur to me,
Thought it was better to leave things that way,
And turn out the light.
Turn out the light.
Turn out the light.

This song was designed to be sung as Colette moves from the music hall set to the set representing her room, where she "comes down" from the excitement of her performance. Colette's feelings of helplessness and loss are summed up in Barbara Spence Potter's repeated melodic phrase "Turn out the light."

By the time Colette is finished singing, we know her brashness is a facade. Inside, she is defeated, lost. The routine of her life merely serves to cover her deep pain. This revelation of her inner character, and the haunting music to which it is sung, perfectly combine to set the mood for the arrival of Colette's new lover, Henri.

Instead of being the confident and defiant woman of Scene 2, she is suddenly confused and vulnerable: in the right condition for a love scene. All this takes place in the space of two and a half minutes of song. Such is the transformational power of a song.

The ensuing scene between Henri and Colette is quite short and filled with information. Henri is a new character. Before he and Colette can sing their love duet, we have to know all about him: who he is, what he does, how he feels about her, what he wants now, and so forth.

In musical theatre, the writer has very little time to establish his or her characters. Singing takes up so much stage time that the "book" (that is, the dialogue part of a musical) is often 50 percent shorter than the script of a regular play, and sometimes even shorter than that. Therefore, a musical-theatre writer must be extremely concentrated and direct in his or her dialogue. No word may be wasted.

For the actor, this presents special challenges. Acting for musical theatre is much more direct and open than ordinary acting. It requires a bravura attack. The actor must make unequivocally clear to the audience, almost from the first moment, exactly who he or she is and what he or she wants. There is no room for slow character development, as in straight dramas, for there is likely a song coming up any minute.

This does not mean, however, that musical-theatre characters are simple caricatures. It means only that their subtlety — their complexities, doubts, contradictions, wild and secret hopes, all that which makes them fascinating and worth watching — is expressed in song. A musical-theatre actor must attack the dialogue with gusto, using clear, bold strokes and save the nuances of feeling and desire for his or her singing.

This brings us to the second song in the scene. The written scene ends at the point where both characters clearly state their opposing points of view. Henri calls Colette a fraud and tells her that she needs him as much as he needs her. Colette replies (defiantly again, but we know better): "I don't need anybody!"

HENRI: I push you, I pull you,
                  I pester, cajole and delight.
                  I beckon, you whistle,
                  I flatter, you bristle with fright.
                  But sometime or other,
                  You're bound to discover
                  Your stiffened lip will get tight.
                  And sooner or later, you're going to give up.

COLETTE: *(sings)* You're right.

HENRI: Be cautious, be wary,
                  Be prudent, be prim and be slow.
                  Be frozen, be firm in
                  Your steadfast refusal to glow.

COLETTE: *(speaks)* Now that was unkind!

HENRI: But someone is certain
                  To bring down the curtain
                  And call an end to the show.
                  And sooner or later, you're going to give in.

COLETTE: *(sings)* I know.

HENRI: See the lonely women in their chairs by the door,
                  Killing time at tables for one.

COLETTE: *(speaks)* I do have a few friends!

HENRI: Quelling their desire,
                  Reading by the fire

COLETTE:	*(speaks)* How sad!
HENRI:	*(picks up book)*
	Philosophy of Socrates.
	For fun?
COLETTE:	*(speaks)* It's fascinating. Really!
HENRI:	So let me caress you,
	And even undress you today.
COLETTE:	I have to confess you're
	The best thing that's happened my way.
HENRI:	There's no need for deadlock
	On something like wedlock,
	Just seize the moment
COLETTE:	*(sings)* And pray!
HENRI:	So dine while the food's on the plate.
COLETTE:	Enjoy it before it's too late?
HENRI:	*(speaks)* Exactly!
BOTH:	*(sing)* Let's hurry before life has slipped away!
	(They are in each other's arms)
COLETTE:	*(speaks)* Oh, Henri! Oh, I am an idiot!

During the course of this song, Colette realizes that Henri is too attractive to pass up and, being the woman that she is, she will give in to him in the end. Her sexual nature will betray her again.

But this revelation comes suddenly and dramatically. Henri sings: "And sooner or later, you're going to give up." Colette answers: "You're right." In prose, such a response might come across as arbitrary, or like a bolt out of the blue. However, in song it is direct and clear because singing reveals what is deep inside us.

The climax of the scene — Colette's acceptance of Henri — happens in the middle of the song. By the end of "Sooner or Later" she is in his arms, a position very different from her earlier one: "I don't need anybody!"

Once again we see the power of song to transform: people change when they sing. It is this specific power that gives musicals an astonishing force in theatre, as well as making the musical such a popular, enduring art form.

Stage versus television: degree of release

Acting for television, film, and sound-recording work, like acting for plays and musicals, involves the process of creating a character. However, the differences in performance techniques between stage and other media are enormous. Major adjustments are necessary to the size of performance when moving between a 500-seat theatre and a television studio.

The most obvious distinction between the two forums is the presence or absence of the audience.

Respect for Acting author Uta Hagen describes the theatre audience as her partner. The audience is the last piece of the jigsaw puzzle that began in the playwright's imagination years before your production and your performance came to be. The audience can bring you energy and communion, or rejection and stony silence. However, if you want to make the transition to electronic forms of acting, you must be able to function without a live audience.

Even in a theatre, the difference between playing to a full house and to a theatre containing just a few people can be enormous. For this reason, the same production can often be given slightly different performances from one theatre space to another, or from one evening to the next — although actors should always strive for consistency and ensemble connection in their performances.

Occasionally, a televised version of a successful stage play is not as exciting because of the performers' inability to move successfully from one medium to the other. The method of creating a character may be the same, but the reality of the medium is different.

Stage blocking is based on an awareness of a specific theatre's seating arrangements and sight lines; the style of the play; and sharing the actors' reactions with the audience. In stage work, actors must search out the maximum freedom of body language. However, with television work, blocking often has to be changed to fit the visual picture of the small screen. Awareness of focus is far more important on camera than on stage.

The basic rule of thumb in stage work is that an actor should play to the last row of the audience. That includes both vocal projection and eye contact. In television and film, however, you are playing to the eye of the camera. The camera, guided by the director and mixer, makes the decision about what the audience will see. It will do all the work of creating energy, finding the vocal projection level, and providing visual variety, as the director cuts from one camera shot to another every few seconds.

The movement of the camera provides an artificial control over the viewer's focus, demanding that the audience follow from one point to the next. However, the eye of the camera can look only at one thing at a time. So bear in mind these points:

- Onstage the director, actors, and lighting designer must have rehearsal time to develop exactly where it is, at specific places and deliberate times, that the audience's eye will be drawn. Even then, the audience still has the freedom to take in the full stage picture. A stage director may guide a character's isolation from others in the scene through use of stage areas, or perhaps by incorporating levels on the set.
- With television, isolation can be achieved through contrast of heights or levels in the visual picture, or a close-up of one character with other characters viewed over a shoulder in the distance. One actor may have to move in unnaturally closely to speak over the shoulder of another performer so that both faces can appear simultaneously on the screen.
- Onstage, two actors having a fight will relate to each other at every moment.
- On television, the actors may not even see each other, but the mixer will cut from one camera shot to another and make it appear that the two actors are face to face. The actors may end up delivering lines in the fight to imaginary projections of their partner. In fact, someone who isn't even a good reader could fill in your scene partner's lines while you are acting in cut-away shots.

There are actors who prefer the exchange of energy that a live audience brings to a performance and there are those who prefer to work playing to the invisible eye of the camera. However, each medium demands different techniques, so a thorough understanding of these distinctions is required — not to mention lots of practice — before the performer can comfortably switch from one form to another. Here are just a few considerations.

Acting for television

Understanding camera shots:

- Television provides certain freedom of artistic expression while restricting the actor in other ways. The angle of the camera, for instance, does some of the actor's work, shooting upward on the face to indicate aggression, shooting downward to create a feeling of despair or exhaustion.
- In rehearsal for television, learn which camera is focused on you, and when and at what range from you — for example, close-ups

versus medium shots. You must know in every shot how far the camera is from where you are standing or sitting so that you can gauge the degree of vocal and physical release necessary for each moment of the action. Although the camera may be several metres away from you, if the lens is in a close-up shot, you need to savour the intimacy of the moment.

- When the picture is a long shot, the camera could be up to 30 or 40 metres from the actor. You become a dot on the screen. At such distance, flexibility and body language are critical to the successful communication of the scene.
- In a medium shot, the actor will be a few metres from the camera. Much less physical action is required but your facial features and eyes are now visible on the screen and must convey the emotion. You need only speak at a normal level; microphones will do the rest of the work for you.
- In a close-up, the camera is just centimetres away from you and your eyes will convey the truth of the moment. The camera is unforgiving and relentless in a close-up shot. Your face becomes larger than life on the screen: 20 centimetres of face can occupy 60 centimetres of television screen. Try carrying on a conversation with someone who is that near and you will soon discover that your volume level must be reduced to an unrealistically low level. In fact, someone a few feet away may not hear what you are saying.

The nature of the industry:

- A lot of preparation goes into directing for television and film. Long before the actors arrive on set, scripts have been finely tuned so that fresh camera shots occur every few seconds. This sustains visual interest through an artistic mix of camera angles in medium close-ups, long shots and extreme close-ups.
- Unlike stage work, where the director is in constant contact with actors during rehearsal, the television director sits in the control booth fixed on several screens simultaneously while the actors are on the studio floor. The director spends much time consulting with others to confirm camera angles, plus lighting and audio levels, and communicating with the floor director who passes along the director's instructions to actors.
- Editing choices can juxtapose images to make a statement that

may not even appear in the script, but which can have a powerful impact on the viewer.

- Scenes may be shot out of context because of technical considerations, such as availability of equipment and personnel, outdoor shooting schedules, and lighting requirements.
- The large number of technicians and creative personnel required for film and television work, not to mention the amount of expensive technology on hand, means directors do not have time to hold actors' hands step by step as they sometimes do in theatre. Actors accustomed to stage work sometimes feel abandoned in such circumstances. But time is money in the world of television and film, and extra pressure is put on the actor to be ready whenever the director calls for action to begin.
- Actors in soap operas must be prepared for the fact that on the day of the shoot — any day — they could be given a different set of lines or an entirely new script for the scene. The plot may have changed for any number of reasons, and this happens often in the world of television. Consequently, it is very important that actors who want to be successful in television should be quick studies. They need first-class skills in reading, memorization, and making immediate connections to the text and their fellow actors.

Rehearsing:

- The only reality in television is what fills the screen. In rehearsal for television work, an actor must know the difference between distance and degree in performance: you must be able to release your character according to the distance between you and the camera. There is little need to worry about what message your body language is sending out if the shot is a close-up of your face. When acting must be expressed in a close-up shot, you must have a heightened awareness of what your face is projecting to the camera
- Use your reading rehearsal time to discover places where you can incorporate your emotional reactions. While still on book in rehearsal, react to the other character before you let yourself glance back down to the script to deliver your next line.
- In close-up work, hands — using props if possible — are often brought near to the face. This device provides another method of illuminating the message of the subtext, as well as varying the visual image of an oversize face filling the screen.

- Some shots may require really awkward blocking to create the appropriate visual picture. Just watch a few commercials to see how artificially pitchmen must handle the products they are selling in order to fit everything onto the screen. Because these television techniques are anti-naturalistic, sometimes actors have difficulty making television acting appear to have its own truth and reality.

Vocal projection:

- Stage vocal projection demands careful articulation to fill the large space of the typical theatre, whereas less projection of under-articulated sound is needed in a television studio. Vocal techniques for consonant sounds are quite different for sound-studio work. Instead of strengthening the muscles used in speech, you must work to relax them. Especially important are tongue-relaxation exercises such as those discussed earlier in Chapter 3. These exercises can even be done as last-minute studio preparation.
- A good audio operator can make any actor sound much better, but only if the actor understands the fundamentals of sound technology. For example, if wearing a body mike, never bring your hands in close to your chest or you will cause distortion of sound, or perhaps even damage the microphone. When asked to do a voice check, always do so in the voice you will be using in the scene, i.e. using the volume, rate of delivery and energy that you have rehearsed, so the audio operator can get an accurate reading of your voice.

Emotional release*:*

- With stage work, actors often tend to play an emotional reaction after speaking the line, to fill the subsequent moment or explore the emotional state following delivery. In television, however, you must learn to work in the reaction before the line or your work will end up on the cutting-room floor. The director will already have switched to another camera fixed on the next character who speaks.
- The camera will accentuate existing problems in emotional delivery, such as eye focus, tight jaw, vocal gusting, or flatness of

inflection. Know your problems and work on them before you come onto the floor of the studio.

Blocking and movement:

- Television blocking is based upon lighting and sound considerations, placement of cameras, and angles of shots. Use your rehearsal time to become aware of your light and know when you are pulling out of it.
- Little movement is necessary because cutting from one camera shot or angle to the next provides us with the constantly changing visual picture. You need to identify which camera will be on you at which point so you can adjust the degree of movement in your acting accordingly. Consequently, you will know when a gesture is appropriate and when it will mask your face.
- For television, actors must learn to speak quickly but move slowly. When physical action, such as rising from a chair, is performed too quickly, the movement will look overly rushed if the camera is only a short distance from the actor. Furthermore, the actor runs the risk of moving off screen.

Auditioning for camera work:

Many people today are attracted to the idea of auditioning for television commercials or cameo appearances in TV and film. The grim reality is that film and television producers will hire actors only through specific agencies that represent talent. This means that if you hope to become involved in media work, you will have to find a reputable agent who is willing to sign you up. There are exceptions in the case of independent or student film projects, where actors can often get experience without having agents. You need to know where to find information about such projects:

- audition notices posted on callboards at film and television schools
- advertisements and articles in alternative newspapers published in the larger cities
- personal contact through "friends of friends" in the industry.

If you are fortunate enough to get an audition for film or television, you are expected to wear the clothing and hairstyle appropriate to the character for which you're auditioning. For example, if the part is that of a rising young lawyer, you should wear a blazer, carry a briefcase, and look professional.

Here are some other points to consider in preparation for auditions and studio work:

- Practise with cold readings. Learn how to look at the script at the right time and practise listening to the person who is speaking to you.
- Give yourself permission to take your time.
- Know your "look" on camera. Are you urban, country, ethnic, trendy, or the person next door? Know what you project and accept it comfortably.
- Allow your emotions to bubble underneath the surface of your cold readings.
- When dressing for an audition, avoid white shirts because they bounce too much light. Blue "reads" better on television.
- If you have a choice, wear something that can work easily with body mikes in case a boom mike fails.
- Never wear clunky or jangling jewellery.
- Keep your hair well off your face. Use gel if you must, but never let your eyes be hidden.
- People get nervous in television studios and, under the intense lighting, begin to perspire. Prepare accordingly.
- Be patient. Most reasons for reshooting scenes have nothing to do with what the actor has said or done in the audition. More likely, they involve lighting or sound problems, or the timing of cuts from one camera to another. The actor must wait until it is time to reshoot the scene and remain ready to hit the same level of energy achieved earlier.
- Hold your last moment after you've finished because you never know how long the camera is staying with you. Wait to be told that it's a wrap.
- Be polite to everyone you meet because you never know the interrelationships of the people you meet.

There are major differences between acting for television and stage. Television is perhaps less forgiving of the performer's own personality, and it certainly lacks the immediate feedback that a live audience can provide. But comparing the two forms of entertainment is really like deciding if you like apples better than oranges. Today, no performer would be wise to refuse either option.

Exercise: The degree of emotional release

Here is a practical exercise to heighten your awareness of the degree of release required in acting. It may make you better appreciate the separate demands of stage and media acting, for it is based on the idea of opening emotions up and bringing them back down. Run through each step in its own natural time frame: don't rush but don't linger.

1. You are sitting in a chair feeling very bored.
2. Something at a distance catches your eye and you express vague interest.
3. This becomes stronger interest.
4. Gradually interest changes to concern.
5. Concern gives way to growing anxiety.
6. Anxiety is replaced by fear.
7. Fear is dissipated by realization.
8. Then relief spreads over you.
9. After some time, relief gives way to boredom again.

Explore each of these levels of energy. Be aware of the importance of breath and sound in this exercise. Breath enables your character to project an emotional state without any dialogue. Notice how the quality and the placement of breath vary with each new development in the exercise.

Now try the exercise again in a variety of ways:

1. with a rigid 10-second count for each stage, marked by a handclap
2. with a focus on individual breath rhythms for each stage, with five full breaths in and out at each emotion regardless of time factors. A variation on this can include the vocalization of sounds on the fifth breath cycle of each section
3. with no movement outside of eye-focus changes and certain stiffening or relaxing of the body at each stage
4. with use of a different physical level (seated, standing and on the floor) and/or use of the chair at each point
5. as a dance drama, seeking a fluidity and free use of all the space
6. placing everything in the face and nothing in the body

7. in a totally realistic style, incorporating whichever of the above techniques seem appropriate to the character and the stages of the situation you have created

The principles of acting for television are very similar to those for film and video. With the development of relatively inexpensive videocam recorders, the general public now has access to equipment that was unheard of just a generation ago. It's not that difficult today for an acting student to borrow or rent a videocam and, with some help from friends, begin to experiment with acting for the camera.

Chapter Nineteen
Approaching Shakespeare

We have seen how human psychology is related to modern acting. Now let's look at a playwright often called "modern" because of his understanding of human feelings and his ability to create real, believable characters with whom the average person can identify. Although William Shakespeare lived 400 years ago, and his characters may seem to be historically and culturally remote from our own lives, his plays nevertheless continue to reward us. His work is a cornerstone in the training of actors today. Although there are other classical writers of the Elizabethan Renaissance, Shakespeare's plays tower over the rest in public appeal.

Almost everyone encounters Shakespeare's plays, whether in school, college, on television, or in the theatre. As with other plays, what we need to bear in mind when reading Shakespeare is that he wrote his plays to be acted on a stage, not read as literature.

Shakespeare was a total theatre person: a writer, actor, company manager, and jack of all trades. He had his own company of actors and was part owner of the Globe Theatre in London (which has been authentically and painstakingly reconstructed in recent years near its original site by Blackfriars Bridge). His plays were written for his own actors to perform and he often wrote roles for specific members of his acting troupe. It was not in his own interests to publish his plays because he wanted people to come to the theatre to see them performed.

Shakespeare from the actor's viewpoint

Approaching Shakespeare from an actor's point of view involves special challenges for the student. In the first place, the language in his plays often presents a barrier to today's student. It takes time to learn the meanings of many of the words, similes, metaphors, classical allusions, and other literary devices that give Shakespeare's plays a richer texture than the story line itself presents.

As you begin to work on the delivery of the lines, you have to be concerned about rhythm and rhyme patterns in his verse. Often, you will have to research the historical and cultural background of the play — especially in his histories, such as those dealing with "the Richards" (II and III) or "the Henrys" (IV, V, and VI). Then you must begin to bring the character to life and make him or her every bit as real and complex as those in today's plays.

In contemporary plays, actors can often find a monologue that is perfect for them. These are roles in which the actors could easily be cast because their personal look is right and the character is easy for them to understand. In Shakespeare's plays, however, you cannot "hide behind" the character. You must do a great deal of work to make the character your own, understanding every syllable of every word, being in touch with the character's emotional life, and sharing Shakespeare's vision of the world.

In turn, these insights will bring you to another level of understanding:

- Characters become real.
- Dramatic conflict makes sense in a personal way.
- Emotions and relationships are better understood when they are experienced.

Focusing on Shakespeare from an actor's perspective does not diminish the literary value of his plays. After all, he had a vocabulary four times greater than that of the average college graduate of today. His use of iambic pentameter rhythm is masterful. His generous and clever use of literary devices — such as soliloquies, extended metaphors, and vivid imagery — enriches his plays immeasurably. Yet an entirely new dimension can be added to understanding Shakespeare's plays if they are approached from the actor's viewpoint. Let's look at some of those issues.

Understanding Shakespeare

Begin your study of a Shakespearean play by reading it to see the plot, characters, style, and shape of the play and to recognize familiar meanings in the text. You must read the entire play first. (In fact, this is a basic prerequisite for any monologue or scene study work. Otherwise your understanding of the character and situation will be limited, or perhaps even misinterpreted.)

Exploring Shakespeare's plays in English literature classes will help you become more familiar with meanings of words and images, shadings of interpretation, and the variety of interpretations to his lines. But reading Shakespearean plays outside the classroom without any help can be an intimidating experience.

There are ways of making the task easier. A good edition such as the *Signet Classic Series* will give you footnotes explaining terms that you may not understand. Asimov's *Guide to Shakespeare* is an excellent reference source that will make any of Shakespeare's plays come to life for you. It provides accurate background material, which is especially helpful in Shakespeare's histories. Asimov also explains all classical and historical references in the script and discusses their influence on the dramatic action of the play. Educational publications such as the series of *Coles Notes* for each of Shakespeare's plays can be helpful to gain an understanding of a particularly complicated plot, obscure characters, or intricate relationships.

Today, recordings and videos of film and television versions of Shakespeare's plays are also available. These range in quality, though, and often the scripts have received extensive editing. In some versions, famous soliloquies have been cut completely in order to free up time for the extended visual elements of the film. In other versions, additional lines and scenes have been worked into the script to illustrate scenes that were originally described on stage by a messenger. Actors are advised when renting videos to sit with an open copy of the script in one hand and the VCR hand-control unit in the other, so they can track where the video is taking liberties with Shakespeare's text.

While the use of these various support materials isn't going to make your performing work any better, it can improve your comfort level in acting by increasing your depth of understanding. Therefore, such "short-cuts" can help in some acting situations.

Once you have worked your way through the script and have isolated the speech or scene you wish to approach, you must begin to do text analysis. Look up the meanings and pronunciations of words you do not understand. Find explanations either in the text footnotes or in one of the Shakespearean lexicons or concordances that are available at most libraries.

Even words that you think you understand might have a different meaning in Shakespeare's vocabulary, so you can't take anything for granted when delving into his plays. For example:

- We do not use the word "wherefore" in conversation today, but because it begins with "where" we might naturally assume it means just that. Following this assumption, we would imagine that Juliet's famous line in Act II, Scene 2 — the balcony scene — of *Romeo and Juliet* (while she is still unaware that Romeo is within earshot) is a rhetorical question asking where Romeo has gone: "Wherefore art thou Romeo?" In fact, "wherefore" means "why" or "for what reason." An accurate modern paraphrase of the line shows the depth of Juliet's distress as she realizes her new love is from the Montague family, sworn enemies of Juliet's family, the Capulets.

- The word "coz" is used frequently in Shakespeare's plays and is derived from the word "cousin." But just because one character addresses another with this term doesn't mean that they share a family relationship. It merely indicates a close degree of familiarity.

- You will often see the word "an" used in a context that does not make sense, given our modern usage. Today we use this indefinite article in front of words beginning with a vowel, as in "an apple." In Shakespeare's day, the word "an" meant "if." Consequently, you will find "an" at the beginning of many questions posed by characters in his plays, and in the often-used expression "an it please you."

- The word "fond" today means "liking" or "loving," but in Shakespeare's day it meant "foolish." To an Elizabethan audience, the word "strange" did not mean "unusual" or "peculiar" as it does today. It had several meanings, one being "reserved" or "distant." In view of the modern meanings of these two words, see the different interpretation that emerges in these lines spoken by Juliet to Romeo in the famous Act II, Scene 2 balcony scene:

> "In truth fair Montague I am too **fond**:
> And therefore thou mayst think my behaviour light,
> But trust me Gentleman, I'll prove more true
> Than those that have more cunning to be **strange**,
> I should have been more **strange**, I must confess ..."

- A young actor today might make an educated guess that "nunnery" means "convent," a building where nuns live in retreat from the world. If it is any consolation, even Richard Burton acknowledged in *John Gielgud Directs Richard Burton in Hamlet* that he played the role of Hamlet for years before knowing the Shakespearean meaning of the word, which is "whorehouse." Understanding the original Shakespearean meaning of "nunnery" gives a very different interpretation than we might originally have expected to Hamlet's charge to Ophelia to "get thee to a nunnery."

- One of the most frequently misspoken words in Shakespeare today is "zounds." Because the word is foreign to us today, it is often mispronounced with the "ou" sounding like the vowels in the word "ouch." Research will identify that the word is a contraction of an oath common in Shakespeare's time, "by God's wounds." This phrase referred to Christ dying on the cross and was considered in its time to be an extreme oath for a Christian to speak. Because this was not always socially polite (it could have offended a well-bred lady), the words were commonly contracted to "zounds."

Attention to language in Shakespeare's plays is the responsibility of the actor. With experience and good footnotes in your copy of Shakespeare's plays, you will come to understand a myriad of new words. You will also discover surprising new shadings and additional meanings in words you already know.

The next steps:

1. After you have examined the text carefully for thorough, accurate meanings of words, take the speech and **paraphrase** it into today's language.
2. Then you can begin to create the **inner monologue** of the character.

These techniques, described earlier in chapters 6 and 11 respectively of this book, work equally well in classical and contemporary theatre. They will help you to discover the objectives, obstacles, and conflict that create the emotional life of the character's speech.

Blocking Shakespeare

Look for staging clues in the script. Shakespeare didn't write stage directions as modern playwrights do today, other than making an occasional reference to characters entering or exiting the scene. However, his writing is filled with clues that, to the experienced eye, give very clear suggestions for staging the action of the play.

For example, in the famous meeting between the headstrong Katharina and the equally obstinate Petruchio in Act II, Scene 1 of *The Taming of the Shrew*, there is room for physical contact and struggle. This does not mean that every suggestion mentioned below must be used, for the scene can be staged effectively in any number of ways. You must discover staging clues first, though, before you can decide whether or not to use them. Here are some of the hints in the text regarding the physical blocking of the scene:

In response to Petruchio's statement that he is moved to woo Katharina for his wife (this is a point at which a prospective suitor in a period play might likely be down on one knee), she replies:

"Mov'd, in good time, let him that mov'd you hither
Remove you hence …"

Visualize the verb "mov'd" and translate it to a physical action. You may decide this is a perfect opportunity for the actor playing Katharina to give Petruchio a strong shove, sending him sprawling onto his back. Petruchio shortly thereafter says:

"Come sit on me."

This line not only suggests that he grabs her and pulls her onto his knee, but such an action opens up further opportunities for visual comic business, with Katharina struggling against his improper familiarity. Later in the scene, Petruchio says:

"Why does the world report that Kate doth limp?"

Without some physical action to illuminate the meaning of this line, the words make no sense. If the text gives no previous hint, then the actors must invent some business to justify the meaning of the line. Because there has been no previous mention that Katharina is handicapped in any manner, the conclusion can probably be this: Katharina has just aimed a swift kick at Petruchio shortly before this line, missed hitting him and accidentally stubbed her toe rather painfully against something very hard. Such an action sets up a laugh for the audience and can double the energy with which Katharina then tries to rebuke him.

These are just three of many staging suggestions that may be found in this encounter in Act II, Scene 1. In fact, since this meeting involves two very energetic characters in conflict, we see the energizing momentum of this scene in stage fighting. Here are ways to capture that energy:

Exercise: Tag-team blocking in Shakespeare

Begin by reviewing the stage-fighting techniques mentioned earlier in Chapter 16. Divide the class into several groups of three. Each threesome consists of:

- one Katharina
- one Petruchio
- one director (or more, if numbers are uneven), who can also prompt when the scene is presented

Allocate eight or 10 lines to each pair of actors and organize the threesomes in sequence: one, two, three, four, five, and so forth. Keep the number of lines to a minimum to allow each pair of actors to get "off book" within the time frame of such an exercise. Larger sections can be allocated if the exercise is to be assigned over a longer period.

Group One must consult with Group Two and decide on a "freeze" position. This stance will mark the end of the first group's lines and the beginning of the second group taking over the scene. Group Two then meets with Group Three and establishes another freeze position to mark the end of the second group's lines. The process continues until every group knows its starting and finishing freezes. Decide, too, on a basic playing area and floor plan that all the actors must use. This will create continuity when presenting the scenes.

Each group is to work independently, discovering appropriate physical action in its own lines. The director of the scene blocks and rehearses the actors. Each group incorporates as much stage fighting as it decides is necessary and justifiable.

When it comes time to put the scenes together, the first pair of actors will present the first segment until they reach their ending freeze position. They hold that position without moving until the second pair runs up and takes over. Then the second scene begins. The two new actors continue until they reach the second freeze position. Then the third pair of actors runs up to continue the action — and so the story line continues to the end of the scene. This makes the scene take on elements of a tag-team match, and is a very fast way of getting to the heart and energy of the scene in a short time.

It is possible to stage two or even three versions of this exercise, depending on the number of students available. Quite often, the versions are remarkably alike because the actors, working independently, make similar discoveries in the text.

Speaking Shakespeare

Shakespeare wrote in a number of different literary styles. Some of these are discussed here and others are addressed in Chapter 20. Before delving further into this chapter, you may also wish to review some of the definitions and issues in verse speaking that are discussed in Chapter 6. Some of those same principles are discussed here, but they are applied more directly to Shakespeare's plays, as opposed to the sonnets analyzed in Chapter 6.

Shakespeare wrote using **iambic pentameter verse, prose, songs, music, lyric verse,** and **sonnets** with great facility. Each of these requires some study for the modern actor because they place specific demands on vocal delivery. We are generally more comfortable with prose than any other form of Shakespearean writing because plays today are written almost exclusively in prose. Consequently, modern actors must be trained to become comfortable with the components of poetry such as rhythm and rhyme, imagery and poetic devices.

It was common in Shakespeare's day for writers to create plays using blank verse — iambic pentameter lines that follow a regular rhythm but are without rhyme. Shakespeare used poetry to express the more elevated thoughts and feelings of his characters. Blank verse accounts for most of the writing in his plays.

The actor in a Shakespearean play must honour the rhythm of iambic pentameter verse in the same way that the singer must honour the rhythm of a song. When a modern actor speaks Shakespeare's text with no acknowledgment of the iambic pentameter rhythm, the lines will sound as if they are written in prose. To the experienced theatre person or professional director, this would sound uneven and inappropriate, much like a song delivered with distorted or erratic rhythms. It offends the ear of the trained listener.

Sometimes Shakespeare broke away from strict adherence to the use of iambic pentameter rhythm, especially in his later plays as his writing matured. He sometimes used four stressed beats per line instead of five, for example. Increasingly he wrote in prose, and this point is discussed more fully in the next chapter.

Don't get bogged down with scansion for there is so much additional work to be built upon its foundation. Scansion is only one of the beginning steps in learning to speak Shakespeare's verse, but it is an important step. It will help you discover the richness of his text.

Why bother with scansion?

Scansion provides many answers to the multitude of questions facing the actor in classical plays. Then you can go on to build your characterization.

1. Pronunciation:

Many of the words that Shakespeare used are foreign to us today and, even with a dictionary, we can hesitate repeatedly when we come to pronounce them. If you have ever tried to sight-read Shakespeare, you will understand how frustrating an experience it can be. But there are other clues about pronunciation that an actor can unearth, and it is wise to identify these before beginning to memorize lines. Anyone who has tried to unlearn an incorrect pronunciation can appreciate how important this point is. Here are some different instances where the correct pronunciation can be determined through scansion of the script:

Example #1: Pronouncing unknown words
In Act II, Scene 3 of *Henry IV, Part 1,* Lady Percy complains to her husband, Hotspur, that he has been ignoring her. Lady Percy worries about the nightmares which have been disturbing Hotspur's sleep. Examine the piece with the iambic rhythm marked out. You will discover that Shakespeare has told you how to pronounce words, even though you may not have had any idea of their meanings at first glance. After all, not many people today are expected to know what is meant by "sallies," "palisadoes," and "basilisks"; these words don't appear in everyday conversation.

Begin by reading the line slowly and exaggerating the alternated unstressed and stressed beats. The correct pronunciation of Shakespeare's words will fall into place. Here is a section of Lady

Percy's speech with scansion applied:

"... And **thou** / hast **talk'd**/
Of **sall**/ies, **and** / retires,/ of **tren**/ches, **tents**,/
Of **pal**/isa/does, **fron**/tiers, **pa**/rapets,/
Of **ba**/silisks,/ of **can**/non, **cul**/verin,/
Of **pris**/oners' **ran**/som **and** / of **sol**/diers **slain**,/
And **all** / the **cur**/rents **of** / a **hea**/dy **fight**./"

Example #2: To "ed" or not to "ed," that is the question
Here is another familiar pronunciation problem in classical text: do you pronounce the "ed" at the end of a word or do you ignore the extra syllable? The answer can always be found through scansion. For example, in Act III, Scene 2 of *Romeo and Juliet,* Juliet has just been told of Romeo's banishment for the murder of Tybalt. Midway through her speech, Juliet says:

"Tybalt is dead, and Romeo banished:
That banished, that one word banished"

If the actor playing Juliet were not aware of the rhythmical structure to the lines, she might read the line with the modern pronunciation of "**ban**-ished" (pronounced with two syllables. Special note: hyphens are used here only to clarify divided syllables for the reader)

"Tybalt is dead, and Romeo **ban**-ished:
That **ban**-ished, that one word **ban**-ished"

You can see how this reading throws out the entire sense of rhythm that Shakespeare has carefully established throughout the rest of his writing. However, by applying the rules of iambic pentameter, it is obvious that the final "ed" must be stressed in all three instances, so the word is pronounced in three syllables as "ban-i-shed." This makes the lines fall into place with the correct rhythm (except for Tybalt's name, which is a trochee, not an iamb; see Chapter 6 for further detail on trochees and iambs). A classically trained actor would say:

"**Tybalt** / is **dead**,/ and **Ro**/meo **ban**/-i-**shed**:/
That **ban**/-i-**shed**,/ that **one** / word **ban**/-i-**shed**"

Example #3: Correct pronunciation of names

One of the common mistakes in modern pronunciation involves Juliet's name. Many people today pronounce it with three syllables and emphasize the final consonant, as "Jul-i-et." In fact, when you apply rules of scansion to Shakespeare's lines, you will find the pronunciation involves just two syllables with emphasis on the first syllable (this makes sense given that the Italian root name "Julia" is correctly pronounced in two beats with stress on the first syllable). Romeo says in Act II, Scene 2:

"But, **soft**,/ what **light** / through **yon**/der **win**/dow **breaks**?/
It **is** / the **East**, / and **Jul**/iet **is** / the **sun** /"

Example #4: Discovering archaic pronunciations

Today in England, the word "parliament" is pronounced by many people with four syllables, as "parl-i-a-ment." We in Canada pronounce it in three beats, as "parl-a-ment." Similar clues can be found from Shakespeare's texts that hint at pronunciations in the 16th century. For example, in *King Henry VI, Part 2*, Act I, Scene 3, the word "proportion" appears and scans with an extra little beat. Queen Margaret says to Suffolk (again, hyphens are used here only to clarify divided syllables for the reader):

"I **thought** / King **Hen**/ry **had** / resem/bled **thee**,/
In **cou**/rage, **court**/ship, **and** / pro**por**/ti-on /"

Shakespeare's text is peppered with clues like this about how words were likely pronounced several hundred years ago in England. The question today is whether the actor should pronounce the word with four syllables and appear pretentious to a modern audience, or stay with the three-syllable pronunciation and sacrifice the rhythm. Most actors today would say "pro-**por**-tion" in three beats rather than four. When you are having trouble scanning a line (particularly from Shakespeare's early plays), the extra kicker syllable can often account for the problem.

Example #5: A reminder about gerunds

As discussed in analyzing Sonnet 29 in Chapter 6, actors should remember to be careful when scanning gerunds (verbs used as nouns and ending with "ing"), especially when they appear in the first foot of iambic pentameter verse. Never scan with emphasis on the "ing" part of the word.

In the Epilogue of *King Henry V,* Chorus uses three gerunds in four lines. (There are also two feminine endings indicated here by brackets, but don't let them distract you from "ing"):

"Thus **far,** / with **rough,** / and **all**-/una/ble **pen,**/
Our **bend**/ing **auth**/or **hath** / pursued/ the **stor**(y)/
In **lit**/tle **room** / confin/ing **migh**/ty **men,**/
Mangling / by **starts** / the **full** / course **of** / their **glor**(y)/"

The third and final gerund, "mangling," falls in the first foot of the line. The foot is a trochee and must be spoken that way by the trained actor.

Example #6: Variety of pronunciation in period style
You might try comparing two videos of the same Shakespearean play, filmed in different decades, to see how an actor's choice and the director's vision can colour the interpretation of character, emotional choices, and delivery of the text. Be prepared to find that many of the "rules" for speaking iambic pentameter verse are broken by different actors and directors. By comparing versions of the same play, we can see how acting styles and public taste change over time.

For instance, in *King Henry V* Henry encourages his troops in Act III, Scene 1 in the speech beginning "Once more unto the breach, dear friends." He later says:

"Then lend the eye a terrible aspect"

In the film version made 50 years ago, you will hear Sir Laurence Olivier give a classical reading of the line in perfect iambic pentameter:

"Then **lend** / the **eye** / a **terr**/-i-**ble** / as**pect** /"

In the more recent film version with Kenneth Branaugh, the line is spoken with a contemporary interpretation (presumably so that it does not alienate the modern audience's ear):

"Then **lend** / the **eye** / a **terr**/-i-**ble** / as**pect** /"

In Act III, Scene 1, Olivier's *Hamlet* says in classical iambic verse (with a feminine ending in brackets):

"To **be**, / or **not** / to **be**,/ that **is** / the **ques**(tion) /"

Mel Gibson's film version gives the line a different but, arguably, a more modern reading:

"To **be**, / or **not** / to **be**,/ **that** is / the **ques**(tion) /"

2. Pointing words:

As discussed thoroughly in the sonnet unit in Chapter 6, these are the emotive, descriptive words that create an impact, paint an image, or capture our imagination. Invariably, they are the words that carry the emotion of the character.

Most important to remember in classical plays is that pointing words always fall on the stressed part of an iambic foot, not the unstressed part. But not every stressed beat automatically becomes a pointing word: that would lead to singsong delivery. Here is scansion applied to a selection from Act III, Scene 2 of *King Richard II*. No attempt has been made here to differentiate between the importance of the stressed beats. This example just identifies the pattern of the iambic rhythm.

Bollingbroke is successfully challenging Richard for the throne, and in a moment filled with self-defeat, Richard says:

"Our **lands**, / our **lives**, / and **all** / are **Bol**/lingbroke's/
And **noth**/ing **can** / we **call** / our **own** / but **death**,/
And **that** / small **mo**/del **of** / the **bar**/ren **earth**/
Which **serves** / as **paste** / and **co**/ver **to** / our **bones**./
For **God's** / sake, **let** / us **sit** / upon / the **ground**/
And **tell** / sad **sto**/ries **of** / the **death** / of **kings**:/
How **some** / have **been** / depos'd, / some **slain** / in **war**,/
Some **haunt**/ed **by** / the **ghosts** / they **have** / depos'd,/
Some **poi**/son'd **by** / their **wives**, / some **sleep**/ing **kill'd**;/
All **mur**/der'd ..."

Scansion shows you that stress or emphasis is placed on five key beats in a line. Now the actor can begin to identify which words to point to make the speech clear and effective. Richard's speech tells us a great deal about the emotional state of the king under pressure.

Pointing words help illuminate Richard's character:

- his mental state
- his emotional state
- his preoccupation with death

In the example below, note how the cumulative increase of powerful words heightens the dramatic intensity in the speech:

"Our lands, / our lives, / and **all** / are **Bol**/lingbroke's/
And **noth**/ing can / we call / our own / but **death**,/
And that / small mo/del of / the bar/ren **earth**/
Which serves / as paste / and co/ver to / our **bones.**/
For **God's** / sake, let / us sit / upon / the **ground**/
And tell / sad sto/ries of / the **death** / of kings:/
How some / have been / de**pos'd**, / some slain / in **war**,/
Some **haunt**/ed by / the **ghosts** / they have / de**pos'd**,/
Some **poi**/son'd by / their wives, / some **sleep**/ing **kill'd**;/
All **mur**/der'd ..."

As discussed in Chapter 6, words that form a suspensive pause at the end of an unpunctuated line of poetry automatically become pointing words. Thus, "earth" and "ground" are examples in this selection and will be discussed in more detail later in this chapter in point #5 on "Breathing." (You will find slight variations in punctuation from one edition to the next, and between them and the First Folio edition of Shakespeare's plays, which is generally considered to be the final arbiter.)

A summary of the pointing words in this excerpt makes for strong reading: "**All, Bollingbroke's, nothing, death, earth, bones, God's, ground, death, depos'd, war, haunted, ghosts, depos'd, poison'd, sleeping kill'd, murder'd.**" What a great, dramatic starting point these words provide for the actor.

3. Dramatic tension and rhythm:

If you look at the following example from Act II, Scene 2 of *Macbeth,* you will notice that the manner in which it is written across the page seems unusual. Why are there all those extra spaces on some of the lines? The technique is called **stichomythia** and it originated with Greeks writers. Shakespeare (and generations of his editors) uses this device to emphasize line-by-line verbal fencing between two people who echo each other's thoughts.

Macbeth has just murdered Duncan and is returning to his wife, who is waiting for news that the deed has been done:

LADY MACBETH:
    Alack, I am afraid they have awak'd,
    And 'tis not done; th' attempt, and not the deed,
    Confounds us. Hark: I lay'd their daggers ready,
    He could not miss 'em. Had he not resembled
    My father as he slept, I had done't. *(Enter Macbeth)* My husband?
MACBETH:
    I have done the deed:
    Didst thou not hear a noise?
LADY MACBETH:
    I heard the owl scream, and the crickets cry.
    Did not you speak?
MACBETH:
            When?
LADY MACBETH:
               Now.
MACBETH:
                  As I descended?
LADY MACBETH:
    Ay.
MACBETH:
    Hark!
    Who lies i' th' second chamber?
LADY MACBETH:
                 Donalbain.
MACBETH *(looking on his hands):*
    This is a sorry sight.
LADY MACBETH:
    A foolish thought, to say a sorry sight.

Consider the dialogue not as a speech being spoken by two people but as one continuous line with a relentless rhythm. There is a deliberately sustained energy created by stichomythia. The following lines also indicate that there is no let-up of the rhythm and no easing in the build of dramatic tension. An intense closeness bonds one character to the other:

LADY MACBETH:
   Did **not** / you **speak**?/
MACBETH:
                When?
LADY MACBETH:
                       Now./
MACBETH:
                             As **I** / de**scen**(ded)?/
LADY MACBETH:
   Ay.

We have one leftover feminine ending in the word "descended" (the unstressed 11th beat at the end of a line of blank verse is expressed in brackets), but otherwise this reads as one unbroken iambic pentameter line. The words spoken by the two characters can collapse into the time it takes to read them as one continuous line. Macbeth and his wife almost overlap their words, reinforcing the urgency and tension of the scene.

There are other examples in *Macbeth,* such as Act IV, Scene 3, where stichomythia builds dramatic tension. But Shakespeare also used it to build comic tension. For example, you will notice stichomythia in a number of comic scenes in *The Taming of the Shrew.*

4. Pace:

Actors study iambic pentameter not only for its rhythmic clues but also for the sense of pace contained in the dialogue. In Shakespeare's day, actors got through his scripts in much less than three hours. Elizabethans obviously spoke at a much faster rate than we do.

Shakespeare's literary structure provides the key to vocal delivery. When you read a speech with appropriate emphasis on stressed syllables, there is a sense of unrelenting energy in the text. Words and thoughts take place simultaneously. Without the numerous "meaningful pauses" so popular in contemporary drama, the Shakespearean play takes on an urgency that enables the passion to build vigorously. Avoid the trap of using the modern formula of thought + pause, thought + pause, thought + pause — along with its attendant vocal patterns — or your three-hour production will stretch into a four-hour marathon.

As his work matured over time, Shakespeare experimented with different forms of verse other than iambic pentameter, occasionally using only two feet (iambic dimeter), three feet (iambic trimeter), or four feet (iambic tetrameter) in a line. Gower's opening speech as Chorus in *Pericles, Prince of Tyre*, is an example of iambic tetrameter that continues for 42 lines. Shakespeare's four great tragedies — *Hamlet, Othello, King Lear,* and *Macbeth* — all contain many irregularities of rhythm and cause students considerable anxiety when applying the rules of scansion.

But there are important clues for the actor when Shakespeare's writing changes within a scene from longer iambic lines to shorter lines.

Example in dramatic form: One of the best examples of Shakespeare's use of verse to heighten pace can be found in Act I, Scene 2 of *King Richard III*. In this scene, Lady Anne is escorting the body of her father-in-law King Henry VI, who has been murdered by Richard, Duke of Gloucester. Prior to the action of the play, Richard murdered Lady Anne's husband (Edward, the crown prince of England), so Lady Anne has a great deal to be angry about. She opens the scene with a monologue delivered to anyone within earshot in the streets of London. It is a very political speech that rails against Richard, who is portrayed in this play as Shakespeare's archetypal villain. She calls down curses on Richard.

Suddenly Richard appears, creating a complex, challenging scene for any two actors. By the end of the scene, Anne has been drawn into Richard's spell and accepts his ring, which is a major turnaround by anyone's definition.

The point is this: if the actors playing this intricate scene begin to analyze the structure of the writing, they will discover that Shakespeare uses a variety of line lengths to reinforce the increasingly passionate exchange of words. Although the scene begins in iambic pentameter verse, Shakespeare uses several devices to increase the tension and tighten the pace. These include stichomythia, antithesis (as Richard and Anne volley lines back and forth over the dead king's corpse), and increasingly shortened lines that build to natural climaxes. In fact, the scene's climax is written in iambic trimeter (with three — not five — iambs per line) as Richard persuades Anne to accept his ring.

It is a powerful scene, but analyzing the structure of the writing can unearth many dramatic clues for the two actors. They will point Richard and Anne in the right direction to express the natural emotional pace of the scene.

Example in comic form: Shakespeare also used shortened lines to build comic pace and tension. You will notice how playing with the structure of the line increases the pace of the scene in the initial meeting of Petruchio and Katharina in Act II, Scene 1 of *The Taming of the Shrew*. The scene suddenly jumps from five iambs per line to two or three (that is, from iambic pentameter to iambic dimeter and iambic tetrameter). This heightens the stakes for the two characters as they exchange comic quips back and forth. Increasing urgency is expressed through the shortened lines, reaching its briefest stage with Kate's "I care not."

Example combining dramatic and comic forms: Sometimes Shakespeare helps keep the pace of a script moving by giving individual lines to characters in sequence. If actors fall into the trap of modern custom and put pauses at cue lines, the pace of the scene will be flat. However, if they almost overlap their voices, a relentless energy will rise to the surface.

A good example can be found in Act III, Scene 2 of *King Henry VI, Part 3,* where King Edward tries to seduce the widowed Lady Grey, while Gloucester and Clarence make ribald comments from a distance. Each character has a different objective and obstacle. Lady Grey must tread a perilously fine line to keep her good name, while King Edward has no hesitation in using intimidation and political power to make his conquest. Gloucester and Clarence provide comic relief. If the four actors in this scene keep the cues tight, the pace will illuminate strongly contrasted characters and intensify the emotional conflict.

5. Breath breaks:

Speaking poetry is not like speaking prose because there are specific guidelines for breath points in verse speaking. You cannot stop midway through a line of poetry to take a breath; you may take a breath only at a punctuation point. Because Shakespeare used suspensive pauses, many of his speeches continue for two or three lines — often longer — without a single mark of punctuation. This deliberate device makes heavy demands on the untrained voice. Looking back at the earlier excerpt from *King Richard II,* there are two examples of suspensive pause. They are clearly marked below:

> "And nothing can we call our own but death,
> And that small model of the barren **earth**
> Which serves as paste and cover to our bones.
> For God's sake, let us sit upon the **ground**
> And tell sad stories of the death of kings:"

Here are the breath breaks in these five lines:

- The first breath continues to the end of the first line, where a brief breath may be taken because the line ends with a comma.

> "And nothing can we call our own but death,"

- The second breath runs through Lines 2 and 3 to the period, which permits you to take a third breath. Remember to "lean" into the suspensive pause and drag out the vowel sounds of "earth."

> "And that small model of the barren **earth**
> Which serves as paste and cover to our bones."

- The new breath is then sustained through the fourth and fifth lines until you reach the colon. If you need to take a quick extra breath after the phrase "For God's sake" you may, because the comma allows you to inhale briefly. Again, remember to honour the suspensive pause on the word "ground."

> "For God's sake, let us sit upon the **ground**
> And tell sad stories of the death of kings:"

It is clear that if you choose to lean consciously or subconsciously on every final word in Shakespeare's verse, you will create a predictable, stilted and boring form of delivery. But suspensive pauses occur only on some lines. Avoid leaning on final words where punctuation exists. When properly delivered, pointing words will alleviate vocal patterns and predictability.

Try reading these five lines aloud on three breaths as if you were speaking to an audience of several hundred people. Then search out other examples in Shakespeare. Punctuation varies considerably from one publisher's edition to another, so skim your own copy to find further examples of suspensive pause.

Rhyme and rhythm

There is no formal rhyme pattern in blank verse, but rhythm is dominant because of the repetition of the five iambs. Rhyme was used more obviously in Shakespeare's earlier plays and a **rhyming couplet** (that is, two lines in a row which rhyme) was often used to indicate to the audience that the actors had reached the end of a scene. This couplet quite often was referred to as a

sententious couplet because it summed up a scene or a character's intention in two lines.

Sometimes Shakespeare wrote entire speeches in rhyming couplets. This rhyme structure is a deliberate device employed by Shakespeare. It occurs in both dramas and comedies, and poses special challenges for the actor. The first challenge is to determine why rhyming couplets are used at that specific point of the play. For example, many of Gower's speeches as Chorus in *Pericles, Prince of Tyre,* are written in rhyme. Because the real-life Gower was a 14th-century poet and friend of Geoffrey Chaucer (the author of *The Canterbury Tales*), it is hardly surprising that his character in the play speaks in the poetic writing style typical of his period.

In the following example from Act I, Scene 1 of *A Midsummer Night's Dream,* the entire speech is written in rhyming couplets. It is used in this scene because Helena is feeling sorry for herself. The rhyming couplets almost echo the whining sound of a petulant child as Helena complains about the fact that the man she loves is in love with her best friend. In many instances in this speech, the first line of the rhyming couplet presents the thought, while the second line counteracts it.

However, rhyming couplets present additional challenges for the actor, who must avoid getting trapped in the vocal patterns of both rhythm and rhyme. Scansion will help the actor avoid these traps. The rhyming couplets can easily be seen below in the final word of each line: "be," "she," "so," "know."

> "How happy some o'er other some can **be**!
> Through Athens I am thought as fair as **she**;
> But what of that? Demetrius thinks not **so**;
> He will not know what all but he do **know**;"

The following section has been marked in stressed and unstressed beats, with oblique lines separating each foot of verse, as was illustrated in Chapter 6.

> "How hap/py some/ o'er oth/er some/ can be!/
>
> Through Ath/ens I/ am thought/ as fair/ as she;/
>
> But what/ of that?/ Deme/trius thinks/ not so;/

˘ ‾ ˘ ‾ ˘ ‾ ˘ ‾ ˘ ‾

He will/ not know/ what all/ but he/ do know;"/

If it is easier for you when reading aloud, here is the same piece with stressed beats marked in boldface:

"How **hap**/py **some** / o'er **oth**/er **some** / can **be**!/
Through **Ath**/ens **I** / am **thought** / as **fair** / as **she**;/
But **what** / of **that**? / Demet/rius **thinks** / not **so**;/
He **will** / not **know** / what **all** / but **he** / do **know**;"/

Read these lines aloud and exaggerate all the stressed beats while underplaying the others. (Just a note of explanation: you may want to pronounce the name of Demetrius with four syllables, as "De-**me**-tri-us." But reading the line within the poetic rhythm, you will see that Shakespeare tells us the name should be pronounced with three syllables as " De-**met**-rius" with the third and fourth syllables being elided together to create one sound.)

Pointing words stand out as being more important than other stressed beats in the line. By experimenting with pointing words, individual interpretation in acting begins to come into play. Each actor approaching this speech will have a different way of inflecting and pointing these four lines, according to her personal interpretation of Helena. Remember the advice given in Chapter 2: there are no rights, no wrongs, just choices. The actor's job is to make the most dramatically effective choices.

Repeat each line five times through, exaggerating in turn one of the five stressed beats, to discover which word it is for you that deserves the extra emphasis.

"How **hap**py some o'er other some can be!
"How happy **some** o'er other some can be!
"How happy some o'er **oth**er some can be!
"How happy some o'er other **some** can be!
"How happy some o'er other some can **be**!
Through **Ath**ens I am thought as fair as she;
Through Athens **I** am thought as fair as she;
Through Athens I am **thought** as fair as she;
Through Athens I am thought as **fair** as she;
Through Athens I am thought as fair as **she**;

But **what** of that? Demetrius thinks not so;
But what of **that**? Demetrius thinks not so;
But what of that? De**me**trius thinks not so;
But what of that? Demetrius **thinks** not so;
But what of that? Demetrius thinks not **so**;
He **will** not know what all but he do know;
He will not **know** what all but he do know;
He will not know what **all** but he do know;
He will not know what all but **he** do know;
He will not know what all but he do **know**;"

It will be obvious that some of the 20 pointing words indicated above are not logical or effective choices, while others sound better to the ear. However, repeating each line five times through is a good place for the novice actor to begin to discover the real intention of the text, to become familiar with various interpretations, and (subconsciously) to begin learning the lines. For the sake of argument, we may decide that the following lines represent one such interpretation:

"How **hap**py some o'er other some can be!
Through Athens **I** am thought as fair as **she**;
But what of that? De**me**trius thinks not so;
He will not know what **all** but he do know;"

You will observe that looking for the pointing words helps to clarify the meaning of the text and the interpretation of character. Since "feeling" comes first as the actor delineates a character, pointing words are merely conveyors of the interpretation you wish to establish:

- "Happy" sets up the theme of these four lines.
- Emphasizing "I," "she," "Demetrius," and "all" illustrates that Helena believes Demetrius is blind to something evident to everyone else: that she is as beautiful as Hermia and, therefore, as worthy of his attention.
- "I" and "she" are balanced in the second line, emphasizing the rivalry between Helena and Hermia through antithesis (that is, the contrast of ideas). The use of two pointing words in this line reinforces the conflict between them.
- In the final line, by setting the second use of the pronoun "he" in a stressed position, Shakespeare has placed Demetrius in a position

against the rest of the world. This is emphasized when choosing "all" as the pointing word for the line.

These interpretations open up emotional choices for Helena of petulance, anger, envy, or sorrow. In choosing these particular pointing words, the problems of being swept up in rhythm and rhyme are also avoided.

Advice about weak and strong pointing words:

One other very important principle is illustrated here. When you examine the alternation of stressed and unstressed syllables in Shakespeare's verse, rarely do you find he has placed emphasis on pronouns. As a general rule, actors should try to minimize the stressing of pronouns. These weak words — such as I, you, me, he, she, they, it, himself, herself, themselves — do little to bring out the meaning of most lines. The same holds true for many weak adjectives, such as: my, his, yours.

When pronouns do fall on stressed beats, there is dramatic justification. Shakespeare has deliberately stressed several pronouns in Helena's lines above and provided actors with strong clues for character interpretation.

Here is an example involving a number of pronouns and adjectives that illustrates the importance of placing the emphasis elsewhere in a Shakespearean line. The excerpt is taken from Act I, Scene 2 of *King Henry VI, Part 1* and the speaker is La Pucelle, known to us today as Joan of Arc. Begin by sight-reading the piece aloud:

"Dauphin, I am by birth a shepherd's daughter,
My wit untrain'd in any kind of art:
Heaven and our Lady gracious hath it pleas'd
To shine on my contemptible estate,
Lo, whilst I waited on my tender lambs,
And to sun's parching heat display'd my cheeks,
God's Mother deigned to appear to me,
And in a vision full of majesty,
Will'd me to leave my base vocation,
And free my country from calamity:
Her aid she promis'd, and assur'd success,
In complete glory she reveal'd herself:
And whereas I was black and swart before,
With those clear rays, which she infused on me,

That beauty am I bless'd with which you see.
Ask me what question thou canst possible,
And I will answer unpremeditated:
My courage try by combat, if thou dar'st,
And thou shalt find that I exceed my sex.
Resolve on this, thou shalt be fortunate,
If thou receive me for thy war-like mate."

To illustrate the importance of avoiding pronouns and weak adjectives, read the speech again. This time, deliberately emphasize each pronoun and pronominal adjective (indicated below in boldface) and see what happens to the character of Joan and her vision of Mary:

"Dauphin, **I** am by birth a shepherd's daughter,
My wit untrain'd in any kind of art:
Heaven and **our** Lady gracious hath **it** pleas'd
To shine on **my** contemptible estate,
Lo, whilst **I** waited on **my** tender lambs,
And to sun's parching heat display'd **my** cheeks,
God's Mother deigned to appear to **me**,
And in a vision full of majesty,
Will'd **me** to leave **my** base vocation,
And free **my** country from calamity:
Her aid **she** promis'd, and assur'd success,
In complete glory **she** reveal'd **herself**:
And whereas **I** was black and swart before,
With those clear rays, which **she** infused on **me**,
That beauty am **I** bless'd with which **you** see.
Ask **me** what question **thou** canst possible,
And **I** will answer unpremeditated:
My courage try by combat, if **thou** dar'st,
And **thou** shalt find that **I** exceed my sex.
Resolve on this, **thou** shalt be fortunate,
If **thou** receive **me** for **thy** war-like mate.

Few actors would stress all 31 of these words on a first reading. But in contemporary plays, actors often lock onto such weak words and overemphasize them at the expense of other, richer words in the text. Do you see here how the continual stressing of pronouns and pronominal adjectives imbalances the meaning of the lines? It changes the character of

Joan of Arc into a petulant, whining egocentric. One of the commonest mistakes in acting — and not just with Shakespeare, either — lies in incorrectly placing the emphasis on pronouns at the expense of the more important pointing words in the line.

Here is the same speech, with the placement of stressed and unstressed syllables clearly indicated through applied scansion. Read the speech again, this time observing the iambic pentameter rhythm. Note how sparingly Shakespeare himself stressed any of the pronouns in his writing: only 13 are stressed within the natural rhythm of the iambic pentameter line. When you add the selective use of pointing words to the speech, the emphasis on pronouns diminishes even further. Shakespeare has written the clues for speaking his lines into the metric structure of his blank verse.

"Dauphin,/ I am / by birth / a shep/herd's daught(er),/   (Line 1)
My wit / untrain'd / in an/y kind / of art:/
Heaven and / our La/dy gra/cious hath / it pleas'd /   (Line 3)
To shine / on my / contempt/ible / estate,/
Lo, whilst / I wait/ed on / my ten/der lambs,/
And to / sun's parch/ing heat / display'd / my cheeks,/
God's Moth/er deign/ed to / appear / to me,/   (Line 7)
And in / a vis/ion full / of ma/jesty,/
Will'd me / to leave / my base / voca/tion,/   (Line 9)
And free / my coun/try from / cala/mity:/
Her aid / she prom/is'd and / assur'd / success,/
In com/plete glor/y she / reveal'd / herself:/   (Line 12)
And where/as I / was black / and swart / before,/
With those / clear rays, / which she / infused / on me,/
That beau/ty am / I bless'd / with which / you see./
Ask me / what ques/tion thou / canst poss/ible,/
And I / will an/swer un/premed/itat(ed):/   (Line 17)
My cour/age try / by com/bat, if / thou dar'st,/   (Line 18)
And thou / shalt find / that I / exceed / my sex./
Resolve / on this, / thou shalt / be for/tunate,/
If thou / receive / me for / thy war-/like mate./

Clues for the actor discovered through scansion:

- **Line 1:** The first line has an 11th extra unstressed syllable, called a feminine ending, at the end of the line. It is used to create a sense of grace and lightness. Be prepared to encounter a good number of feminine endings in Shakespeare's writing. (Remember, both the anapest and the dactyl have three syllables each to the foot, too.)

- **Line 3**: This line should be spoken with the two syllables in the first word eliding together into one sound, as "Heav'n." Some editions, in fact, spell the word in this contracted form so the actor is reminded that the word is spoken as a single sound.

- **Line 7**: You will notice the actor must pronounce the final "ed" of "deigned." Otherwise the rhythm is thrown off.

- **Line 9**: Today we pronounce the word "vocation" with three syllables. If that's how you pronounce it here, you will once again throw off the rhythm. But if you throw in an extra little "kick" — making four syllables in the word, not three — it will scan fluidly. (This point is discussed earlier in this chapter in the section on pronunciation.) Most actors today would opt for sacrificing rhythm so as not to distance their character from the audience. "Vo-**ca**-ti-**on**" sounds awkward compared with "Vo-**ca**-tion."

- **Line 12**: Scansion of this line, with emphasis on the first syllable of "complete," hints at a possible different Shakespearean pronunciation of the word than we are used to hearing today. The word scans similarly in many other pieces of Shakespeare's writing, so we can assume this word was likely pronounced in his day with emphasis on the first syllable.

- **Line 17**: There is another feminine ending in this line.

- **Line 18**: "Dar'st" is another word that today might be pronounced with two syllables, but in Shakespeare's usage they are elided together to create one sound.

Now the actor working on La Pucelle can begin to play with stressed and unstressed beats and make some choices in pointing words. By the time the actor has explored each line at least five times through, the subconscious mind will have begun to make inroads in memorization. More importantly, the meaning will begin to fall into place and much of the actor's initial apprehension will evaporate.

By breaking down Shakespeare's verse into concrete steps and methodology, as outlined in this chapter, elevated language will become less intimidating than it might have first appeared to the novice Shakespearean actor. It's just a matter of taking text work one step at a time. All the answers will be there in the fullness of time.

Here is your checklist for literary analysis. Search Shakespeare's text for clues to support your acting choices through:

- scansion
- paraphrasing
- inner monologue
- blocking ideas
- pronunciation
- pointing words
- dramatic tension and rhythm
- pace
- breath breaks
- rhythm and rhyme

These will allow your interpretation of character development, emotional life, and relationships to emerge radiantly through the language of Renaissance England.

Chapter Twenty
Shakespeare and the Actor

Forms of Shakespeare's writing

Although the greatest part of Shakespeare's work is written in iambic pentameter blank verse, he used other forms and devices in writing, too. One has already been mentioned in Chapter 19: rhyming couplets. This chapter will explore other literary styles that Shakespeare employed.

1. Sonnet:

The sonnet, discussed at some length in Chapter 6, is a form of poetry written in 14 lines of iambic pentameter verse with a specific structure and rhyme scheme. In his plays, Shakespeare occasionally used sonnets as prologues to introduce the plot, to outline basic facts we need so we can understand the opening scene of the play, and often to foreshadow what is about to unfold. One example of the sonnet form can be found in the Prologue to *Romeo and Juliet*:

> "Two households, both alike in dignity,
> In fair Verona, where we lay our scene,
> From ancient grudge break to new mutiny,
> Where civil blood makes civil hands unclean.
> From forth the fatal loins of these two foes

A pair of star-cross'd lovers take their life;
Whose misadventured piteous overthrows
Do with their death bury their parents' strife.
The fearful passage of their death-mark'd love,
And the continuance of their parents' rage,
Which, but their children's end, nought could remove,
Is now the two hours' traffic of our stage;
The which if you with patient ears attend,
What here shall miss, our toil shall strive to mend."

When Romeo and Juliet meet at the end of Act I, their first words interweave to form another sonnet but, in this instance, it is followed by an additional quatrain for a total of 18 lines. Shakespeare was ever creative in experimenting with literary form.

2. Lyric verse:

Another form of writing that Shakespeare used was lyric verse. This is a short poem expressing personal emotion, but it is not necessarily written in iambic pentameter form. Shakespeare pokes gentle fun at the theme of "love" through the device of both lyric verse and sonnets in *Love's Labour's Lost.* The king and his courtiers, living in self-imposed isolation in the woods, resolved to fast, study, and give up contact with others — especially ladies — in order to meditate on a spiritual level. Each of them in turn falls in love with a woman, however, and in Act IV, Scene 3, the deep emotions of their new-found love are expressed, one after the other, through sonnets and lyric verse.

Here is an example of lyric verse from that scene. It is an ode written by Dumain:

"On a day, alack the day:
Love, whose month is ever May,
Spied a blossom passing fair,
Playing in the wanton air:
Through the velvet leaves the wind,
All unseen, can passage find;
That the lover, sick to death,
Wish himself the heaven's breath.
Air (quoth he) thy cheeks may blow;
Air, would I might triumph so.

But alack my hand is sworn
Ne'er to pluck thee from thy throne:
Vow alack for youth unmeet,
Youth so apt to pluck a sweet..."
Dumain continues in a similar fashion for several more lines.

3. Song:

Shakespeare used songs freely. Most of his plays contain examples that help create the spectacle of Elizabethan festivities — banquets, weddings, and celebrations. Spirits, sprites, and fairies, such as we see in *The Tempest* or *A Midsummer Night's Dream,* provide many charming moments that heighten the sense of fantasy through the use of song. Because songs have the potential to create charming harmonious diversions, they can enhance the mood of a scene. One instance occurs when the fairies in *A Midsummer Night's Dream* lull Bottom to sleep with their singing.

Songs can also take the audience on a different tack. An example of this appears in Ophelia's mad scene in *Hamlet.* Here in Act IV, Scene 5, Ophelia enters singing:

"How should I your true love know
　From another one?
By his cockle hat and staff,
　And his sandal shoon.
He is dead and gone, lady,
　He is dead and gone;
At his head a grass-green turf,
　At his heels a stone.
White his shroud as the mountain snow,
　Larded with sweet flowers;
Which bewept to the grave did not go
　With true-love showers."

This song vividly expresses the disintegration of Ophelia's mental condition and is more dramatic than if her condition were merely described by someone else such as a messenger. Throughout this song, she is unaware of the interjected lines from Gertrude and Claudius, which gives strong dramatic tension to the scene. Ophelia can sing "out of tune" to reinforce that her character is "out of tune" with the real world as a result of the events thus far in the play.

4. Music:

Shakespeare's plays incorporated the talents of a number of musicians because music can reinforce the fantasy world of the stage. Fanfares and incidental music helped link scenes together in seamless continuous action. Music was used to create a mood, to mark the passing of time, or perhaps to help the dramatic action of the play.

One of the challenges facing you when approaching a Shakespearean song is to compose your own melody line. There is no written music from the original plays, although suggested tunes for all Shakespeare's songs do exist. But every actor has the freedom to create his or her own music for such songs.

5. Prose:

Just as the emotional climax in the modern musical scene comes with a character bursting into song, so in Shakespeare's day a character would speak elevated emotions in blank verse. However, Shakespeare wrote a number of scenes in prose when he wanted to express less lofty thoughts or reveal character change. For example, Hamlet speaks in blank verse when he is expressing deep thoughts and feelings. At other times — when he is "mad" or "not himself" — he speaks in prose.

In Shakespeare's plays, prose is the language of less educated people or characters from a lower social position. Because prose has fewer literary conventions than verse, a natural "everyday life" speech pattern is possible. Most of his servants and soldiers speak in prose and letters were generally written in that style. The realism of prose helps to reinforce the sense of everydayness contained in the letter.

When you encounter a scene that is written in prose, Shakespeare is giving you a clue that the content of the scene is not emotionally elevated, even though your character may speak in verse elsewhere in the play. Identify why the form of the language has changed and you will find an important aspect of the development of your character.

Additionally, Shakespeare used prose to free up language patterns for comedy, which was viewed in his day as a less heightened and less noble form of expression. It is difficult to create and sustain believable, lively banter in comic exchanges while trying to remain within the confines of blank verse. Shakespeare overcame this problem by settling on prose for comedy.

Falstaff, one of Shakespeare's most exaggerated comic creations, speaks in prose in *King Henry IV, Part 1.* In speaking to Falstaff throughout the play, Prince Hal also talks in prose: he is not his "noble" self so he speaks in prose. Here, Prince Hal is seen teasing Falstaff in Act I, Scene 2. Falstaff has languidly asked, "Now, Hal, what time of day is it, lad?" Prince Hal replies:

"Thou art so fat-witted with drinking of old sack, and unbuttoning thee after supper, and sleeping upon benches the afternoon, that thou hast forgotten to demand that truly which thou wouldst truly know. What a devil hast thou to do with the time of the day? Unless hours were cups of sack, and minutes capons, and clocks the tongues of bawds, and dials the signs of leaping-houses, and the blessed sun himself a fair hot wench in flame-colour'd taffeta; I see no reason why thou shouldst be so superfluous to demand the time of the day."

Prince Hal speaks eloquently in blank verse throughout the play in addressing his father, the king. He also speaks in verse when assuming some measure of nobility in his battle with his father's enemy, Hotspur. This excerpt is from the final scene, Act V, Scene 4, when Prince Hal is about to fight Hotspur (whose family name is Percy). Prince Hal says:

"I am the Prince of Wales, and think not Percy,
To share with me in glory any more:
Two stars keep not their motion in one sphere,
Nor can one England brook a double reign,
Of Harry Percy, and the Prince of Wales."

Another clear example that contrasts integrity of character is found in *King Henry VI, Part 2,* Act IV, Scene 10. Here, the traitorous Cade is escaping after having failed to overthrow the monarchy. He stumbles into the garden of Iden, the staunch and patriotic English yeoman. The sharp contrast between the two characters is provided not just by the words they use, but also by the form of expression they use throughout their one scene. The villain Cade speaks exclusively in prose, while Iden speaks in blank verse.

In *Measure for Measure* and *A Winter's Tale,* Shakespeare easily shifts back and forth between blank verse and prose, as he moves from tragedy to comedy; from darker, evil and ignoble situations to moments of individual reflection, enlightenment, forgiveness, and reconciliation.

There are many such examples that can provide guidance for the actor. The more you delve into Shakespeare's plays, the more you will see how cleverly he used forms of expression to express character, conflict, and emotion.

Forms of dramatic action in Shakespeare's plays

1. Soliloquy:

The actor uses this device to talk directly to the audience in an intimate manner. Today's actor must be aware of the nature of the soliloquy, its intended purpose, and its style of delivery. In the soliloquy, the character reveals issues he or she is facing, debates the pros and cons and by the end resolves to pursue a course of action. This device, usually presented from a downstage position, allows an actor to communicate deep inner feelings that cannot be expressed in dialogue to other characters in the play.

Today in film and television, the same effect is created by the use of voice-overs. When a character's personal feelings or reflective comments are superimposed on the opening moments of a television show or movie, we can see what is occurring right now while the voice-over fills us in on important background information. At other times, the voice-over can permit us to see a discrepancy between what a character is saying to others and what he or she is really thinking.

Here is a portion from a soliloquy in *Hamlet* that appears in Act III, Scene 1. Claudius, uncle to Hamlet, murdered Hamlet's father (the king of Denmark), then seized the throne and married Hamlet's mother. Hamlet, his emotions profoundly shaken by these events, is unable to resolve on a singular course of action. Here he is speculating on the nature of life and death:

> "To be, or not to be, that is the question:
> Whether 'tis nobler in the mind to suffer
> The slings and arrows of outrageous fortune,
> Or to take arms against a sea of troubles,
> And by opposing end them: to die, to sleep
> No more; and by a sleep, to say we end
> The heart-ache, and the thousand natural shocks
> That flesh is heir to? 'Tis a consummation
> Devoutly to be wish'd. To die to sleep,
> To sleep, perchance to dream: ay, there's the rub ..."

Through the device of the soliloquy, we are allowed to see into Hamlet's mental and emotional state at that point in the play. We can share the struggle that is churning inside him as he is attempting to decide on a course of action, and we learn his thoughts on the nature of life and death. Without the insight expressed in Hamlet's various soliloquies, our deep knowledge of his true character would be dramatically reduced.

2. Monologue:

The monologue was never spoken "to oneself," as was the soliloquy. Rather, it was meant for the benefit of those listening nearby. This might include the audience members, but it could be that the actor was speaking to God, fate, or the elements of nature.

The monologue could be an invocation or a denunciation. It was sometimes used to reflect on events or to disclose a sudden revelation. Sometimes, the monologue could approach the intimacy of the soliloquy, but other characters present in the scene would be understood to "hear" the monologue. At other times, however, the monologue can be seen as an extended form of normal dramatic dialogue.

There are numerous examples of the monologue form in Shakespeare, but one of the best known can be found in *King Lear*. Before Act III, Scene 2, King Lear has divided his kingdom between his daughters. Subsequently, he has been treated shabbily by them. Dismissed from court, he wanders in exile. In this scene, Lear berates the cruel elements in the famous "storm-on-the-heath" scene. Although his faithful Fool is with Lear at this time, Lear is not addressing him. Indeed, Lear is oblivious to him for many lines as he rages at the forces of nature. Rejected and alienated, he cries out:

"Blow winds, and crack your cheeks; Rage, blow
You cataracts, and hurricanoes spout,
Till you have drench'd our steeples, drown the cocks,
You sulph'rous and thought-executing fires,
Vaunt-couriers of oak-cleaving thunderbolts,
Singe my white head ..."

3. Prologues and epilogues:

Shakespeare occasionally began a play with a prologue and/or ended it with an epilogue. Sometimes these lines were delivered by a character who appeared several times during the play, as with Gower's opening lines in *Pericles, Prince of Tyre*. At other times, these direct addresses were spoken by an actor called Chorus, as in the Prologue to *King Henry V.*

In any case, the lines framing the show were delivered to all members of the audience to "warm up the crowd." This tradition dates back to the days of travelling troubadours who passed the hat at the end of shows performed in makeshift settings. In the same way today, a television presenter may open and close a program, but may not otherwise have anything directly to do with the program itself.

The prologue, as discussed earlier in this chapter on sonnets, serves to outline what the play is about by introducing theme and characters. Prologues and epilogues were not restricted to 14 lines, as were sonnets. For example, the Prologue to *King Henry VIII* goes on for 32 lines. The epilogue was designed to sum up the play and usually included a plea for a round of applause from the audience. This can be seen in Puck's final charge to the audience at the end of *A Midsummer Night's Dream*. Puck, also known as Robin Goodfellow, says:

"So goodnight unto you all.
Give me your hands, if we be friends,
And Robin shall restore amends."

4. Aside:

Shakespeare also used this device, which was very popular later in 17th- and 18th-century theatre. The aside allows an actor to talk directly to the audience for a brief line or two, usually without other characters in the scene being allowed to "hear." Other actors present in the scene generally remain in a semi-freeze during an aside, in order not to upstage the focus on the actor who is delivering the aside. Today in film and television, the same effect is created when the camera zooms in on the face of a speaker who "confides" in the camera.

This technique is used mostly in comedy. To stage an aside, the actor usually leans out toward the audience, cups an upstage hand around his or her mouth (to prevent other characters from hearing), and semi-whispers the line.

For example, some individual lines spoken by the drunken Stephano — on first discovering the monster Caliban in *The Tempest* in Act II, Scene 1 — can be thrown directly out to the audience. This would suit both the spirit of Stephano's character — his character is broad and full of gusto — and the comic nature of the scene.

5. Dialogue:

During the balance of Shakespeare's plays, dialogue is the conventional speech pattern. In dialogue, the actors within the scene do not concern themselves with the audience in the manner demanded by the soliloquy, the monologue, or the aside. They are concerned only with the other characters appearing in the scene.

Advice on approaching elaborate speeches

Shakespeare considered himself primarily to be a poet and his use of poetic devices throughout his plays is extensive. He used elaborate imagery and extended descriptive passages to embellish the text, provide layers in characterization, and illuminate his ideas. Although beautiful to read, literary devices and classical allusions can often intimidate, confuse, or tongue-tie a novice actor. The length and complexity of Shakespeare's lines pose special challenges for the modern actor, whose speech patterns may be based on shorter lines and a more concise vocabulary.

Many literary terms are discussed in Chapter 6, and you may wish to review those definitions now that we are addressing Shakespeare's plays.

Juliet says, in Act III, Scene 2 of *Romeo and Juliet*:

"Gallop apace, you fiery-footed steeds,
Toward Phœbus' lodging; such a waggoner
As Phæthon would whip you to the west,
And bring in cloudy night immediately.
Spread thy close curtain, love-performing night,
That runaway's eyes may wink, and Romeo
Leap to these arms, untalk'd of and unseen!
Lovers can see to do their amorous rites
By their own beauties; or, if love be blind,
It best agrees with night. Come, civil night,
Thou sober-suited matron, all in black,
And learn me how to lose a winning match,
Play'd for a pair of stainless maidenhoods:
Hood my unmann'd blood, bating in my cheeks,
With thy black mantle; till strange love, grown bold,
Think true love acted simple modesty:
Come, night: come, Romeo; come, thou day in night;
For thou wilt lie upon the wings of night

Whiter than new snow on a raven's back.
Come, gentle night, come, loving, black-brow'd night,
Give me my Romeo; and, when he shall die,
Take him and cut him out in little stars,
And he will make the face of heaven so fine
That all the world will be in love with night,
And pay no worship to the garish sun.
O! I have bought the mansion of a love,
But not possess'd it, and, though I am sold,
Not yet enjoyed. So tedious is this day
As is the night before some festival
To an impatient child that hath new robes
And may not wear them ..."

There are key elements here for the actor to take into consideration:

1. the speed of movement provided by words like "leap," "see," and "come"
2. the appeal for darkness found in words like "cloudy night," "blind," and "black"
3. the use of strong colour in the imagery, particularly black, white, and red

This speech is a good example of the problems a novice actor encounters when first trying to speak lines written with extended imagery. Read the scene several times, allowing yourself to see and feel the images in your own mind. Include all classical allusions, personification, and comparisons of similes and metaphors. The words involved in the imagery will affect your emotional delivery. Work patiently through the feelings and details of the images. Allow your voice to express the full meaning of those images, or the major thought of the line may get lost.

- To find the momentum of the lines, begin by marking your script with a **highlighter** to isolate the minimum number of key words that provide the core to the sentence. This will provide you with the **through-line** and will include a couple of nouns, some verbs, and other essential words. It will not include weak words, such as conjunctions, comparisons contained in similes and metaphors, embellishments of language, excessive adjectives, or classical allusions.

- Begin with the essential **verbs**. This will enable you to discover words such as: Gallop, bring, spread, leap, see, and come. Not all verbs will be used, for you are aiming for economy in your selection of key words, but you can see how these few verbs provide tempo and energy.
- Skim your passage to find other key words that speak a strong, personal message. You may locate a vivid image, an emotive word, or a logical connection to the verb you have already chosen.
- If you are unsure whether to include a specific word, leave it out. You want to include only those words that carry an unquestionable impact for you. By doing this you will often create "short sentences."

On skimming Juliet's lines to detect the minimum key words, you may discover the following: (Note that these key words are expressed below in italics, as opposed to the boldface font used in illustrating iambic pentameter rhythm, because they may or may not be pointing words. In your script, they should be highlighted for easy reading.)

" *Gallop apace*, you fiery-footed steeds,
Towards Phœbus' *lodging;* such a waggoner
As Phæthon would *whip* you to the *west,*
And *bring in* cloudy *night* immediately.
Spread thy close curtain, *love-performing night,*
That runaway's eyes may wink, and *Romeo*
Leap to these arms, untalk'd of and unseen!
Lovers can *see* to do their amorous rites
By their own *beauties;* or, if love be blind,
It best agrees with night. *Come,* civil *night,*
Thou sober-suited matron, all in black,
And *learn me* how *to lose* a winning match,
Play'd for a pair of *stainless maidenhoods.*"
Hood my unmann'd *blood,* bating in my cheeks,
With thy *black mantle;* till strange love, grown bold,
Think true love *acted* simple modesty:
Come, night: come, Romeo; come, thou day in night;
For thou wilt *lie* upon the *wings* of *night*
Whiter than new *snow* on a *raven's back.*
Come, gentle night, *come, loving, black-*brow'd night,
Give me my *Romeo;* and, when he shall die,

415

Take him and cut him out *in little stars,*
And he will make the face of heaven so fine
That *all the world* will be *in love* with night,
And pay no worship to the garish sun.
O! I have *bought* the mansion of a love,
But not possess'd it, and, though I am sold,
Not yet enjoyed. So *tedious* is this *day*
As is the night before some festival
To an impatient child that hath new robes
And may not wear them ..."

To sum up the key words for your through-line, then, you might decide on:

Gallop apace, lodging. Whip west. Bring in night. Spread love-performing night. Romeo leap. Lovers see beauties. Come night, learn me to lose stainless maidenhoods. Hood blood, black mantle, acted. Come, night: come, Romeo; come, lie wings night whiter snow raven's back. Come, come, loving, black. Give Romeo. Take him in little stars. All the world in love. Bought, but not possessed, not yet enjoyed. Tedious day.

What we have in summary, then, are the most passionate words that capture the essence of the scene. The actor peels away the excessive words to get to the "bare bones" through-line of the speech. This prevents you from getting bogged down in extended imagery or antiquated language. The end result will connect the you to the emotional life of the character and make your acting more truthful.

Developing a through-line in verse

You may wonder how the actor reconciles the choice of through-line words with the choice of pointing words, especially because some through-line words fall on apparently unstressed beats (such as "leap" and "hood" in Juliet's speech). But there are different, specific vocal skills required. These skills involve inflection, pitch, and rate of delivery.

Earlier it was discussed how some film actors and their directors make different choices when delivering the same speeches in various versions of Shakespeare's plays. Contrasted through-lines and pointing words bring personal interpretation to the text. This is one reason why people can sit through several versions of the same Shakespearean play during their lifetimes. No two productions will be alike.

Speaking the through-line:

When the time comes to work on delivery of the lines, actors should speak the words that comprise the through-line on the middle pitch of their voice. Other words that are not part of the through-line can either be lifted to a higher pitch or dropped to a lower note according to the emotional content of the words in question. The actor plays with variables, including rate of delivery and volume, so that certain phrases that expand an image can be spoken more quickly and/or quietly as appropriate. (The actor's phrase is to "throw away" a line.)

Here is an example using a section of Juliet's speech above. Italicized key words are spoken on the mid-range, while other phrases are lifted or dropped and are spoken at a faster or slower rate. Pointing words, as determined through scansion, are inflected within the given pitch and rate of delivery. They are layered on top of the through-line, but no attempt has been made here to indicate pointing words.

This is simply a demonstration of how an actor can vary the pitch and rate of speaking to reveal the through-line in Shakespeare's complicated text:

- Mid-range   *"Gallop apace,*
- Lower range and faster rate   you fiery-footed steeds,

- Upper range and slower rate   such a waggoner
- Mid range   Towards Phœbus' *lodging;*

- Continuing upper/slower   As Phæthon would
- Mid-range   *whip* you to the *west,*

- Mid-range   And *bring in* cloudy *night*
- Lower range and slower rate   immediately.

- Mid-range   *Spread*   *love-performing night,*
- Lower range and slower rate   thy close curtain,

- Upper range and faster rate   That runaway's eyes may wink, and
- Mid-range   *Romeo*

- Mid-range   *Leap* to these arms,
- Lower range and slower rate   untalk'd of and unseen!

By this means, then, the main message of the lines will be heard. This may sound like an overly clinical approach to Shakespearean text work, but the audience's ear will not be bogged down by equal importance being attributed to each and every word.

This technique will help you make sense out of long, embellished images that can slow down a speech. After you have analyzed the script for the through-line, the meaning will become clearer for you. Your interpretation will take on a natural sound with practice and you will feel much more comfortable delivering the lines. Over time, as you become more practised with Shakespeare's language in a variety of his plays, you will achieve an easy, natural confidence with through-lines.

The foundation for the delivery of the speech rests on the iambic pentameter rhythm. Despite the variations in pitch, rate and volume that the through-line technique encompasses, a sense of the rhythm must still be heard in the spoken voice.

Some advice for the novice Shakespearean actor

Initially, when new actors prepare a scene from Shakespeare, they fall into the trap of excessive amounts of "I should":

- "I should speak beautifully with lovely rounded vocal tones" (because that's what all Shakespearean actors are supposed to sound like, isn't it?).
- "I should look noble and grand" (because I am meant to be in a tragedy).
- "I should be very deep and serious in my manner" (because I am doing a scene from the Bard, after all).
- I should affect a British dialect (because Shakespeare was English)

When an actor "assumes" a voice, he or she sounds insincere. You become involved with how you sound rather than what you are saying. To express it differently: you are playing the effect, not the cause. There is no substance behind an artificial "Shakespearean" dialect or accent. The reason for Shakespeare's enduring international appeal throughout the centuries does not lie in beautifully produced plummy vowels. The answer is found in the universal appeal of his plays: the emotions, fun, drama, stories, characters, energy, themes, and understanding of our heritage.

1. In first approaching the creation of a character from Shakespeare's

plays, discover the **natural voice** of the character. Because voice is so important in expressing the emotional life of a character, sound must come from within you and not be assumed or imposed.

Accents and dialects may be added, using any regional variation of the English language, so long as the emotional truth of the speech provides the foundation for the words. For example, the porter in *Macbeth* (who provides the only comic relief in the play) can be presented just as successfully with a rural Canadian dialect as with a British working-class sound or an authentic Scottish dialect. The Stratford Shakespearean Festival (Ontario) has recognized this reality for some time now, and it is very common in this country today to hear Shakespeare's plays spoken with a variety of North American sounds.

The actor's task is to pursue the character's emotional intention with full honesty.

2. A second major problem for the novice Shakespearean actor lies in discovering the **natural energy** of the character. This energy will provide the source of all physical action. It will also convey the intention behind the spoken word.

Let's look at the role of Juliet in *Romeo and Juliet*. Most young actors are tempted to see Juliet as a self-indulgent or self-absorbed sentimentalist — much as Romeo himself behaves early in the play. Before he meets Juliet, Romeo thinks he is in love with another girl but in reality, he is more in love with the idea of being in love. Sentimentality leads to weak emotional choices.

In preparing for the role of Juliet, don't fall into the common trap of visualizing the character through pastel-coloured filters. That is the fastest way to make Juliet a sighing and fluttery character. And she isn't. She is young, she knows what she wants, she is impetuous and she is persistent. Most important, Juliet is just discovering her sexuality. All these elements should be kept firmly in mind when rehearsing any of Juliet's speeches or scenes.

Here is an example where sentimentality would kill the energy of a scene. Act III, Scene 5 begins at dawn. Romeo has married Juliet and has secretly spent the night in her room. The time has come for them to part, before his presence could be discovered and he could be arrested for the murder of Tybalt. The young lovers must part, but they long for just one more embrace, just one more kiss.

On first reading, many actors will focus on the text and allow the lyricism and eloquence of the language to carry them. Yet, before the Nurse comes to interrupt them 36 lines into the scene, Romeo and Juliet experience each of the following emotions (albeit in different orders at different times):

- fear that dawn is arriving
- realization that they must part
- denial that dawn has yet begun
- defiance of the fate awaiting Romeo if he stays
- an attempt to seduce the other
- resentment of the unalterable forces of nature

Exercise:

To help the actors discover the sense of desperation that runs through the scene, begin by reading the first 36 lines of the scene. Then, Romeo and Juliet must embrace each other and retain a solid grasp no matter what happens. Surround the couple by a large number of students. On a given sign, the other students are to attempt to separate Romeo and Juliet, trying to pull them apart with unrelenting effort. At the same time, Romeo and Juliet must reread their lines without letting go of each other, all the while ignoring the efforts of those who would separate them. Sometimes it helps if two students are assigned the task of holding the scripts in front of Romeo and Juliet during this exercise, as it can be difficult for the actors to hold each other and their scripts.

After they have completed this step, Romeo and Juliet should reread the lines again. This time, they should retain the breath centres and breath patterns that they have just been forced to use. They will discover the natural source of energy for their characters and for their relationship in this scene.

3. These two points go hand in hand with finding the **natural emotional content** in Shakespeare's writing. One of the actor's biggest challenges is to discover interesting and appropriate emotional levels in Shakespeare's lines. There is often a great temptation to ride through his speeches on one emotional note. This is a common problem in contemporary plays, too, of course. But when the language is as complex and rich as Shakespeare's, and four centuries old, there is a special need to keep the emotional life vibrant.

Emotional texturing in Shakespeare

Discovering emotional texturing can be a very helpful step in the actor's work process. Here is a scene from Act II, Scene 2 of *Twelfth Night*. At this point in the play, Viola is disguised as a man in order to protect her identity following a shipwreck at sea. While working in disguise for Duke Orsino, she is sent as an emissary to the Countess Olivia to plead the Duke's devotion to Olivia on his behalf.

Viola has fallen in love with the Duke, but she must not reveal this secret while she is assuming the role of a man. Olivia, meanwhile, is quite smitten with Viola (in disguise) and she sends Malvolio chasing after Viola to give her a ring. Here is a portion of Viola's speech immediately after Malvolio has tossed the ring on the ground and departed. This speech is very popular with actors because it contains great comic potential.

> "I left no ring with her: what means this lady?
> Fortune forbid my outside hath not charm'd her!
> She made good view of me; indeed, so much,
> That sure methought her eyes had lost her tongue,
> For she did speak in starts distractedly.
> She loves me, sure; the cunning of her passion
> Invites me in this churlish messenger.
> None of my lord's ring! why, he sent her none.
> I am the man: if it be so, as 'tis,
> Poor lady, she were better love a dream.
> Disguise, I see, thou art a wickedness,
> Wherein the pregnant enemy does much."

Read the speech once through for content. Then take some time to find images wherever you can in the piece. The right image will help make the emotions real for you. Now read it aloud twelve additional times, each time trying to focus consistently on only one of the points listed below:

1. disbelief
2. annoyance
3. confusion
4. anger
5. giddiness
6. horror
7. exasperation

8. outrage
9. bewilderment
10. indifference
11. sexual tension
12 offhandedness

Forget about iambic pentameter for the moment. Concentrate only on the emotional content. Incorporate a lot of sound as you read and add noises wherever possible. Consider the importance of:

- breath centre
- breath rhythm
- energy level

You may discover that the image or emotion on which you are concentrating works more strongly on one line than another. Don't worry if that happens. You may also feel that one or two of the qualities are more difficult for you to deal with than the others. But don't use that as an excuse to give up.

What you will likely discover is that one of those emotions works well with one line, or even part of a line. Another will work equally strongly with another moment. Perhaps a third will be an obvious choice for yet another part of the speech. Experiment with these interpretations, and then pick and choose what works best for you. Eventually, you will be able to piece together a reasonably well-textured emotional interpretation of Viola's speech.

This exercise is particularly important when approaching a dramatic piece. Often an actor will become so caught up in the high drama of the piece, exploring all kinds of heavy-duty feelings, that he or she will completely lose sight of lighter moments in the script. This leads to less effective acting that borders on "soap opera" intensity. Fifty lines of unrelenting anger can get very tedious for any audience unless interspersed with a generous helping of many softer emotions to texture the speech.

Even the most powerful dramatic speech will have some elements of humour waiting to be discovered. Comic moments in dramatic scenes provide contrast just as they do in real life when a wisecrack can break the tension of a situation. If you were to get into the rehearsal habit of laughing your way once or twice through a given speech — giggling, in fact — you would discover that humour naturally emerges on some of the most surprising lines.

When exploring emotional texturing, keep in mind the theatrical principle of opposites discussed earlier in this book. Two strongly contrasted emotions placed immediately together will always provide a strong dramatic or comic moment, both for the actor and the audience. Some rehearsal time should always be devoted to discovering and developing those contrasted moments.

Other acting exercises explained elsewhere in this book will work well with Shakespeare. Both internal and external approaches to creating a character can be useful, depending on which of his plays you are rehearsing and the challenges inherent in rehearsing that style of play — comedy, tragedy, history, or romance.

However, you have to work with Shakespeare. You can't fake it. If you are required to present a piece from one of Shakespeare's plays, the person auditioning you will know in a few seconds exactly what level of instinct, bravura attack, skill, understanding, insight, and training you can bring to your acting. Shakespeare really is the ultimate test. Your acting strengths will be clearly evident, and so will your weaknesses. The auditioner will know exactly what he or she can expect from you as an actor.

That is why preparation in Shakespearean monologues and scenes form part of the foundation in the training of every serious actor.

Part Three

The "Outside Eye"
The Actor as Director/Coach

Chapter Twenty-One
How to Help the Actor with Problems in Acting

When novice actors first present a monologue or scene, unusual things happen to them — that is, until they acquire a sense of what they are doing and what acting should involve. Here are a dozen of the most frequent problems that I have encountered in acting classes over the years, along with suggestions to take the "acting-ness" out of acting.

Each of these problems is discussed in greater detail from the actor's viewpoint in other parts of this book. However, I have condensed the problems and solutions in this chapter for easy reference by the teacher/director. For although this book is aimed principally at students, it is common in the classroom that one student will end up directing others in a scene. The distinction between director and teacher is so blurred in most classrooms that the term teacher/director seems simpler, and it is to this person that this chapter is devoted.

Some of the exercises should be done on a one-to-one basis, especially with inexperienced actors. This isn't always possible, of course, but it does get faster and better results. Sometimes, too, you will work with a student for weeks or months on a particular acting problem, with no apparent results. All of a sudden, the right combination of time, experience, material, insight, and courage will result in an amazing breakthrough.

You'll be thrilled when a breakthrough happens, then equally dismayed to discover that the student has yet another monumental acting problem. It was there all the time, but until you resolved the first one, the second one wasn't clearly visible.

Twelve common problems in acting and how to deal with them

1. The School of Internalized Acting

Diagnosis:

These students may have done all the preparatory work but they don't have the vaguest idea of how to present the scene effectively. This is not simply a case of learning the basics of blocking and stage design. It is a much more serious problem that is deeply rooted, but its origins are not the concern of the acting coach.

These actors may have no sense of how to use the body to express emotion, and are so physically inhibited that they feel disconnected from gestures and physical impulse. They feel clumsy and ill at ease. Given half a chance, they will sit on chairs or sofas throughout the scene because these are "safe places." (There's a lot to be said for using uncomfortable furniture in rehearsals; it encourages actors to search for physical action.)

In performance, Internalized Actors rely heavily on the use of the face, eyes, and voice. If a television camera were present and could provide close-ups and visual variety, their work might suffice. But there is generally not sufficient emotional release for stage purposes. An intelligent performance may be going on inside the actor's mind, but he or she just cannot get it out. What you must try to do is release that interpretation. Help the actor find the appropriate physical expression of the character.

Remedy:

The first step in dealing with this problem is to take away all the words from the scene. Have the student work on a few lines from the speech using just movement and body language to convey the emotional content. The source of this emotion will be found in the breath. If students can get in touch with the right breath level behind each emotion, body action and gestures will take care of themselves:

(a) Isolate the first emotion in the speech and have actor repeat several breath cycles while concentrating only on that one emotion. The deeper the breath goes into the actor's body, the more easily emotion can be felt.
(b) Use gibberish sounds or nonsense words in accompaniment with the breath.

(c) At the end of an exhaled breath, have the actor speak the one most important word in the sentence.

(d) Finally, allow the actor to say the whole sentence through synthesizing breath, text, and movement.

If students still have a problem developing breath and energy, a more physical approach to acting may release the emotion in the speech. Here is a "tug-of-war" exercise that may help. Seat two actors on the floor in the middle of the room facing each other, and have them lock right hands. Actor A (for whom this exercise is designed) picks a focal point on the wall as far over his or her left shoulder as possible. It is to this spot that Actor A must direct the lines of the speech while simultaneously trying to drag Actor B as close as possible to that focal point. Actor B's job is to try to drag Actor A away from the focal point. On the word "go," Actor A begins to speak while both A and B engage in a tug-of-war.

During this exercise, Actor A will likely encounter line problems because of the split focus and physical energy required to succeed. That does not matter. If the actor simply repeats the same line over and over, jumps from one part of the script to another, or paraphrases dialogue, the exercise will still work.

Immediately the speech is over (or when one person "wins"), have Actor A stand up and deliver the speech again. The physical effort of the exercise will have stimulated deep breathing and, as long as Actor A sustains strong diaphragmatic breathing, emotions will be much more easily released. In addition, this exercise helps students feel a "need" to speak that they can then connect to the character's intention in the scene.

Another exercise is to have the actor paint a long, tall, imaginary wall using three different colours of paint and three contrasted sizes of brushes or paint rollers. This is done while speaking the lines of the scene to another unseen person on the opposite side of the wall. Increase the speed of action while the actor is painting the wall.

Have the actor deliver the speech "for real" once the exercise is complete, and see what changes occur. This exercise works to free up the action of the rib cage and diaphragm, thanks to the extensive physical use of the arms while painting the imaginary wall. Bigger projection and exaggerated physical activity will cause the actor to discover necessary energy and freedom in performance.

2. *The School of Approval Seekers*

Diagnosis:

These actors are known by their use of, "Am I doing it right? Huh? Huh?" The phrase is not verbalized, you understand, but it's telegraphed. The message consistently pervades the performance. Their introduction generally contains rising inflections at the ends of lines. Approval Seekers are afraid to state, but feel content to ask.

How does this subliminal message override everything else in acting? It's simple. Approval Seekers keep darting little, fleeting glances at you — the teacher/director — every few seconds. They constantly monitor you throughout the speech or scene looking for reassurance that their work is successful by assessing your reactions. They need to be advised that they should concentrate less on the director's pleased response and more on pleasing themselves.

Approval Seekers will panic and lose their lines if the director is diverted or begins to make notes. Line dries are often accompanied by awkward laughter, too. Approval Seekers often express their discomfort through giggles that, for them, are a socially safe form of releasing embarrassment.

Remedy:

A daily routine of concentration exercises is helpful to such students. However, to cure this problem — which is a nervous habit, really — run the scene again with one change: make it impossible for actor to watch you. There are a couple of ways to ensure that the actor cannot monitor your reactions:

If the scene has a lot of blocking and props, reposition the scene so the actor's back is to you throughout as much of the action as possible.

If the scene is relatively static, have the actor present it with eyes closed or blindfolded. Through analysis of the text, make the student aware of specific points of focus at every step of the scene. That focal point will never include you, the teacher/director.

It does not hurt to have a chat with them about believing in their own abilities. See what happens to their discussions when you ban the use of "right" and "wrong" from all their rehearsals. If they ever begin to use either word, immediately speak up and require them to rephrase their point.

3. *The School of Flounce Acting*

Diagnosis:

Students from this school of acting are those who embellish the moments before beginning to present a speech. Occasionally, their face takes on a "special look" ("Watch me, I'm about to act. See? Now I'm acting!") Sometimes, physical tension is manifested in the arms or body in a very strange way. It might involve a shoulder roll, hand tension, or a fixed tilt of the head. Invariably the voice is artificial and unbelievable.

Remedy:

The way to deal with that problem is to show the actors that saying the lines of the speech should be no different from talking about what they did last weekend:

   (a) Turn two chairs back-to-back and place them about a metre apart. Position the actor in one chair while you sit in the other with your arms resting on the backs of the chairs. In this position, you will be very close to each other and can speak at a low, easy vocal level.

   (b) Ask them to begin recounting something trivial that happened to them recently, but using an intimate voice. They will be unable to use the personal "flounce" mannerisms with this physical position and verbal approach. They must make the story as real as possible.

   (c) After a minute or so of this story, tell them to begin the acting monologue over again at exactly the same level of intimacy as the trivial story. If bad habits begin to reappear because the actor associates them with the text of the speech, stop them and go back to the beginning again.

   (d) Once students are comfortable working with natural ease in such close proximity, you can begin to increase the distance between the chairs. Ultimately, you will be able to have them achieve the same results from a standing position.

4. *The School of Perfection*

Diagnosis:

Students from this school have serious concentration problems. They may be overly concerned with the accuracy of memory work and may be convinced that you, the teacher/director, can read minds and therefore know that they forgot a word. This kind of student generally does well with academic detail in written assignments, but panics when perfection doesn't happen in performance.

Students from the School of Perfection seem to think that all acting teachers know every speech in theatrical literature word-perfectly. They have two favourite expressions:

- "Oh no, I made a mistake. Can I start over again?"
- "But you should have seen it last night at home in front of my mirror!"

For this reason, a director should never follow the script of a speech when novice actors are presenting something. It spooks them too much. There is a time to stress complete fidelity to the text, but that time is some distance down the road. Try to make the student understand that memory work is only a small portion of an actor's job. In fact, sustaining a character through line problems is a much more important skill than memorization.

Remedy:

The more flexible you remain with blocking and movement choices, the less likely you are to panic and blank out when line problems occur:

(a) Have these students say each line through three, four, or five times, but specifically not the words that the playwright has written. Each time the actors say the line, they should find yet another way of expressing the character's intention. These students can use their own words or ad lib around the subject, but must never say the lines as written.

(b) Involve different types of movement or blocking in this exercise. Have them move in contrasted ways, each time beginning from a new starting point. For example, try sitting the first time, leaning against a wall the second time, pacing around the room a third time, reclining on the floor the next time, and so forth. This will help to build their concentration and confidence.

Student actors should be encouraged to try many physical positions when beginning to work on a new piece. When the time comes to memorize the text, they will not feel totally "married" to every word of the text or every prepared action.

You can fool 99 percent of your audience 99 percent of the time when you dry, if you keep your wits about you and if you understand the intention of the lines in the script. This skill improves with experience.

5. The School of "Bleaaauugh" Acting

Diagnosis:

These students throw themselves into a piece with great gusto. They love the emotional content and ride it to the hilt. Generally, these actors lose perspective on the nuances of emotion and the need for texturing the speech with subtlety and emotional variety.

For instance, if they discover anger in the speech, wow — does the audience ever get anger! This anger is released non-stop on every word of every line. Hence, the anger lands "bleaaauugh" in front of you a little bit like an unfortunate digestive upset.

Remedy:

Script analysis is the first step toward improvement for those who remain locked in one strong emotion:

(a) Have them look through the speech for the variety of emotions and list these.

(b) They should consult a dictionary and a thesaurus to discover the shadings of each of the words.

(c) Ask them to select five or six strongly contrasted emotions and read the speech through several times in the manner discussed in the previous chapter under "emotional texturing." Each time, they are to read every line concentrating on only one emotional intention throughout the whole speech.

(d) Have them look for the use of emotional opposites. Whatever emotion they have served up to you, ask them to explore the opposite. For example, if they expressed only anger, have them deliver the entire speech as if it were the funniest joke of the year. The chances are that one or two moments in the script will actually work with some levity.

Students from the School of "Bleaaauuugh" Acting do not naturally discover the humour in a speech and need help in finding it. Remind them frequently that in every speech there is humour. There is love in every speech. Don't forget to look for these elements.

6. The Laidback School of Mellowspeak

Diagnosis:

These students have trouble understanding the importance of energy in performance. They must be made to experience the ways that energy can serve their acting physically and vocally.

Remedy:

These students must experience the connection between the depth of breath in the body, projection of energy in acting, and free emotional release:

(a) If the weather is nice, send Laidback students outside for a few minutes of jogging. Otherwise, suggest some general indoor calisthenics, skipping, sit-ups, or jumping jacks. Whatever exercise you choose will end up dropping their breath deeper into the body. Continue physical exercise until these students are really winded.

(b) Ask the actor to begin delivering the speech while continuing to exercise or jog. A natural rhythm will emerge (which is particularly helpful and supportive when working on iambic pentameter verse in classical text).

(c) Ask the actor to stop moving and repeat the speech while rooted to one spot. He or she must keep the same degree of breath support and projection level. If support or volume slips, begin exercising again.

Die-hard cases should carry skipping ropes with them to acting classes and rehearsals.

7. The School of Semaphore Acting

Diagnosis:

The graduates of this school have so much energy they don't know what to do with it. Generally it is sent to their hands and they gesticulate and wave their way through every acting piece. If you have them repeat the piece while sitting on their hands, to prevent them from upstaging themselves, they will often send the energy elsewhere in their bodies.

Remedy:

Semaphore actors are trying too hard to act. They have lost touch with the simplicity and power of the words in the script:

- Return the actor's focus to the text. Place the actor a corner of the room and ask him or her to deliver the speech a metre away from the wall. This turns the speech into a radio play: all the expression has to be revealed through use of the voice.
- Try some extensive resonance work using exaggeration of vowel sounds to reconnect the actor with with the script. Slow the rate of delivery and find the key pointing words in the speech.
- To prevent excessive use of gestures, "manacle" the actor to the wall while running the lines of the scene. In addition, keep the actor's head in contact with the wall during this exercise.

Once these students have made renewed contact with the meaning and intention behind the lines, the problem will ease.

8. The School of Turning Blue

Diagnosis:

Students who turn blue do so for one reason: they forget to breathe. Even when you can manage to get them to inhale a deep breath before speaking, they insist on either releasing most of the air during the first few words or keeping the breath trapped inside their bodies.

Blue actors usually lock their nervous tension high in the chest so that the rigidity of the rib cage traps their breath in the throat. They have a problem understanding that there must be a fluid, easy connection between breath and the spoken word.

Remedy:

The first thing to do is to encourage the students to breathe from deeper in their bodies:

(a) Put them through the spinal-twist exercise mentioned in Chapter 3. The interesting thing about this position is that they cannot breathe using the upper chest. Breath must come from deep down in the abdomen.

(b) Have them inhale a full deep breath and release it again. Then have them take a second breath.

(c) Once this second inhalation is complete, they should begin to speak as the air is exhaled. Then take a third breath and release it. Take a fourth breath and speak the second line as this air is exhaled.

(d) Have them continue in this manner, adding a complete breath cycle after each line. Most actors will want to skip over half the intervening breath cycle, whether consciously or subconsciously, so they can get back to the text as quickly as possible. Don't let this happen. Keep them focused on each breath cycle. Gradually they will find the connection between full breath support and easy vocal delivery of a speech.

(e) Be careful when you transfer breath exercises to standing positions: hyperventilation can be a real problem for actors who are not used to filling their lungs with extra oxygen in a given time. It is a wise idea to keep a chair nearby in case a Blue actor becomes dizzy.

You might also wish to try this exercise with them: have them stand in the middle of the room and do a series of rag-doll flops, ensuring the head and arms remain loose. Add some gentle spins to the flopping action. Then ask them to pretend they are three years old and are "building into" throwing a tantrum. These physical actions will bring looseness to their upper torso. Once the maximum tantrum levels and limber physicality have been realized, allow them to begin to say the words of the speech. Ensure that the vocal interpretation matches the physical action of the tantrum, and does not revert to a "prepared speech" delivery.

9. The School of Shhhh — Someone Might Hear Me Acting

Diagnosis:

These students are battling against 15 or more years of habitual speech patterns. They seem incapable of speaking above a whisper and your repeated requests for them to speak louder have an effect only for a few seconds. When they do manage to speak up, it seems to them that they are shouting. This belief makes them cringe with embarrassment. In reality, these students are barely up to normal conversational level, let alone the volume level necessary to project to the back wall of the average theatre space.

Remedy:

Resonance work can help them. Working on "heavy-duty" emotional release scenes and monologues may also help. If possible, work with the actor in front of a window:

(a) Begin with a focal point inside the room the first time through the speech.

(b) Then choose an exterior focal point. Have them focus their energy on this spot the second time through.

(c) Gradually move the focal point farther and farther away each time they deliver the speech until they are projecting as far as possible.

(d) Encourage these students to speak at a slower rate as the volume increases. Stand well off to the side yourself, or behind them if possible, so that you don't allow them to play to you subconsciously. They won't feel as inhibited when they cannot easily see you.

Students from the School of "Shhhh — Someone Might Hear Me Acting" generally speak quietly throughout the day, so this problem must be addressed outside the acting class as well. Give such students an assignment: three times each day, they are to deliberately increase vocal projection level for a limited period. For example, these students could go into a store and sustain a larger vocal projection for the entire time because no one knows them. The sales clerk has no expectation of their behaviour or vocal quality, so the student will feel less awkward when donning a new persona. Eventually, once they get used to hearing a larger sound emanating from within, speaking confidently will become easier.

It is often difficult for these actors to overcome this problem because they are up against many years of social conditioning. They are often reluctant to become assertive, whereas improvement in vocal size is tied into personal development, taking control of one's life, and processes of maturing.

10. *The School of Mild Acting*

Diagnosis:

Students from this school have a rare ability to do everything smoothly. They can move easily around a set, deliver lines with vocal variety, and work well with others.

One major problem is that a lot of their work has a quality of sameness. The character in one speech is very much like the character in every other monologue this actor has ever presented. The more challenging the role, the less likely you are to see anything exciting. This type of actor tends to stick to nice, safe, generalized emotions and carry them through entire scenes. The lights do not go on in their eyes and their faces are mask-like, making scene work very boring to watch.

Remedy:

You have to try harder with these students than with most. They are a very difficult case to deal with because they are hiding from emotions. They have likely been getting away with it for years, not just in acting but in real life: striking attitudes, assuming "pretend" emotions and playing at feeling these:.

(a) Try sitting such students down for a long chat. You must discover the barriers to deeply rooted emotions.

(b) Buried inside each of us is a secret we have never shared with anyone. Ask these actors to identify and think about a personal secret for a minute or two. Then leave them alone for five minutes, ensuring that no one else is around or within earshot. Instruct them to "confess" the secret aloud (when they are alone) to an imagined "witness."

(c) What will make the exercise even more difficult for them is that they must imagine they are confessing this to the one person in the world that they least want to know their appalling secret.

(d) When you return (armed with tissues), ask the actor to repeat the most emotional part of the scene being studied. If the actor has been honest with him or herself while you were out of the room, you can be in for a remarkably different interpretation to the truth of the scene when emotions are transferred laterally from real life to the character's life.

This exercise must be treated with tremendous care and can work only if there is mutual trust and respect. It is not meant to meddle with another person's mind. The acting coach must never ask what the actor's personal secret was or to whom it was revealed. These are immaterial issues and asking questions about those topics is the most terrible invasion of the actor's privacy.

Confessing and witnessing are rooted in theology, psychology, philosophy and literature, and are a beneficial — even therapeutic — aid to these actors. As Hippolyta says in *A Midsummer Night's Dream* (Act V, Scene 1):

"But all the story of the night told over,
And all their minds transfigur'd so together,
More witnesseth than fancy's images,
And grows to something of great constancy;
But howsoever, strange, and admirable."

The interesting fact to remember is that lightning doesn't strike you down for harbouring thoughts or expressing them in such an exercise. But these actors must put thoughts into words. Just thinking about them isn't strong enough. The students need to hear themselves say the words aloud. Speaking secrets aloud in safe, controlled circumstances can help the actor get in touch with honest emotions that have remained buried inside for many years.

The exercise is an attempt to free actors to draw on real-life emotions and experiences to improve their acting in a safe and nurturing environment, and turn them from mild actors to exciting ones.

11. The School of Value Judgments

Diagnosis:

These actors are related to those in the School of Mild Acting because they are cheating the character of depth. In this case, it is not fear of emotions that blocks the work but the notion that one's opinions on everything are so superior as to stifle the truth and uniqueness of the character. The real nature of the character under study is layered with the veneer of the actor's value judgments that are based on personal, religious, cultural, or social mores.

For example, such actors may portray the character of a prostitute in an antiseptic, sanitized manner, fearing that to do otherwise will incriminate their own reputation. These actors usually have serious problems developing a character with a different sexual orientation to their own. They are trapped by a lofty but rigid moral code, where personal inflexibility makes teamwork impossible.

Remedy:

Such actors need to be shown how to distinguish between a character on stage and their own personal identity.

(a) To illustrate the difference, divide a page into two columns and contrast and compare the character and the actor point by point.
(b) These actors must focus on characterization exercises and carry the exercises beyond the rehearsal or classroom into the real world. The student should create a similar character to the one demanded by the script, and take that character in little forays out into shops, grocery stores, and so forth.
(c) Develop this over week or so, then put the actors as their characters into a question-and-answer situation:

- being questioned politely by a television interviewer
- being interrogated in a hostile manner on some pretext by an authority figure

This exercise will help such individuals to sustain a character without worrying about script work, yet give the actors a chance to experiment with a number of emotions.

Moral inflexibility is one of the most intractable problems in acting because acting requires imagination and moral release before a role can be approached.

12. The "But I Can't" School of Acting

Diagnosis:

This school is filled with a number of different types of students. Sometimes "But I Can't" really is a matter of "I haven't done enough work" — in which case, replace "can't" with "didn't" and treat accordingly. Other times it means "I don't like this material" or "I don't like this exercise" or "I don't like" ... (another student in this scene, my teacher, Friday morning classes, or myself). It doesn't matter particularly what is causing this mental block. The block is enabling these students to dump responsibility and take the easy way out. "It's not my fault. I just can't do it."

Most often, such students want immediate results. When their work doesn't meet their expected level of achievement, they are overly self-critical. Another problem is that such actors constantly compare their work with other people's acting. Natural insecurities are magnified in the mind to the point where it paralyzes all work.

Remedy:

Such students need to learn to replace "But I Can't" with "I have not yet learned how to" ... (substitute appropriate word) or "I'm having temporary difficulty with...." There is nothing in acting classes that students cannot learn if they let go of unreal demands or self-imposed expectations.

(a) Occasionally, you can change their approach to acting problems by refusing to allow them to begin a sentence with the word "But."

(b) Set them to researching biographies of established performers. They will be hard-pressed to find a success story where the individual didn't share their insecurities and doubts.

(c) Break their work assignments into smaller, self-contained components until their confidence begins to grow.

(d) Stress to the students that an acting class is the place to experiment, to have the opportunity to fail. An acting class is a place to focus upon the process, not the final product. It doesn't matter if the work falls flat because that is how the actor grows. Work should not be viewed as a performance, but rather as a rehearsal. What is important in the acting classroom is honesty and effort.

These are just a dozen of the major problems one encounters in students. As indicated earlier in the book, there are others like the "This Was Nice, Wasn't It?" School of Acting referred to on page 170. Instead of sharing a journey through the life of a character with the audience, the actor rushes like lightning through the work, unaware of the excessive speed of the presentation. Cure this problem by working on one word or phrase at a time.

An imaginative teacher/director will keep an open mind in rehearsals, constantly looking for methods to help actors discover their physical and emotional blocks, then finding or creating exercises to address these acting problems. If you take a physical approach in certain acting coaching situations, such as the "tug-of-war" exercise to build breath work, you may discover immediate and exciting results. Try "intimidation games" with actors to elicit stronger emotional responses, arm-wrestling while delivering a speech to connect with physical tension and energy, or whatever seems appropriate to the occasion. Imaginative approaches make acting more fun, both for the actor and the teacher/director.

When Joshua Logan visited Constantin Stanislavski in Moscow during the winter of 1930–31, he asked this most famous grandfather of modern acting technique about his method. Stanislavski told Logan to make up his own method, something that would work for him, and encouraged him to keep breaking traditions.

It worked for Logan, it works for me, and it will work for you.

Chapter Twenty-Two
Advice for the Novice Director

Finding the right script

One of the biggest headaches for a teacher/director is finding the right script to match up with the available student actors in the theatre arts classroom. Theatre adjudicators are often asked for suggestions on festival entries: plays suitable for 19 girls and three boys! There are many problems finding the right script to meet:

- the needs of the students
- the interests of the director and, if applicable, the music director and choreographer
- the nature of the school, the audience, the community
- the realities of the budget

Most acting companies look for a subject that will stimulate discussion in rehearsal. Others settle for farcical comedies of limited social value or commentary, which leave you feeling that you can't be bothered working on them for six weeks. Well, if it doesn't excite you, you're hardly likely to be able to share a vision with your actors and excite their theatrical energy.

Sometimes the scripts offer great challenges for male students but not for females. Many plays are written with two or three leads, perhaps a few minor characters, with a number of walk-ons or cameo appearances. We all understand the boredom that can overtake some students in rehearsal when the only thing they are called upon to do is participate in a crowd scene. A bored student is not learning very much. Despite the saying that "there are no small parts, just small actors," some students do want to be challenged more than crowd-scene work provides.

How often do you find a play that matches the male-female split of the class? Until very recent writing trends, the male-to-female ratio of roles was approximately 3:1. The ratio of male-to-female in the typical theatre arts class is much more likely to be the reverse — 1:3, if not more imbalanced. Therefore, it is usually the females in the class who are left short-changed in the scripts selected for production. Double-casting some female roles provides only limited compensation, its value often undermined by competition between the two actors, disagreements about who will be performing on opening and closing nights, and doubled wardrobe costs.

Creating a good script

One solution to these problems is to create your own ensemble script. Although at first the idea may seem intimidating, there are many aspects to such a project that make it an attractive alternative to working on a traditional scripted play.

The docudrama form, or collective creation, generally incorporates the following elements:

- A theme is developed in dramatic and/or comic episodes, with some action evolving from improvised sources and some emerging from existing writing.
- All the actors are involved in assembling material to work on and develop, which exponentially increases both the quantity and diversity of raw material.
- Music, songs, and choreographed movement are used to develop the story line and are interspersed between dramatic and comic excerpts.
- Several actors can be featured and given the chance to play one or several characters, depending on the needs of the play and the abilities, interests, and proven commitment of the individual.
- There is generally a chorus that provides a large number of inexperienced actors with performance opportunities through choral speech or cameo lines. The members of the chorus can

emerge to become one or several characters as required in various scenes and songs.

- Unity of ensemble demands complete precision in performance.
- Flexibility in staging is the watchword.
- The teacher/director functions more as an animateur, the stimulus within the group collective, and the developer of the idea behind the text.

There are several very important advantages to creating your own play, as opposed to producing an existing script:

1. Subject matter

The play can be created around a theme that is important to your particular actors at that specific period in their lives. Discussion surrounding the selection of a subject will help you get to know your students better and assist them in seeing you as a person, as well as a teacher/director.

- Themes can range from political-social topics (such as war or the arms race) to a "one-time only" theme (such as the International Year of Whatever).
- Perhaps a historical subject would give students an understanding of their roots (see "Building a docudrama" below for further suggestions of themes and subjects).

2. Shared tasks and responsibilities

Group collective productions demonstrate processes of shared responsibility, teamwork, collective problem-solving, and goal-oriented multi-task activity:

- Untrained actors who are keen to be challenged can learn through research assignments and group chorus work. These tasks will keep them actively involved in the play throughout the rehearsal period, without putting too much responsibility on inexperienced individuals.
- Chorus members will acquire an understanding of the disciplines of theatre as well as experience the basic process of putting a play together.
- Future principal actors will improve their performance skills in a non-competitive environment.

- Those who prove to be most reliable and committed can be given increased responsibilities. For example, the most disciplined member of the chorus can be appointed chorus master and be given the task of supervising daily choral-speech rehearsals.

3. Fairness in casting

When you create your own play, roles can be much more evenly and fairly distributed throughout the group. You are limited only by the collective imagination, scene by scene:

- It is possible to create several equally important lead roles. This avoids the problem of creating the "star," which is inherent in many conventional scripts.
- You can create roles that more accurately reflect your group's particular male-female split.
- Cross-dressing (e.g. a woman emerges from the chorus to play the role of a male in a scene) is widely accepted in collective creations or ensemble shows. Rarely does this device work effectively in a traditional scripted play.
- The chorus provides a workable theatrical medium where the gender and male/female ratio of those involved is of no real importance.
- Don't think that the actors need play only traditional character parts. In some docudramas, actors perform a multiplicity of roles, ranging from traditional characters to animals or inanimate objects.
- The chorus can be used to heighten the power of a particular moment, or to provide explosions of energy when the production requires a dramatic or comic lift. After all, 15 people saying the same lines in unison can be 15 times more powerful than one individual saying the line alone.

4. Utilization of talents

Creating your own script allows you to incorporate into the production the special talents and abilities of your students. These include:

- singing
- dancing
- gymnastics

- playing musical instruments
- performing magic tricks

Someone with years of dance experience can generally function as a choreographer. Perhaps the experienced pianist can help train the singing voices of others in the class. There could be a songwriting team just waiting to be discovered and matched up.

5. Ensemble

Group cohesion can be a difficult thing to achieve in some styles of theatre. In a collective creation, where each member is totally involved in all aspects of the show, the feeling of ensemble is heightened. The students feel a commitment to:

- their research
- the script they develop through rehearsal
- their ability to present the message of the play through effective dramatic, comic, and musical forms

6. Artistic and creative freedom

Another advantage of the collective creation is that it places emphasis on imaginative acting rather than production values. Because scenes move rapidly from one time and place to another, staging the show demands utter simplicity in setting. This means that it can be presented as a very portable production:

- appropriate to a wide variety of performing spaces
- using a simple set
- involving the minimum amount of technical complication
- with an ensemble "company costume" of limited expense (e.g. dark trousers, matching T-shirts with logos, and running shoes)
- with limited, inexpensive, or home-made props

7. Budgetary considerations

By limiting technical requirements, the production can be mounted on a shoestring budget:

- Unless you must make payments for excerpts from existing plays, songs, or books, you avoid royalty costs.
- Because technical aspects are simplified, it is possible to spread the responsibility for set, costumes, and props equally throughout the group.
- Outside of the company costume costs, specific characters can be created by adding one or two well-selected costume pieces.

8. *Taking the show on the road, or how to increase your public relations efforts*

For all of these reasons, docudrama is a popular style of theatre for touring plays. By approaching a play of this genre, you open up the possibility of touring the show throughout a network of theatre arts classes in other schools or the community at large:

- Taking a play into the community forges a link between school and the real world.
- It promotes the talents and expertise of your particular school within the community.
- Many places, such as hospitals, service groups and seniors homes, appreciate live entertainment throughout the year.
- Sometimes a specific event, such as a community's centennial celebration, will offer a unique opportunity for involvement in civic festivities with a theatrical presentation.
- Touring to such places need not be expensive. For little more than the cost of transportation, you can bring live theatre to people who otherwise might not be able to get out to a conventional theatre. Sometimes, the places to which you take your play will contribute to your transportation costs.
- Perhaps most importantly, touring a production provides a chance for acknowledging students who have no other outlet for public recognition. This includes students who don't excel at sports, are not academically strong, are not involved in extra-curricular activities for any number of reasons, or who simply lack social and interpersonal skills. Touring a show provides individual growth opportunities for students as they meet the challenges and self-discipline demanded of them.

Building a docudrama

How do you begin to create a play from nothing? Where do you begin? Here are some ideas that can be applied to numerous dramatic or comic subjects to create widely different plays:

1. Find a subject or theme. A subject might be "war"; a theme, "war is bad." Consider the following suggestions, which simply represent a few possibilities in a limitless field:

   - contemporary social problems (drugs, drinking and driving)
   - politics (nuclear proliferation, peace activism)
   - a particular topic that has been studied for a semester in English class, such as 19th-century Romantic poets
   - local history (a popular subject for touring within the community)
   - world history (World War II or the exploration and settlement of western North America)
   - natural and supernatural phenomena
   - relationships (between the sexes, races, cultures, or different generations)
   - cultural influences (the media, pop music of different decades, peer problems, or the role of television or the computer in modern society)
   - musical forms in the 20th century
   - the life and achievements of a well-known individual
   - current events — a never-ending source of inspiration

2. Divide your subject into episodes that, by consensus, seem to be worth developing within a general dramatic framework. At this stage, an episode is just a single incident — perhaps an idea for a piece of music, or an excerpt from a book — that can be developed in rehearsal. Allocate specific responsibilities for developing these episodes to groups of actors according to their expressed interest and/or individual talents.

3. Make a list of all the possible sources from which to research the project and allocate actors fairly to each source. Maybe some research can be integrated with other class assignments. For example, an English lesson in letter writing could be incorporated into writing to resource people for information

on your topic. Send the students out to research the subject:

- through direct sources such as interviews with people, if possible and appropriate
- through secondary research sources at the library
- through Internet research assignments
- through individual or group field trips
- finding music appropriate to the time frame and subject matter

4. Assemble and edit the information that has been collated. Some of it will be useful as direct dialogue, while other material may provide interesting subjects and situations for improvisation. Much of it will likely have to be discarded. While it is hoped that actors can participate in this decision-making, the director has the final word.

5. Arrange the information, alternating excerpts and styles regularly. For example, look for existing material such as:

- prose
- poetry
- songs
- jokes
- limericks
- quotations from the classics
- sayings
- excerpts from other plays

Between these, work in:

- improvisations
- original writing
- music

The more talented the writers in the group are, the less you will need to rely on secondary sources.

6. Apply the theatrical principle of opposites to achieve a dramatic effect:

- Comic scenes should alternate with serious ones.
- Use individual monologues interspersed with large company numbers to constantly vary the energy level of the show.

- Place upbeat songs immediately after dramatic moments.
- Discreetly move the chorus out of a scene to bring a sense of isolation to a dramatic monologue.

7. It is important that music be incorporated every so often and that the styles and treatment of music be quite different. You don't want three ballads in a row. For each piece of music you find in research, ask:

   - Do you want musical accompaniment for this song? If so, what instrumentation is required?
   - Will the song work better *a cappella* (that is, without instrumental accompaniment)?
   - Can it be made into a round and/or be echoed elsewhere in the show?
   - Should this music be used as underscoring to heighten a dramatic or comic moment?
   - Will humming this song be more effective than singing?

   Look for a theme song that sums up the idea and overall style of the play. If you cannot find one, write a song with lyrics that incorporate the diverse themes of the production. The theme song, with minor adjustments, can provide both an opening number and a finale for your show. Repetition enables the audience to leave the theatre space humming your theme song, and with it your message.

8. Create some warm-up exercises that reflect the style of the collective creation. Here are three examples of exercises — all of which have been discussed earlier — that can provide the foundation for preliminary work on a docudrama:

   - Cartoon-acting exercises are helpful in creating an awareness of the visual element of theatre, and can provide a good foundation for a comedic docudrama. See Chapter 17.
   - Vocal masques can serve as a challenging introduction to the range of the human voice. Masques can be assigned individually or as groups. They can either be part of the general theme of the docudrama itself, or be self-contained in their own right as warm-up exercises. See Chapter 5.
   - Choral speech work will help to establish a collective

awareness and communication fundamental to the process. See Chapter 6.

9. Begin to develop improvisations that are designed as a means to an end. These can be assigned individually, or the same subject can be given to all groups. The best ideas can then be drawn out of each improvisation and pooled into one strong collective. Each company member should participate equally, giving feedback on what works dramatically and what doesn't.

10. Then start to rehearse various parts of the play. You need not begin at the beginning. Working on a collective creation is very much like writing a mathematics examination: start with the questions you can answer first and worry about the rest of it later. In this instance, start with the parts of the script that seem to excite you and your group the most and allocate responsibilities equally throughout the class.

   You may end up at one point of rehearsal with 10 minutes of cohesive material and two or three other snippets of scenes that don't yet seem to belong to the major section. Don't worry. Further rehearsals will enable you to link your material together or replace it with stronger examples.

11. In presentation, remember that clarity is critical. Always keep in mind the value of simplicity and appropriateness in staging and selecting props and costume pieces.

   • The right piece of costume or prop will make the necessary and correct statement. For example, you can create an immediate statement merely by wrapping a piece of masking tape over the bridge of an unfashionable pair of glasses. Good acting will create the rest of the characterization.
   • Use mime as much as possible because the action keeps moving even faster when you don't have to set and strike props.
   • Ask yourself continually: do we really need this prop or can we do without it? Precision and clarity in mime work are critical, so reduce all mimed physical action to its minimum.
   • Keep the staging of the production moving as rapidly as possible between one scene and the next by using the minimum amount of furniture and by multiplying the uses of each piece. For example, let one basic box perform as many functions as possible throughout the play — and not just for something predictable such as sitting. The manner in which

the box is used will tell us what it is meant to represent — whether a ladder, an automobile, or a kitchen stove.

12. Be imaginative with your staging concepts. Don't get trapped by traditional staging approaches and techniques, for that limits the full realization of the potential that collective creations offer. Be flexible:

- Remember the impact a chorus can have on the dramatic energy of the show and try to incorporate the general chorus in different scenes.
- Decide when and where you want to incorporate this energy — the opening, finale, at certain dramatic or comic moments — and develop the use of the chorus in those moments.
- Does the play work better with a slow beginning, or should it start with a bang?
- Try each scene with only those individuals necessary to the action, then try it again with some or all of the chorus worked in as traditionally integrated characters within the scene.
- Chorus members can be used imaginatively (on stage, from the wings or in the house):

(a) as inanimate objects
(b) as visual symbols to heighten a moment
(c) to vocally underscore moments of the scene with sound and/or words

13. Continue to work each section. Over time, the play will take on its natural shape:

- Keep a free mind about the running order of the sequences and the workability of the material.
- Often something that has been discussed, developed, and refined will end up appearing out of place or heavy-handed. Cut it from the show if it doesn't belong.
- Don't be too upset about throwing out work because the simple creation of the material had its educational value. However, there are certain facts of life in theatre and the bottom line must always be the dramatic or comic effectiveness of the material.

- Some things that have individual merit may not be dramatically effective in the overall shape of the production. It's the director's function to make those decisions, painful as they may sometimes be.
- Don't panic if it seems to take a long time to realize concrete theatre from the morass of research and improvisation. Although early rehearsals may not seem to go very quickly (especially if the genre is new to the participants), later stages of rehearsal will move progressively faster as the discipline, style, and theatrical conventions are established and understood.

14. Begin each rehearsal with a run-through of the material that has been finalized thus far:

    - In the early rehearsals, this will be an erratic exercise and consist merely of bits and pieces of scenes.
    - There is no existing traditional script for the student to take home to study.
    - Because the physical action and the text are being developed simultaneously, regular reinforcement is essential.

15. Now you are ready to present the group collective effort. Find an audience for it, even if it is "once-only" workshop presentation. Invite guests who will value the thematic message and show them the presentation in the classroom, if need be. Remember that it is very important in an effort like this that both individual and collective work be recognized.

    Creating your own play can be a liberating experience for the actors and the teacher/director. Because of its imaginative demands and open-ended nature, docudrama can be approached more freely than a traditional play. Having done the exercise once, you will appreciate the educational values of such a project.

    As the students become equally and equably involved in a show, so they will share a sense of individual and collective commitment to the production. The greater the sense of ensemble:

- the more disciplined the working environment will be
- the more the actors will learn
- the more sophisticated the artistic standard will become

Theatre festivals and adjudication

As one who has adjudicated extensively over the past 25 years for the Sears Ontario Drama Festival; other regional school theatre festivals; and community theatre festivals at state, regional, and national levels in the United States, I am often asked for advice regarding plays in the school environment.

These queries include suggestions of scripts for curriculum study material — especially Canadian plays — and for production. Sometimes the questions involve advice for the teacher/director about the process of creating or producing a play.

Theatre festivals:

The debate about the value of competitive festivals, in both the educational and community theatre sectors, will always be with us. The purpose and value of theatre festivals in the school system is quite clear. Festivals offer a chance for students from a variety of different schools, backgrounds, and levels of experience to get together and share in the diversity of theatrical forms and themes that are offered by the variety of plays. Festivals offer:

- special fellowship with like-minded people
- opportunities for acquiring new skills
- forums for the exchange of perceptions and opinions

Theatre festivals, competitive and non-competitive alike, offer arts students an experience that may otherwise be missing in their school careers. For serious theatre students, there is generally no other outlet for competitive excellence. Few students are equally at home on the playing field and the stage, and many schools have a natural division between dedicated athletes and dedicated theatre arts supporters. Surely arts students deserve the same kind of opportunities for competing and promoting excellence that athletes get through inter-collegiate sports.

Dilemmas of adjudicating:

Sports events are pretty clear-cut: there are winners and losers. But competitive theatre festivals, which by their nature compare apples and oranges, are more complex. That is why the term "outstanding" seems to have replaced "best" in most theatre awards today. The selection of winners is the prerogative of the theatre adjudicator. Unlike sports competitions, the recognition of winning productions is based entirely on the subjective standards of one person. That is an awesome responsibility for the adjudicator. This fact may be understandably irrelevant to participants, especially when the awards are all given out to competing plays and none to one's own show.

Therefore, the purpose of an adjudicated festival should be stressed to every member of the production at the beginning of rehearsal and again on adjudication night — to the director, actors, designers, technicians, and stage crew alike:

- An adjudicator voices one person's opinion of excellence, based on specialized educational training and practical experience.
- It is a completely subjective view based on the execution of acting work, artistic achievement, and technical skill in one production in one theatre space at one particular moment in time: no more, no less.

The adjudicator's responsibility is to offer a detached and impersonal view (both positive and negative) of the overall success and unity of the production — a view that often escapes us as we become caught up in rehearsals and grow emotionally committed to the show. Criticism offered by an adjudicator is most helpful when seen by actors and technicians as coming from an educational base. The emphasis should be on growth of theatre skills, stimulation of fresh ideas for discussion, and encouragement to apply newly understood theatrical principles in future productions.

Guidelines for festival productions:

Many of the production problems to which adjudicators allude can be avoided by considering some of the following points. While such a "festival formula" offers no guarantee that your production will win, it does help avoid frequent problems that plague the teacher/director.

1. Look for a play that has some educational merit and redeeming literary style or you will short-change your students. Personally, I also feel strongly that it is important to expose Canadian students to Canadian scripts. For most students, this will be their first introduction to our national dramatic literature. For a few, it will be their only high school exposure to Canadian theatre.

Some theatre arts students go further with their interest and enrol at colleges for the next level of theatre training. At their college-level audition, most applicants are hard-pressed to name three major Canadian plays and playwrights. If teacher/directors in schools aren't going to introduce young people to our writers, who is?

2. Try to find something new and different. There are a great many plays, collectively called "pot-boilers," that are over-exposed simply because people don't look far enough afield when searching for a festival entry.

Every adjudicator has had the experience of seeing two or three versions of the same play in the same festival. One extreme instance was an adjudicator who sat through 11 performances in one festival, nine of which were the same absurdist script. Moreover, the first production was superb, making the others suffer by comparison. That is the luck of the draw, of course, and an occupational hazard of adjudication.

Every adjudicator must wipe out preconceived ideas, especially those based on successful prior productions, and view each show as an entity unto itself. Nevertheless, it is sometimes excruciatingly difficult to accept a second-rate standard when you know the show can be done so much better and you've seen it done better many times before. If the play is a new script you've never encountered before, you don't face that problem. (You may, of course, find that the production you see doesn't live up to the expectations that reading the script raised in your mind, but that's another problem entirely.)

Thousands of new plays are created each year throughout the English-speaking world. In addition, many successful companies in educational, community, and professional theatre create their own plays to suit the needs of their performers. Why not consider such a venture yourself?

3. If you are entering a festival, you should make the entry as strong as possible. Shoot for the top and incorporate your strongest talent. This suggestion has a natural corollary: restrict your festival entry to a smaller cast and crew. The larger the number of the cast and crew, the more difficult it is to achieve artistic excellence. It's not impossible, just more difficult. With a large company, you have more chance of encountering a situation where a cast member is withdrawn from a show at the last moment (for any number of

legitimate reasons). A smaller company is generally more tightly knit, sharing the same vision of excellence and discipline.

A festival entry should not be the first acting experience for novice performers, except in rare cases. The pressure of competing in a theatre festival combined with the myriad of skills to be acquired in a short time can overwhelm many students. Their introduction to festivals might better come from supporting the school entry in less pressured capacities, as well as participating in all festival workshops and discussing the relative merits of each show in competition. Use other productions in the school year to provide the initial training for your new performers. This will keep the festival play as something special to which novices can aspire in future years. Additionally, it will make the festival a more valid educational experience for those who are selected to represent the school.

4. Consider what rewrites you will make to alter a script before you audition the show. Make certain that obvious weak spots in a production are removed by taking strong directorial decisions before casting the show.

One obvious example is the show that has 15 male parts, eight of which are servants. If the extracurricular theatre group has only five committed male actors, the director must go pleading to find 10 additional male actors. Rarely will you stumble upon 10 gifted, committed new actors just waiting to be discovered. In such an instance, consider casting some of the servant roles with females, or combine servant roles into a couple of larger, more substantial roles. Maybe one or two could be entirely eliminated without diminishing the effectiveness of the play.

Make sure you have played with your rewriting ideas before you audition the show so that you know the options available to you. You can be quite vague at auditions about the actual final number of people you plan to cast. Wait until you see what talent emerges at the auditions.

If you can avoid it, do not cast several impossibly weak performers hoping they will improve with rehearsal. Some might improve sufficiently, but many won't. At the very worst, keep your options open until you have held the first read-through. You may even be able to get away with not making your final editing decisions until a couple of weeks into rehearsal. Indeed, this might make some individuals work harder on their roles.

Sometimes directors concede that they should have eliminated a particular role but that they couldn't take the lines away once the actor had begun to rehearse the part. Bearing in mind the philosophical goals of education, I agree. But foresight and trusting one's instincts would have prevented the problem from arising in the first place.

If you are going to make alterations to a script, you must have permission from the playwright to do so. However, it is rare that a writer will not grant permission for such alterations to a school production if the teacher/director outlines the realities of the situation in a letter to the copyright holder. This should be attended to long before opening night so that if the playwright attaches provisos, the teacher/director has time to consider the impact of such requirements.

5. Simplify the technical design concept of the show. Be able to justify your technical decisions. The full width of a stage, which can sometimes be 30 metres or more in a school auditorium, is unnecessary for the living-room setting in a comedy where there are just two people in the cast. Excessive space on the set undermines the potential for comedy. Imagine how much time it takes just for entrances and exits in such a production. Having a lot of room doesn't mean you have to spread your set out. Enclose the space by lighting and make your "stage world" only as large as necessary.

   Some schools are particularly fortunate with their theatre facilities and sometimes their shows are based upon technical wizardry. However, most festivals involve travelling to other theatre spaces with each new level of competition. Often a previously successful show will fall apart in a new theatre environment because what worked at home unravelled on stage at the next facility.

6. Find a show that incorporates the best talents and skills of your available students. Such a concentration of abilities is the reason that the docudramas and collective creations are successful at festivals.

7. The success of the private adjudication may depend on the director having trained the company members to arrive with notebooks in hand. Such a gesture assures the adjudicator of the committed and serious intent of the students. Sessions become stimulating and rewarding for all. At other times, an adjudicator will enter the room and read body-language messages that say, "So? Try to teach me!"

Sadly, the openness that should attend all learning situations is nowhere in sight.

Like everything else in theatre, what you put into the project at hand is directly proportional to what you will get out of it. For the process of adjudication to be valid for actors and technicians, the director should spend time during the rehearsal period dealing with what participants should expect in a festival. Similarly, time should be spent putting the festival into perspective when it is finally over and everyone has returned to life in the real world.

Festivals are meant to be times of sharing, learning, and acquiring new skills and insight. The expression that "all theatre is theft" means that festival participants should "steal" ideas from the experience: from the adjudicator, other productions, workshops, seminars, and peers. One of the oft-quoted remarks is that there are no losers in a festival. We all win by participating. Adjudicators learn just as much as the participants do, through analysis, discussion, and shared experiences.

Finding Canadian scripts

There is an annual search by every professional, community and educational group in the country to discover the "definitive" Canadian script, the play that is going to capture the imagination of audiences across the country and bring endless glory to the original production company. Where does one begin looking for plays? This can be difficult, especially when you live in a small rural town that is hours away from the larger cities. Here are some suggestions, regardless of geography:

- Everyone seriously interested in theatre should acquire a catalogue from every Canadian publisher of plays. Look them up on the Internet and visit their home Web pages. Write to them, phone them, or e-mail them annually for updates.
- Read. Incessantly.
- Get your local and school libraries to inform you of new acquisitions. Better still, you can supply them with lists of plays that you have found to be important. Help them on behalf of others in your community to develop their resources.
- Read theatre reviews in the larger national newspapers and magazines to see what scripts are current.
- Follow the annual announcement of plays being presented in

forthcoming seasons, in order to keep up with trends. Theatres across the country issue information regularly in news releases and it generally appears in newspapers. Pay particular attention to theatres that specialize in producing new scripts.

- Talk to others who are interested in theatre in your area, whether they are involved in community or professional theatre. They may be a source of information about good, new plays.
- When you attend theatre festivals, you will be exposed to many new ideas through other participants and their productions. Talk with these participants and discover what new scripts they have encountered.
- Secure catalogues by writing to shops that specialize in scripts and theatre-related books, such as Theatrebooks in Toronto. Include a visit to theatre bookshops whenever possible. Write to them, phone them, browse their Internet Web sites regularly, or e-mail them annually for updates.
- Contact organizations that sponsor annual playwriting competitions and ask how to obtain copies of scripts that reached at least the level of semifinalist.

You can always write your own play, of course.

Some advice about law, morality, playwrights, and publishers

There are a few final points to be made about royalty fees and permissions to produce shows. Playwrights make their money from two sources: one is the sale of scripts, which affects the writers' income from publishers; the other is royalty payment from productions of their plays. Agents make a commission on these sales. A publisher's only source of income is the sale of scripts.

Even neophyte directors know that you must pay certain fees to present plays, that such monies are dependent upon a number of variables to be determined through correspondence with the individual or organization holding the rights, and that permission must be obtained before the play can be presented.

Generally, agents are quite sympathetic to the special educational limitations of cheaper ticket prices, small audiences, and short runs. Royalty costs take all these factors into consideration.

Everyone at one time or another has read the copyright information at the beginning of scripts, but few people pay any attention to it. The invention of the photocopy machine has made copying dozens of scripts very simple. Yet, such photocopying is illegal without the permission of the publisher. A teacher may buy one copy of a script, photocopy a couple of dozen excerpts and distribute them to students. If this is being done with an entire script that is about to go into rehearsal for production, the procedure is highly illegal and immoral. It is just as wrong as neglecting to get permission or to pay royalties for any public performance of a script.

It is difficult enough to make money as a playwright, but these practices constitute robbing the playwright, not to mention the publisher. Canadian publishers, in fact, face steep expenses when producing scripts because the country has a limited population base on which to amortize publishing costs.

It is most important that each director bear these facts in mind and pass along the information to students who view the photocopy machine as a quick way to save the effort of writing out a speech by hand. It is a necessary part of teaching acting students professionalism in theatre.

Chapter Twenty-Three
Advice for Further Studies

Auditioning for theatre schools

From time to time, some high-school theatre arts students entertain the idea of enrolling in a college or university theatre course. Because the acting profession is notoriously underpaid and suffers from particularly high unemployment rates, families of such students often try to discourage them from pursuing their dreams.

Not only does the student often lack family support, but he or she rapidly discovers how daunting it can be to research the merits of different theatre programs and to prepare appropriate audition material. Endless questions spring to mind when you have limited knowledge of post-secondary theatre training and the acting profession:

- What is the difference between university theatre programs, college theatre programs, and conservatory or private training?
- What are the relative merits of the various theatre programs?
- Should I consider studying theatre in New York or London?
- What is involved in a theatre-school audition?
- How do I prepare for an audition?
- What are the auditioners looking for?
- What is demanded of the student in full-time theatre studies?
- Is it possible to make a living as an actor?

- How do actors gravitate toward film and television work?

Good guidance counsellors can answer many of these questions but, depending on your experience and connections, you may have to delve deeper to find answers to industry-specific issues. If the accident of geography works for you, you may have access to people who can help. Or you may not. Sometimes it can be nearly impossible to visit theatre schools and talk with faculty and staff who have first-hand knowledge of the different programs. Writing for literature, scouring Internet Web sites, and phoning registrar offices can tell you only so much.

But during the academic year prior to when you would like to enrol, make every effort to tour the sites of theatre programs in which you are interested. Go see the productions they mount. With sufficient advance notice, you can often arrange to audit classes for a day. This will provide answers to many of your questions and, as an added benefit, you will meet contact people at the institution whom you can phone with follow-up questions.

Most importantly, you will meet currently enrolled students who will be able to tell you what the program really offers and what it does not. It takes time to find the right school for you at the right stage of your development. After all, any institution can produce a glossy brochure but it takes perseverance to look beyond the photographs and "soft sell." You owe it to yourself to thoroughly investigate each program that interests you, because the training you receive and the network of professional contacts you establish while in school will serve you throughout your professional career.

Here is some advice for those who may want to audition for entrance into a post-secondary theatre-training program. It differs from what you might read in material advising actors on how to enter the theatre industry. The two audition processes are quite different, based as they are on separate levels of experience, training, goals, skill, and outcomes.

However, the following suggestions and ideas could make your college or university preparation a little easier.

General advice*:*

- Read all the college and university literature carefully because every school has a different process of auditioning students. Often critical material can be overlooked when you are under pressure. Use a highlighting marker to flag any important points in the information that arrives from each institution and review these points carefully when selecting material and preparing your application.

- If an institution requires you to send a résumé, photo, or letters of reference, make sure you do so. You don't want to run the risk of losing a position in a theatre program because you failed to complete paperwork on time.

- Make sure all letters of reference are written on letterhead and signed by the person who wrote the letter. With the development of personal computers, anyone today can forge a letter of reference and this certainly has been known to happen. Some institutions automatically telephone anyone whose letter is not on appropriate business letterhead and/or properly signed. Worse still, they may discard your application as being incomplete.

- Punctuality and deadlines are critical. Theatre is founded on absolute deadlines. If a professional actor isn't in place at curtain time, he or she could be fined, fired, or blacklisted by Canadian Actors' Equity Association (CAEA is the union for stage actors). How you handle deadlines prior to beginning theatre training can be an important factor in assessing your suitability for the program or the industry.

- Your audition is not just about presenting your material. It involves finding the correct match of student and program. Your job that day is to present the most positive image of yourself as a serious theatre student. This means dressing as if it were an important day, because it is, and conducting yourself likewise. If you look smart and professional, people will respond to you in that manner. After all, theatre is a business of image. If you look as though you don't care about your appearance, people will respond accordingly.

- Remember that the audition panel wants to like you. No matter how nervous you may feel, assure yourself of this point. When you walk in the room, they want to think you're the strongest candidate to walk through the door that day. After all, when the curtain rises on a show and you are sitting in your seat, you want to love the play that's about to begin, don't you? You are already on the actors' side. It's a similar situation in auditions. Those people who are assessing you want to like you, so there's no real need to be nervous. Besides, they have been on the other side of the fence themselves many times so they understand the pressures you are facing and the effects of adrenaline.

Selecting your audition material:

- Never choose a piece from a monologue book. They are overdone. Most audition panelists to whom you present such material will have seen it many times and know its full potential. They may have directed the show, and there is a strong chance they have worked on the material in the past with their own students. In choosing a piece from a monologue book, you run the risk of appearing too idle to read plays and search for your own material. Professional actors take months to find one new, interesting, and appropriate monologue for their repertoire, so you should start now to invest time looking for effective audition material.

- If you are asked to choose two pieces, ensure they are contrasted — one comic and one dramatic — so you can show your range of talent. Where possible, try to select a Canadian piece since it is assumed you hope to work in Canadian theatre one day. Your choice of material will reveal some understanding of Canadian theatrical literacy.

- Find material that takes your character on an emotional journey with a clear beginning, middle, and end. Ideally, audition panels want to see your character present a situation at the top of the monologue, debate the problem in the body of the piece and, by the end, reach a decision to take action.

- If the school asks to see a "classical" piece, that generally means anything written prior to the late 19th century. Shakespeare and his English contemporaries are always a safe bet for classical monologues. You can also look at pieces from Greek theatre, the English Restoration period, plays by Molière, and anyone writing up to the time of Chekhov and Ibsen in the late 1800s. It is then that the "modern" period of theatre is agreed to have begun, as writers began explore to real people in real situations grappling with difficult issues.

- Do not write your own material or choose something from an original or little-known script. The audition panel will want to see a piece from a reasonably well-known play by an established playwright in order to assess your ability to create a character in a context they know.

- Choose a character of your own gender, close to your own age, and someone who does not use a strong dialect or accent (unless you are very comfortable with that sound and can reproduce it easily).

You don't want to end up worrying about how you sound rather than what your character is saying and why he or she is saying it.

- Unless otherwise stated in literature from the school, your monologue should run between one and two minutes in length. If it is less than one minute, the script may not offer you sufficient emotional range to display your ability. Anything over two minutes is excessive and the audition panel may lose focus.

Preparing your material:

- Always begin by reading the entire play through so you have an accurate framework for your character.
- Begin with the fundamental character questions discussed in Chapter 11. Here are some of the key questions:

  1. Who am I?
  2. Where am I?
  3. What surrounds me?
  4. What are my given circumstances?
  5. What is my relationship to others?
  6. What do I want?
  7. What is in my way?
  8. What do I do to get what I want?

- Avoid using a lot of props. You won't have time to do much setting up of props and furniture. It is quite acceptable to bring along one important hand prop, but it must be manageable and appropriate. That means you must avoid using ballpoint pens to represent daggers.
- Wear something that is appropriate to your character. Lady Macbeth would not wear jeans and running shoes, and most audition panelists would like to see such attire banned from all auditions. Find something that makes you look good and which (perhaps with an accessory) can transform you into another character in seconds.
- Explore images and linger over the sensory opportunities provided in your monologue. Don't skip over powerful words because they will serve you well if you delve into them and savour them.
- Quite bluntly, if you don't see the images and feel the emotions before you begin to speak the line, do not assume your audition

panel will be able to see and feel them either.

- When rehearsing movement, avoid the trap of static or repetitive blocking patterns. If you don't know what to do with your hands, leave them by your side. If you are going to gesture, make it definite and clean, and when you are done, let it go. Do not let nervous tension override this advice.

At the audition:

- Arrive a little early in case you have trouble finding the audition site on campus. You will have to fill out paperwork anyway, and administrative details take time.
- Be friendly, professional, and courteous with everyone you meet that day, including the other applicants. Personal dynamics are very important in theatre and everyone participating in the auditions will be assessing you, whether as a future student or peer.
- When you walk into the audition room, how you conduct yourself and what you project will be assessed from the first moment. But assessment is a two-way street. Don't just launch into a prepared introductory speech. Be prepared to size up the atmosphere of the room and look for signals from the audition panel. Not every panel member, for example, might be interested in shaking hands with you. The auditioners will provide clues and you must be prepared to accept that information intuitively and go with it.
- Do not go to a lot of trouble setting up furniture, and be fast. One chair is generally all that's needed or all that's provided. Your acting skill is being assessed, not your ability to arrange a room. Try not to complain that the chair is different from the one that you've rehearsed with. As an actor, you should be flexible and able to adapt to the circumstances of the moment.
- Introduce your material briefly. All the panel will need to know is the name of the play, the act and scene, the playwright and the character you are presenting (you cannot imagine how frequently some of this information is forgotten by applicants in the panic of introducing the piece). Consequently, your introduction should be every bit as rehearsed as your actual monologue. You might take one additional sentence to set the scene. Don't go into any more detail than that: no extensive plot summaries and definitely no explaining what the monologue is about since your acting should illustrate that in the near future.

- When you are about to start, take two or three breaths and begin to become your character. Use that breath to focus on your character's "moment before" and be really specific in connecting to the emotion and energy leading into your first line. That is all the time you should take when "grounding" yourself or the auditioners may become restless. (Make sure you have rehearsed your material with that time limitation in mind.)
- Experienced audition panelists make their minds up within 10 seconds whether you have something to offer that interests them. This sounds tough, but it's very true and accounts for the infamous 30-second "cattle call" auditions on Broadway where actors are cut off in mid-sentence, thanked, and then asked to leave stage. Owing to pressures of time during the theatre-school audition process, you may well, in fact, be stopped before you have presented all your material — although it is hoped not as drastically as with Broadway's cattle calls. Make sure you hit your stride early in your monologue. Don't slide into your acting.
- In circumstances where so much is at stake, you cannot always trust that you will be able to control your nerves. Your own adrenaline may cause you to rush your speech. Be careful with the rate of delivery and use breath control to help keep you focused.
- If you have problems, do not apologize, break character, or stop. Just take a couple of breaths in and out, stay with the moment, and the lines will return. When actors dry, they stop breathing. It never fails. Just remember to breathe and you will recover (unless you are under-rehearsed, of course, in which case you should have cancelled your audition a week earlier and decided to pursue another career).
- It is often said that the eyes are the mirrors of the soul. They are also described as the windows into the mind. If we can't see your eyes, we cannot connect with you. Interestingly, 99 percent of the time when actors lose their lines, their eye level drops to the floor. Keep your eyes up most of the time, just slightly over the heads of the audition panel. Set your images at that level to ensure the auditioners can see into your eyes clearly.
- Do not get trapped in profile, speaking to imaginary characters in your monologue, because if you do, half your energy will disappear offstage. Place your imaginary characters between you and the audition panel, and you can sustain your eye level and remain in an open position.

- Never apologize for your work. Do not point out that you have a sore throat. Theatre auditioners are sufficiently experienced that they can hear it in your voice without being told. You don't want to sound as if you are making excuses for yourself.
- You should be prepared to present your material a second time with some directorial changes. Normally, such suggestions are very different from how you presented your material the first time through. These requests are designed to see how completely you are able to take direction. To prepare for this, make sure you rehearse your material in as many different ways as possible so that you remain loose and flexible with the text. If you simply parrot your piece in the same manner as you did originally, you will end up on the cutting-room floor.
- The audition panel is looking for candidates who will become flexible, creative, spontaneous actors. They want to be assured, too, that you are a nice person to work with because life in a theatre school is difficult enough to begin with. The manner in which you take their suggestions will form part of their decision-making process.
- If part of the audition process that day involves an interview, what you say and how you say it are equally important. This is where you let the auditioners know who you are, what you have to offer to the world of theatre, and how realistic your expectations are. Consequently, you will likely be asked questions that have no right or wrong answers. Be honest, not coy. The questions are designed so your responses tell the panel something about you. Be prepared for questions like these:

  - Who is your favourite actor, character, or director?
  - What is your favourite play, musical, film, or novel?
  - Why do you want to be an actor?
  - Why did you choose to audition for this school and where else have you applied? (Be honest with these responses because flattery can often work against you.)
  - Where do you see yourself in one year, five years, or 10 years?
  - What role did you most enjoy of all those you have performed in class or in a show?
  - What hobbies do you have?
  - What do your family and best friends think of this career field?

- Who is the current artistic director of the Stratford Festival Theatre? The Shaw Festival?
- Who is your favourite playwright and why?
- What is the most recent professional production you saw, and what aspect of the show was most memorable for you?
- What is the average annual salary for an actor who is a member of Canadian Actors' Equity Association?
- What will you do if you are not accepted at this school?
- What would you do if your career plans for theatre didn't work out?

Every institution has its own way of auditioning prospective acting students. Some conduct individual auditions, while others do group work and improvization. Some have callback procedures, while others do one-session processing. Most involve several steps during the audition process, the better to assess your suitability for their program and the theatre industry.

Finding the right school can be daunting. Indeed, it might take two or three years before your audition result is successful. If you must take more than one kick at the can before you are accepted at your school of choice, remember that the personal growth you experience during the intervening period will count for you. In a second or third audition, you can expect that the auditioners will be very interested in what you have been doing to pursue your training during that time, and what you have learned about yourself and your craft.

As people with an impressive collective history of professional theatre experience, they know full well that determination and perseverance form the foundation of a successful theatre career.

Conclusion ... on a lighter note

I once heard a learned Polish director musing why it was that he could go into a restaurant and have a superb meal, yet feel no compunction to give up everything to become a chef. Yet, he said, an individual would go to see a play, emerge emotionally touched by the experience, and want to forsake everything else in his or her life to become an actor.

To this I add a corollary. Why is it that, because an actor can read a script and learn some lines, he or she feels after a couple of years' study that a professional career is within easy reach? You would not expect a dancer to begin a professional career after two years of part-time dance classes.

Neither would you expect a singer to land a major recording contract, or successfully audition for a professional opera company, with little more than a couple of years of singing lessons.

Why, then, do actors feel that it's easy to begin a professional career?

It is a source of constant wonder to me that many people view acting as a simple process and a career that would be fun. Few things are further from the truth. Not many subjects seem to give rise to unreal expectations to the degree that acting does.

Yet, interest in the study of acting and theatre in general seems to be growing every year. This is true in educational, community, and professional theatre. It seems that, despite the advances of modern media, nothing can replace the special electricity that is generated between actors and their audience.

The study of acting is a lifelong pastime, one that offers many rewards in personal development and appreciation. Not the rewards of applause and attention, for they are transitory and superficial. The rewards of theatre come through confidence, insight, understanding, and the discovery of truth.

May this book, in some measure, help you along the path.

"Oh no! Look at all the lines I have to memorize! Cram, cram, cram. Memorize, memorize, memorize."

Since reading those lines in the first pages of this book, you have probably come to realize there are numerous other steps in the process of acting that the actor must consider before even beginning to worry about memorizing lines. If you are ever tempted to begin your performing work with sheer memory work, think on this: it is very much like buying an expensive car and then pushing it everywhere you go. You can do it, of course, but it makes little sense; it's a lot harder work, and it will not get you there very quickly.

There is a lot more work to acting than many people realize. Luck has little to do with success in theatre. As Toronto actor Bryan Foster puts it, "Good luck is just opportunity meeting solid preparation."

Break a leg ...

When you finally get the role and you are waiting to go on, here is an exercise from Antony Parr, who has been acting for decades in Canada and the United States. This exercise takes only two or three minutes to do. It comes from an ancient Druid ritual — and you may wonder at the connection of a Druid ritual with modern theatre. But one of the most important things to learn in theatre is that each person develops his or her own method of approaching performance work. You must always respect your fellow actor and find for yourself the technique that works best for you.

Mr. Parr has used this concentration exercise for many years, finding that it helps him relax into a role rather than straining up to it. He also finds it helps him to avoid a "second performance letdown" and gives uniformity to his acting whatever the conditions.

I particularly like the exercise because it is based on the sense of the actor's craft being handed down from one generation to another. What I learned from my teachers many years ago at drama school was taught to them by others in decades gone by. In turn, they were taught by ... who knows? The art of theatre has an ancient and mystical heritage.

Here is Mr. Parr's exercise:

- At the "five minute" call, explain to the stage manager that you have an exercise you wish to do and get his or her clearance.
- Position yourself about a metre upstage centre behind the curtain facing the audience. If there is no curtain, position yourself in the wings behind a flat or "black," on an angle toward the audience.
- Stand firmly with your feet at shoulder width, fingers stretched as wide apart as possible, arms and hands stretched as high as they can reach. Pull in your pelvis and strain upward as much as you can. Now ask for the power.
- "Give me the power. It's mine, give it to me. I'll use it well and return it." Repeat this in your own words but you must believe you will get the power. You must use it for good: your own good, the good of the show, for the benefit of the audience.
- Then say, "I want the power for ..." (mention your parents and visualize them smiling at you with love). Go on to include your director, the cast (individually see them approve of you), the crew, teachers, friends — anyone at all.
- Keep erect, keep your fingers wide apart, and soon you will feel your fingers twitch. Allow the pressure to relax in your fingers, through your hands, down your arms, slipping the energy down into your torso as you slowly twist to each side. Take a deep breath and walk away tall. Very tall.

Bibliography

Asimov, Isaac. *Asimov's Guide to Shakespeare, Volumes I & II*. New York, NY: Avenel Books, 1978

Avital, Samuel. *Mime Workshop*. Venice, CA: Wisdom Garden Books, 1977

Baker, Sarah. *The Alexander Technique*. Toronto, ON: Bantam Books, 1981

Barry, Cicely. *Voice and the Actor*. London, UK: Harrap, 1976

Benedetti, Robert L. *The Actor at Work*. Englewood Cliffs, NJ: Prentice-Hall, Inc., 1976

Cameron, Ron and Ross, Mary, eds. *Behind the Scenes Volume One*. Toronto, ON: Simon & Pierre, 1990

Cameron, Ron and Ross, Mary, eds. *Behind the Scenes Volume Two*. Toronto, ON: Simon & Pierre, 1990

Campbell, Oscar James, ed. *The Reader's Encyclopedia of Shakespeare*. New York, NY: Thomas Y. Crowell Company, Inc., 1966

Courtney, Richard. *Play, Drama & Thought*. Toronto, ON: Simon & Pierre, 1989

Delgado, Ramon. *Acting with Both Sides of Your Brain*. Toronto, ON: Holt, Rinehart and Winston, 1986

Deszeran, Louis John. *The Student Actor's Handbook*. Palo Alto, CA: Mayfield Publishing, 1975

Esslin, Martin. *An Anatomy of Drama*. New York, NY: Hill and Wang, 1976

Frye, Northrop. *Northrop Frye on Shakespeare*. Markham, ON: Fitzhenry & Whiteside, 1986

Glenn, Stanley L. *The Complete Actor*. Boston, MA: Allyn and Bacon Inc., 1977

Hagen, Uta. *Respect for Acting*. New York, NY: Macmillan Publishing Company, 1973

Hall, C. and Nordby, V. *A Primer of Jungian Psychology*. Scarborough, ON: Mentor Books, 1979

Harrison, G. B. *Introducing Shakespeare*. Harmondswoth, UK: Penguin Books Ltd., 1981

Hilgard, Ernest R. *An Introduction to Psychology*. New York, NY: Harcourt, Brace and World, 1962

Hill, Harry. *A Voice for the Theatre*. Toronto, ON: Holt, Rinehart and Winston, 1985

James, Muriel and Jongeward, Dorothy. *Born to Win*. New York, NY: Signet Books, 1978

Kahan, Stanley. *Introduction to Acting*. Boston, MA: Allyn and Bacon Inc., 1985

King, Nancy R. *A Movement Approach to Acting*. Englewood Cliffs, NJ: Prentice-Hall, Inc., 1981

Linklater, Kristin. *Freeing the Natural Voice*. New York, NY: Drama Book Publishers, 1976

Manderino, Ned. *The Transpersonal Actor*. Venice, CA: Wisdom Garden Books, 1976

McGaw, Charles. *Acting is Believing*. Toronto, ON: Holt, Rinehart and Winston, 1980

Moore, Sonia. *The Stanislavski System*. New York, NY: Penguin Books, 1978

Morris, Eric. *Being and Doing*. Los Angeles, CA: Whitehouse/Spelling, 1981

Schmidt, Alexander, ed. *Shakespearean Lexicon and Quotation Dictionary, Volumes I & II*. New York, NY: Dover Publications, Inc., 1971

Shakespeare, William. *The First Folio of Shakespeare: The Norton Facsimile*. Edited by Charles Hinman. New York, NY: W. W. Norton & Co., 1968

Shakespeare, William. *The Complete Illustrated Shakespeare, Volumes I, II & III*. Edited by Howard Staunton. New York, NY: Platinum Press, 1995

Shurtleff, Michael. *Audition*. New York, NY: Walker & Co., 1978

Spolin, Viola. *Improvisation for the Theatre*. Evanston, IL: Northwestern University Press, 1977

Stanislavski, Constantin. *An Actor Prepares.* New York, NY: Theatre Arts
  Books, 1973
Sterne, Richard L. *John Gielgud Directs Richard Burton in Hamlet.*
  London, UK: Heinemann, 1968
Swann, Robert, and Sidgwick, Frank. *The Making of Verse: A Guide to
  English Metres.* London, UK: Sidgwick & Jackson, Ltd., 1966

Special thanks to the following people for their assistance in developing
some of the content in this book:

- the late Christopher Covert, Toronto: Chapter 18
- Paul Lampert, Toronto: chapters 5, 8, and 10
- David Leong, Northern Kentucky University and Fight Master
  of the Society of American Fight Directors: Chapter 16
- Dr. Iris MacGregor-Bannerman, Toronto: chapters 3 and 4
- Teresa Sears and David Switzer, Toronto: Chapter 14
- David Smuckler, Toronto: Chapter 5

Index